Invitation to Community Music Therapy

Invitation to Community Music Therapy presents the main perspectives and principles of community music therapy as it is practiced around the world. A relatively recent development within the broader field of music therapy, community music therapy emphasizes human connectedness, health promotion, and social change. This textbook surveys the history, theory, and current practice of community music therapy to develop a comprehensive picture of the field. Along the way it takes full measure of the diverse and vibrant ways community music therapy is practiced around the globe. Including dozens of photographs and pedagogical tools such as chapter questions, textboxes, figures, key terms, and discussion topics, *Invitation to Community Music Therapy* is the ideal introduction to a growing area of music therapy.

Brynjulf Stige is Professor of Music Therapy at the Grieg Academy, University of Bergen, and Head of Research at GAMUT, Uni Health, Uni Research, Bergen, Norway.

Leif Edvard Aarø is Chief Scientist at the Division of Mental Health, Norwegian Institute of Public Health, Oslo, and Adjunct Professor of Social Psychology at the University of Bergen, Norway.

Invitation to Community Music Therapy

Brynjulf Stige and
Leif Edvard Aarø

Routledge
Taylor & Francis Group

NEW YORK AND LONDON

Please visit the eResources website at www.routledge.com/9780415805544

First published 2012
by Routledge
711 Third Avenue, New York, NY 10017

Simultaneously published in the UK
by Routledge
2 Park Square, Milton Park, Abingdon, Oxon OX14 4RN

Routledge is an imprint of the Taylor & Francis Group, an informa business

© 2012 Taylor & Francis

Library of Congress Cataloging-in-Publication Data
Stige, Brynjulf.
  Invitation to community music therapy/Brynjulf Stige &
Leif Edvard Aarø. – 1st ed.
  p. cm.
  1. Music therapy.   2. Music – Social aspects.
  I. Aarø, Leif Edvard.   II. Title.
  ML3920.S819 2011
  615.8′5154 – dc22
  2011012012

ISBN: 978–0–415–89760–0 (hbk)
ISBN: 978–0–415–80554–4 (pbk)
ISBN: 978–0–203–80354–7 (ebk)

Senior Editor: Constance Ditzel
Editorial Assistants: Denny Tek and Mike Andrews
Production Editor: Sarah Stone
Marketing Manager: Chris Bowers
Copy Editor: Ruth Jeavons
Text Design: Susan R. Leaper at Florence Production Ltd
Proofreader: Jane Canvin
Cover Design: Jayne Varney

Typeset in Times New Roman and Futura
by Florence Production Ltd, Stoodleigh, Devon

Brief Contents

Contents

List of Figures

List of Text Boxes

Preface

MUSIC has the potential of bringing people together, often in exhilarating ways that create a sense of meaning and belonging. It is not surprising that researchers in a range of disciplines now take interest in music as a resource for positive health and community development. The tradition of community music therapy is a notable part of this picture. It is a tradition that goes back several decades, but the documentation in the literature has been varied. Since 2000 the international interest and debate has increased rapidly and several research-based articles and books have been published. In our opinion, it is time for a textbook to bring the existing knowledge together, and to discuss and contextualize it for students.

Writing *Invitation to Community Music Therapy* was inspired by Brynjulf's doctoral dissertation in 2003. He has been a dedicated advocate, committed to developing community music therapy practice, theory, and research. His holistic involvement has been both a resource and a challenge in the process of writing this textbook. An active role in the field is an advantage in relation to access to information and understanding, but a potential difficulty in relation to balance in perspective and presentation. By involving Leif, we have tried to establish a fruitful dialogue between insider and outsider perspectives.

Leif is a social psychologist (teaching community psychology since 2001) and a quantitatively oriented researcher. For him, contributing to this book and being associated with music therapy has been a fascinating journey. In many ways, music therapy can be close to clinical psychology in terms of challenges and orientations. Similarly, community music therapy is adjacent to community psychology and also to public health, which is another research area in which Leif takes interest. He thinks that music represents a resource that deserves to be more fully utilized and explored in health care and community settings and that the emergence of community music therapy as an academic discipline will contribute to inspiring further developments and applications.

The collaborative writing of this book started in 2004 and intensified in 2006, when Leif became a research scholar at the Department of Psychology at Stanford University. We met in California for a concentrated writing period. The writing has then progressed over the years through our connection to GAMUT, The Grieg Academy Music Therapy Research Centre at Uni Health, and the University of Bergen, Norway. We are pleased that our research and collaboration has resulted in a textbook that we hope will prepare students to step boldly into the field of community music therapy. As the pages of this book will demonstrate; contemporary societies invite explorations of the possibilities of community music therapy. We invite you to investigate these possibilities!

GOALS

In writing this book, our ambition has been to produce an accessible text, focusing on theory and research, practice, and profession. We hope we have succeeded with the following features:

■ **Global outreach**. This textbook is published in the US, written by two European scholars, with input from colleagues around the world, including Australia, Asia, Africa, and South America. It reflects a truly international effort and we hope to engage readers around the world in continued deliberations on the future of community music therapy.

■ **Reflective writing style**. The book includes more discussion and argument than some textbooks. This writing style has been chosen because community music therapy is multifaceted and complex. Both concepts and practices can be explored from several perspectives.

■ **Pedagogical features**. In order to increase accessibility, the reflective writing style is supplemented by pedagogical tools such as chapter questions, textboxes, figures, key terms, and discussion topics.

■ **Focused presentation**. We have tried to represent various theoretical perspectives as respectfully as possible, but we do believe that a textbook needs to clarify its own main viewpoint in order to be useful and interesting. We focus on transactions between people in context, which involves exploring the interdependent relationships between personal agency and social structure. Examples of such theoretical perspectives will be presented throughout the book.

■ **An inclusive, participating role for the reader/student**. Our goal has been not only to summarize existing knowledge, but also to contribute to the development of a theoretically informed discourse that might enable future practitioners and researchers to engage with, critique, and develop community music therapy.

HOW TO USE THIS BOOK

An invitation may function as stimulation, provocation, or temptation. We hope that *Invitation to Community Music Therapy* will be read as a call for action and reflection. The book is divided into four parts which represent different entries to the field. In Part I we introduce the tradition of community music therapy and present the historical developments that led to its emergence. In Part II we explore basic concepts of community music therapy, such as health, community, and music. In Part III we examine the practice dimension of community music therapy, with a focus on issues, values, and processes. In Part IV we examine implications for discipline and profession, with chapters on community music therapy research and on the professional role of the music therapist.

Each of the ten chapters includes several pedagogical features, which we will list here with some suggestions as to how they can be used:

■ **Chapter questions**. These questions provide you with an outline of central topics to be discussed in the chapter. They can be used for preparation and orientation as well as for reflection on your pre-understanding of these topics.

■ **Textboxes**. Each box presents a case in point, usually from the community music therapy literature. The boxes are often presented as exemplars clarifying aspects of more general themes discussed elsewhere in the text. Each textbox can be read in relationship to its surrounding text and in relationship to its surrounding textboxes, so that explanations and examples can be compared and considered.

■ **Figures**. The book includes a substantial number of photos from practices around the world, also, drawn figures that illuminate information presented in the text. In contrast to the drawn figures, the photos could not be said to illuminate concrete information. We have made no attempts at using photos as illustrations and have not linked textboxes and photos, for instance. This choice, we hope, will clarify the role the photos play in communicating some essential dimensions of the work, such as the aesthetic, emotional, and social qualities that make community music therapy a very rich experience.

■ **Key terms**. At the end of each chapter there is a list of key terms. These can be used as a checklist, to ensure that the basic terms used in the book are understood. More creative usages of these key terms are also imaginable. They can be used in class for collaborative construction of new discussion topics, for instance.

■ **Discussion topics**. Three topics for discussion are presented after each chapter. The topics refer to central discussions in the text and also to possible implications of the argument given. The discussion topics can be used as a basis for personal reflection but are designed to work in the setting of a class or group studying community music therapy. Learning is in many ways a social process, in community music therapy as well as in the study of it.

Acknowledgements

COMMUNITY music therapy invites collaboration, and the processes that have led to the articulation of the ideas presented in this book have also been collaborative. A large group of colleagues, friends, clients, and project participants over a considerable number of years deserve our warmest gratitude. This book would not have been written if not for you.

It is tempting to mention no names so that no one is forgotten, but we do need to make a few exceptions. Clive Robbins, Even Ruud, Carolyn Kenny, and Kenneth Bruscia have been friends and music therapy colleagues for decades and have supported and challenged the idea of community music therapy in ways that have stimulated our thinking continuously. From the related field of music sociology, a scholar such as Tia DeNora has been of immense importance. Kirsti Malterud also deserves to be mentioned, for stimulating dialogues on qualitative research on health and resources in everyday life.

For a period of several years, starting from 2004, we worked in a research group with Gary Ansdell, Cochavit Elefant, and Mercédès Pavlicevic. Randi Rolvsjord and Christian Gold were also part of the same research milieu. Needless to say, these scholars have inspired and challenged our thinking in a multitude of ways which are reflected throughout the pages of this book. In the broader community of music therapy there are also several scholars who in various ways have influenced and inspired our work. This list includes names such as Trygve Aasgaard, Kenneth Aigen, Lia Rejane Barcellos, Leslie Bunt, Simon Procter, and Yu Wakao.

We want to express our special thanks to scholars who have read and commented on chapters of the manuscript. This includes Simon Gilbertson, Lucy O'Grady, Jill Halstead, Viggo Krüger, Katrina McFerran, Lars Tuastad, and the three anonymous reviewers recruited by Routledge. Their comments have challenged and stimulated us in ways that led to important enhancements in the manuscript. Warm thanks also to our editor at Routledge, Constance Ditzel, for her patience and wise advice in the process of balancing various inputs and ideas in the writing of the book. We also thank editorial assistants Mike Andrews and Denny Tek, and our production editor, Sarah Stone.

Thank you with deep appreciation to the many colleagues who have contributed photographs for this book (see "List of Figures" and "Photo Credits"). These photos bring

Acknowledge-ments

the reality (and the wonders) of the work itself closer. We extend our appreciation to the following publishers that kindly have given us permission to use four figures previously published in other books. Thanks to Ashgate Publishing, Barcelona Publishers, Cambridge University Press, and Cengage Learning (previously Wadsworth/Thomson Learning).

Finally, we thank our families. When we were close to submitting the manuscript, we wrote our editor, "This is a message from two Norwegian professors who for some weeks now have been neglecting their wives and university jobs in order to be able to submit the manuscript for *Invitation to Community Music Therapy*. Hopefully wives and jobs will survive." We are most grateful to them—and all seem to have survived.

Brynjulf Stige and Leif Edvard Aarø
Bergen, Norway, February 2011

Part I

Introduction to Community Music Therapy

Pₐᵣₜ I introduces the reader to the idea and practice of community music therapy and to the historical developments that led to the emergence of community music therapy as an international discourse and field of study.

Chapter 1 introduces community music therapy, first by discussing one of the basic metaphors that informs it and then by presenting examples of community music therapy practices around the world. Definitions of community music therapy and ways of describing the family of practices that might enable us to recognize community music therapy are discussed, before community music therapy as a continuation of and contrast to conventional music therapy is considered.

Chapter 2 explores the history of community music therapy. Many of the pioneers of modern music therapy, especially in the 1960s and 1970s, paid attention to a broad, social way of thinking about music and health. In addition to individual sessions they explored the use of improvisation groups, music clubs, therapeutic teaching, chamber music, record sessions, and performances. The pioneers never theorized or researched these broader ways of thinking about music therapy and in many countries their successors paid less attention to these social–musical traditions than to clinical work with individuals and groups. Important undercurrents have existed in several countries, however, and after 2000 a strong international interest in community music therapy emerged, with provocative discussion papers and intriguing practical examples from a range of contexts to fuel the process. We need to understand how and why this happened.

An Overview

After studying Chapter 1, you will be able to discuss questions such as:

■ How does the metaphor of "attending to unheard voices" relate to community music therapy?

■ How is community music therapy practiced in various contexts around the world?

■ How has community music therapy been defined by various authors?

■ What are the challenges in defining community music therapy?

■ What are the seven qualities communicated by the acronym PREPARE?

■ How could community music therapy be considered a continuation of as well as a contrast to more conventional forms of music therapy?

■ Why is community music therapy relevant and significant in contemporary societies?

ATTENDING TO UNHEARD VOICES

MUSIC can be used to mobilize resources in the service of health, wellbeing, and development. This is something humans have "always" known and acted upon. The idea that music can help has been cultivated over millennia in a range of cultural contexts. Since World War II professional music therapists have gradually developed a body of research-based literature to refine this idea and to support the development of professional music therapy practice. Traditionally, the literature on professional music therapy has focused on problems and solutions as they relate to individuals. The dominating view in modern music therapy, as in many other health-related disciplines, has been that therapists work with individuals and their pathology, often in clinical settings.

Community music therapy practices question this tradition by employing social and ecological perspectives on music and health, which implies that health-promoting connections between individuals and various communities are explored. To study community music therapy involves exploring a broad family of practices and perspectives that enable music therapists to be open for the needs, rights, and possibilities of persons and groups in challenging situations. Part of what is new about community music therapy is its radical willingness to explore the relationships between individual and communal change and development (Pavlicevic & Ansdell, 2004).

Community music therapy ideas and practices are not new in every respect and consequently some have questioned the need for and legitimacy of a separate label. The most heated debates are already some years old and contemporary community music therapy has grown into an international discourse with an ability to cross geographical as well as academic borders. Acknowledgement of the value of **human connectedness** is part of the identity of contemporary community music therapy, which has emerged as

FIGURE 1.1 | Hear my voice! A child from a foster home visited by the Music Therapy Community Clinic in the Greater Cape Town area, South Africa.

Photo: India Baird.

a vital interdisciplinary field of study and practice. In considering its legitimacy it is no longer necessary to measure it against standards established by other traditions. Community music therapy has developed its own relational agenda.

The issues and values of this agenda will be intimated later in this chapter and elaborated in Part III of the book. **Attending to unheard voices** is one of the metaphors that inform it. The related image of therapy as "giving voice" to experiences that have been silenced has been used within narrative therapy, for instance (Stige, 2002). It is an open metaphor which points to the possibility that the processes leading to silencing can have personal, interpersonal, social, cultural, and material origins. In this book we use "attending to unheard voices" instead of "giving voice," as voice is a personal performance in social context. We cannot give people a voice, but we can contribute to the construction of conditions that allow for previously unheard voices to be heard. The metaphor links the interest in each individual with the community. It opens a space for a social agenda without neglecting the personal issues of the participants. It also opens a space for visions of a better world.[1]

To attend to unheard voices is not an intervention instigated by a therapist; it is a collaborative process balancing values such as liberty and parity. The metaphor therefore implies a multi-voiced community (Stige, 2003, p. 283). Community music therapy encourages musical participation and social inclusion, equitable access to resources, and collaborative efforts for health and wellbeing in contemporary societies. It could be characterized as solidarity in practice. In this way community music therapy can be quite different from individual treatment, sometimes closer to practices such as community music, social work, and community work.

CONTEXTS OF CONTEMPORARY PRACTICE

We will illuminate contemporary developments in community music therapy through presentation of six practice examples, selected from various continents, countries, and cultural contexts. We will start with an example from South Africa, a country with a short history of professional music therapy but a long history of health-related and community-oriented musical practice.

Box 1.1 | THE MUSIC THERAPY COMMUNITY CLINIC IN THE GREATER CAPE TOWN AREA

In Cape Town, South Africa, a group of music therapists including Sunelle Fouché and Kerryn Torrance (2005) have formed a non-profit organization called the *Music Therapy Community Clinic,* which provides professional music therapy to disadvantaged people from poorer communities within the Greater Cape Town area. Fouché and Torrance describe one of the neighborhoods where they are working in the following way:

Box 1.1 |

> Most of Heideveld's older generation remember being moved here in the 1960's from inner city suburbs as part of the apartheid government's Group Areas Act. Where extended families used to live in the same house or in close proximity to relatives in Cape Town city, they became scattered over the different settlements in the Cape Flats, in the 'hinterland'. These forced removals to Heideveld and other areas of the Cape Flats meant moving into a world of strangers. The social and emotional support which family members and neighbours once provided each other was lost (Fouché & Torrance, 2005).

In Heideveld the music therapists work with adolescents facing the danger of becoming immersed in the gang culture of the suburb. The authors explain that for adolescents who live in a socially fragmented community, gangs provide some social and emotional support. While families often have few resources for providing support, gangs can offer an identity, a sense of belonging, and a feeling of acceptance, power and purpose. After having worked with children in this community, the two music therapists were approached by the police, who asked them to see adolescents at risk; young people involved in local gangs, drug abuse, and acts of crime:

> The Police were reluctant to place these youngsters into the criminal justice system as the rehabilitation statistics in Southern African prisons are exceedingly low, with notorious prison gangs constantly recruiting young adolescents to a life of organized crime. The Police saw music therapy as an alternative form of intervention. Each week, the Police fetch the youngsters, disarm them and deliver them to our Music Therapy door. Police supervision ends and the musicking begins. . . .

> While the police fetch the youngsters each week, their attendance is not compulsory. Although the group appeared very sceptical and aloof at the first meeting, they have returned willingly and eagerly every week. Music seems to be the magnet. It is a 'cool' thing to do. Within the gangs' Rap/Hip-Hop culture, the musicians are the 'heroes', looked up to by the youth; the ones who give social commentary. (Fouché & Torrance, 2005).

The music therapists observe how music energizes the adolescents and gives them a purpose and an opportunity to create new social identities. Creating and relating through involvement in music and movement is motivating and meaningful in itself and also establishes a platform for telling and sharing stories (Fouché & Torrance, 2005).

The above example illuminates several themes that will be discussed throughout the book, such as community music therapy's potential in relation to social problems, the importance of prevention of problems rather than just treatment, and the need to think and act ecologically, exemplified with the necessary alliance that was developed with the local community and the police in this case.

In describing the active music-making, Fouché and Torrance (2005) employ a term that has become central to the community music therapy discourse, namely **musicking**.[2] Instead of thinking of music mainly as an artifact (as a work of art, for instance), the term *musicking* suggests that we can think of music as an activity that we take part in. If we start considering music as an activity in a given situation, we are also invited to think about the relationships between those who make sounds and those who make sounds possible. In a concert situation, the importance of the audience is pretty obvious. In the example above, police supervision (*and* the end of it) made music possible and can be considered part of the musicking, broadly conceptualized. We will elaborate on this term and its ecological implications in Chapter 5.

From this example we will move to South America, where social and contextualized approaches to music therapy have been developed since the 1970s. In a comment about the prospects of the profession in a new millennium, Brazilian music therapist Marly Chagas suggests that the music therapist "will be engaged in situations that involve collective health, awareness of creating expression, artistic expression, or even social life through musical symbols. He/she might contribute to the effective analysis and intervention in local communities" (Chagas, 2000, cited in Zanini & Leao, 2006). This view might be exemplified by descriptions of how Brazilian music therapists have tried to work in relation to the problem of homeless people:

Box 1.2 | SEARCHING FOR PATHS THROUGH ARTS IN RIO DE JANEIRO

In Rio de Janeiro, Brazil, music therapists have taken interest in trying to improve the conditions of the many homeless people in this city. Lia Rejane Mendes Barcellos (2002, 2005) writes about how music therapists try to work with this. One specific example is the project *Searching for Paths through Art* (2002–2004), developed in adult homeless shelters and coordinated by the music therapist Marly Chagas. It offered many kinds of art activities, such as music therapy, storytelling, drama, dancing, and workshops where people could make their own musical instruments. One goal of the project was to "humanize" the relationships between the interns and staff members. Barcellos (2005) labels this practice "social music therapy" and explains that it is an established element of the Brazilian music therapy tradition.

Chagas (2007) explains how some of the goals of the project were related to the development of each individual while others were more social or political, with focus on the enhancement of the milieu and the relationships between people in various roles and situations:

> New situations are brought to light: we were able to get a wheelchair; harmonicas; at Carnival the youth drum ensemble from Mangueira (Rio shanty town and home of the *Estação Primeira da Mangueira samba* school) provided an emotional generational integration and the boys' trip outside Rio offered the entranced *mangueirenses* (those

> **Box 1.2** |
>
> from Mangueira) the possibility of crossing the Rio de Janeiro–Niteroi bridge for the first time; one long-term care infirmary sings a *samba* march about a leafy tree on the patio of the institution, the lyrical composition of which is theirs, the melody having been composed by the music therapists of the Project. An instrumental group is formed, a group of women go to the theatre, a group of men, aided by the employees, organized a music festival, another group a poetry festival. We danced *cirandas* (children's dance of Portuguese origin) and *forros* (musical style from northeastern Brazil) together. We created stories, we drew, we made instruments—in several senses of this term, we are here thinking, examining ideas, exchanging shared experiences. We heard exceptional stories, amazing stories! (Chagas, 2007).
>
> Valued outcomes in this project went beyond those typically focused on by health professionals and included the discovery of new performers and the beginning of new ensembles and stories.

Music therapists can choose to relate actively to the broader social situations they belong to, in this case the glaring inequalities in the Brazilian society, and to combine this with sensitivity for musical and narrative resources in each individual. An ecological and systemic perspective is implied here (as in the South African example). This is a dimension that is quite prominent in the next example, which is from Bergen in Western Norway:

> **Box 1.3 | MUSIC IN CUSTODY AND LIBERTY IN BERGEN**
>
> Norwegian music therapists Lars Tuastad and Roar Finsås (2008) have for several years worked with rock bands in the *Music in Custody and Liberty* program in Bergen, Norway. The program evolved from a national project that was initiated by music therapist Venja Ruud Nilsen in Oslo in the early 1990s. Today, most prisons in the country offer inmates the possibility to play in bands while they are incarcerated and to take part in music leisure activities in the community after the period is served. The project *Music in Custody and Liberty* is part of the rehabilitation philosophy of the Norwegian Correctional Services but also represents a critical force in relation to this.
>
> In a study on how involvement in the project is experienced by participants, Tuastad and Finsås (2008) examined the existing research on the life histories and living conditions of the population found in Norwegian prisons. This review suggested that life before imprisonment is characterized by less access to resources than what is typical in the society at large. Many inmates have little education and have had problems with getting a job. They are relatively poor and they often have health problems and drug addiction problems.

Box 1.3

With reference to research and theory within the discipline of criminology, the music therapists in this project concluded that individualized rehabilitation programs are not sufficient. It is also necessary to acknowledge how these people have been marginalized in society. The music therapists therefore decided that their approach should be informed by empowerment philosophy, and not just at the level of the individual but with a clear focus on possibilities for having a voice and participating in the community.

Music in Custody and Liberty is organized in three phases: 1) Intramural band activities while participants are in custody, 2) Supported band activities in a community culture center when participants have regained their liberty, 3) Self-initiated musical activities as a hobby or occupation when participants maintain their liberty. The same music therapists facilitate the band activities of phases 1 and 2 and offer support and supervision in phase 3. This way of organizing the program is in line with ecological thinking, as it supports the participants' transition from one context and life phase to another and as it takes specific interest in possible ripple effects. Public or semi-public performances are central to the process.

The history of one participant exemplifies the work: For very many years he lived a complicated life of drug addiction and criminality. Repeatedly he went in and out of prison. At one time when he was incarcerated he decided to join *Music in Custody and Liberty*. He discovered the program accidentally and afterwards claimed that he "decided to check it out merely because the information sheet looked kind of cool." In the beginning he just wanted to observe the activities but after a while he got "hooked" and wanted to take part. "It was kind of like something that made the time in prison worthwhile," he explained in a later interview. Participation in music created a change in his life situation, but only slowly. For some years he still lived a troubled life and experienced several new rounds in and out of prison. Every time he came back to prison he immediately registered for the music activities, however, and gradually he got more and more involved in music performances. A strong interest in music had become part of his identity. An important change occurred when he was granted a transfer from prison to a drug rehabilitation center. He played music intensively during the period of rehabilitation and when he was released he joined phase 2 of *Music in Custody and Liberty*. He participated in the band activities in the community culture center and decided not to return to the milieu of drugs and criminality. To play in the band gradually grew into more than a leisure activity and his participation evolved into phase 3. Today he works in the drug rehabilitation center where he was once treated and he is responsible for a music program in this institution, strongly influenced by the philosophy of *Music in Custody and Liberty* (Tuastad & Finsås, 2008, pp. 64–65).

Not all participants experienced this kind of dramatic transformation, of course, but the story illuminates important assets of this practice, in its focus on the empowerment of participants in phases of ecological transition.

The music therapist's willingness to investigate the directions suggested by the client or participant is often central in community music therapy.[3] This participatory dimension is illustrated well by the next example, from American music therapy:

> **Box 1.4 | FACING CANCER, DARKNESS, AND FEAR: FROM MUSIC THERAPY TO COMMUNITY IN NEW YORK**
>
> In New York, Alan Turry has explored the use of performance in music therapy, together with one of his clients, Maria Logis. Or, a more accurate description would perhaps be that Maria has explored the use of performance in music therapy, together with her music therapist, her friends, and her social network (Logis & Turry, 1999; Turry, 2005). Maria describes the beginning in the following way:
>
>> I was diagnosed with non-Hodgkin's lymphoma in the fall of 1994. I was in shock. I could feel nothing; silence and paralysis took over. In the midst of all my anguish, I turned to God for help, and the help that came was not at all what I would have imagined. I found music and, in it, a balm that made it possible for me to resist the crushing silence that enveloped me when I learnt that I was sick (Maria in Logis & Turry, 1999, p. 97).
>
> Music was not what Maria expected to find. Her relationship to music was far from simple; she had taken piano lessons as a child and tried to learn and sing as an adult, but it had not worked out so well for her. Some 10 years before the diagnosis she had tried to sing in a choir, in addition to taking classes and private singing lessons, but the experience was tough:
>
>> I wasn't good enough; I didn't practice enough; I lacked discipline; I couldn't read music; it was taking too much of my time. I dropped the choir and then I dropped the classes, hoping to salvage the singing lessons. But after 2 years of singing lessons, I gave up, totally frustrated and defeated. It was absolutely clear that I could not keep up with even the most minimal standards. I kicked myself for ever thinking I could sing (Maria in Logis & Turry, 1999, p. 98).
>
> The recurrence of the thought that she should sing seemed pretty ridiculous to her, but she pursued it and started searching for singing teachers. Her dentist gave her a name that turned out to be Alan's colleague who then referred her to Alan.
>
>> The first time we met, we made lots of sounds, and I found myself laughing for the first time in the weeks since the diagnosis. I decided to come back. What began in November 1994 and continues to this day is a process that has completely transformed my life.
>>
>> My struggle to accept my diagnosis and my great fear of treatment came up as soon as I started to sing. . . . The words just kept coming. . . . Alan treated my music and

Box 1.4 |

words like they were important; he kept me going by improvising on the piano. So I kept singing and more and more words and feelings came out (Maria in Logis & Turry, 1999, pp. 98–99).

While working with Alan, Maria also met Janet Savage, a singer and coach. Maria started to work with her too. After having heard recordings that Maria had shared from the improvised music therapy sessions, Janet came up with the idea of treating the improvisations as songs and suggested for Maria that she could perform them for friends. Maria "prayed about Janet's suggestions and discussed it with Alan" and soon they were planning a celebration of one year without chemotherapy, a celebration in song. Maria invited her friends to a concert of original music at her house.

Singing the songs for my friends was one of the happiest days of my life, and I have had very few days in my life that I could describe as happy. When I look at the photographs, I see myself smiling in joyous exuberance. I was celebrating a year without chemotherapy. It was like flying. I felt so alive. I was "singing my way through" the anguish of this illness.

The freedom of the music therapy process was exhilarating. I could not get over the fact that I could not make any mistakes in improvisation. I sang not only about being sick but about my lifelong sadness and despair (Maria in Logis & Turry, 1999, pp. 103–104).

The process continued with alterations between exploring pain, darkness and hope in improvisational music therapy and sharing songs with friends in semi-public events. In summing up the experience of sharing songs, Maria says:

A few months after the concert in my home, I had one at my church for a larger group of friends. Their support and love was deeply satisfying. In the spring of 1996, Alan arranged for me to share the music with students and faculty at a local university. Each experience of sharing the music publicly has helped me to claim my "voice."

I was amazed by the process. Dwelling within the embrace of music has helped me to create images about the many painful issues in my life, and the whole process of singing about silence is a way of defeating it. As I sing, I claim my voice (Maria in Logis & Turry, 1999, p. 114).

In an article written a few years after, Turry (2005) discusses problems and possibilities linked to an expansion of contexts for music therapy practice. He links this to the perspectives on practice developed within the emerging tradition of community music therapy.

The music therapy process described by Logis and Turry is collaborative; there is a shared willingness to explore new territory and there is reflexivity involved in dealing with the possibilities and pitfalls of the process. This is an example of community music therapy growing out of more conventional music therapy, emerging "from within," so to say.

The next example is taken from the Japanese context and has a very different starting point. Here, community music therapy does not grow from more conventional therapeutic practices but from musical and cultural ideas and visions.

Box 1.5 | WHERE EVERYBODY CAN COME AND SHARE MUSIC: THE OTOASOBI PROJECT IN KOBE

In Kobe in Japan, Rii Numata works as a music therapist, leads music workshops in a community space, and directs The Otoasobi Project, which is an improvisation collective for musicians with and without intellectual disabilities. In a paper called "EinScream!," she discusses how new musical ideas can create new possibilities to form community (Numata, 2009).

Numata discusses how music therapists pioneering improvisational music therapy have given different appraisals of the value of new music and she suggests that new music should be explored more actively in music therapy. In the context of the workshops that she leads, she has found Bailey's (1992) ideas on free improvisation especially helpful, in combination with modern principles of composition, such as the experimental principles of the "Shogi Composition" of the Japanese composer Makoto Nomura and the "game piece" *Cobra*, composed by the American avant-garde composer John Zorn.

The game pieces and experimental improvisations that Numata and her participants engage with are collaborative and unfold flexibly, according to certain rules that enable participants to understand and engage with the flow of events. Numata (2009) describes "a place where plural individual participants with different cultural resources meet and communicate with each other to create improvisational music." A participatory ethics is here transformed to a participatory aesthetics, so to say. Numata discusses the possibilities of new musical forms with coexistence of different values, skills, and intentions:

> From September 2004 to March 2005, I participated in a Community Music Therapy Project in Ashiya, Japan. During the project, the idea from free improvisation, Shogi Composition and Cobra were adopted so that every participant could take part and play freely and lively.
>
> . . . Based on the discussions about the process of improvisation, we tried to interweave each participant's musical resources into the music.
>
> My motivation in this project was to create a place where participants can concentrate on music-making itself and be able to communicate through music. This project aroused my interest in how it would be if music therapists, people with learning disabilities, and musicians who play free improvisation work together to create new music. It is still not known how participants will be if not intending therapeutic change but concentrating on exploring new musical expressions (Numata, 2009).

The author underlines that the creative space established was not "restricted only to clients such as people with learning disabilities, the elderly, and psychiatric patients but a place where anybody in the society could come and share music" (Numata, 2009).

The Japanese example illuminates how music is often a driving and motivating force in the development of community music therapy practice. Frequently the musical motivation is linked to broader cultural and social concerns, as the following example of interdisciplinary practice in Australia illustrates:

Box 1.6 | ARTSTORIES AND INTERDISCIPLINARY PRACTICE IN AUSTRALIA'S NORTHERN TERRITORY

The Northern Territory of Australia is vast and culturally diverse; The Northern Territory Aboriginal Interpreter Service has registered more than one hundred Indigenous languages and dialects. There are also a broad range of immigrant languages in the Territory. Many communities are therefore highly diverse, culturally and linguistically, while other communities are remote and isolated. This situation creates serious challenges in relation to learning and literacy.

Anja Tait, an Australian researcher, music educator, and music therapist, established ArtStories in 2006, in order to enhance possibilities for arts participation and partnership building, with learning and wellbeing as two of the goals. Music, as a medium for personal expression and cultural development was central to the initiative. Catherine Threlfall, another Australian music therapist, joined Tait in this project, together with workers from other professions. ArtStories developed as a transdisciplinary project, with the goal of connecting the language and practice of the arts with education, health, and wellbeing. Peer-coaching with school staff was also an important component of the project, with the goal of developing practices that are flexible and sustainable over time.

The activities of ArtStories include listening, singing, playing, dancing, writing, drawing, painting, constructing, and multimedia. In addition to being interdisciplinary, the approach is participatory and intergenerational. Younger people often work together with adults in ways that stimulate transmission of knowledge between generations. For example, in one of the remote Indigenous communities involved in the project, young men worked together with senior women and they produced two CDs and a series of instructional DVDs. This collaboration required the skills of both generations and served to promote Indigenous language and culture.

In 2008 an impact evaluation concluded that ArtStories played a critical pedagogical role in children's literacy learning and also generated wider community involvement. With funding support from government and philanthropic sectors ArtStories practices therefore continue to evolve, in education, health and community settings (Tait & Murrungun, 2010).

This Australian example demonstrates how community music therapy can be a partnered endeavor, culturally sensitive, and socially engaged.

FIGURE 1.2 | Lyric writing for the song "Life is Crazy" in the Hear Our Voices songwriting program, with music therapists Mike Viega and Scott MacDonald, Philadelphia, USA.

Photo: Ryan Brandenberg.

DEFINING COMMUNITY MUSIC THERAPY

To define community music therapy is not straight forward. For some, "community music therapy" is a contradiction in terms, since the term "therapy" quite often is used as a synonym to "treatment" or "curative intervention" at the individual level. We find it relevant to retain the term, both because we consider the relationships to the larger discipline of music therapy important and because **therapy** might be understood in broader terms, including meanings such as "care" and "service." This also links to popular language use, where music is often described as **therapeutic**, since many people find music helpful in various ways in their **everyday life activities** (see e.g. DeNora, 2000). As we have seen in the examples from the previous section, community music therapy goes beyond this to also embrace practices of **health promotion** and **social change**.

We could compare the term "community music therapy" to another other seemingly self-contradictory but still quite productive term, namely the "prose poem." The dictionary definition of prose is "speech or writing without metrical structure: opposed to verse or poetry."[4] In other words, prose and poetry are traditionally considered as mutually exclusive genres. When Baudelaire and others pioneered the genre of the prose poem in the nineteenth century, standard conceptions of both prose and poetry were challenged and a broader way of thinking about literature proposed. Later, this has influenced our conception of poetry in verse and of various prose genres such as the short story. New productive relationships were established (Janss & Refsum, 2003).

Each of the three terms constituting the compound *community music therapy* is multifaceted and complex. Take the term **community**. We touch the surface of the complexity by noting four simple observations. First, communities might be of various types, not just neighborhoods and localities, but voluntary or accidental gatherings also. Second, a community is not necessarily a given, it can emerge in and as we participate in social activities. Third, people will participate in communities in a range of ways, depending on how they perceive the relationship between their own project and the culture of the community. Fourth, a community is nested in, and thus both influencing and influenced by, various other social and cultural systems.

How one defines community music therapy depends in part on how one defines music therapy. There are general music therapy definitions that leave little space for community music therapy but there are also definitions that offer assistance when approaching the question of what community music therapy could be. One of these is proposed by Ruud (1980, 1998), who suggests that music therapy is aimed at increasing people's **possibilities for action**. This view is based on a sociological understanding of health problems. "Possibilities of action" are not only challenged because of individual problems but also because of structural barriers in society. Ruud's definition, developed in the late 1970s, foreshadowed aspects of the current discourse on community music therapy.[5]

One of the first specific definitions of community music therapy was presented by Kenneth Bruscia in *Defining Music Therapy*:

> In *Community Music Therapy*, the therapist works with clients in traditional individual or group music therapy settings, while also working with the community. The purpose is twofold: to prepare the client to participate in community functions and become a valued member of the community; and to prepare the community to accept and embrace the clients by helping its members understand and interact with the clients.
>
> (Bruscia, 1998, p. 237)

Bruscia's definition is less extended than several of the definitions of community music therapy that have been developed after 2000. For instance; Bruscia focused on individual or group music therapy in local communities, while contemporary community music therapy covers a range of different practices and communities. In an elaboration of the notion of community music therapy, Stige (2003, p. 454) proposes that community music therapy can be defined at three levels:

> Community Music Therapy as an area of professional practice is situated health musicking in a community, as a planned process of collaboration between client and therapist with a specific focus upon promotion of sociocultural and communal change

through a participatory approach where music as ecology of performed relationships is used in non-clinical and inclusive settings.

Community Music Therapy as emerging sub-discipline is the study and learning of relationships between music and health as these develop through interactions between people and the communities they belong to.

Community Music Therapy as emerging professional specialty is a community of scholar-practitioners with a training and competence qualifying them for taking an active musical and social role in a community, with specific focus upon the promotion of justice, equitable distribution of resources, and inclusive conditions for health-promoting sociocultural participation.

(Stige, 2003, p. 454)

This definition illuminates how practice must be understood in relation to the branch of learning and the profession it is associated with. The definition is long and complex, however, and it is understandable that many authors have wanted to present shorter and simpler definitions. One such definition was put forward by Ruud in 2004, in a statement that combines one practice characteristic with one theory characteristic: "Community music therapy, then, may be defined as 'the reflexive use of performance-based music therapy within a systemic perspective'" (Ruud, 2004).

Ruud's definition stimulated an intense discussion in *Voices: A World Forum for Music Therapy*. The importance of reflexivity and of systemic perspectives was acknowledged by many, but the proposal that community music therapy could be defined as performance-based practice was controversial. Several participants in the discussion acknowledged that community music therapy processes often include musical performances but were not willing to give this aspect a defining status. Some of the arguments can be summarized by suggesting that community music therapy is perhaps performative (see below) but not necessarily performance-based. Other participants in the debate focused less on the specific claims made in Ruud's definition and instead problematized the whole idea of defining community music therapy.[6]

In short, definitions of community music therapy tend to be complex or controversial, or both. In the next section we will examine some reasons why this is so and also suggest a possible alternative approach to the task of developing language for descriptions and reflections on the identity of community music therapy.

RECOGNIZING COMMUNITY MUSIC THERAPY

Community music therapy is being developed in various ways in relation to a range of local contexts, cultures, and social situations. There are therefore limits to how clarifying general definitions can be. Ansdell (2005a) argues that we do not necessarily improve communication by establishing boundaries and definitions separately from contextual use. Another reason why definitions do not always clarify, Ansdell contends, is that there is an endless regress involved; the definition of one term implies use of terms that also call for definition. One is made to realize that there are many "fuzzy" terms involved in any

FIGURE 1.3 | Exploring music, exploring collaboration. The Otoasobi Project, an improvisation collective for musicians with and without intellectual disabilities, Kobe, Japan.
Photo: Kaneko Yoshiro.

language statement. "Seen from an analytical or positivist perspective this is a bad state of affairs!" Ansdell asserts, but he argues that this should not be considered a defect, since it invites us to explore concepts in context. He proposes the following alternative to exact definitions of community music therapy:

> Instead of abstract synoptic definition of a phenomenon (achieved by hovering above it), we instead make a horizontal, 'on-the-ground' characterization: in terms seeing the pattern of it in everyday use, within its local contexts (which themselves shift constantly). This is a form of understanding by seeing what everyone actually already sees, but then emphasising its key elements so the pattern really stands out. So instead of saying 'the central defining element of CoMT is either x, y or z' we instead look at how the pattern of its elements is rearranged in *new relationships* within any given context. So CoMT is not defined by anything new, or anything 'particular'—but by a new arrangement of known elements: in short, a new *pattern* (or, perhaps to avoid this also sounding too fixed, new *patterning* within a specific context, or need, or use).

> (Ansdell, 2005a)

Limitations of definition are not distinctive to community music therapy. Related disciplines, such as community psychology, encounter similar problems. Nelson and Prilleltensky (2005) argue that it is generally accepted that no definition can capture the complexities of community psychology's theory and practice in any accurate way. Instead of producing a single definition, it has therefore become common to outline a series of themes that characterize this field. For purposes of illustration we will present a description of the list that the community psychology pioneer Julian Rappaport developed as early as in 1977:

> its ecological nature . . . the importance of cultural relativity and diversity so that people are not judged against one single standard or value . . . and a focus on social change. . . . Moreover, Rappaport (1977) argued that CP is concerned with human resource development, political activity and scientific inquiry, three elements that are often in conflict with one another. As the subtitle of his book *Community Psychology: Values, Research and Action,* suggests, CP is a balancing act between values, research and action.
>
> (Nelson & Prilleltensky, 2005, p. 4)

Similar ideas are typical in the community music therapy literature. On the basis of several theoretical discussions developed during the 1990s, Stige (2002, pp. 129–131) proposed a framework for description of community music therapy with a focus on: *health promotion* (prophylactic health work through the strengthening of social networks), *ethics-driven practice and research* (with an activist focus on conditions for cultural and social participation), and an *ecological approach* that supports work that goes beyond the individual or the microsystem level. Based on eight case studies from four different countries, Stige, Ansdell, Elefant and Pavlicevic (2010b) proposed five broad key features, suggesting that community music therapy practice is typically *ecological, participatory, performative, resource-oriented,* and *actively reflective.*

We will use the term **qualities** to refer to a synthesized and modified formulation and sequence of the frames and key features mentioned above. The term "quality" refers to features that characterize community music therapy and that can be reviewed for their significance and relevance in relation to issues of practice. We offer the acronym of PREPARE for communication of seven qualities that characterize community music therapy:

P – Participatory
R – Resource-oriented
E – Ecological
P – Performative
A – Activist
R – Reflective
E – Ethics-driven.

These qualities relate to practice as well as to research and they are examined in the theories and meta-theories that inform practice and research. The qualities also relate to musical as well as paramusical aspects (this is a distinction we will introduce in Chapter 5, where we will discuss how musical processes are embedded in cultural contexts and developed in interaction with related processes of movement, language, and social communication). Many of the seven qualities can be illustrated by revisiting the first example that we presented in this chapter.

In the brief example we gave from the practice of the Music Therapy Community Clinic in the Greater Cape Town area, the *participatory* quality is not particularly striking at first sight. The police had to fetch the youngsters, disarm them, and deliver them to the music therapy door. The youngsters came back voluntarily, however, drawn by their interest for music. Participatory qualities have to be nurtured before they can grow. The *resource-oriented* quality is clearly present; music is a magnet that attracts the youngsters; it is a "cool" thing to do that affords the experience of community as well as the expression of social commentary. The *ecological* quality in this specific example seems to be emerging. The music therapy activities that are described are based in the micro-system that a group of youngsters and the two music therapists create, but the practice relates to processes in the local community and is established in interaction with other significant agents in the broader community. The *performative* quality is unmistakably there; to take part in the music therapy activities affords the possibility of performing new identities, as band members rather than gang members. The *activist* quality is not highlighted in the music therapists' presentation of their work but is perhaps implicit in how they and the participants relate to the issue that instigated the process, namely the problematic role of gangs in the cultural and social life of this local community. The *reflective* quality seems to be prominent. The music therapists describe one aspect of this in the following way:

> From the 2nd session, the group spontaneously began telling us their stories. At first we were concerned that this was taking up too much of the 'music' session time, as it was completely unrelated to the music. We soon changed our minds. . . . explanations provide an opportunity for group members to process their experiences and to express aspects of their lives, which they would usually choose to keep to themselves.
>
> (Fouché & Torrance, 2005)

The final *ethics-driven* quality is primary in this example; what initiates the process is not a concern about individual pathology but a socially engaged perspective on neighborhood challenges, the risks that youngsters face, and the inadequacy of the criminal justice system to deal with these problems in any constructive way. The processes that followed led to change for the youngsters as well as the music therapists involved:

> The role of gangs in an area such as Heideveld, is immensely complex. On the surface, and especially to 'outsiders', gangs appear to be exclusively 'bad' and destructive. It is only after understanding the complicated social networks and historical legacies on which gangs are founded, that one begins to understand their appeal—and indeed, their necessity. Within the Music Therapy room, our experience is that gang members'

roles and identities are shed, and replaced by vulnerable and open young people. Music therapy provides an opportunity to explore different ways of relating, creating and expressing. As therapists we too have learnt to leave our stereotypes of gangs and adolescent gang members well beyond the walls of the Music Therapy room. This helps us to relate to the gang members as young persons in music therapy, and also enables them to experiment and create other social identities.

(Fouché & Torrance, 2005)

The qualities described here are hardly unique for community music therapy in every aspect. The combination of them is characteristic. Even if this is so, each practice usually stresses some of the qualities more than others, depending on needs and possibilities in a given situation. The relevance of a specific quality usually also changes over time. Taken together the seven qualities help us to recognize community music therapy. The interesting question is rarely whether or not a practice should be labeled community music therapy. What counts more is to be able to assess when and how and to what degree each one of the seven qualities—and combinations of them—are relevant in relation to a situation. The information, insights, and discussions in the community music therapy literature can be pertinent to consider also when only some of the qualities discussed here are character-istic of the practice in question. If some qualities are less characteristic, the literature can instigate reflections on why this is so and whether it should continue to be so.

A way of contextualizing the acronym of PREPARE is to relate it to the argument previously made by Bruscia (1998, p. 237) who claimed that there is a twofold purpose of community music therapy; to *prepare* individuals to participate in community functions and to *prepare* the community to accept and support each individual. Community music therapy practices should neither neglect the needs for individual change nor the needs for social change; the focus is on enhanced mutual relationships. The many disadvantages that characterize the local community that we have just visited create difficult challenges for youngsters. Enhanced mutual relationships do not always come easy. As a celebration of human connectedness in music, community music therapy can often be a lot of fun. As a practice addressing issues such as inequity and marginalization, community music therapy is concurrently serious and demanding work that requires solid competencies and valid collaborations. In the next sections we will give a brief explication of each of the seven qualities of the PREPARE acronym and outline where these qualities will be discussed in more detail throughout the book. The seven qualities interact in myriad ways, which will be evident from the examples and discussions of qualities throughout the book.

PARTICIPATORY AND RESOURCE-ORIENTED QUALITIES

The **participatory** quality of community music therapy refers to how processes afford opportunities for individual and social participation, how participation is valued, and how the idea of partnership is supported. The expertise of the music therapist is often crucial but so is the expertise of the participants; community music therapy is not an expert-

FIGURE 1.4 | Performing health and wellbeing. A Children's Welfare Musical, Bergen, Norway. Photo: Astrid Merete Nordhaug.

directed practice. A participatory approach involves the willingness to listen to all voices involved and to acknowledge that there might be several change leaders in a social process. Instead of using terms such as client or patient in therapy or treatment, it is therefore usually more relevant to talk of participants in a collaborative process.

The participatory quality is linked to the issue of human rights and requests a focus on mutual empowerment and democracy in processes of decision making. The participatory quality is central to the discussions throughout the book and will be given specific treatment in the discussions of practice in Chapters 6 to 8 and in the discussions of research in Chapter 9 and (re)professionalization in Chapter 10.

The **resource-oriented** quality of community music therapy reflects a focus on (collaborative) mobilization of personal strengths and social, cultural, and material resources. We usually associate the term resource with reserves and supplies of various sorts. In sociological theory and research there is a tradition for using "resource" or "capital" as metaphors for the reserves and supplies people appropriate in their daily life in order to be able to tackle problems and explore possibilities.

In community music therapy, resources can be of different types, for instance the personal strengths of participants, such as musical talents and interests, relational resources, such as trust and emotional support, and community resources, such as music organizations and traditions. Personal problems and disorders might well be part of the picture in community music therapy practices. Often it is essential to take this into consideration when planning activities and processes, but diagnosis and treatment is not central in community music therapy (see Chapters 6 to 8). The challenge of living with and relating to personal troubles is dealt with in the context of processes that seek to nurture personal resources and, when relevant, to increase access to social, cultural, and material resources. This involves taking social and cultural problems seriously, for instance with the objective of building down social and cultural barriers for participation. The resource-oriented quality therefore does not exclude the possibility of critique and confrontation in the service of social change.

Resources are tangible and intangible, then, as they refer to relational processes as well as to material goods that can be appropriated by members of a community. Inequities in the distribution of health resources are discussed in Chapter 3. Social capital and other social resources are discussed in Chapter 4. In Chapter 5, music is discussed as a health resource and social resource, building and relying on paramusical resources. Chapters 6 to 8 give several examples of how resources are produced, appropriated, and (re)distributed in community music therapy practice.

ECOLOGICAL AND PERFORMATIVE QUALITIES

The **ecological** quality of community music therapy involves working with the reciprocal relationships between individuals, groups, and networks in social context.

The modern usage of the term "ecology" was developed in biology, to describe the reciprocal influences between organisms and their environments. Since the 1960s this term has become influential as a metaphor also for the description of human sociocultural life. In the psychological literature, for instance, many models to describe the ecological character of human life have been proposed, usually with an account of various levels of analysis.[7]

All human practices can be understood ecologically (changes at the level of the individual will have implications for various social systems and vice versa). Community music therapy practices actively work with ecological relationships, for instance by exploring relationships between various groups or between individual and community. What systems and ecological levels that are involved can vary considerably, depending on the needs and resources of each project and context.

In Chapter 4 we clarify how the ecological metaphor has influenced the social sciences, while in Chapter 5 we discuss ecological perspectives on music. The ecological metaphor is also central to the discussion of practice that we will present in Chapters 6 to 8.

The **performative** quality of community music therapy refers to the focus on human development through action and performance of relationships in ecological contexts. This does not suggest that reflection is subordinate (see below) but that reflection is inevitably related to performances of self and social systems.

The performative quality is crucial for exploration of the role of music in community music therapy. It also characterizes community music therapy's proactive role in relation to health and development. The main focus is *promotion of health* and *prevention of problems* rather than curative interventions. Community music therapy practices at times collaborate with the health care sector, but they are not necessarily part of this sector and usually not oriented towards treatment. The focus is on the collaborative efforts for health and wellbeing and the question of how persons, groups, or communities live with and deal with health problems comes into focus. Consequently, the promotion of positive health and quality of life in everyday contexts is vital. Many community music therapy practices therefore involve activities that are not labeled therapy. Groups and projects often identify themselves with proper names, for instance, which demonstrates how these practices may be important for the musical identity of the participants.

Concepts of health and wellbeing in various contexts will be discussed in Chapter 3, followed by a discussion of human development in social context in Chapter 4. The performative qualities of music are elaborated further in Chapter 5.

ACTIVIST, REFLECTIVE, AND ETHICS-DRIVEN QUALITIES

The **activist** quality of community music therapy involves acknowledgement of the fact that people's problems are related to limitations in society, such as unequal access to resources. It also involves willingness to act in relation to this. The activist quality suggests that social change is part of the community music therapy agenda. Participants and music therapists work together, often in collaboration and partnership with others, in order to change the world, if only a bit. The activist quality is perhaps more controversial than most of the other qualities, but logically goes together with, for instance, the participatory quality and the quality of ethics-driven practice.

Activist work requires negotiation and reflection, and must be balanced with the other qualities of community music therapy, as we will explicate in more detail in Chapters 6 to 10.

The **reflective** quality of community music therapy practices refers to dialogic and collaborative attempts at appreciating and understanding processes, outcomes, and broader implications. This often involves thinking and discussing but not exclusively; actions, interactions, and reactions also contribute to understanding. The participatory ethos described above invites negotiation with all involved parties and talks against the idea of the music therapist as the sole expert. Lay and local knowledge is therefore central to the idea of reflection in community music therapy. It still makes sense to focus on research as a central component in these negotiations and collective processes. Research-informed knowledge is a resource when taking an active musical and social role in a community. In order to be relevant as a resource, research in community music therapy must build on multidisciplinary and multilevel perspectives. Openness for the integration of research, theory, and action is also helpful.

Practice characterized by dialogues and collective processes of reflection are explicated in Chapters 6 to 8. In Chapter 9 we discuss community music therapy research and in Chapter 10 implications for the notion of professionalization in community music therapy.

The **ethics-driven** quality of community music therapy refers to how practice, theory, and research is rights-based; the values informing the human rights and the intention of realizing rights guide the activity. Health and wellbeing, community, and music are central to community music therapy practices and these goals are sought to be realized in practices that are nurtured by values such as freedom, respect, equality, and solidarity. What these values involve varies somewhat from one context to another, however, and most people have experienced tensions between values, for instance those between the values of freedom and equality. The ethical foundation of community music therapy practices is therefore negotiated in context.

Issues related to values inform the chapters throughout the book. In Chapter 3, relationships between health and equality are discussed. In Chapter 7 we specifically discuss the notion of community music therapy as a rights-based practice and the central values that support this notion.

CONTINUATION OF AND CONTRAST TO CONVENTIONAL MUSIC THERAPY[8]

Community music therapy practices focus on collaborative possibilities and actualize music therapy's responsibilities in relation to the social domain. A context for this can be established by making a comparison with an established definition of music therapy. One of the larger and more influential music therapy associations in the world, the American Music Therapy Association (AMTA) has defined music therapy in the following way:

> Music Therapy is the clinical and evidence-based use of music interventions to accomplish individualized goals within a therapeutic relationship by a credentialed professional who has completed an approved music therapy program.
>
> (American Music Therapy Association, 2011)

There is tension between this definition and the ideas presented in this chapter. Community music therapy is not necessarily clinical. Goals are sometimes individualized, sometimes not. The pursuit of these goals is not restricted to the realm of a therapeutic relationship. The "interventions" in community music therapy are usually more accurately described by broader terms such as "involvement" and "initiative." And, while community music therapy is informed by research, the phrase "evidence-based use of music interventions" is quite limited in light of the participatory and context-sensitive nature of community music therapy.

The previous paragraph highlights differences between community music therapy and one established view of music therapy. We have to ask: Is community music therapy compatible with received views of how music therapy should be defined and practiced? Instead of answering positively or negatively to this question, we must remember that there is a multitude of definitions of music therapy around the world and that no definition can be made free of cultural or theoretical influences. These influences might be subtle and attenuated, but transparent language free of influence is not achievable. A rough appraisal would be that AMTA's definition is influenced by biomedical and psychological assumptions that are not very compatible with the perspectives informing community music therapy practices. Other definitions of music therapy, such as Even Ruud's sociologically informed definition discussed earlier in the chapter, are much more in agreement with community music therapy perspectives. It is futile to hope for a neutral or comprehensive understanding of music therapy. It is probably more helpful to examine how various perceptions supplement and challenge each other and thus provide impetus for scholarly debate and development.

How community music therapy can be described as a continuation of and contrast to conventional music therapy will be a topic throughout this book. This links to the question of the identity of music therapy as a field of practice and study. The multiplicity of perspectives and ideas that characterize music therapy is a resource for scholarly debate and development, as long as there is contact between various traditions and some exchange of knowledge and ideas. In this way, new ideas in community music therapy can inform and challenge notions accepted as given in more conventional practices, and vice versa. What the conventions are will change over time. Community music therapy can play a constructive role in relation to more conventional fields of the discipline by challenging established notions in ways that encourage continued dialogue and discussion.

Rather than being based on expert-defined diagnoses of individuals, community music therapy processes grow out of negotiated understandings of specific situations. There is less focus on "fixing" people's problems and more focus on mobilizing resources that might help people to grow in the context of improved practices and policies. The examples at the beginning of the chapter also reveal how community music therapy can open up new aesthetic possibilities through its focus on collaboration, participation, and inclusion in music. In this respect, community music therapy can be considered part of broader social and cultural processes, as a practice that supports and empowers people to regain their rights for music and community (Ruud, 2004). This can be seen in relation to increasing evidence suggesting that communication through sound and movement is an innate human capacity that makes both music and companionship possible (Malloch & Trevarthen, 2009).

Community music therapy is related to various processes of sociocultural change in late modern societies. One dimension of this can be described as an increasing tendency to individualization contrasted by a renewed interest in community and fellowship. Another dimension can be described as an accelerating specialization of expert-driven health services contrasted by lay initiatives stressing empowerment and collaboration, often with reference to human rights, such as the right to participation in society. The emergence of community music therapy should be understood in the context of these tendencies and struggles, not as the answer to the dilemmas they reveal but as one practical and academic response (Stige, 2003).

In other words: In reflecting on the importance and relevance of community music therapy, several factors need to be taken into consideration. Universal human capacities make musical community and collaborative musicking possible. Local circumstances define the opportunities and barriers to participation. Universal human rights make participation in society and access to health, education, and culture burning issues. Again, local circumstances define the needs and priorities. Individualized treatment is of course legitimate and significant in many cases but can never eliminate or substantially reduce large scale health problems in a society. Fields such as community psychology, social work, and health promotion have taken this challenge seriously. Individualized treatment must be supplemented by more proactive, social, and cultural approaches to health and development. Community music therapy is part of such complementary strategies.

FIGURE 1.5 | Shared willingness to explore new territory. Maria Logis and Alan Turry in New York, in a process that led from music psychotherapy to community music therapy.

Photo: Jun Oshima.

CONCLUSION

Much of the development of music therapy as a modern discipline has concentrated on individualized treatment, but sub-currents of community-oriented and health promoting practices have existed in several countries. Since the late 1990s, this trend has gained strength internationally.

Community music therapy practices are focused on the linking of individuals and communities through health-promoting musicking. Linking of individuals and communities is multifaceted, as are the relationships between private and public aspects of human life. Community music therapy could therefore not be described exclusively as a contrast to more conventional practices of modern music therapy; it should also be described as a complementary movement. This does not exclude the possibility of community music therapy developing "dangerous knowledge," that is; knowledge that challenges taken-for-granted assumptions in established practices.

Community music therapy can be defined at three levels, as practice, sub-discipline, and professional specialty. As *practice*, community music therapy should be thought of in open terms, as a set of related practices rather than as one specific form of practice. These practices might have some shared characteristics, but there is also considerable diversity between practices, due to differences in local values and circumstances. What can be shared across contexts are not specific activities and techniques, then, but the interest in exploring collaborative music-making informed by certain values and tools for reflection. As *sub-discipline*, community music therapy can be understood as the study of music, health, and social change, in the context of human social life and in the light of human social needs and capacities. Community music therapy is a broad field of study, not least because of the multiple ecological levels involved. As *professional specialty*, community music therapy is based on many of the established skills of the music therapy profession, such as an ability to work with emotionally challenging communication problems and to invite people into musical participation, whatever their musical skills might be. In addition, community music therapy requires attention to an expanded set of professional competencies, such as the ability to understand problems in relation to social situations, to work with collaborative musicking (often including public performances), to articulate one's own values in relation to community problems, to establish alliances across contexts, and to mediate between diverse community members.

Given the multifaceted and contextualized character of community music therapy, any definition tends to grow either too complex or too simple. As one possible way of dealing with the dilemma of definition, we have offered the acronym PREPARE to communicate seven qualities that tend to characterize community music therapy as practice, discipline, and profession.

The emergence of community music therapy represents an invitation to the discipline of music therapy to become more socially involved. But community music therapy is also a continuation and development of values and knowledge that have been cultivated in music therapy for decades. The emergence of community music therapy implies that music therapists allow themselves to use these skills in the service of communities and processes of social change. The relevance of the invitation to community music therapy can be outlined both in relation to the biologically grounded human capacity for connectivity in and through music and in relation to late modern developments that make human connectivity a burning issue in contemporary societies.

KEY TERMS, DISCUSSION TOPICS, AND NOTES

Key Terms

Key terms in order of appearance:

> Human connectedness
> Attending to unheard voices
> Musicking
> Therapy
> Therapeutic
> Everyday life
> Health promotion
> Social change
> Community
> Possibilities for action
> Defining community music therapy
> Limitations of definition

Qualities of community music therapy (PREPARE):

> Participatory
> Resource-oriented
> Ecological
> Performative
> Activist
> Reflective
> Ethics-driven

Discussion Topics

The following critical thinking questions can be discussed in class or in groups, or used by the individual student for critical reflection on topics discussed in the chapter. Extra resources can be found on the website of the book.

1. Many people use music as a resource in their everyday lives. This usage includes music for health and wellbeing. Some people therefore think and talk of music as "therapeutic." Discuss possible implications for the profession of music therapy.

2. While many advocate that definitions are essential for clear scholarly communication, we have seen in this chapter that some scholars argue that we do not necessarily improve communication by establishing boundaries and definitions separately from contextual use. One implication of taking this view would be to seek out various exemplars that can help us understand. Whatever stance you take in this discussion, describe in some detail one exemplar of community music therapy. Try to explain why you find this example illuminating.

3. The final quality in the acronym PREPARE (E for ethics-driven) suggests that community music therapy is driven by negotiated visions of music, health, and community rather than by expert decisions in relation to the pathology of the individual. In the UK, Simon Procter has discussed music therapy's relationship to non-medical initiatives in mental health:

> Services offered in such provision vary, but since the aim is empowerment by focusing on people's ability and potential for wellness (rather than disability and illness), the emphasis tends to be on the practical (counselling, welfare and benefits advice, language/literacy classes, etc.) and the creative (musical, artistic, literary). Given this double emphasis on the practical and the creative, it seems odd that music therapy is rarely available.
>
> (Procter, 2001)

Similar non-medical initiatives as those described by Procter exist in many countries, with or without the inclusion of music therapy. What are the relationships between music therapy and these initiatives in your country and what is your appraisal of the situation?

Notes

1   The metaphor of attending to the voices of all participants is salient in international peace research (Galtung, 1999). If everybody is allowed to use his or her voice, the risk that people will use violence to attack the community—or that they turn the frustrations inward and attack themselves—is reduced.

2   "Musicking" is a term introduced by Small (1998). A similar notion, spelled "musicing," was developed by Elliott (1995) but with less focus on music-making as the performance of relationships in a social situation. Our conceptual understanding of "musicking" is influenced by Small's work as well as by theories in cultural psychology and music sociology on how agents, activities, and artifacts interact and thus constitute each other. In some of the literature cited in this book (notably several texts by Ansdell and Pavlicevic), Elliott's spelling "musicing" is used even when the conceptual understanding is closer to Small's "musicking."

3   Some community music therapy processes grow out of traditional clinical contexts, and authors therefore sometimes find it relevant to use terms such as "client" or even "patient" when describing practice. The general term that we will employ in this book is *participant*, given the participatory perspective taken when we describe the basic principles of community music therapy.

4   This wording is taken from The New International Webster's Dictionary and Thesaurus of the English Language, the 2000 edition.

5   This perspective on music therapy became important for Norwegian community music therapy practices in the 1980s and 1990s (Kleive & Stige, 1988; Byrkjedal, 1992; Einbu, 1993; Stige, 1993, 1993/1999).

6   Ruud's definition and the discussion of it has been published under the heading "Debating the Winds of Change in Community Music Therapy," see: http://www.voices.no.

7   Bronfenbrenner's (1979) model of microsystems embedded by mesosystems, exosystems, and macrosystems has been influential and has informed other models describing the interplay between individuals, groups, organizations, localities, and various larger systems (see Chapter 4).

8   The term "conventional music therapy" is not an exact term, given the fact that music therapy is practiced and discussed in a multitude of ways. The conventions that we refer to by using this term are: to examine symptoms and health problems at the level of the individual, to focus the interventions at this level, and to work within the boundaries of a clinical arena (the "therapeutic space" of a clinic, institution, or private office).

A Brief History

After studying Chapter 2, you will be able to discuss questions such as:

■ How do traditional practices of musical healing resemble and differ from the practices of contemporary community music therapy?

■ What were the central community-related ideas in the literature of the pioneering decades of modern music therapy?

■ What characterized the systemic and sociocultural turn in music therapy theories of the 1980s?

■ What kind of sociocultural change contributed to a renewed practical interest in community-based and community-oriented music therapy in the 1980s and 1990s?

■ Why did community music therapy emerge as an international discourse and field of study in the early years of the twenty-first century?

■ Which metaphors can best describe the historical development of community music therapy?

TRADITIONAL COMMUNAL PRACTICES OF MUSIC AND HEALTH

THE development of music therapy as a discipline and profession is best understood when seen in relation to various contemporary and historical contexts. In the final chapter of this book we will discuss how current developments in late modern societies influence the music therapy profession. In this chapter, we will take a historical perspective and look at some of the processes that have stimulated the materialization of community music therapy as a field of study and practice.

Throughout the history of modern music therapy, various community development initiatives based on an appreciation of human rights and visions of social justice have instigated efforts at making health, education, and valued cultural participation attainable for all citizens.[1] Music therapists that have linked their work to such initiatives have demonstrated how music therapy has something to offer other than individualized treatment (Stige, 2003). If we look at how music is and has been used in traditional societies, we might also understand more of the social and cultural possibilities in collaborative music-making and how these relate to health, wellbeing, and community development.

Traditional practices that in some ways resemble those found in contemporary community music therapy have been present in earlier times and still exist and flourish in many cultures. A current example such as the various **ngoma** traditions in Central, Eastern, and Southern Africa might on the surface look quite different from most community music therapy practices, but there are similarities in the focus on health-related music-making in a collaborative and participatory process. There are a large number of ngoma traditions, a famous example being the Tumbuka tradition of "dancing prophets" in Malawi, studied by Friedson (1996, 2000). In the Tumbuka tradition, Friedson claims, illness, suffering, and healing are events and processes saturated with music. The rituals of healing are semi-public social–musical events designed to address the spirits of the

FIGURE 2.1 | Ngoma healing in the Kamba tradition in Kenya.
Photo: Muriithi Kigunda.

Tumbuka tradition, but also to activate a wider social field. In the rituals that Friedson describes, trance is a central element. This is related to the cosmology of the Tumbuka people, where the spirits of the ancestors play a central role. Trance therefore becomes a vehicle for establishing contact with the spirits.

The spiritual dimension is typical of many African musical traditions of healing (Kigunda, 2004), but there are also ngoma traditions with less explicit reference to spiritual domains and more focus on the social and political dimensions of human existence (Schumaker, 2000). Barz (2006) has studied how music has been used in relation to the HIV/AIDS pandemic in Uganda. While HIV/AIDS at one level is a medical crisis, it is obviously a personal, social, cultural, spiritual, and economic crisis as well. In this situation, the collaborative music-making of the ngoma tradition is invaluable, Barz argues. He describes how people use music to educate themselves and their neighbors about how the disease spreads and about what counteractions could be taken to reduce the infection rates. Barz also documents how music activities can empower participants, build a sense of support and community, and challenge gender stereotypes that contribute to the reproduction of the problem. In this way music becomes part of **multiple healing systems**, where traditional healers, lay practices, and medical services co-exist and supplement each other.

Traditional practices that employ communal and musical rituals of healing do exist in all continents. These practices are often considered "worlds apart" from the professional and research-informed practices of modern music therapy. Often the music therapy literature mentions these practices in the passing, as examples of pre-scientific practices. There have been some voices, however, claiming that music therapists should be more knowledgeable and aware of these traditional practices (Kenny, 1982, 2006; Moreno, 1988, 1995a, 1995b; Rohrbacher, 1993, 2008; Ruud, 1992a, 1995; Sekeles, 1996; Stige, 1983, 2002). Many of these scholars have taken an interest in how traditional rituals integrate musical, social, and healing processes.

This can be seen in relation to anthropologist Janzen's (2000) discussion of the need for an interdisciplinary platform for the study of music and health. Janzen suggests that the segregated character of modern disciplines and universities, where health studies and music studies are usually located in different departments and faculties, contributes to a situation where the totality of traditional healing rituals is seldom understood because researchers tend to take an interest in selected aspects instead of the whole ritual with its interacting components. Janzen argues that music therapy could have the capacity to contribute with integrative efforts in relation to this schism, but claims that this challenge and possibility has not been taken seriously enough among music therapists.

EARLY COMMUNITY-RELATED IDEAS IN THE MUSIC THERAPY LITERATURE

When music therapy established itself as a new profession in the 1940s and 50s, medical and behavioral ideas were prominent. There was some interest in ethnographic investigations of traditional practices, as documented in the book *Music and Medicine*

(Schullian & Schoen, 1948), but as Gouk (2000) has argued, these traditional practices were thought of as unscientific precedent cases of limited relevance for current practice. An early critique of this way of thinking was developed by the American ethnomusicologist Bruno Nettl (1956). He argued that there is therapeutic value in the way traditional cultures integrate music, words, and movement in ritual settings. Nettl contrasted this to the more limited study of the direct effect of music on behavior, which he understood was the focus of modern American music therapy.

In the next two decades, the 1960s and 70s, behaviorist theory and practice dominated American music therapy. It is still not correct to claim that community-related issues were ignored. In one of the first textbooks in music therapy, Gaston's (1968) *Music in Therapy,* a whole section was devoted to music therapy in the community. One of the statements made was:

> Certainly, music therapists will have to become increasingly aware of the greater integration of community and treatment if they are to be current in their practice. Imagination, improvisation, and continued learning directed toward community-centered institutions will characterize the successful music therapist.
>
> (Folsom, 1968, p. 361)

Florence Tyson was one of the American pioneers who contributed with insights on relationships between community and music therapy (see Box 2.1). In the 1950s, 60s, and 70s, Tyson published several texts that focused on issues such as "outpatient music therapy" and "music therapy in the community." Tyson's work illuminated how clinical practice is influenced by context, but she did relatively little to develop new theoretical perspectives that can inform community-based and community-oriented music therapy. This challenge was taken up in the 1980s by Carolyn Kenny (see below), who pioneered culture-sensitive and systemic perspectives to music therapy theory.

In the 1960s and '70s, a few American music therapists explored social perspectives on music therapy (e.g. Hadsell, 1974). In an article called "Community Music Therapy with Adolescents," for instance, Ragland and Apprey (1974) documented a choir project with a population of delinquent adolescents. As the choir performed publicly, the singers received recognition for their performance work. In discussing the project, the authors highlight gains in attendance and motivation in relation to school work. The previously delinquent students developed better school attendance and performance and exhibited better work habits and behaviors.

Some community-related ideas are also found in the music therapy literature of the early years of British music therapy. The work of the pioneer **Juliette Alvin** is a case in point. She never developed a systematic discussion of music therapy and community, but in the 1960s she did publish some reflections on community care and implications for music therapy. She also developed ideas about the necessary fit between music therapy practices and the place in which sessions are held. In her influential book *Music Therapy,* she discussed how the "work has to be conceived in order to fit not only the patient but the place in which the music sessions are held" (Alvin, 1966/1975, p. 159). Alvin was also concerned about increasing possibilities for participation in the community beyond

Box 2.1 | FLORENCE TYSON: THE COMMUNITY MUSIC THERAPY CENTER

Already in the late 1950s Florence Tyson discussed what she called "outpatient music therapy," in response to the de-hospitalization of American psychiatry (Tyson, 1959). Some years later, she wrote a short piece called "The Community Music Therapy Center," where she discussed the history, goals, and organization of a center she had built up in New York (Tyson, 1968). The backdrop was the development of community-based rehabilitative centers throughout the US in the 1960s.

Tyson was one of the first music therapists to regularly use the term "community music therapy," but her concept of community music therapy was probably different from current understandings of the term. She never defined the term, but seems to have used it in ways that reflect less of a radical shift from conventional music therapy. Still, Tyson argued that community-based services present the music therapist with new responsibilities and challenges:

> Music therapy acquires different dimensions in community practice. The music therapist seems to become even more aware of the patient as a whole person and of the fact that each interpersonal contact may have immediate and crucial implications for the patient's total life situation. (It is not merely a question of his adjustment on a sheltered hospital ward.) The *constant impinging of the entire community environment on the music therapy contact* creates the necessity for a broad framework within which music therapy can serve the outpatient's needs (Tyson, 1968, p. 383).

Tyson argued that the main goal of music therapy in a community center is the same as that of hospital music therapy; the re-socialization of the patient. She proposed, however, that the possibilities for working with this are different. Tyson introduced annual Musicales with performances and collective music-making as part of the music therapy center's activities and she argued for a range of positive outcomes from these events, both for the individual clients, for the milieu at the center, and for the relationships between the center and the community. A collection of Tyson's writings, including "Guidelines toward the Organization of Clinical Music Therapy Programs in the Community" from 1973 has been published (McGuire, 2004).

the music therapy room. She speculated that: "a flexible program of music therapy may give the patient an incentive to continue music activities when he returns to the community, provided the community can offer him the necessary facilities to do so." (Alvin, 1968, p. 390). In this way Alvin demonstrated awareness of the fact that the outcomes of music therapy processes depend on social and cultural conditions. She followed this up with reflections on the British amateur music-making tradition as a cultural context of music therapy in that country, and suggested that this tradition is "not only cultural beneficial; it may be preventive of mental trouble." Alvin imagined that: "The music therapist may become a kind of social worker whose tool is music, and has to relate his work to the medical and social services available in the community" (Alvin, 1966/1975, p. 161).

Mary Priestley's work is another case in point. Many music therapists are aware of her model of Analytical Music Therapy, which is an individualized psychotherapeutic approach. But Priestley's own practice was guided by a broad interpretation of what music therapy could be. In her work, she used structures such as improvisation groups, vocal groups, record sessions, therapeutic teaching, chamber music, and music clubs. The latter structure was an open event with voluntary attendance at the psychiatric hospital where Priestley worked, and for "those to whom the hospital is home, it is the nearest thing to a musical evening in a friend's house that they will experience" (Priestley, 1975/1985, p. 95). In discussing whether the music club is an activity group or a therapeutic group, Priestley suggested that the "music offers the opportunity to become a live, vibrating member of such a group and this is the therapeutic experience" (Priestley, 1975/1985, p. 95). This argument places parts of Priestley's practice and therapeutic theory at a smaller distance from contemporary music-centered and community-oriented approaches than is commonly assumed.

The pioneering work of **Paul Nordoff** and **Clive Robbins** (1965/2004, 1971/1983, 1977/2007) is perhaps especially pertinent in relation to community music therapy. They worked partly in the UK, partly in the US, and their approach included transitions from individual music therapy to group work to performances in a broader community. The client's evolving relationship to music was central to their work and they wrote several musical pieces and plays that were performed publicly. Their influence is a lasting one and some of the music therapists that have pioneered community music therapy in the British context, including Gary Ansdell and Mercédès Pavlicevic, are trained in the Nordoff–Robbins tradition.

In this section we have described American and British examples but it is important to note that pioneering work on the relationships between music therapy and community were developed in this time period in several countries, such as Germany, Norway, Argentina, Brazil, and Australia. Examples from these and other contexts will be given throughout the book.

A SYSTEMIC AND SOCIOCULTURAL TURN IN MUSIC THERAPY THEORY

According to Ansdell (2002), the way music therapy was professionalized in the UK from the late 1970s to the late 1990s led to a stronger focus on the treatment of individual clients and less focus on music's social and communal possibilities. Accordingly, theories in music therapy to a large degree were inspired by premises defined by disciplines such as psychology and medicine, with a concurrent focus on individualized problems and solutions. Parallel developments could perhaps be tracked in many countries but nuances need to be added to the picture too. Processes of professionalization vary somewhat from country to country.

The same decades also fostered contributions in music therapy theory and research that led the way to more communal, culture-oriented, and context-sensitive understandings of discipline and profession. We will discuss some of the theoretical perspectives developed in this era, as they grew stronger in the 1980s.

Carolyn Kenny is an American theorist who has contributed to an increasing interest in systems-oriented perspectives in music therapy. Her first book clarified the relevance of seeing music as part of broader cultural systems of health (Kenny, 1982). Taking the ecological work of Gregory Bateson as one of her points of departure, Kenny advocated relational definitions. She suggested that music in music therapy should not be considered a "medication" and that music therapists should encourage and support people in taking responsibility for their health and life. Kenny also argued that the sociocultural function of therapy should be examined. Throughout the 1980s, Kenny developed her thinking in an ecological and systems-oriented direction, and she developed ideas of clear relevance for contemporary community music therapy (see Box.2.2).

Another music therapist who developed important theoretical perspectives on community and society in the 1980s, is the Norwegian theorist **Even Ruud**. In his doctoral dissertation, Ruud (1987/1990) situated music therapy in relation to contemporary theories

Box 2.2 | CAROLYN KENNY: MYTHS AND FIELDS, RITUALS AND RESPONSIBILITIES

American music therapy in the 1960s and 1970s to an increasing degree became behavioral in orientation, but there were several divergent voices advocating broader perspectives. One of the more powerful voices has been that of Carolyn Kenny. The specific term *community music therapy* does not appear in Kenny's writing, but several of her contributions to music therapy theory are of relevance to the present discussion. A continuing thread in Kenny's argument is the search for a synthesis between traditional human wisdom and contemporary knowledge and practice.

In *The Mythic Artery*, Kenny (1982) made a specific case for the value of working with and through myths and rituals. Three years later Kenny (1985) discussed the relevance of *systems theory* to music therapy. In 1989 Kenny published *The Field of Play* with a relational and context-sensitive contribution to music therapy theory. *The Field of Play* to some degree integrated the argument of *The Mythic Artery* with systems theory. The theory that Kenny developed was based on the premise that music therapy is a process-oriented practice. Kenny's notion of *field* is related to an environmental approach and linked to the presence of sounds as well as of persons, symbols, and rituals.

More recently Kenny has been advocating the social responsibility of the music therapy researcher (Kenny, 1999), which is also relevant to the current discourse on community music therapy, as is her turn to a more explicit anthropological focus, with the role of arts in the revitalization of indigenous societies as her main research topic (Kenny, 2002a, b). A collection of her writings includes the contributions to music therapy theory as well as texts informed by ritual studies and anthropology (Kenny, 2006).

FIGURE 2.2 | Signed Song music performers in concert. Milledgeville, GA, USA.

Photo: University Television, Georgia College & State University.

of science and the humanities. One notable feature of this work was its theory about humankind. Ruud contended that no theory about humans is complete unless biological as well as psychological and sociological dimensions have been included. On this premise he developed a pluralistic and multi-factorial theory of conditions for communication in music. Ruud (1987/1990) thus argued that theories that reduce music to a means are not sufficient; the acts of the improvising individual as well as processes of socialization and enculturation must be included in music therapy theory.

Box 2.3 | EVEN RUUD: MUSIC THERAPY IN AND AS A SOCIAL FIELD

In the book *What is Music Therapy?*[2] Ruud (1980) clarifies the implications of taking a more socially oriented perspective on music therapy. He goes beyond the scope of conventional individual and health-specific goals and suggests that music therapy is important because it brings music to people that traditionally have been excluded from taking part. Ruud's premise is that the biomedical and psychological views on health problems tend to neglect the social and cultural dimensions of human life. The problems and limitations experienced by a person coming to music therapy are not linked to the individual only but also to various social and cultural conditions. Ruud therefore argues that music therapy must be directed towards the context and milieu of the client, and that prophylactic and political dimensions become crucial. Interpersonal sensitivity is not always enough, Ruud argues. The music therapist also needs to be sensitive in relation to the *social field* to which music therapy belongs. Sometimes the therapist will need to deal with the political and social forces that shape this field and that create the conditions within which people live, grow, and develop.

Ruud has explored several aspects of this argument in later publications, for instance in a collection of papers on music and health (Ruud, 1986), in music studies using theory and research methods from anthropology (Berkaak & Ruud, 1992, 1994), in studies of music and identity (Ruud, 1997a, b), and in studies of music and health in various contexts (Ruud, 2002; Batt-Rawden, Bjerke, DeNora & Ruud, 2005; Storsve, Westby & Ruud, 2010).

The texts of Kenny and Ruud have been influential in the development of contemporary community music therapy. There are other theoretical contributions from the same era that perhaps are less known internationally but which are also pertinent. Some of the contributions to German music therapy theory exemplify this. There is a tradition for discussing *social* and *political* dimensions of music therapy in the German music therapy literature. Geck's (1972/1977) critical book on music therapy and society illuminates this trend. His argument is that if therapists uncritically try to normalize individuals with no awareness of problems of social power and interpersonal estrangement (the possibility of "collective abnormality"), therapy could become oppressive. In such cases, Geck argues, music therapy represents (political) apathy rather than (personal) remedy.

Until the unification of East and West Germany in 1990, there were two separate German traditions of scholarship in music therapy. **Christoph Schwabe**, the central pioneer of the East German tradition, is also a pioneer of social perspectives on music therapy. He developed many of his theoretical ideas in the 1980s. In the 1990s he rearticulated some of these perspectives, partly in response to changes in culture and society (Schwabe & Haase, 1996, 1998).[3] Schwabe's theoretical considerations are significant for the field of community music therapy, even though there are also discrepancies between Schwabe's ideas and the community music therapy literature. Schwabe presents a model that he labels Social Music Therapy,[4] and describes this as a form of psychotherapy with specific *indications* for referral (Schwabe & Haase, 1998). This argument is based on a notion of "social illness." In contrast, most of the community music therapy literature has been explicit about the relevance of thinking outside notions of illness and diagnosis.

Box 2.4 | CHRISTOPH SCHWABE: SOCIAL MUSIC THERAPY

In 1969 Christoph Schwabe was co-founder of the music therapy section of the East German Society for Arts Psychotherapies and he was a central pioneer of the music therapy discipline in this country. Schwabe's two most renowned books are *Aktive Gruppenmusiktherapie für erwachsene Patienten* (1983) and *Regulative Musiktherapie* (1987), about active group music therapy and receptive music therapy respectively. The text that is most relevant in relation to community music therapy is the more recent *Sozialmusiktherapie* [Social Music Therapy] (Schwabe & Haase, 1998).

Schwabe's theoretical argument is grounded in a discussion of the human condition and a specific notion of the individual. Schwabe underlines that individuals are never completely isolated; they interact with, relate to, and are dependent on others (in various ways and to various degrees). Consequently, a specific notion of the *social*—in which the individual and the collective reciprocally constitute each other—is used as the core theoretical notion in Schwabe's work. Individual development always relates to development in communities and societies.

Box 2.4 |

On this premise Schwabe describes social life through use of the notions *Nähe und Distanz* (proximity and distance). Proximity is related to being *open*, to the experience of *connection*, and is therefore also linked to a certain *lack of protection*. Distance is related to *being different*, to the establishment of *boundaries*, and therefore to *self-protection*. Taken together this illuminates how social contact is the path to liberation while it also represents *hazards* and *risks*. Social health, as defined by Schwabe, is therefore the capacity for balancing proximity and distance in encounters with other persons as well as with one's own inner life (Schwabe & Haase, 1998, p. 15).

EXPANDING THE AGENDA FOR MUSIC THERAPY

In spite of the pioneering efforts of community-based practice in the 1960s and 1970s and the systemic and sociocultural turn in (parts of) the music therapy theory, in the late 1980s Marcia Broucek still suggested that American music therapy needed to be deinstitutionalized:

> Historically, music therapy has been an "institutionalized therapy." Institutionalized people, however, constitute only a small proportion of the larger population. In an attempt to expand perspective beyond the traditional scope of music therapy practice, a review of music therapy from a humanistic perspective is offered, and three levels of music therapy are proposed: for people in crisis, for "average" people, and for people open to self-discovery.
>
> (Broucek, 1987, p. 50)

Broucek argued that music therapy has been "institutionalized" both because of historical precedence and financial realities. She suggested that music therapists should consider what resources they have to offer beyond the institutional setting, and argued that this could open up music therapy in fruitful ways. This argument was made in the North American context. The theme is more general. Deinstitutionalization of music therapy has been a topic of discussion and interest in many countries, in various ways due to varying circumstances.

The contemporary concept of community music therapy implies something more and different than deinstitutionalized music therapy, however. The emergence of community music therapy is part of a broader picture of sociocultural change. Its identity seems to go beyond community as context (music therapy in a community) to encompass approaches that embrace a larger agenda for music therapy (music therapy for community change). This necessarily involves also embracing new arenas and activities. We will present two examples of this trend, from the same decade that produced Broucek's critique.

The first example is from the Norwegian context, where the country's social democratic tradition, as well as Ruud's socially informed music therapy theory, constituted a context for a culturally and socially engaged music therapy. In the early 1980s, **Brynjulf Stige** and colleagues started exploring how music therapy can contribute to the development of inclusive local communities (see Box 2.5). This work was inspired by national debates on the rights of people with disabilities. By linking music therapy to concrete social and cultural challenges in a given local community, the role of the music therapist was redefined. Various ways of using music therapy to enhance community engagement and help people re-integrate into the wider community were explored. Community-based music therapy practices were developed in collaboration with local musicians, music educators, and cultural workers. The project was not officially conducted as a research project but was informed by the literature on ethnographic field studies and the tradition of participatory action research (Kleive & Stige, 1988).

Throughout the 1990s, Stige engaged in several other community music therapy projects on a regional and national scale and also revisited the descriptions of the original work several times in order to develop it theoretically.

Box 2.5 | BRYNJULF STIGE: CULTURAL ENGAGEMENT, OR: HOW TO CHANGE THE WORLD IF ONLY A BIT

Stige's first experience with community-oriented music therapy grew out of a government-funded cultural project in an area of Western Norway in the 1980s. Possible roles of the music therapist in local communities were explored and the project was seen in relation to political and sociocultural developments in the Norwegian society, where universal rights to cultural participation were central:

My interest for Community Music Therapy began one Monday afternoon in August 1983. I then had an experience that has guided much of my thinking as a music therapist since. . . . Together with my colleague Ingunn Byrkjedal I was welcoming a group that later would take the name Upbeat. The group members—six adult persons with Down's syndrome—entered a music room that in many ways looked like any music therapy room, but it was also different: It did not belong to the institution where they lived and we usually worked but to the community music school of the town.

This difference turned out to make a difference. The same room was also being used by local choirs as well as by the local marching band, of which there were several pictures on one of the walls. As the group members entered the room they did not head for the chairs that the music therapists had put out for them in a nice semicircle. Instead they went right over to that wall in order to be able to study the pictures more closely. A great enthusiasm spread among the group members: "The [marching] band!" "Look at that! The drum! The uniforms!" When we finally gathered around the semicircle of chairs that had been arranged, Knut, one of the group members, asked: "May we too play in the [marching] band?"

Box 2.5 |

Knut's short and simple question got me thinking. It challenged so much of what I had learnt as a music therapy student. I think it is fair to say that the culture of music therapy that I belonged to did not favor taking such a question very seriously. I had been told that music therapy was about creative improvisation and interpersonal relationships, or about the use of music carefully composed or arranged to meet the specific needs of each client. It was not about leaving the music therapy room to play with a local marching band! Still, my colleague and I felt that Knut's question was important, and that it called for a serious rethinking of our approach (Stige, 2003, pp. 4–5).

Isolation was a huge challenge for the members of Knut's group, and negotiations with bands and choirs of the local community revealed that it was possible to establish social inclusion as a goal to work with. It therefore made sense to depart from the traditional rules that regulate therapy practice. A participatory and ecological approach was chosen, where the participants' dreams and voices led the way within the broader community's musical and social networks.

When the work was first presented internationally, a title communicating cultural engagement and social activism was used "Music Therapy as Cultural Engagement, or: How to Change the World if Only a Bit." (Stige, 1993/1999). The term "community music therapy" was appropriated after the 7th World Congress of Music Therapy in Vitoria-Gasteiz in 1993, inspired by discussions with Kenneth Bruscia and Leslie Bunt. The fact that it took this author 10 years of work to find a suitable term was partly related to differences between the Norwegian and English languages. There is no equivalent to the English term "community" in the Norwegian language. Instead there are multiple terms, referring to facets such as society, locality, and the experience of togetherness. This illuminates a general point, namely how differences in language and culture constitute both resources and challenges for the international discourse on community music therapy.

The second example is from the USA, where a humanistic approach to music therapy was developed in urban East Coast areas in the 1970s (Vinader, 2008). **Edith Hillman Boxill**, one of the pioneers of humanistic music therapy, also developed a vision for a socially engaged music therapy. Boxill (1985) first developed an approach to music therapy with people with developmental disabilities. Inspired by humanistic psychology, she focused on awareness of self, awareness of others, and awareness of environment, and linked these notions to creativity, emotional wellbeing, growth, self-actualization, and responsibility. Boxill related concepts such as intrinsic learning to an expanded awareness "which leads the person toward participation in the external world and affords personal fulfillment and wholeness" (Boxill, 1985, p. 72).

Informed by ideas in Gestalt therapy and Carl Roger's client-centered approach, Boxill applied a broad notion of *a continuum of awareness*, which she described as: "going beyond the treatment room, reaching out to extend the benefits—the healing power—of

FIGURE 2.3 | How to change the world, if only a bit: Music therapy as cultural engagement. Sandane, Western Norway in the 1980s.

Photo: Ragnar Albertsen.

music therapy to all peoples of our planet Earth" (Boxill, 1997a, p. 2). Her vision was an engaged and activist music therapy that could promote peace throughout the world. In order to take steps in this direction, she became the Founder-Director of Music Therapists for Peace in 1988 and later also took some initiative in the establishment of Students Against Violence Everywhere (SAVE). Boxill envisioned music therapy as a conscious, activist, and open discipline in collaboration with other fields and professions (see Box 2.6). Boxill's influence is continuing, in relation to a person-centered music therapy (Noone, 2008) as well as in relation to the expanded agenda of music therapy for peace and leadership (Ng, 2005; Vaillancourt, 2007, 2009; Vinader, 2008).

RENEWED INTEREST AND NEW INITIATIVES

The theoretical work of Kenny, Ruud, and Schwabe illustrates social perspectives on music therapy developed in the 1980s. In the same decade, ideas of an expanded agenda

Box 2.6 | EDITH BOXILL: MUSIC THERAPY FOR PEACE

Edith Hillman Boxill lived from 1916 to 2005 and spoke for an activist music therapy. In 1988, the same year as *Music Therapists for Peace* was established, she edited a special issue of *Music Therapy*, the journal of the *American Association for Music Therapy*.[5] In the invitation for this issue, she focused on nothing less than the survival of the planet and argued that the field of music therapy could bring about states of consonance and resonance that reach beyond the "parochial walls of our practice." Her vision was an engaged music therapy that could assume a world perspective and promote global peace:

> There's a change in the making, and you are invited to participate . . . *Music Therapy*, the journal of the American Association for Music Therapy (AAMT), is expanding its vistas. We are opening up a dialogue among music therapists, music educators, musicians, psychologists, physicists, physicians, and other health professionals, designed to explore the unique potential of music to affect wholeness/health in this modern age (Boxill, 1988, p. 5).

The pilot project *Students Against Violence Everywhere* (SAVE) and peace school programs also emerged from *Music Therapists for Peace* (Boxill, 1997c). In 2001, Boxill with other professionals, artists, scientists, and politicians participated in a panel to advocate the use of music to encourage healing and peace around the world. The panel was hosted by the UN as part of *United Nations Year of Dialogue among Civilizations*.

for music therapy practice were also developed, as exemplified by the work of Stige and Boxill. These ideas were probably relatively marginal in international music therapy at that time, but in the 1990s these and other influences led to a renewed interest in the relationship between music therapy and community, as evidenced in some of the textbooks from this decade. Again, we will include two examples.

In *Music Therapy. An Art Beyond Words,* **Leslie Bunt** (1994) devotes one of eight chapters to a discussion of music therapy as a resource for the community. He contextualizes this discussion by referring to changes in society and the health and welfare services:

> [M]uch of the early work of the professional music therapist began in the large institutions for mentally handicapped and mentally ill people, to use the terminology of the day. Only forty years later we are currently witnessing major changes in the way in which society is adapting to people with such problems. The terminology is shifting, with the current terms 'learning difficulties' and 'mental health problems' replacing the older ones. A further radical change is the closing-down of these large institutions and their replacements by more community-based day centres, small units and hostels. We are currently living through the difficult implementation stages, with the concomitant implications of additional human and financial resources. The start

of the 1990s has also seen an increase in unemployment, homelessness and further strain in our probation and prison service. What is the music therapist's response to all these changes?

(Bunt, 1994, p. 160)

This question can be read as having a double edge to it: Do music therapists engage with people in need outside the institutional setting to the degree that is warranted? And: Do they have the knowledge and expertise to meet these new challenges? Bunt also follows up with a third question, related to the increasing multicultural character of most contemporary societies: "How will music therapy adapt to this growing culture mix when we are realising with increasing clarity that music of all kinds is a key link with what it is to be human?" (Bunt, 1994, p. 161). Bunt's intention seems not to have been to provide comprehensive answers but to voice questions and demonstrate their importance. He discussed the relevance of a *partnership model* to research and the value of *working links* with other disciplines. Also, Bunt saw the possibility of developing community-based teams in which music therapy could become a complementary practice. Finally, he envisioned a future of freelance "peripatetic music therapists" collaborating with musical and cultural community initiatives.

In the second edition of *Defining Music Therapy,* **Kenneth Bruscia** (1998) included some influential discussions on music therapy, ecology, and community. In the first edition (published in 1989), Bruscia had defined eleven areas of practice but had not included community music therapy practices. In the second edition he reduced the number of areas from eleven to six. The areas of practice included in this edition were didactic, medical, healing, psychotherapeutic, recreational, and ecological practices. In describing ecological practices in general and community music therapy specifically, Bruscia referred to the work of Kenny, Ruud, Boxill, Stige, and others. He described the ecological area of practice in the following way:

The ecological area of practice includes all applications of music and music therapy where the primary focus is in promoting health within and between various layers of the sociocultural community and/or physical environment. This includes all work which focuses on the family, workplace, community, society, culture, or physical environment, either because the health of the ecological unit itself is at risk and therefore in need of intervention, or because the unit in some way causes or contributes to the health problems of its members. Also included are any efforts to form, build or sustain communities through music therapy. Thus, this area of practice expands the notion of "client" to include a community, environment, ecological context, or individual whose health problem is ecological in nature.

(Bruscia, 1998, p. 229)

Bruscia underlined the relational character of ecological music therapy. While therapists work to facilitate changes in the individual or community, the basic ecological premise is that changes in one will lead to changes in the other. To help an individual is not then a separate enterprise from working with contextual change (Bruscia, 1998, p. 229).

Bruscia argued that ecological practices can be quite different from other practices, not only because music therapy is extended beyond the treatment room but also because the client–therapist relationship is transformed to include many layers of relationship with and within a community. "Going even further, the process of intervention itself is different, sometimes not anything like traditional therapy" (Bruscia, 1998, p. 231).

THE EMERGENCE OF AN INTERNATIONAL FIELD

Even though community-oriented practices were included in some influential textbooks in the 1990s, community music therapy was still not part of the general conception of music therapy at the beginning of the millennium. The year 2002 came to be a turning point concerning international awareness. This year saw the publication of several articles that focused specifically on community music therapy, of which **Gary Ansdell**'s (2002) "Community Music Therapy and the Winds of Change" published in the journal *Voices* was probably the most influential. Two books that featured chapters on community music therapy (Stige, 2002; Kenny & Stige, 2002) were also published this year. In the 10th World Congress in Music Therapy in Oxford the same year, community music therapy was a central topic of discussion. What is the story behind this "sudden" interest?

Stige (2003) has argued that before the new millennium, community music therapy initiatives were mainly local or regional in their character. In the beginning of the twenty-first century this situation changed. The discourse of music therapy grew international. When electronic forums such as *Voices* were established in 2001, a thought-provoking essay such as the one written by Ansdell (2002) could be read across countries and cultures. The scene was set for international dialogue and debate.

Box 2.7 | GARY ANSDELL: COMMUNITY MUSIC THERAPY AND THE WINDS OF CHANGE

In the discussion paper "Community Music Therapy and the Winds of Change," Gary Ansdell (2002) suggested that a "paradigm shift" was in progress in music therapy, towards greater awareness of social and cultural factors. According to Ansdell, the "perennial" music-and-health link in European cultural history developed two progeny in Britain in the twentieth century. One offspring gradually led to the development of the British branch of the modern profession of music therapy, while the other led to the development of the British tradition of community music. Ansdell described the divergence of these two traditions and depicted how music therapy gradually became more and more individual in its focus, while community music practices remained social:

What lies between the two positions? Is a less polarised approach possible? Which situation would be in the best interests of clients, or of musicians who train as Music Therapists, or Community Musicians, or the institutions in which any of this work takes place? (Ansdell, 2002).

Box 2.7 |

Ansdell acknowledged that many music therapists had already explored a broader spectrum of the individual–communal continuum. His errand was therefore to develop an argument for the legitimization of this. The most controversial section of his paper is probably a discussion of the relationship between community music therapy and what he called the "consensus model" in music therapy. He used this term to reflect what he considered the basic assumptions underlying music therapy practice in Britain. His discussion focused on identities and roles, sites and boundaries, aims and means, and assumptions and attitudes. Here is an excerpt from the argument:

> The consensus model focuses on clients' problems and their emotional reactions to these. Following the basic assumptions of psychoanalytic thinking, clients' problems are seen as essentially intra-psychic ones, which manifest through emotional and interpersonal difficulties. The priority for the Music Therapist is to help clients with their underlying problems through the means of the therapeutic relationship, and to prevent external intrusions into the process. This therapeutic agenda is supported by an *individual* psychological model, where the client is identified as both the site of the problem and the hope for the 'cure.' Cultural and social determinants of selfhood are seldom theorised or worked with. The consensus model's assumptions about music also follow this model: music is largely seen as an introspective phenomenon, and as a dynamic representation of states of mind, feelings, and patterns of relating. The core analogy underlying this is of musical improvisation being a corollary to psycho-analytic free-association. This leads to the belief that the primary function of music is as an expressive or projective device, or as a container (and possibly re-organiser) of the forces of feeling.
>
> Community Music Therapy derives its assumptions from a social (or perhaps *ecological*) phenomenology of music – believing that Music Therapy must work in the ways in which music itself commonly works in individual and social life. The Community Music Therapist's practice follows where music's natural tendencies lead: both *inwards* in terms of its unique effects on individuals, but also *outwards* towards participation and connection in *communitas*. . . . Rather than focus directly on clients' problems, a Community Music Therapist aims to enlist musicking's ability to generate well-being and potential in individuals, relationships, milieus, and communities (Ansdell, 2002).

The enhanced interest in community music therapy in the twenty-first century can be related to sociocultural developments that have consequences for health and wellbeing in late modern societies. One aspect of this is how personal identity has changed from being defined by a given tradition to being a continuous personal project for each individual. This includes a greater concern with health and meaning in life. As Chaney (2002) has argued, the search for meaning in or through a healthy life cannot easily be contained in the science of expert-driven medicine.

Paradoxically, these tendencies in direction of individualization can be one of the factors leading to a renewed interest in community-oriented perspectives. Community music therapy is representative of a cultural and reflexive movement, in that it fosters increased awareness of culture and context and the need for reflexivity in relation to each person's identity project, which inevitably is linked to other persons' projects. In this way, community music therapy represents important prospects for music therapy in posing new questions about people's access to the resources of music and health in everyday life (Stige, 2003).

Community music therapy can then be understood both as the emergence of new perspectives and practices in the discipline of music therapy and as a set of responses to social and cultural change in the contexts where music therapists work. The emergence of an international discourse in community music therapy made local and regional insights and developments accessible for a broader international audience. At the same time, community music therapy demonstrated its relevance in contexts where music therapy is in the process of being established in the beginning of the twenty-first century. The work of **Mercédès Pavlicevic** in South Africa is a case in point here. As one of the founders of the first university training program in music therapy in this country, she realized that the fit between the South African context and Western individualized ideas about music therapy was not good. She therefore gradually developed a community music therapy perspective adjusted to the South African cultural and social situation (Pavlicevic, 2004).

Box 2.8 | MERCÉDÈS PAVLICEVIC: REFRAMING PROFESSIONAL PRACTICE FOR TIME AND PLACE

Until 2006, Mercédès Pavlicevic had lived in, and engaged with, the social context of South Africa for 15 years. In 1998, together with Kobie Temmingh, she set up the first music therapy training program in Africa; at the University of Pretoria. She was head of this training program for many years. Pavlicevic (2004) has explained how the experience of traditional African music healing ceremonies and also her practical work with people from urban and rural areas of the country constantly nudged at her clinician's mind, "uncomfortably in the main." The Western individualized models of music therapy did not seem feasible or sensible in the South African context. Over the years Pavlicevic and her graduate students immersed themselves in various innovative community music therapy projects, in an attempt to reframe professional practice for the time and place in question.

In 2004 Mercédès Pavlicevic and Gary Ansdell edited the first anthology to be published on community music therapy, and Pavlicevic has later produced several influential studies of relevance for the field, in relation to topics such as musical companionship (Ansdell & Pavlicevic, 2005), collaborative musicking (Pavlicevic & Ansdell, 2009; Pavlicevic, 2010a), and social activism (Pavlicevic, 2010b).

FIGURE 2.4 | Collective improvisation. The Otoasobi Project, an improvisation collective for musicians with and without intellectual disabilities, Kobe, Japan.

Photo: Kaneko Yoshiro.

ROOTS, RIVERS, AND RELATIVES

The emergence of an international discourse on community music therapy led to the "rediscovery" of various local and national traditions that were informed by related ideas and values. It quickly became clear, for instance, that the Australian, Canadian, and South American contexts had their own traditions of community-based and community-oriented music therapy. We will visit these contexts briefly.

According to O'Grady and McFerran (2006), there is a long tradition for community music therapy in Australia, grounded in strong community values and a system of community care. In a qualitative study, these researchers investigated questions of delimitation between community music and community music therapy in the Australian context (O'Grady & McFerran 2007). Their results suggest that there are differences as to where on the "health-care continuum" the two groups of professionals are engaged. They also found differences concerning how music versus the persons involved are the main focus of attention. Finally, they found differences concerning how ethical boundaries are understood and worked with. The two researchers argue that Australian music therapists have much to learn from community musicians and vice versa.

One of the music therapy pioneers in Canada, Fran Herman, developed an approach that was partly oriented towards performance and community. She started her work with children with multiple disabilities in the 1950s:

> The Wheelchair Players (1956–1964) was the first group music therapy project in Canada. Designed as a vehicle for exploration in the expressive arts, the youngsters living in The Home for Incurable Children (later known as *Bloorview Hospital*) became advocates, seeking access to the arts as their basic human rights.
>
> These youngsters, who because of their obstacles were perceived as receivers and consumers, wanted to be viewed as contributors and sharers. They understood that through the sharing and development of creative activities, they could move beyond the confines of their disabilities.
>
> (Herman in Buchanan, 2009)[6]

Carolyn Kenny's work has also been influential in Canada and several perspectives and initiatives of relevance for community music therapy have been explored in this country, including the use of systems and environmental perspectives (Woodward, 2002/2004), the exploration of possibilities for therapeutic interventions in large-scale community performances (Oddy, 2001/2005), and the development of partnered community mental health music therapy programs (Baines, 2000/2003).

In South American music therapy there have been several initiatives that are of relevance for a contemporary understanding of community music therapy. For instance, Barcellos (2005) has described the tradition of a "social music therapy" in Brazil, of which the work of Chagas (2007) is one example. In Colombia, Gonzalez and associates (2008) have developed a transdisciplinary vision in music therapy, linking music, education, and society. In Argentina, the idea of a preventive psychosocial music therapy has been explored by Pellizzari and Rodríguez (2005).

These examples remind us of the complexity of the history of community music therapy. We can sum this up in three points. First, community music therapy is an emerging movement and perspective. While discussions of music therapy and community can be traced in the music therapy literature of previous decades, the specific term *community music therapy* was established internationally only this millennium. Second, the English term "community" does not translate directly to some central languages in music therapy (such as for instance Japanese, Spanish, Portuguese, German, and the Scandinavian languages), which makes shared delineation even more complex to achieve. Third, a central tenet in community music therapy is that practice, theory, and research are localized, so we are talking about a set of more or less interrelated histories, not one single development. These points, of course, represent a challenge for anyone attempting to trace the origins and development of community music therapy.

The authors and writings referred to in this chapter take quite different frames of reference. All texts represent a call for change in the theory and practice of music therapy, but while some authors advocate minor to moderate evolutions, others advocate more radical solutions. Several new notions have been proposed, such as Community

Music Therapy, Ecological Music Therapy, Music Environmental Therapy, Music Milieu Therapy, Music Sociotherapy, and Social Music Therapy (Stige, 2003, p. 121). While these terms and the discourses they belong to are related in various ways, our understanding will be hindered if we treat them as interchangeable. Some contributions represent context-bound arguments for pragmatic adjustments of professional practice. Other texts propose new approaches to music therapy and some indicate new theoretical or metatheoretical perspectives. The texts we have referred to in this chapter are hardly about the same "thing," then, in any concrete or restricted way. They do share some family resemblances, however. We can probably not assume that all authors referred to would accept or appreciate the term community music therapy as their family name, but relationships between texts can still be identified.[7]

This invites some reflection concerning **metaphors to describe historical develop-ments**. When people talk about history it is very common to talk of *roots*. In the situation we have described above it makes limited sense to think of roots as having a shared core and ancestry. This image does not seem to fit the development of community music therapy; there are many origins from various contexts. Another aspect of the "root" metaphor makes more sense, namely how roots provide nourishment for growth. In response to this aspect, Stige (2003, p. 401) has proposed the specific image of *aerial roots*. When banyan trees and other plants with aerial roots grow, new roots descend from the branches, push into the ground and form new trunks. This version of the root metaphor shows that history is not separate from the phenomenon that interests us; it is an integral part of it. Early roots are almost always interesting but we might also need to acknowledge that younger "aerial roots" can be more important in providing nourishment for contemporary developments.

Another and perhaps simpler metaphor would be to think of community music therapy as a *river*. In a river there is usually water from several smaller streams. Sometimes, several large rivers meet and establish even larger rivers. Other times, rivers branch out and create smaller rivers moving in different directions. This does not depend on the river itself as much as it depends on landscape and climate conditions. This image illuminates the hybrid character of community music therapy; there is "water" from music therapy mixed with water from social work, health promotion, and community development, to mention some of the possibilities. The image also illuminates the idea that transformations are due not only to factors internal to the discipline; they relate also to political, social, and cultural change in society.

A limitation of the metaphors referred to above is that they suggest the image of community music therapy as something "natural," something that grows or flows due to internal dispositions and external conditions. This illuminates some aspects of the process, but there are also aspects of *agency* involved. Social and cultural developments such as community music therapy are due to the interplay of various conditions, also the activities and choices of the human agents involved. A third metaphor, namely community music therapy as a *family*, captures some of these aspects. The development of a family, and the possibility of change (such as whether it will stay together or split up), are consequences of choices and acts as well as of the traditions and conditions surrounding

FIGURE 2.5 | Musical pride. Music education in a Palestinian refugee camp in Lebanon.
Photo: Vegar Storsve.

the family. Some family members are more distant, others are closer, but there are not necessarily any clear-cut or "natural" boundaries between families. New families are formed from previous families and there are various types of connections within and between larger families. As a "family," community music therapy can be compared to and related to other "families," such as community psychology or community music. The family metaphor might help us see that the flexibility that characterizes many community music therapy practices is not the same as amorphous or boundless practice (Stige, 2003).

CONCLUSION

Music invites participation and collaboration and often builds a strong sense of community. Many people are aware of these possibilities and many traditional cultures have explored them in rituals that incorporate and capitalize on collaborative music-making. In exploring the history of professional community music therapy it is therefore relevant to discuss relationships to other practices, such as various traditional practices.

The term "community music therapy" was in use in the literature already in the 1960s. Florence Tyson, for instance, discussed the establishment of music therapy as part of community health services. The context of her discussion was the de-institutionalization of certain health services in many industrialized countries in this decade. While Tyson discussed how new contexts affected the roles and responsibilities of the music therapist, her practice was mainly in congruence with conventional conceptions of modern music therapy. In several of the other texts referred to in this chapter, more radical change has been advocated.

Several pioneers of music therapy—such as Alvin, Priestley, and Nordoff–Robbins—developed practices and ideas in the 1960s and 1970s that took the human need for connectivity and community into consideration. In the following decades of professionalization, individual and group approaches to music therapy dominated in several countries. Counter-currents existed, though, such as the work of Kenny, Ruud, and Schwabe. In the 1980s they developed contributions to music therapy theory that led the way for more communal, culture-oriented, and context-sensitive understandings. The same decade also saw emergence of community-oriented practical projects that embraced a broader agenda for music therapy. In Norway, for example, Stige and colleagues started exploring how music therapy could contribute to realization of the rights of people with disabilities in relation to cultural and social participation. In the USA, Boxill developed a vision for an engaged and activist music therapy for peace and non-violence.

In the 1990s, these new developments started to find their way into influential music therapy textbooks, by authors such as Bunt and Bruscia. At the beginning of the twenty-first century an international scholarly discourse of community music therapy emerged. Proponents of community music therapy, such as Ansdell and Pavlicevic, claimed that a paradigm shift was on its way. A tendency of more far-reaching departure from conventional therapy practice emerged, where music therapists were ready to take psychosocial roles in the communities where they worked. In consequence, many music therapists currently find themselves as participants in broader partnerships for health, where lay people and professionals work together in developing creative strategies for community development and health promotion.

Three metaphors illuminate different aspects of how we can think about the history of community music therapy. The metaphor of *root* is one of them. Some of the original roots may be less prominent today, while younger aerial roots—including relationships to fields such as community music and community psychology—can be of increasing importance. *River* is another metaphor. There is much water from the river of music therapy in current community music therapy, but also streams coming from other sources. As waters blend, community music therapy is not music therapy as it used to be plus community; it is a new combination with its own identity. *Family* is the third metaphor. In the same way as people make choices as to how they cultivate relationships to the family members and extended families that they are connected to, students of community music therapy will have to reflexively work with their relational identities as practitioners and scholars.

KEY TERMS, DISCUSSION TOPICS, AND NOTES

Key Terms

Key terms in order of appearance:

Traditional practices
Ngoma
Multiple healing systems
Florence Tyson
Juliette Alvin
Mary Priestley
Nordoff and Robbins
Carolyn Kenny
Even Ruud
Christoph Schwabe
Brynjulf Stige
Edith Hillman Boxill
Leslie Bunt
Kenneth Bruscia
Gary Ansdell
Mercédès Pavlicevic
Metaphors for description

Discussion Topics

The following critical thinking questions can be discussed in class or in groups or used by the individual student for critical reflection on topics discussed in the chapter. Extra resources can be found on the book's website.

1. Several scholars have argued that music therapists can learn from traditional practices of ritual healing. However, the arguments that are used to support this claim vary among authors. Can you outline some of the arguments and discuss their strengths and limitations in relation to contemporary areas of practice in your country?
2. Edith Hillman Boxill established Music Therapists for Peace in 1988 and envisioned an engaged and activist music therapy that promotes peace throughout the world. More recently, scholars of related disciplines have argued that music can be an important medium for conflict transformation (Urbain, 2008). Critics would argue that this is too tall an order for a small discipline such as music therapy. Discuss the possibilities and limitations of music therapy in relation to peace and conflict transformation.
3. The emergence of an international discourse on community music therapy in the twenty-first century has been met with a range of reactions, ranging from enthusiasm, to criticism, to indifference. What characterizes responses in your country? Have

responses varied over time? Which cultural, social, political, and scholarly factors influence the discourse in your context?

Notes

1   Initiatives for realization of the human rights of people with intellectual disabilities exemplify this development, see (Owen & Griffiths, 2009).

2   Our translation of the original Norwegian title of Ruud's (1980) book: *Hva er musikkterapi?*

3   In addition to Schwabe, important German perspectives on music therapy and community include those of Almut Seidel (1992, 1996), who linked music therapy to social work, and Isabelle Frohne-Hagemann (1986, 2001), who discussed relationships between music psychotherapy and sociotherapy.

4   Our translation of the original German title of Schwabe and Haase's (1998) book: *Die Sozialmusiktherapie.*

5   In 1988 there were two music therapy associations in the US, the National Association for Music Therapy and the American Association for Music Therapy. The two associations merged in 1998 to found the American Music Therapy Association. The journal *Music Therapy* was discontinued at that point.

6   The interview (Buchanan, 2009) from which this quote is taken includes clips from a film that was made about the Wheelchair Players.

7   The metaphor of "family resemblance" was employed by Wittgenstein (1953/1967) in an argument explaining why he did not define the essence of language but instead developed the notion of "language games." The meaning of language is linked to the contexts of its use, and these are multifaceted and ever-changing. The idea of defining a shared essence in language is thus problematic, according to Wittgenstein. This is not to say that similarities could not be detected. Wittgenstein uses the "family resemblance" metaphor to illustrate this. You do not recognize a family because of one shared and essential feature. There is a web of features that characterize a family, with some features more prominent in certain members and other features in other members.

Part II

Basic Concepts of Community Music Therapy

IN Part II we explore some basic concepts of community music therapy, derived from the three terms that construct the label itself; community, music, and therapy. In doing this, we acknowledge that community music therapy cannot only be understood as a compound of these three notions and the practices they refer to. As we discussed in Chapter 2; a range of hybrid traditions such as community work, community psychology, community music, music therapy, social work, and health promotion have influenced the contemporary field of community music therapy.

Chapter 3 focuses on health and wellbeing. Community music therapy is based on the assumption that health is more than absence of pathology and disease. Resources that enable wellbeing and positive dimensions of health are highlighted. Community music therapy also draws attention to health as a process influenced by social and cultural factors.

Chapter 4 discusses the social dimension of human life, with a focus on notions such as community, social support, social stress, social capital, inclusion, and exclusion. Modern societies are often said to be characterized by individualization. There is a need to examine whether individuality excludes or accentuates the possibility and necessity of community.

Chapter 5 elaborates on the notion of music and relates it to health and community. Is music a means that enables community, which again leads to health and wellbeing, or are there other ways of conceptualizing relationships between health, community, and music?

Chapter 3

Health and Wellbeing

After studying Chapter 3, you will be able to discuss questions such as:

- How could health and wellbeing be described?
- What are the possible relationships between disease, illness, and sickness?
- How are different dimensions of health linked to various levels of analysis (human beings characterized as organisms, persons, and/or social beings, for instance)?
- Why is the field of mental health particularly challenging when it comes to definition and conceptual clarification?
- How does health vary across regions of the world?
- How do socioeconomic inequalities influence health?
- Is wellbeing related to material wealth?

HEALTH AS ABSENCE OF DISEASE

COMMUNITY music therapy is a field concerned with health and wellbeing, but it is not restricted to working with clients in hospitals or other health care settings. Community music therapy often takes place in community settings such as schools or other places where people spend time and live their lives. The purpose of community music therapy is not primarily healing and treatment but the promotion of health in the widest possible meaning of the word. In this chapter we will present various conceptions of health and wellbeing and also discuss the labels we use to describe health problems. Given the international character of community music therapy we will then provide an overview of the diseases and disorders that threaten health across the world and also look into statistics on the positive aspects of health and wellbeing.

There are a number of definitions of the concept of health. In medical contexts **health** has often been defined as the absence of disease, and this definition still has its proponents

(Saracci, 1997). A widely used phrase is that health is the state of the organism when it functions optimally without evidence of disease or abnormality.

Disease has been defined as "any condition associated with discomfort, pain, disability, death, or an increased liability to these states, regarded by physicians and the general public as properly the responsibility of the medical profession" (Guze, 1978, p. 296). The words used when describing disease all have negative connotations (discomfort, pain, disability, death). The presence of such states is not sufficient to classify a condition as a disease, however. There also has to be an agreement between experts and the general public that the condition is a responsibility of the medical profession.

Although this definition contains elements of social construction perspectives (the understanding of health as a product of communication among experts and lay people), everyday language use is often more straightforward. Sarafino (2002) claims that people commonly think about health in terms of the absence of a) subjective symptoms of disease and injury, such as nausea or pain, or b) objective signs that the body is not functioning properly, such as high blood pressure. A person is considered healthy to the extent that he or she has not contracted cancer, stroke, myocardial infarction, HIV/AIDS, depression, schizophrenia, or any other known disorder. The list of possible diseases is comprehensive, however, from the most frequent ones to the less frequent, from purely somatic diseases to mental health disorders, from easily diagnosed to rather vague syndromes.

In order to be healthy according to these definitions, a person does not have to experience a high quality of life or be a productive member of society. It is sufficient that the person has no specific disease or symptoms of disease. This definition of health is rather narrow and it is sometimes referred to as a purely medical definition, reflecting the priorities and approaches of modern medicine. The person is seen as composed of a number of organ systems (lung, heart, vascular system, central nervous system, etc.), and hospital departments as well as fields of medical specialization are defined according to these organ systems. The de-composition of the person into organ systems has become so dominant in the practices of modern medicine that critical voices have called for a more holistic approach. Patients should be treated as persons and communication between health personnel and patients should reflect respect and concern for the person as a whole and not focus exclusively on specific organ systems. In order to communicate such ideas, the concepts of *illness* and *sickness* have sometimes been employed.

Often the word **illness** is used interchangeably with the word disease. In the scientific literature, however, a distinction is made. Illness refers to people's perception of their own health, irrespective of the presence or absence of disease. In principle a person with a disease can perceive his or her own health as good. More often, however, the discrepancy will be in the other direction; the doctors may not be able to identify any known disease and still the patient may feel ill. **Sickness** adds a social dimension to the picture. In the sociologically informed literature, the concept of sickness is sometimes employed to denote the socially constructed label of being unhealthy. Sickness therefore can be independent of both disease and illness. A person could be considered unhealthy by a community without having a disease in the medical sense or feeling ill. All sorts of patterns of congruence and incongruence between disease, illness, and sickness are therefore imaginable (Boyd, 2011).

FIGURE 3.1 | Rehearsal and relaxation. The CeleBRation Choir, Auckland, New Zealand. Photo: Neil Shepherd.

PRESENCE OF POSITIVE HEALTH AND WELLBEING

In the constitution of the World Health Organization (WHO) of 1946, it is stated that:

> Health is a state of complete physical, mental and social wellbeing and not merely the absence of disease or infirmity. The enjoyment of the highest attainable standard of health is one of the fundamental rights of every human being without distinction of race, religion, political belief, economic or social condition.
>
> (World Health Organization, 1946)

The most cited part of the statement is the words "*a state of complete physical, mental and social wellbeing and not only the absence of disease or infirmity.*" This phrase means that obtaining good health is for all practical purposes impossible. Who can claim that he or she experiences a state of complete wellbeing? And if the goal is permanent perfect wellbeing for all, the absurdity becomes even more obvious. What about the inevitable frustrations that we meet during any normal day? What about challenges we meet at work or at school? Is good health incompatible with a normal life?

In spite of being rather *utopian*, the definition has influenced people's way of thinking about health quite a lot. It has opened up health concerns beyond treatment, prevention, and rehabilitation. Health has important positive aspects that should not be neglected. In a practical health policy and health promotion context, the definition also implies that the disease prevention perspective is far too narrow. In addition to the prevention of disease, an important task for health professions, NGO's,[1] and any group involved in the field of public health is to promote positive aspects of health. The Alma Ata conference on primary health care, a conference set up by the WHO in 1978, agreed on a declaration that was also inspired by a positive notion of health.

> The Conference strongly reaffirms that health . . . is a fundamental human right and that the attainment of the highest possible level of health is a most important world-wide social goal whose realization requires the action of many other social and economic sectors in addition to the health sector.
>
> (World Health Organization, 1978)

According to this perspective, promotion of health involves many other sectors than health. Since health to a large extent is shaped by policies, practices, and contexts outside the health care sector, it is an obligation of these other sectors to be concerned about health consequences of their actions, to contribute to the prevention of diseases, injuries, and premature death, and to promote wellbeing and positive health. This involves sectors such as education, work, culture, and transport. WHO's definition of health and the implication that health promotion is linked to people's everyday life activities and to many other sectors than the health care sector, is an important context for community music therapy. Music therapists do not need to accept the premise that health-related work is necessarily curative and focused on the individual. The promotion of positive social and cultural factors may be equally important and this is often the focus of community music therapy projects.

When describing positive aspects of health, concepts such as *wellbeing, quality of life*, and *life satisfaction* have to be defined. Some researchers regard these (and related concepts) as synonyms. Easterlin (2003, p. 4), for instance, says that "I take the terms wellbeing, utility, happiness, life satisfaction and welfare to be interchangeable." Other researchers are concerned about the fact that there is no consensus on how the various concepts should be defined. According to Susan Hird, there are as many definitions of wellbeing as there are people studying the phenomenon (Hird, 2003).

The WHO has used the concept **wellbeing** in statements and charters and it is therefore worthwhile taking a closer look at this concept in particular. The concept is used in a number of sciences and disciplines, such as psychology, sociology, medicine, geography, economics, philosophy, and marketing research. A major distinction is made between *subjective* and *objective wellbeing*. In order to explain what subjective wellbeing is, one often uses phrases like contentment and happiness. The term emphasizes the subjective aspect of life and is often used as kind of a catch-all phrase meaning global satisfaction when all aspects of life are considered.

Hird (2003) has developed a slightly more elaborate model. She says that **subjective wellbeing** can be deconstructed into three aspects: pleasant affect (happiness), unpleasant affect (unhappiness), and cognitive aspects of wellbeing, the latter being the same as *satisfaction with life*. Satisfaction with life can be global, or it can be domain-specific (family, job, income). While those who measure objective wellbeing focus on objective indicators (i.e. income, years of education, quality of housing), domain-specific satisfaction with life is measured by obtaining informants' evaluations of various aspects of their life. In principle these aspects could be the same as for objective wellbeing (see Figure 3.2). Consistent with this, Diener (1984)[2] has defined subjective wellbeing as consisting of four components: a) pleasant emotions (joy, happiness), b) unpleasant emotions (anger, sadness), c) general life fulfillment and d) satisfaction with specific life domains (such as work, health, marriage).

The notion of **objective wellbeing** is based on the assumption that there are a number of needs that are common to all individuals. Satisfaction of such needs is understood as contributing to wellbeing. Objective indicators of wellbeing would be based on statistics regarding factors such as education attainment, housing conditions, and health (as absence of disease). Felce and Perry (1995) suggested that it is possible to distinguish between five aspects of life with regard to the measurement of objective wellbeing; physical wellbeing, material wellbeing, development and activity, social wellbeing, and emotional wellbeing.

Since subjective and objective wellbeing are two different aspects of the joint concept of wellbeing, one could imagine that there was a strong and clear correlation between indicators of these two aspects. There is, however, no simple and direct relationship between objective and subjective indicators. There are a number of studies showing a marked decline in happiness among people living in the United States at the same time as standards of living were rising. This indicates that money does not equal happiness (Kahn & Juster, 2002). Tim Kasser has suggested that our value orientations are related to wellbeing and that this is in conflict with materialistic values:

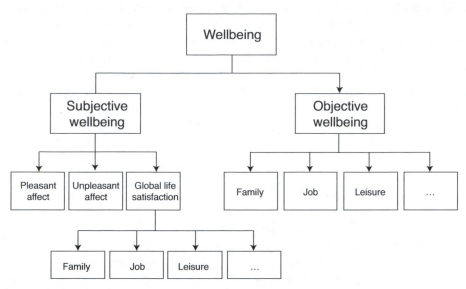

FIGURE 3.2 | Aspects of wellbeing.

People who are highly focused on materialistic values have lower personal well-being and psychological health than those who believe that materialistic pursuits are relatively unimportant. These relationships have been documented in samples of people ranging from the wealthy to the poor, from teenagers to elderly, and from Australians to South Koreans. Several investigators have reported similar results using a variety of ways of measuring materialism. The studies document that strong, materialistic values are associated with a pervasive undermining of people's well-being, from low life satisfaction and happiness, to depression and anxiety, to physical problems such as headaches, and to personality disorders, narcissism, and antisocial behavior.

(Kasser, 2002, p. 22)

In order to explain why a materialistic orientation undermines wellbeing, Kasser (2002) assumes that all humans are equipped with a set of basic needs such as the need to feel competent, the need to be related to other people, and the need for autonomy. Satisfaction of these needs is seen as a prerequisite for wellbeing. If these needs are systematically frustrated, this will lead to a lower level of wellbeing. Materialistic values lead people to organize their lives in ways that do a poor job of satisfying their needs, and thus contribute to people's misery. Kasser adds that when people feel the emptiness of material success or failure, they often persist in believing that more will be better, and thus continue to strive for what they think will make them happier. In this process they receive relatively poor satisfaction of their needs for competence and esteem and they fail to correct the underlying psychological issues that led them to such an empty pursuit in the first place.

Kasser's (2002) findings regarding the relationship between a materialist orientation and wellbeing do not mean that wealth is associated with low quality of life. According to a study carried out by *The Economist,* material welfare in a country is associated with high scores on subjective wellbeing. But so also are health, political stability and security, family relations, and community life (Economist, 2005). A materialist orientation may be associated with reduced quality of life. A materialist orientation is, however, not the same as being successful and rich. Also, lack of material resources can be associated with strain and stress, while possessing plenty of material resources tends to protect people from many frustrations and hassles of daily life. Kasser's research could therefore not be used as an argument for legitimizing socioeconomic inequality.

Researchers in psychology and social sciences do not make any clear distinction between wellbeing and **quality of life**. The concepts are often used interchangeably. The quality of life concept, however, has been used in a particular context that is of interest to anyone concerned with public health. Quality adjusted life years (QUALY) is sometimes used as an indicator of success in public health interventions. One year of life in good health counts as a full year. One year with strongly reduced health could for instance count as 0.5 (half a year). The poorer the health, the lower the number assigned to a particular year. This way of operationalizing health contributes to a change in focus from maximizing life expectancy towards maximizing the number of years in good health. The concept of disability adjusted life years (DALY) is related to, but also different from the concept of quality adjusted life years. It is a measure of the gap between the actual health situation and an ideal situation where everyone lives into old age, free from disease and disability. Not only years of lost life due to premature mortality, but also years lost as a result of disability (weighted by the severity of the disability) are taken into account (Lopez et al., 2006).

Research on human wellbeing and quality of life suggests that the traditional and narrow disease prevention approach should be replaced by a health promotion way of thinking. Community music therapy, therefore, is probably more closely related to fields such as health promotion and community psychology than fields such as medicine and psychotherapy.

Box 3.1 | HEALTH AS PROCESS AND PERFORMANCE

In the second edition *of Defining Music Therapy*, Kenneth Bruscia (1998) advocates a different conception of health from that advocated in the first edition of this influential book. In the first edition Bruscia (1989) treats health as a state of wellbeing. In this view there is a dichotomy involved; either you are in a state of health or you are not. In the second edition he gives a criticism of this view and adopts Antonovsky's (1987/1991) "salutogenic" orientation, where a person's health can be described along a continuum, depending on how well he or she is coping with health threats. Health is then not a state, but a process of building resources. Based on these premises, Bruscia gives this definition

Box 3.1 |

of health: "Health is the process of becoming one's fullest potential for individual and ecological wholeness" (Bruscia, 1998, p. 84). In developing this definition, Bruscia draws on the work of, for instance, Even Ruud and David Aldridge, who stress that health is related to social context and that it is a way of "being-in-the-world."

Even Ruud (1987/1990, 1998, 2010) stresses the need for what he calls a humanized concept of health. Health is something more than and different from "not being sick," he argues. We therefore need a broader concept of health than is typically found within medicine. He relates the concept of health to the notion of *quality of life*, and also suggests that health extends beyond the individual to include community and culture. He argues that there is a reciprocal influence between the individual and collective levels, and that the health of either will influence the other, hence his definition of music therapy as the effort to increase a person's possibilities for action (Ruud, 1998, p. 52).

David Aldridge (1996) links perception and the performance of music to health. In a discussion of health as performance he argues that health is related to process and identity:

> In modern times, health is no longer a state of not being sick. Individuals are choosing to become healthy and, in some cases, declare themselves as pursuing the activity of being well. This change, from attributing the status "being sick" to engaging in the activity of "becoming well," is a reflection of a modern trend whereby individuals are taking the definitions of themselves into their own hands rather than relying upon an identity being imposed by another (Aldridge, 1996, p. 20).

Aldridge adds that clients, as a consequence of this, have begun to demand that their understandings about health play a role in their care. He suggests that when health is subject to social and individual definition, professional practitioners will start to seek complementary understandings.

A RELATIONAL CONCEPT OF HEALTH

Health is sometimes understood as one's ability to cope with and master the *challenges of daily life*. This perspective adds a lot to our understanding of health. Health is no longer simply a property of the person only. Health becomes a relational concept. Health is about the relationship between the person and his or her surroundings. Within mental health this is often called the interpersonal approach (Kiesler, 1991; Kaslow, 1996). Various societies impose different kinds of strains and demands on the individual. Across continents there are huge differences between the strains and demands in a rural setting and in a big and modern city, for instance. It is possible that mental health symptoms that would be disastrous to a businessperson's job in a city would have only minor consequences for a farmer. On the other side, it is also possible that a physical problem that would create trivial challenges to an urban clerk could be critical to a rural carpenter.

It could be argued that the higher the level of job demands concerning factors such as speed, precision, and social skills, the more challenging it is to function at an adequate level. Productivity demands are, however, not the only aspect of the psychosocial context which is important. Another aspect is the degree to which members of a certain social system are tolerant or intolerant of deviance. If problems and behaviors are met with tolerance, understanding, and perhaps even trigger care and support from the surrounding social environment, the strains and demands are substantially lower than would be the case in a less tolerant social context.

The charter from the Alma Ata conference of 1978 mentions three aspects of health; physical wellbeing, mental wellbeing, and social wellbeing. These three aspects are sometimes referred to as physical, mental, and social health. Occasionally spiritual health is defined as a fourth aspect. Instead of limiting the concept of health down to denote the properties of a person (or a person's ability to cope with his or her environment), we sometimes also see phrases like the health of a community, the health of a group, or the health of a nation.

FIGURE 3.3 | Singing and improvising on the experience of diabetes treatment. Grupo Autocuidado em diabetes; an assisted self-help group in Goiânia, Brazil.
Photo: Dalma Pereira.

In this book we will not expand the concept of health to the level of community or society, however. Instead of building the context into the concept, relevant aspects of reality can be regarded as predictors, mediators, moderators, or simply correlates within more comprehensive theoretical and conceptual models. By relating the concept of health to factors and processes that are captured by other concepts, health promotion can be understood in relation to broader processes. Health is influenced and molded by the social, cultural, and societal context in which we live, as we will discuss in more detail in the next chapter. An individual's relationship to spirituality and religion can have important health aspects and health consequences as well. In the way that we will use the concept of health, these are factors extrinsic to health itself, but they may be very relevant in health-related work such as community music therapy.

Box 3.2 | HEALTH AS PARTICIPATION

Taking a relational perspective, Brynjulf Stige (2003) discusses concepts of health in relation to community music therapy. He argues that in defining health, there is a need to navigate between ideas of biological and sociocultural determinism on one side and ideas about the autonomous and self-sufficient individual on the other. The latter position, although perhaps more appealing than determinism, is problematic because it leads to the creation of a dichotomy between the individual and the collective, Stige argues.

In an attempt to get beyond objectivist and relativist notions of health, Stige takes inspiration from the Danish theorist Ole Dreier's (1994) attempts to outline a dialectical concept of health. Dreier acknowledges individual aspects of health but also stresses that health is related to people's *mutual care*. The dialectics between the conditions under which people live and their personal qualifications for participation in social life should be taken into consideration. In this way Dreier locates health neither in body, person, nor society, but as a quality of the *interaction and activity* that humans engage in. To state this does not mean that conventional conceptions of health stressing individual factors are irrelevant, only that they are partial. Dreier's intention is hardly to define health in any exact manner, but to suggest an alternative path for reflections on the notion of health, Stige (2003) argues. In relation to community music therapy, this path would imply that we take an interest in how mutual care for each person's possibilities can be expressed through shared music-making. Stige therefore proposes the following notion of health:

> Health is a quality of mutual care in human co-existence and a set of developing personal qualifications for participation. As such, health is the process of building resources for the individual, the community, and the relationship between individual and community (Stige, 2003, p. 207).

Stige (2003) suggests that health understood as a quality of human co-existence implies that community music therapy practices need to be concerned with a participatory approach and a *partnership model*; that is, a model where the role responsibilities between lay people and professionals are negotiated in each situation, depending on the problems and resources at hand (see Chapter 10).

DIMENSIONS OF HEALTH

Instead of providing a new definition of health, we would like to briefly summarize what we have described, as three **dimensions of health**.

First, health can be defined as absence of disease. This is a narrow definition of health but even this definition brings forward something of importance for community music therapy. In order to have good health it is a great advantage to avoid diseases that could create pain and suffering and reduce one's ability to live an active life. After all, absence of disease contributes to wellbeing. This is not in conflict with the idea that even people with serious physical or mental impairments can experience positive aspects of health and have a good life. It is reasonable to regard avoidance of injury and disease as basic contributions to good health.

Second, health defined as wellbeing reminds us of the important point that health is more than absence of disease. Health means positive affect and satisfaction with central aspects of one's life, such as family, work, and leisure time. We hesitate, however, to agree with the idea that avoidance of negative affect is an important prerequisite for good health. Life will never be free of daily hassles, frustrations, and periods when we feel less good about things. A life with no frustrations and only positive affect is not possible and probably not what we want to achieve. Challenges can lead to learning and growth and negative emotions can represent a contrast, thus boosting our positive affective reactions. The concept of wellbeing points to important aspects of health, but should not lead to an unrealistic notion of good health as a permanent state of happiness.

Third, we would like to emphasize that health is not only a property of the individual. One's ability to cope with and master the challenges we meet in daily life are relative to the person as well as the situation. Health is a relational concept; it is about relationships to other people, to demands and challenges, to social, organizational, cultural, and societal contexts. Contexts that exert overpowering demands and cultures with a lack of tolerance for deviance contribute to the exclusion of individuals from participation in school, work, and social life. In order to understand health, it is important to understand the person, his or her contexts, and the relationships between the person and their contexts.

The three dimensions that we have outlined to a large degree reflect three perspectives on humankind; the human being as an organism, a person, and a social being (Ruud, 1987/1990; 1998). They also reflect levels of analysis as outlined in WHO's International Classification of Functioning, Disability, and Health (ICF), which complements the more established document ICD (International Classification of Diseases, see below). ICF attempts to give a picture of the person-in-context, describing human function as interactions and relationships between the condition of the individual and various contextual factors.[3]

Taken together, these dimensions suggest that music therapists take **relational and contextual factors** into consideration in their work without neglecting impairments in body function and structure and the personal experience of illness and wellbeing. This is in line with a concept developed within the community music therapy literature, suggesting that the needs of clients and the situations in which they find themselves might call for action across the whole "individual–communal continuum" (Ansdell, 2002). Community music therapy as a field of study and practice can acknowledge this continuum and explore practical, theoretical, ethical, and political implications.

FIGURE 3.4 | A music therapy group on the women's ward at a TB hospital. The Music Therapy Community Clinic in the Greater Cape Town area, South Africa.

Photo: Magriet Theron.

THE SOCIAL CONSTRUCTION OF MENTAL HEALTH

The definitions of disease and the notions of health mentioned in the previous sections cover a broad range of disorders and health resources. In the context of a textbook on community music therapy, mental health deserves special attention, not only because this is an important area of practice but because it exemplifies relationships between disorders and discourses. When it comes to definition and conceptual clarification, the field of mental health is particularly challenging.

Two widespread systems for defining and diagnosing mental health disorders are the DSM-IV TR (the Diagnostic and Statistical Manual of Mental Disorders) and the ICD-10 (the International Classification of Diseases), which also covers somatic disease. The DSM manuals are published by the American Psychiatric Association and the ICD manuals are produced by the World Health Organization.[4] As far as mental disorders are concerned, there is considerable overlap between the two systems. DSM was launched in 1952. The first edition of ICD, known as the International List of Causes of Death, was adopted by the International Statistical Institute (ISI) in 1893. In 1948, WHO took over the responsibility for the Sixth Revision of the ICD, which also included causes of morbidity. Both systems, in their present versions, are characterized by the importance ascribed to sorting disorders into distinct and discrete categories. The rationale is similar to the medical rationale for somatic diseases. The idea is that in order to find the right remedies and treatments, you first need to know as exactly as possible what the problem is. In order to make the diagnostic system as reliable as possible, a rather detailed system of criteria is applied, such as inclusion criteria, order of symptom occurrence, duration of symptoms, level of functioning, and exclusion of other possible diagnoses. In each case, multiple diagnoses may apply.

DSM-IV TR conceptualizes *mental disorder* as a clinically significant behavioral or psychological syndrome or pattern that occurs in an individual and that is associated with present distress (e.g., a painful symptom) or disability (i.e., impairment in one or more important areas of functioning) or with a significantly increased risk of suffering, death, pain, disability, or an important loss of freedom, and which reflects a psychological or biological dysfunction of the individual (American Psychiatric Association, 2000, p. xxxi). Mental health problems often have organic etiological factors, correlates, or manifestations, but while somatic diseases are located in organ systems, mental disorders are "psychological" or "behavioral." This means that such problems can sometimes be diagnosed with no reference to organ systems or somatic symptoms, as simply based on behavioral or psychological criteria. When DSM-III was introduced in 1980, the editors admitted that there is no satisfactory definition that specifies exact boundaries for the concept of "mental disorder." This is repeated in later editions of the DSM manuals (Berganza, Mezzich & Pouncey, 2005).

Earlier versions of DSM (DSM-I and DSM-II from 1952 and 1968) were strongly influenced by a psychodynamic approach. There was no sharp distinction between "normal" and "abnormal." Good or less good health was a matter of position on a scale from good health to disorder. In DSM-III, which was published in 1980, the psychodynamic approach was replaced by a biomedical notion of health and disease. A distinction between normal and abnormal was introduced. The DSM-III manual has been characterized as a "watershed document," "a scientific revolution," and as having brought about a "transformation of American Psychiatry" (Wilson, 1993). There have also been numerous critical voices, questioning the implications of the fact that the number of diagnostic categories has increased with each new version of DSM. The next edition, DSM-5, is scheduled for publication in May 2013.

In order to function adequately, a diagnostic system has to be reliable. Reliability in this context can be defined as the extent to which clinicians agree on the same diagnoses when independently assessing a number of patients. It has been claimed that the reliability of the diagnostic categories of the DSM-III was much better than in previous versions of the DSM system and that the problem of reliability after the publishing of DSM-IV was largely solved. Serious doubts about the scientific soundness and the reliability of the diagnostic system have been raised, however. After reviewing the available evidence, Kirk and Kutchins (1994) concluded that the reliability of DSM-III as well as earlier versions of the DSM system was rather low and they criticized the extent to which the reliability problem has been ignored.

According to the World Health Organization, there is no such thing as a single, "official" notion of mental health (World Health Organization, 2001b). Mental health may refer to absence of specific mental disorders or a state of positive emotional and cognitive wellbeing. The sociologist David Mechanic has defined mental disorders as deviant behavior which arises when the individual's thought processes, feelings or behaviors deviate from the usual expectations or experience and the person affected or others in the community define it as a problem that requires intervention (Mechanic, 1999).

A more fundamental critique of the diagnostic systems comes from social constructionists. Maddux (2008) maintains that mental health diagnoses do not refer to facts but to social constructions: "conceptions of psychological normality and abnormality and specific diagnostic labels and categories are not facts about people but socially constructed abstract concepts that reflect shared worldviews that were developed and agreed upon collaboratively over time by the members of society (e.g. theorists, researchers, professionals, their clients, the media, and the culture in which all are embedded)" (Maddux, 2008, p. 63). In a previous publication, Maddux (2002) develops a similar argument and argues strongly against the DSM and ICD systems. He is particularly critical on three points: a) the categorization and pathologization of humans, b) the assumption that mental disorders exist within individuals rather than in their relationships with other individuals and their context at large, and c) the notion that understanding what is worst and weakest in human beings is more important than understanding what is best and strongest.[5]

Social scientists have maintained that use of mental health diagnoses may even contribute to making life as well as prognosis worse for patients. In Labeling theory a distinction is made between primary and secondary deviance. Primary deviances are seen as violations of social norms which are interpreted as symptoms of mental disorders. Primary deviance may originate from four sources. It could be caused by an organic deficit, by psychological dynamics, by external stress, or by volitional acts in defiance of social rules. Secondary deviance is the process that takes place when individuals accept their identity as deviant. **Labeling theory** sets out to explain how being labeled as a patient with mental health problems, or more specifically, as a person with a particular diagnosis such as schizophrenia, may contribute to more deviant behaviors (Scheff, 1966). Erving Goffman added to this picture with his descriptions and analyses of how mental health diagnoses can lead to stigmatization. Stigma is defined as a deeply discredited attribute. In societal and cultural contexts where mental health diagnoses are perceived as discrediting, stigmatization may add burdens to the lives of people. According to Goffman, when we institutionalize illness, its deviance is exaggerated. There are two factors contributing to this; the impact of institutional regimes, and separation from the world of normality (Goffman, 1963; Rogers, 1991).

Notions such as **secondary deviance** and **stigmatization** remind us about how social context and social norms inform the rationale guiding practice, which illuminates how professional practices relate to values. This theme will become clearer as we now approach the issue of world health, which elucidates how we cannot discuss health without also discussing justice and equity.

Box 3.3 | DO WE NEED DIAGNOSTIC LABELS IN MUSIC THERAPY?

In the music therapy literature, problematic aspects of mental health diagnoses have been discussed from various angles. Christian Gold and associates (Gold, Rolvsjord et al. 2005) argued that the medical premise that you need a diagnosis before action is of limited relevance in music therapy, where other information such as the context and severity of problems and the client's relationship to music can be more important.

Randi Rolvsjord (2007, 2010) has explored the implications for music therapy theory and practice of focusing on resources and processes of empowerment rather than pathology and problems. In a similar, vein, Brynjulf Stige (2003) has argued that in community music therapy it can create bias in the direction of an individualistic focus to define problems according to DSM-IV or ICD 10 criteria. Such a definition would be grounded in the medical assumption that problems belong to the individual and solutions to the professional expert. One alternative would be to take contextual factors into consideration and think of disadvantage as relative to context and community. To work with the relatively disadvantaged links to the metaphor of music therapy as *attending to unheard voices* and involves concern for voices that have been silenced. The value of social justice and equity then becomes part of the rationale guiding the practice.

Simon Procter (2001, 2004) has discussed cultural differences between medical and non-medical mental health provision, in relation to issues such as diagnosis, personal history, and hierarchy. He has asked questions such as: "As music therapists, do we need diagnosis? Could we work without it?" and "Do we need access to a documented history of the client authored not by the client but by professionals? Could we work without it?" (Procter, 2001). He admits that some could label him as a naïve maverick when asking questions like this, but argues for non-medical mental health provision focusing on *personhood, enablement,* and *empowerment.*

FIGURE 3.5 | Felicia singing with Ariel on the guitar. Baltic Street Clinic, New York.
Photo: South Beach Psychiatric Center.

INEQUITIES AND INEQUALITIES IN HEALTH

The concept of **inequity** has sometimes been understood as synonymous with the concept of **inequality**. It is, however, important to differentiate between the two. While inequality refers to differences, for instance in life expectancy or other indicators of health between individuals or population groups, inequity refers to differences which are unnecessary and avoidable but, in addition, are also considered unfair and unjust.[6] "Not all inequalities are unjust, but all inequities are the product of unjust inequalities" (Pan American Health Organization, 1999).

In the World Health Report of 2003, there is a description of the lives of two young women, one from Japan and one from Sierra Leone:

> While a baby girl born in Japan today can expect to live for about 85 years, a girl born at the same moment in Sierra Leone has a life expectancy of 36 years. The Japanese child will receive vaccinations, adequate nutrition and good schooling. If she becomes a mother she will benefit from high-quality maternity care. Growing older, she may eventually develop chronic diseases, but excellent treatment and rehabilitation services will be available; she can expect to receive, on average, medications worth about US$ 550 per year and much more if needed.
>
> Meanwhile, the girl in Sierra Leone has a low chance of receiving immunizations and a high probability of being underweight throughout childhood. She will probably marry in adolescence and go on to give birth to six or more children without the assistance of a trained birth attendant. One or more of her babies will die in infancy, and she herself will be at high risk of death in childbirth. If she falls ill, she can expect, on average, medicines worth about US$ 3 per year. If she survives middle age she, too, will develop chronic diseases but, without access to adequate treatment, she will die prematurely.
>
> (World Health Organization, 2003, p. ix)

The contrast between these two scenarios illustrates the huge inequity in health that exists between rich countries and poor countries and between affluent and less affluent regions of the world.

According to a report from the United Nations Development Programme (2005), life expectancy in high income countries for the period 2000–2005 was 78.8 years. The corresponding figure for sub-Saharan Africa was 46.1 years. As shown in Figure 3.6, all other regions of the world were positioned between these two extremes. As compared with the period 1970–1975, there had been a substantial increase in life expectancy in all regions of the world, except two: In sub-Saharan Africa there was almost no change, and in countries belonging to the Soviet bloc (Countries in Central and Eastern Europe (CEE) and Commonwealth of Independent States (CIS) there was a decrease in life expectancy. In sub-Saharan Africa the HIV/AIDS epidemic has contributed to reducing life expectancy. In CEE and CIS countries the breakdown of their planning economies and welfare systems as well as problems during their economic transition has had dramatic negative impact on the health of their populations. Coronary heart disease, injuries, and other health problems related to unhealthy lifestyles such as smoking, physical inactivity, unhealthy eating habits, and alcohol consumption have reached pandemic proportions.[7]

Inequalities in health are also pronounced within countries, poor countries as well as rich countries (World Health Organization, 2007a). Differences in health occur along a number of axes of social stratification including political, socioeconomic, and cultural. Socioeconomic status is usually defined by level of education, income (personal or family), job in the occupational hierarchy, or geographical location. In all countries where there are indigenous groups of people, they have life expectancy lower than the national average (World Health Organization, 2007b).[8]

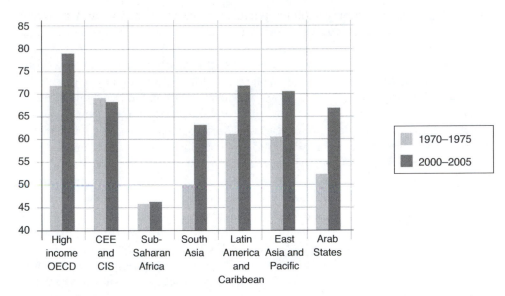

FIGURE 3.6 | Life expectancy at birth by region (OECD—consists of e.g. Australia, Canada, USA, and most Western European countries, CEE—Countries in Central and Eastern Europe; CIS—Commonwealth of Independent States, i.e. former USSR states).

In their presentation of the global burden of disease, Lopez and associates (2006) distinguish between two large regions of the world: a) High-income economies (Western Europe, USA and Canada, Australia, New Zealand, Japan and South Korea), and b) Low- and middle-income countries (Latin America and the Caribbean, Middle East and North Africa, sub-Saharan Africa, South Asia, East Asia and the Pacific, and Eastern Europe and Central Asia). Fifteen percent of the world's population lives in high-income countries. The proportion is declining.

Furthermore a distinction is made between three classes of diseases. Group I: Communicable diseases, maternal and perinatal conditions, and nutritional deficiencies. Group II: Noncommunicable diseases (i.e. cancer, diabetes, coronary heart disease, stroke, alcohol use disorders, unipolar depression). Group III: Injuries (including self-inflicted injuries and violence).

Let us first have a look at mortality statistics as described in the Global Burden of Disease report (Lopez et al., 2006). Worldwide, 56 million people died in 2001. Nearly 20% were children younger than five years of age. The burden of disease is much higher among children and adolescents in low- and middle-income countries than is the case in high-income countries. In high-income countries, only 7% of all deaths are due to group I diseases. The corresponding figure for low- and middle-income countries is 36%. In high-income countries, 87% of all deaths are due to Group II (noncommunicable) diseases, while in low- and middle-income countries the corresponding figure is 54%. Group III diseases (injuries, suicide and violence) constitute 6% of all deaths in high-income countries and 10% of all deaths in low- and middle-income countries (see Figure 3.7).

Almost all Group I diseases (communicable diseases, maternal and perinatal conditions, and nutritional deficiencies) are in low- and middle-income countries. The HIV/AIDS problem is growing fast in these countries, from 2% of Group I diseases in 1990 to 14% in 2001. The HIV/AIDS pandemic is particularly overwhelming in sub-Saharan Africa. Sub-Saharan Africa has less than 10% of the population in the world, but more than 70% of those who are HIV infected live in this region.

Group II diseases (such as cancer, diabetes, coronary heart disease, stroke, alcohol use disorders, and unipolar depression) used to be the diseases of rich countries. These diseases are, however, now responsible for more than 50% of all deaths among 15 to 59 year olds in low- and middle-income countries, except from two regions; sub-Saharan Africa and South Asia. This means that the populations of five regions of the world (Latin America and the Caribbean, Middle East and North Africa, East Asia and the Pacific, and Eastern Europe and Central Asia) are facing new health challenges. Since also Group III diseases (injuries and violence) are highly prevalent in these countries, they are confronted with three challenges simultaneously.

In all regions of the world, neuropsychiatric conditions are the most important causes of disability, accounting for more than 37% of years of healthy life lost as a result of disability among adults aged 15 years and older. The disability burden of these conditions is almost the same for men and women, but the major contributing causes are different. Depression is the leading cause of disability for both males and females, but the burden of depression is about 50% higher among women. Females also have higher burdens due to anxiety disorders, migraine, and senile dementia. The male burden due

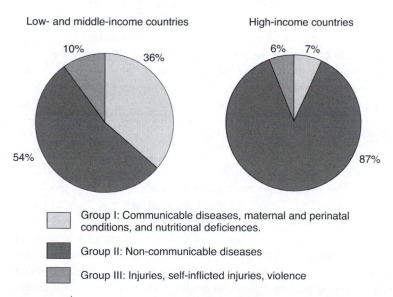

Low- and middle-income countries

High-income countries

Group I: Communicable diseases, maternal and perinatal conditions, and nutritional deficiences.

Group II: Non-communicable diseases

Group III: Injuries, self-inflicted injuries, violence

FIGURE 3.7 | Proportional distribution of total deaths by broad cause group.
Based on data from Mathers, Lopez & Murray, 2006.

to alcohol and drug use disorders is nearly six times higher than that for females and amounts to one quarter of the male neuropsychiatric burden (Lopez et al., 2006).

EXPLAINING INEQUALITIES IN HEALTH

The global variation in the burden of disease demonstrates that medical perspectives may be important but not sufficient in our understanding of health and health problems (as we suggested when discussing dimensions of health previously in this chapter). In describing global differences in health problems, medical language is often used for specification of diseases and disorders, while sociological and economic knowledge is necessary for an understanding of the conditions and processes that create some of these differences.

This also suggests that music therapy practices need to relate to very different realities from context to context as to which problems are the most pertinent to relate to and how to approach them. For instance, music therapy with people with HIV/AIDS patients is an important but small field in European and American music therapy, and the music therapists working in this field have mainly chosen to develop an individualized approach (see e.g. Lee, 1996). In contrast, it can be argued that HIV/AIDS is one of the essential issues when working with music and health in an East African context and that this issue cannot be approached in an individualized manner but requires community-oriented approaches informed by sociocultural perspectives (Barz, 2006; Stige, 2008b).

Wilkinson (1996) and Wilkinson and Pickett (2010) have pointed at a possible link between socioeconomic inequalities within countries and inequalities across countries. These authors maintain that populations of egalitarian countries, at all levels of development, have better health than countries with more pronounced socioeconomic inequalities. The main explanation is related to social cohesion. More egalitarian societies and smaller socioeconomic differences are associated with social cohesion, and social cohesion is associated with better health (see the next chapter). Wilkinson suggests that the egalitarian quality of social relations and public values explains why the so-called communist countries in Eastern Europe traditionally had higher standards of health than would be expected given their per capita income. Based on available empirical evidence, Kawachi (2000) concludes that the size of the economic gap is an important predictor of health, independent of the absolute standard of living. Kawachi and Berkman (2000) defines social cohesion as "the extent of social connectedness and solidarity among groups in society," and they define social capital as "those features of societal structures—such as levels of interpersonal trust and norms of reciprocity and mutual aid—which act as resources for individuals and facilitate collective action." Social cohesion and social capital are collective dimensions of society, distinguishable from concepts such as social networks and social support, which are usually applied on the level of individuals and their interaction with others. Kawachi and Berkman suggest that these two concepts, social cohesion and social capital, are important for public health.

A large number of factors may contribute to explaining socioeconomic inequalities in health. One important factor is related to socioeconomic differences in health-related behaviors such as smoking, eating habits, and physical activity. Huisman, Kunst and Mackenbach (2005) have examined inequalities in the prevalence of smoking in the European Union. In both genders, the proportion of smokers increases with lower socioeconomic status. This is just one example of an association that seems to be present across a large number of countries and several health behaviors: Unhealthy behaviors are generally more common among low-status groups. Health behaviors are obviously one of the factors which contribute to explaining the association between socioeconomic status and morbidity/mortality.

Inequalities in health are not limited to the adult parts of populations. Socioeconomic health inequalities among children and adolescents exist in all parts of the world. According to the Black Report from 1980, health inequalities among children in the Nordic countries had almost been eradicated. More recent research has, however, shown that relative inequalities are pronounced even in these rather affluent countries (Halldorsson et al., 2000). It is still the case that poverty among children is much less widespread in countries with universal social welfare systems, free access to health care, and free education. In wealthy countries which have given less priority to socioeconomic equity, such as the United States, poverty in families with children is more widespread (World Health Organization, 2007a).

In the Ottawa Charter on Health Promotion (World Health Organization, 1986) there is a list of what is termed **prerequisites for health**: "The fundamental conditions and resources for health are peace, shelter, education, food, income, a stable eco-system, sustainable resources, social justice and equity. Improvement in health requires a secure foundation in these basic prerequisites." This simply means that economic processes, legal systems, and political decisions have consequences for people's health. Action for public health and health promotion involves all sectors of society and goes far beyond the mandates of health professionals and the health care system. Poverty is the most important challenge to the health of the populations in most regions of the world.

Box 3.4 | MUSIC THERAPY, DIVERSITY, AND POVERTY

How do music therapists prioritize when encountering diversity and poverty? This is the main question in Helen Oosthuizen's (2006) article on diversity and community in South African music therapy. Oosthuizen is one of just a few music therapists that work in the Johannesburg area and she describes how she finds it necessary to carefully consider her priorities when deciding which work opportunities to accept:

> Some wealthier institutions and parents are willing to consider the services of a music therapist and community centres are beginning to ask questions, to offer possibilities. I have many options and there are not music therapists to fill those places I reject. Besides questions around how I could best work in one community, I need to consider whether my resources will be best utilised in one community or another. The choices I make in how I utilise my skills, whilst holding great value for a particular community,

Box 3.4 |

may serve to grow or *inhibit* our profession and may serve to address or *compound* pertinent issues affecting the country as a whole (Oosthuizen, 2006).

Oosthuizen describes her work as a music therapist within different South African communities:

> As I introduce music therapy to an affluent school community, I find the cultural understandings I share with community members a helpful advantage, and yet I need to consider that by working only in wealthy, resourced communities similar to my own community, I may be highlighting the divide between wealth and poverty. In this way, I compound our country's struggle with social inequality. As I initiate a short term music therapy group in a community very different to my own, I struggle with questions of whether music therapy has any relevance here, and find myself adapting my thinking, and working closely with the community to form a music therapy practice that has value in this context. These diverse work experiences challenge music therapists to increase our awareness of pertinent national and global issues and the possibilities our profession holds for addressing these issues (Oosthuizen, 2006).

In concluding her article, Oosthuizen argues that as music therapists we need to consider our work within broader social contexts, even if this involves changing our ways of working:

> This is not to suggest that all music therapists need to seek out work in a range of different communities, but rather that we need to carefully consider our work in any community. I find it easy to become ignorant of the poverty that surrounds me, allowing this ignorance to excuse my lack of investment in impoverished communities, increasing the divide between rich and poor (Oosthuizen, 2006).

WELLBEING AND OBJECTIVE CONDITIONS OF LIFE

So far we have described world health by providing statistics on mortality, morbidity, and disability. However, as stated earlier in this chapter, health is more than absence of disease. And the concept of wellbeing calls for an emphasis on the more positive aspects of life. Attempts have been made to analyze happiness across nations. Veenhoven (1995) distinguishes between three **theories of happiness**: Comparison Theory, Folklore Theory, and Livability Theory.

In *Comparison Theory* it is assumed that evaluations of life are based on a sort of mental calculus, in which perceptions of life as it is experienced by the individual are weighted against standards of how life ideally should be. In other words, we judge life on the basis of what we think it realistically could be. As a result of these comparison processes, one's subjective appreciation of life would be unrelated to its objective quality. The *Folklore Theory* does not see happiness as an individual evaluation of life, but as a reflection of culturally shaped notions of life. Also according to this theory, happiness should be largely unrelated to the present quality of life in a particular country or culture. *Livability Theory* claims that one's subjective appreciation of life first of all depends on the objective quality of life. The better the living conditions, the happier a population is likely to be. Livability Theory focuses on absolute quality of life, rather than on relative differences.

Based on analyses of data collected among university students in 38 nations and general population surveys in 28 countries, Veenhoven (1995) concluded that the predictions from Comparison Theory and Folklore Theory were largely unconfirmed, while the predictions from Livability Theory were all confirmed. Happiness does to a large extent reflect objective conditions of life. If we go back to the discussion of relationships between subjective and objective wellbeing previously in the chapter, Veenhoven's conclusion could be somewhat surprising. A range of studies have demonstrated that there is no

FIGURE 3.8 | Music and wellbeing. ArtStories students from Henbury School participate in Making Music Being Well, Northern Territory, Australia.

Photo. Christine Carrigg.

simple and direct relationship between objective and subjective indicators of wellbeing. Money does not equal happiness. A materialistic orientation could even undermine well-being. At the same time, lack of material resources is often associated with strain and stress, lack of choice and options, and increased vulnerability.

Relationships between the objective conditions of life and the experience of wellbeing are complex and multifaceted and relative to time, person, and place. Some of the important mediating factors are the degree of social support and amount of social capital available, and this will be the theme of discussion in the next chapter.

CONCLUSION

Health concerns and ideas about health vary over time and between places. In medical contexts *health* has often been defined as *the absence of disease*, for instance as a state when the organism functions optimally without evidence of disease or abnormality. In order to be healthy, according to this perspective, a person does not need to feel healthy or be a productive member of society. It is sufficient that the person has no specific disease or symptoms of disease. Critical voices have called for a more holistic approach to health where patients are treated as persons. In order to communicate such ideas, the concepts of *illness* and *sickness* have sometimes been employed. In this literature, illness refers to people's perception of their own health, while *sickness* is used to denote the socially constructed label of being unhealthy.

WHO's utopian definition of health from 1946 has influenced people's way of thinking about health considerably. Health has important positive aspects that should not be neglected and WHO's definition has opened up for practices that are not only concerned with treatment, prevention, and rehabilitation but also on health promotion, enablement, empowerment, and social change. When we direct our attention to positive aspects of health, concepts such as *wellbeing*, *quality of life,* and *life satisfaction* become central. Wellbeing, for instance, could be understood in relation to the dimension of subjective wellbeing (emotions, global judgment of life, and satisfaction with specific life domains) and in relation to objective indicators of wellbeing (regarding education attainment, housing conditions, and absence of disease). There is no simple and direct relationship between objective and subjective indicators. There are, for instance, a number of studies showing a marked decline in happiness among people living in the United States at the same time as standards of living were rising.

Various societies impose different kinds of strain and demands on the individual. Health can therefore also be defined as one's ability to cope with and master the challenges of daily life. This is a relational concept; health is a quality in the relationship between a person and their surroundings. This perspective is central to community music therapy. It would be a mistake, however, to think that we could do without an understanding of health as absence of disease or as positive experience of wellbeing. The three dimensions of health that we have outlined suggest that relational and contextual factors should be taken into consideration without neglecting diseases, disorders, and experiences at the individual level.

The field of mental health illuminates this point quite well. A diagnosis is a social construction; it is based on observations of violations of social norms and these are then interpreted as symptoms of mental disorder. The deviance could originate from sources such as organic deficit, psychological dynamics, or external stress. It could also represent volitional acts in defiance of social rules. According to many social scientists, the act of labeling influences the field that the labeling is part of. When a person is given a diagnostic label this influences his or her self-concept as well as other people's conception of this person. In some instances it could contribute to more deviant behaviors. This is one of the reasons why resource-oriented perspectives to mental health might be very useful.

It is impossible to discuss health without also discussing the value of social justice. There are huge inequities in world health. The World Health Report of 2003 exemplified this with an example showing that a baby girl born in Japan could expect to live for about 85 years while a girl born at the same moment in Sierra Leone would have a life expectancy of 36 years. If a citizen in Japan becomes chronically ill she could expect excellent treatment and rehabilitation services and medications worth about US$ 550 per year on average. In contrast, a citizen in Sierra Leone could expect, on average, medicines worth about US$ 3 per year if she falls ill. Inequities exist not only between countries, but also within countries, in some countries to quite an extreme degree. The question of how to prioritize when encountering poverty and inequities in health is therefore relevant for music therapists everywhere.

KEY TERMS, DISCUSSION TOPICS, AND NOTES

Key Terms

Key terms in order of appearance:

Health
Disease
Illness
Sickness
Wellbeing
Subjective wellbeing
Objective wellbeing
Quality of life
Dimensions of health
Relational and contextual factors
Labeling theory
Secondary deviance
Stigmatization
Inequities in health
Inequalities in health
Prerequisites for health
Theories of happiness

Discussion Topics

The following critical thinking questions can be discussed in class or in groups or used by the individual student for critical reflection on topics discussed in the chapter. Extra resources can be found on the website of the book.

1. In the previous chapter we discussed the systemic and sociocultural turn in music therapy theory in the 1980s. This can in part be related to a range of ecological theories that emerged in psychology and related disciplines in the 1960s and 1970s, as discussed at the beginning of this chapter. One implication for practice would be to work with relationships between the immediate systems of the troubled person (such as the family and classroom milieu of a child). More drastic departures from traditional therapeutic practice are also thinkable. Discuss if and how ecological thinking characterizes the theory and practice of music therapy in your country. Do you feel that the range of possibilities proposed by ecological thinking has been fully explored? If not, what factors have contributed to the current situation?

2. Many people resist activities that are labeled therapy, possibly because the term is associated with stigma or with situations in which experts dominate. For music therapists working in non-medical contexts this could sometimes create dilemmas. When is it respectful and when is it dishonest not to use the label music therapy for the work? Discuss examples and various ways of dealing with such dilemmas.

3. Inequities in health is not one of the issues that has been discussed extensively in the music therapy literature, but some music therapists have chosen to actively relate to this problem (see e.g. Box 3.4). Delineate inequities of health in your context and discuss if and how music therapists could work with this issue.

Notes

1   NGO is an established abbreviation for Non-Governmental Organizations.
2   Diener is former president of the International Society of Quality of Life Studies and editor of the *Journal of Happiness Studies*.
3   ICF is organized around the following components: Body functions and body structures, activities and participation, and environmental factors. In relation to body functions and/or structures, a person may experience *impairments*, such as significant deviation or loss. *Activities* refer to an individual's execution of a task or action, while *participation* is understood as involvement in a life situation. A person may not only experience impairments then, but also *activity limitations* (difficulties in executing activities) or *participation restrictions* (problems with involvement in life situations). Environmental factors, as described in ICF, include natural environment, technology, support and relationships, attitudes, services, systems, and policies. These factors increase or diminish the consequences of impairments, activity limitations, and participation restrictions (World Health Organization, 2001a).
4   Other classification schemes may be used in non-western cultures, such as the Chinese Classification of Mental Disorders.
5   Conceptualizations of problems and disorders contribute to the construction of professions, as Foucault's (1961/1991) seminal work *Madness and Civilization* demonstrated, see Chapter 10.
6   There are various notions of equality with different definitions of what constitutes equity (see Chapter 7).

7 Recent reports from the new EU member states in Central and Eastern Europe have shown that the negative trends taking place during the economic transition have already been reversed (Zatonski & Jha, 2000).

8 Inequalities in health are not necessarily stable. In the Russian Federation there are presently increasing variations in life expectancy by level of education among men as well as among women (Murphy et al., 2006).

85

Health and Wellbeing

Chapter 4

Community and Social Resources

After studying Chapter 4, you will be able to discuss questions such as:

- What do we mean by levels of analysis when we discuss human development?
- What are the roots of the concept of community?
- How closely is each one of us linked to the rest of the world through our social networks?
- What is the difference between the direct effect hypothesis and the buffer effect hypothesis in research on the effects of social support?
- How can non-events (something that does not happen) represent stress?
- What is social capital and how can it be studied?
- How can music therapists contribute in relation to the situation of marginalized groups?

HUMAN DEVELOPMENT WITHIN SOCIAL CONTEXT

THE lives of human beings are characterized by continuous interaction with others. Newborn children can only survive if taken care of by their parents or other caretakers immediately after birth and if the care continues for years. Reciprocity, cooperation, and sharing are—to various degrees and in various ways—important characteristics of our lives. In the evolution of the human species there seems to have been a gene-culture co-evolution and a selection for specific traits that enable humans to function especially well within groups, both to their own individual benefit and to the advantage of the group (Stige, 2002). Belongingness and relatedness have been suggested as basic psychological or social needs so fundamental that if systematically frustrated the health consequences may be quite serious (Baumeister & Leary, 1995; Berkman & Glass, 2000). Our social surroundings are, however, not only a resource and a positive factor in life. Other people may also be a burden and a source of stress. Interpersonal relationships can be associated with attraction, positive experiences, and love, but can also be dominated by aggression, jealousy, and sadness. This chapter is about the social contexts of people's lives.

There are a number of conceptual models describing the elements of such contexts. Bronfenbrenner's (1979) **ecological model** describing relationships between micro-systems, mesosystems, exosystems, and macrosystems has been influential. According to Bronfenbrenner (1979, pp. 16–42), *microsystems* consist of patterns of activities, roles, and interpersonal relationships experienced by the developing person in a given setting (such as a family or a peer group). *Mesosystems* refer to the interrelations among two or more microsystems in which the developing person actively participates (such as the relations between home and school for a child). *Exosystems* refer to systems that do not involve the active participation of the developing person but which influence the systems containing the developing person (a local council or a school administration are examples of exosystems). *Macrosystems* refer to textures and consistencies at higher levels of organization, such as society. Such levels can be understood as nested, where lower levels are embedded in higher levels.

Dalton, Elias and Wandersman (2007) have suggested a related model, with the person at the center, surrounded by layers defined by concentric circles (or ellipses; see Figure 4.1). The layer closest to the person consists of *microsystems*, which are defined

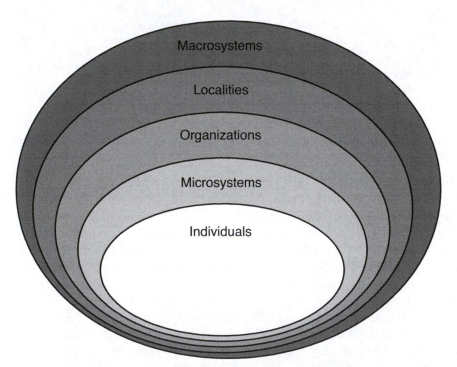

FIGURE 4.1 | The person in context: levels of analysis.

Adapted from Dalton, Elias, and Wandersman (2007, p. 18), with permission from Cengage Learning (previously Wadsworth/Thomson Learning).

as environments in which the person engages in direct, personal interaction with others over time. The next layer is *organizations* which consist of sets of microsystems, such as teams and other divisions of employees in workplaces. Geographic *localities* constitute the next level. Typical examples include villages, neighborhoods, and suburbs. Localities can be understood as sets of organizations and microsystems. And the final layer consists of the *macrosystems*, which consist of cultures, governmental and economic institutions, legal systems, and so forth. This ecological model illustrates how our lives are formed by circumstances. Some are close, others more distal, but all of them exert direct or indirect influences on our lives.

Several key concepts are needed in order to describe relevant features of these contexts.[1] Each of the terms presented in this chapter captures important aspects of social life.

Box 4.1 | RESTORING COMMUNAL EXPERIENCES DURING MUSIC THERAPY

David Ramsey is one of the music therapists who have explored music as a resource for human connectivity. He worked as a music therapist at Beth Abraham Health Services in New York for many years. In his doctoral dissertation, Ramsey (2002) examines his own work with a group of patients with aphasia. In describing and analyzing the transformations the clients went through, he ends up with a focus on communal music experiences as central to the process.

> While analyzing my group I was aware of the various individual personalities demonstrated during the group process. Greta seemed to be the compliant one, while Mary was the challenger. Ross would agitate the group at times, and Pam could demand attention and divert group activities. I was the demonstrated leader. The traditional way of observing each member as to role function however did not take into consideration the "personality" and "role" of the music. The task commitment on one level was the production of the familiar song. On another level the song exerted a power and leadership of its own that ultimately determined group process.
>
> I came to view the group from a perspective that focused on unified group responses rather than individual differences. The traditional view of group dynamics whereby individuals interact to determine process was replaced with an overview of the "chorus effect" whereby individuals, rather than demonstrate personal preferences, submit to the musical experience. The musical experience in this case provided for them, held them, and restored essentials that no other thing could provide. Through the group engagement and unified production of the well-known song, the participants could immerse themselves in expressive presentations that reflected the shared human necessity related to need for community (Ramsey 2002, pp. 107–108).

Restoration of community became a core category in Ramsey's study; community as shared experience, as connection and sense of togetherness, as psychological and social support, and as emotional rapport and sharing.

COMMUNITY

The word **community** is derived from the Latin *communitas* (of common), and the modern English word is linked to a variety of related meanings, ranging from personal and experiential dimensions to institutional and structural dimensions. The word is even used about large associations of countries like the European Community. The word "communicate" has the same Latin roots (*communicare*). To communicate means to make something common.

The concept of community is used in a wide range of disciplines, for instance biology, anthropology, sociology, and psychology. There is no single definition which is generally accepted. According to Hillery (1955), 94 definitions had been suggested already in the 1950s. An important distinction is between the **geographical notion of community** (neighborhood, village) and the **relational** one (quality of human relation-ships) (Gusfield, 1975, cited in McMillan & Chavis, 1986). In the context of community music therapy, both uses are relevant.

A community is often defined as a *group of individuals* who are *interacting* over time in a specific *location*. MacQueen and associates (2001) define community as a group of people with diverse characteristics who are linked by social ties, share common perspectives, and engage in joint action in geographical locations or settings. In late modern societies there is a tendency that communities develop out of common interests. These communities are defined by relations rather than locations. In the age of Internet communication, communities can develop involving individuals who live far away from each other.

McMillan and Chavis (1986) have developed a theory of **sense of community**, based on previous work by McMillan (1976). Their definition of this concept is based on four elements; *membership* (the feeling of belonging or of sharing a sense of personal relatedness), *influence* (a sense of mattering or making a difference to the group), *integration and fulfillment of needs* (the feeling that members' needs will be met), and *shared emotional connection* (the commitment and belief that members have and will have a shared history, common places, time together, and similar experiences). The term "sense of community" has strong, positive connotations and points at important psychological aspects of well functioning communities. Community as a geographical or relational concept is more descriptive but it has not always been treated as neutral.

A stable little community, in the image of say a village, often comes to mind when the concept of community is discussed. This is only one of many forms that human social organization has taken but it has sometimes been treated as a prototype. Take *The Little Community,* written by a renowned scholar in mid-twentieth century anthropology, where the argument goes as follows:

> The small community has been the very predominant form of human living throughout the history of mankind. The city is a few thousand years old, and while isolated homesteads appeared in early times . . ., it was probably not until the settlement of the New World that they made their "first appearance on a large scale".
>
> (Redfield, 1953/1963)

This treatment of the notion of community can be criticized for naturalizing one way of human social organization, by concentrating more on the village communities than on the complex fission–fusion patterns of nomadic communities.[2] Redfield's (1953/1963) ideas exemplify that the notion of community in social theory has a problematic history. There has been a tendency to privilege certain forms of community over others and to treat the selected forms as positive per definition. In other words; normative and descriptive elements have been confused. A one-sided focus on stable little communities is problematic because it neglects human diversity and also under-communicates negative aspects of human social life and thus the confining functions of a community.[3]

In urbanized late modern societies, there has been a diversification of communities with complex patterns of connectivity (Walker, 1993). Processes of individualization have also accelerated. This transforms rather than eradicates communal initiatives:

Individualization does not imply that all forms of collectivity disappear, it only gives community new, late modern forms. The need for ordering structures to orient oneself in daily social life makes people invent restrictions for their actions even where

FIGURE 4.2 | Music therapy as Street Party. "Rock am Ring" in Krefeld, Germany.
Photo: Peter Neumann.

they are not given a priori. Collective schemata therefore appear even where everyone must choose by her or himself, which is increasingly the case in late modernity.

(Fornäs, 1995, pp. 100–101)

Several of the notions of community described above have been found relevant in the community music therapy literature. The psychological sense of community is often stressed (Ramsey, 2002) and linked to community defined by relations (Ansdell, 2002, 2004) and/or locations (Kleive & Stige, 1988). In a theoretical discussion of the notion, Stige (2003, pp. 198–201) argues that community involves *shared practice* and a *culture of commitment*. Similar ideas have been developed in the literature through reference to the notion of musical **communities of practice** (Stige, 2002; Krüger, 2004; Ansdell, 2010a; Storsve, Westby & Ruud, 2010) (see Box 4.2 and Chapter 5).

Box 4.2 | EXPLORATIONS OF MUSICAL COMMUNITY

In an essay based on a qualitative case study of the group Musical Minds, Gary Ansdell (2010a) explores various notions of community. The members of Musical Minds live in a deprived area of East London and they meet once a week under the auspices of an organization that helps adults with long-term mental health problems. Ansdell describes how he witnessed and participated in a social and musical world where community was neither a given nor a comfortable state but a vulnerable yet vital process; music and singing was for the group unique ways of finding meaning and a sense of *belonging* in a difficult environment. The case of Musical Minds, Ansdell claims, highlights complex relationships between individuality and community, identity and belonging, and collaboration and negotiation. The following field note illuminates this point:

> The "performance space" is now set up, and members of Musical Minds suggest songs and sing them individually at first—each of them absolutely singular in style, delivery, taste. Concentration on each others' performance seems fragile to begin with. People move around, talk to someone else, go out for a cigarette. But concentration grows as the session settles, with people joining in the chorus of the more well-known (and easy to sing) solo songs. There's a ragged togetherness at these moments. In the interval one man comes up to me and says: "They don't sing in the same way as I do—then I get my breathing wrong!" Then he adds, "But I know it's good to sing together—I've got to keep trying" (Ansdell, 2010a, p. 45).

Ansdell contextualizes this description by referring to Gerald Delanty's discussion of the notion of community in contemporary society: "If anything unites [the] very diverse conceptions of community it is the idea that community concerns belonging" (Delanty, 2003, p. 4). Rather than just happening, Ansdell claims, contemporary community must be performed. Ansdell suggests that the best model for description of the group is to think of it as a *community of musical practice*:

Box **4.2** |

One possible model for Musical Minds is a "community of practice," a concept developed by the social learning theorist Etienne Wenger (Wenger, 1998; Wenger, McDermott & Snyder, 2002). It emerged from studies of the participatory learning of work groups, where the social, educational and productional aspects were closely connected. Wenger suggests that the concept "community of practice" characterizes the everyday experience of people engaged in doing and learning something together— where this is more than a transitory encounter, but less than a formal social structure. Wenger's concept has increasingly been used to describe all kinds of small-scale groups which exemplify how learning is social. It brings our attention to how such "communities of practice" catalyze fundamental social processes of participation, meaning-making, identity, and belonging (Ansdell, 2010a, p. 48).

Subsequent sections of Ansdell's essay explore particular aspects of a community of musical practice, such as its value for people as a focus for belonging and learning and for negotiation of the delicate balance between identity and difference. He suggests that a prime function of a community music therapy endeavor can be to cultivate, nurture, and sustain communities of musical practice in circumstances where they are otherwise difficult (see also Box 7.3).

SOCIAL NETWORKS

Beyond the concept of community, there are a number of other concepts relevant for describing social contexts and human connectivity. One of these was first used by Barnes when he carried out a study in a small fishing village in western Norway in the 1950s (Barnes, 1954). In order to describe aspects of social interaction he used the term **social network**. The term social networks refers to the web of contacts between people in their daily lives. Our social networks consist of all the people that we interact with, for instance family members, friends at school, colleagues at work, neighbors, or anyone that we meet repeatedly and communicate with. People whom we pass on the street incidentally and do not know or communicate with do not belong to our social network. But people that we regularly talk with at a bus stop, even if we don't know their names or their background, are part of our social network.

The concept of social network also takes into account the fact that contact between two people represents indirect contact between those who belong to the social network of both of them. Through members of your social network you are indirectly in contact with all people on earth. Researchers have actually tried to find out how many steps are necessary to get from one arbitrarily chosen person on earth to a specific other one, unknown to the first one, and living far away. The Hungarian author Frigyes Karinthy in 1929 wrote a novel where it was suggested that on the average only five intermediaries are needed. This is similar to what the well known social psychologist Stanley Milgram called "six degrees of separation." Milgram actually tested this hypothesis by randomly selecting a number of people in the American mid west and asking them to send a package to a specific person living in Massachusetts. They were, however, not allowed to use the post office, but instead they had to send it to someone they knew, who could send it to someone else that he or she knew and so on, in order to get the package across to the target person with as few intermediaries as possible. For those packages that actually reached the target person, it took on average between five and seven intermediaries to get to its destination (Milgram, 1967).

In 2003, Columbia University researchers carried out another study similar to the one by Milgram, but this time with senders in New York and receivers spread around in different countries. Again they found that the average number of intermediaries was five to seven (Saxbe, 2003). Seen from a social network perspective, we certainly live in a small world. It must be added, however, that in the Milgram study fewer than 100 out of 300 packages reached their destination. In the Columbia University study only 324 out of 61,168 messages reached their destination. The researchers attributed the high attrition to the participants' lack of motivation.

Within social networks, the connections between two individuals are called "ties." A distinction is often made between *weak ties* and *strong ties*. A strong tie is a relationship which is characterized by regular encounters, real conversations about matters that are perceived to be important, and mutual positive feelings. Weak ties are more transitory and may appear to be less important to each of us. Weak ties are still important. Saying hello to neighbors or colleagues that you don't know too well, may still give you an impression of being noticed and a feeling of belonging.

Networks can be described in a number of ways (Berkman & Glass, 2000). *Size* is the total number of people in the network of a person. *Density* is the extent to which members of a network are connected to each other. Density is sometimes more precisely defined as the number of bilateral connections out of all possible such connections among a defined group of people. Among 10 persons, there are 45 possible bilateral connections. If there in fact are only nine such connections, the density is 20%. *Inclusiveness* is the number of non-isolated individuals within a defined social network. A non-isolated person is a person who has at least one tie with one of the others. *Homogeneity* is the extent to which people within a specific network are similar to each other with regard to characteristics such as age, educational background and lifestyles. *Multiplexity* denotes the number of different types of transactions or support that flow through a specific set of ties. The multiplexity is low if your relationship to members of the local choir relates to the fact that you are all members of the same choir only. The multiplexity is higher if you also know several of them from other contexts, for instance as neighbors, colleagues, teachers of your children, friends of your parents, or members of the same congregation.

Within social networks there are several kinds of possible relationships and connections among people. Some concepts are used to describe bilateral ties between individuals within social networks. Important aspects are frequency of contact, duration of ties, and reciprocity. Reciprocity is high if both persons in a relationship give and take to the same extent. If one person is always the "helper" and the other one is always the

FIGURE 4.3 | Improvisation in an inclusive summer workshop. Kublank, Germany.
Photo: Kristin Richter.

one who receives help or support, then the relationship is characterized by lack of reciprocity and is potentially a source of stress to both parties (Mittelmark et al., 2004). To be *socially integrated* means to participate in a broad range of social relationships.

The concept of social networks is useful in several arenas, for instance as regards health and lifestyles. Networks of sexual contacts determine the spread of HIV-infection across communities and populations, our health-related behaviors are to a large extent influenced by significant others in our lives, and well functioning social connections are important to mental health. The concept of social networks is, however, insufficient when we want to understand the processes that determine the impact of social relationships on individuals. So far, our way of describing networks or relationships between persons within a network is primarily quantitative. In order to describe these processes more extensively, we need other concepts, concepts that capture important qualities of interpersonal relationships, such as how people provide support or create stress for each other socially.

SOCIAL SUPPORT

Social support has been defined in a number of different ways. The simplest possible explanation is that social support refers to the process which takes place when one person helps another (Feldman & Cohen, 2000). Barrera (2000, p. 215) has used slightly different words: "It is a concept that attempts to capture helping transactions that occur between people who share the same households, workplaces, organizations, and other community settings." Social support has also been defined as an exchange of resources perceived by either the provider or the recipient or both to be intended to enhance the wellbeing of the recipient (Shumaker & Brownell, 1984). While the first definitions take an outsider perspective and regard social support as a kind of transaction between people, the latter one emphasizes the perceived aspects making a distinction between provider and recipient. In a communication theory framework we would instead say "sender" and "receiver." Both perspectives are valid. The perceived aspect allows for providers and recipients to perceive their relationship in different ways. One person may for instance believe that he or she provides important support, while the other one may experience their interaction as more stressful than supportive.

Social support has been called a "natural resource" which exists in communities everywhere. Help from others is important in a myriad of different situations: Small children need comfort when they stumble and fall. Schoolchildren may need help with their schoolwork. An adolescent may need someone to talk to after being dumped by his or her boyfriend or girlfriend. Pregnant women may need to talk with other women about how to tackle their situation. Those who experience the death of a spouse may need someone to talk with about their grief and their sorrow. Social support is an important remedy to be used against a variety of stressful experiences in life.

House (1981) distinguishes between four categories of social support: *Emotional support* is associated with sharing life experiences and involves the provision of trust, caring, and empathy. *Instrumental support* implies provision of help and tangible aid for persons directly in need. *Informational support* involves the provision of information and advice that can be useful for a person to address or solve specific problems. *Appraisal support* means provision of information (feedback and affirmation) that is useful for someone in order to learn more about himself or herself. All forms of social support may contribute to improve health and wellbeing. Emotional support is the category that has been paid most attention to in research.

The importance of friendships and positive social relationships for health has probably been part of folk wisdom for millennia ("friends can be good medicine"). It was only in the 1970s, however, that systematic empirical evidence began to emerge (Reis, 1995). According to Cohen, Gottlieb and Underwood (2000) there are two traditions of research on social relationships and health. In the sociological perspective originally developed by Durkheim, there has been a focus on social integration, participation, and social roles. Research in this tradition has confirmed that social integration is associated with lower levels of mortality and morbidity (Berkman & Glass, 2000). Measures used in this line of research include assessments of network size, diversity, and reciprocity (Steptoe & Ayers, 2004). This is known as the **direct effect hypothesis** which simply postulates that high levels of social support are associated with low levels of distress, psychological complaints, and psychiatric symptoms.

The second tradition was inspired by Cassel (1976). In this tradition another hypothesis was suggested. According to the **buffer effect hypothesis**, social support represents a resource when we are exposed to various stressors. The association between

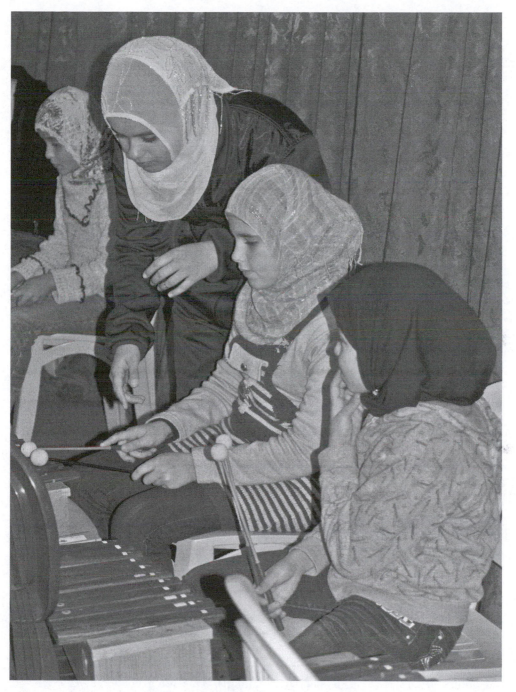

FIGURE 4.4 | Learning from more experienced learners. Music education in a Palestinian refugee camp in Lebanon.

Photo: Even Ruud.

such stressors and aspects of, for instance mental health, is strong for those who score low on social support and weak among those who score high on social support. In statistical terms this is an *interaction effect*: The association between a predictor (in this case degree of exposure to a source of stress) and a dependent variable (score on a scale for measurement of mental distress) depends on the level of a third variable (level of social support). From the perspective of the buffer effect hypothesis, social support is first of all a resource when people are confronted with stressful demands or stressful situations.[4]

High levels of social support are related to lower mortality and better mental health, such as lower levels of depression (Stansfeld, 2006). Much of the evidence, however, comes from studies with cross-sectional designs (studies where data are collected in one wave only and not repeatedly over time, see Chapter 9). There are, however, also a number of studies with a prospective design. These studies show that on average, persons with low support have two to three times higher mortality compared with those who report high support (Uchino, 2004, cited in Wills & Ainette, 2007). The mechanisms by which social support is related to mortality are, however, not well explored. There is a need for more prospective, longitudinal studies, with measurement of those factors that lead to a better understanding of these processes.

The consequences of musical participation for social networks and social support have been discussed in some of the community music therapy literature. In two studies of a senior choir in a rural town in Norway, both Knardal (2007) and Stige (2010b) found that the participants valued the choir as a social experience generating social support within networks. Social isolation is a challenge for many elderly people living in a local community. Partners and friends might pass away and their social network might shrink or grow weaker in various ways. Many participants described the choir as an important source of new supportive relationships. Friendships evolved, people started to help each other with transportation and other mundane challenges, and some of the choir members started to meet in between rehearsals. Increased multiplexity was also frequently described. Stige (2010b) used the term *culture of mutual care* to portray the multiple roles and relationships the singers cultivated in relation to each others, as neighbors, co-singers, drivers, helpers, board members, advocates, and so forth. The variety of roles taken by the music therapist was also described in similar terms.[5]

SOCIAL STRESS

As mentioned at the beginning of this chapter, people's relationships to others are not only a source of wellbeing and good health. Other people may also represent a burden and a source of frustration. This has led social epidemiologists to talk about **social stress**.

The word stress has several meanings. It refers to external demands which may exceed our ability to cope (stressors—the stress stimuli). This refers to our perception and evaluation of those demands (the stress experience). It also refers to internal psychological and physiological reactions to the demands that we meet (stress response). A fourth aspect is our experience of the stress response, which may add to the feeling of being stressed

(Ursin & Eriksen, 2004).[6] Responses to strain are normally adaptive and contribute towards increasing the individual's chances of coping. The term **positive stress** is often used to refer to forms of stress that the person is able to cope with. In all people's lives there is stress, and as long as we can cope we may learn from our stressful experiences and become even better able to cope with stress. When the burdens we are confronted with are so intense or so long-lasting that we are unable to cope adequately, the term **negative stress** is used.

Wheaton (1999) describes a number of different forms of stress as well as the continuum between the most discrete, sudden, and traumatic forms of stress to the more continuous ones (see Figure 4.5). *Chronic stress* refers to stress that does not start as a specific event. It may develop slowly and gradually, for instance as problematic aspects of our relationships with others. *Non-events* are defined as events that are desired or anticipated, but do not occur. A young boy in the early teens is invited to birthday parties of his classmates but when his own birthday arrives his parents or caregivers are unwilling or unable to hold a birthday party. *Daily hassles* have been defined as irritating and frustrating demands of everyday life, such as traffic jams or other people demanding too much.[7] *Stressful life events* are discrete and observable events such as life changes with distinct onsets and outcomes, such as death of a family member or a divorce.[8] *Sudden traumas* are more dramatic and include events such as natural disasters, plane crashes, and similar catastrophic events beyond what we can imagine covered by the term social stress.

Wheaton's scheme also contains a most interesting category called *macrosystem stressors*. These stressors are caused by processes at the macrosystem level and include socioeconomic inequality, unemployment, high crime rates, and so forth. These stressors may be mediated by stressors at the personal and interpersonal levels, but it is also easy to imagine that there may be aspects of societies that impose direct stress on the individual, for instance increasing individualism and materialism or simply the complexity of modern societies.

It is easy to see that many forms of stress are caused by other people. Several lines of research have confirmed the impact of such stress on psychological complaints and mental health. In the Midtown Manhattan Study (Langner & Michael, 1963) it was shown that mental health problems were related to factors such as parents being divorced, parental conflict, negative impression of parents, and inadequate relations to other people in one's social network. Rutter and associates (1975) identified family discord or disruption as one of the most important predictors of psychiatric disorder among children. Other factors that have been shown to be associated with poor health are poverty and unemployment (Bartley, Ferrie & Montgomery, 2006) and job stress (Marmot, Siegrist & Theorell, 2006).

People react differently to stress. Experiences which may be perceived as quite stressful by some individuals are rather easily dealt with by others. Lazarus and Folkman (1984) defined two interrelated appraisal processes. *Primary appraisal* refers to a person's estimate of the strength or intensity of one or more stressors. For one person, giving a speech at a public meeting may represent quite a challenge and be perceived as stressful. For another person giving such a speech may be perceived as not stressful at all.

*Basic
Concepts of
Community
Music
Therapy*

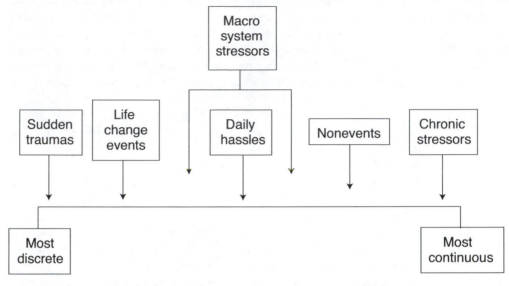

FIGURE 4.5 | The stress continuum.
Source: Wheaton, 1999. Reprinted with permission from Cambridge University Press.

Secondary appraisal refers to the person's estimate of available resources and coping options for responding to the stressors. *Reappraisal* means "reframing" or changing one's perception of the intensity of the stressor or of available coping resources.

To work with musical performance might create stressful situations for some participants in community music therapy. To participate in appraisals of the situation and to nurture constructive reappraisals is then part of the music therapist's responsibility (Ansdell, 2005b; Dahle & Slettebakk, 2006; O'Grady, 2009; Ansdell, 2010b).

Coping resources refer to personal and social characteristics that people may utilize when dealing with stressors. An important category of coping resources is well functioning social networks where social support can be mobilized. Personal coping characteristics include self esteem and self efficacy. In a review of relevant research, Cohen and Edwards (1989) came to the conclusion that there was only limited evidence for the importance of personality characteristics as buffers against stress.

Box 4.3 | THE COMMUNITY AS "THE OTHERS"

Communities unify and differentiate, include and exclude people. A study of a Canadian choir for homeless men illuminates this point quite clearly. Consider for instance this statement, made by one member of the choir:

Box **4.3**

Jean: The system . . . has been built for the community . . . the whole one, but there's so many . . . there's so (many) different character within the community, the system is good for a couple one but for about the half of it, it's garbage, it's not properly fit for those kind of character, so that's why I, I went down the drain, and I lost even my dignity. People used to spit on me on [First Street] because . . . you're nothing (Bailey & Davidson, 2003).

The assertion is made in the context of a qualitative research interview, in a study examining the formation of the choir and the subsequent positive life transformations that occurred for many of the participants. The researchers conclude:

Through participation in the choir, it appears that these previously destitute and powerless men have found their voice in a society in which they were despised and ridiculed during times of destitution. While they are singing their addictions and traumas are overcome and the disencumbered selves are allowed to soar beyond the mundane yet ever constant demands of food and shelter. The use of the singing voice has provided the members of the Homeless Choir with a vehicle to express what is worthwhile within themselves and to share this worth in a public forum (Bailey & Davidson, 2003).

There are tensions as well as positive interactions between individuals, groups, and communities, depending upon the quality of social networks and degrees of social support and social stress. This study exemplifies how these relationships can be worked with through communal amateur singing (see also Box 10.2).

SOCIAL CAPITAL

Concepts like social networks, social support, social stress, and coping are all describing phenomena and processes taking place at the personal and interpersonal levels. The term **social capital** has been proposed to characterize larger units, such as local communities, municipalities, counties, and countries. Use of the term can be traced back to the early twentieth century (e.g. Hanifan, 1916) but the concept is nowadays strongly tied to the name of the French sociologist Pierre Bourdieu (1986). Bourdieu distinguished between four forms of capital: *economic capital* (command over economic resources), *social capital* (resources connected to group membership, relationships to others, and social networks), *cultural capital* (education and knowledge), and *symbolic capital* (prestige and honor). Kawachi and Berkman (2000) have described social capital in a way which is highly relevant in our context. They define social capital as "those features of social structures—such as levels of interpersonal trust and norms of reciprocity and mutual aid—which act as resources for individuals and facilitate collective action." These authors claim that social capital forms a subset of the notion of **social cohesion**.

In a more recent publication, Kawachi, Subramanian, and Kim (2010) distinguish between two kinds of definitions of social capital. The social cohesion approach defines social capital as a property of organizations or communities (such as the definition provided above). The network-based approach defines social capital as the resources embedded within an individual's social network. In our opinion, the latter definition makes it more difficult to distinguish between social support (defined earlier in this chapter) and social capital. If the term social capital is used more narrowly to describe the resources available to individuals, it does not add much to terms like social network and social support. As an ecological concept focused on higher levels of analysis, it brings new perspectives to our understanding of how social factors influence health.[9]

Since social capital is defined as aspects of social communities that represent resources to its individual members, it may seem contradictory to look for its possible negative consequences. This is, however, exactly what Portes (1998) did in an influential article. He identified four such negative consequences of high levels of social capital: a) excessive demands placed upon members of cohesive groups to provide support to others, b) conformity pressure that may lead to intolerance and restrictions on individual freedom, c) oppression or exclusion of members of out-groups, and d) hindering of upward social mobility. This has led Kawachi, Subramanian, and Kim (2010) to conclude that definitions of social capital should not be based on the assumption that consequences of high levels of social capital are always positive.[10]

Scales for measuring social capital demonstrate clearly the multifaceted nature of this concept. One scale was developed by Robert D. Putnam of Harvard University. The scale consists of measures of behavior, opinions, organization memberships, positions in clubs or organizations, number of organizations in a certain geographical unit, and turnouts at presidential elections (Putnam, 2000). In a sense this makes the concept of social capital rather unspecific. Still it may capture aspects of social life which are important in order to characterize communities, states or even countries.

Putnam (2000, p. 22) distinguishes between two forms of social capital; **bonding** and **bridging**, and maintains that this may be the most important of the dimensions along which social capital can be described. *Bonding* is defined as the social capital associated with social networks of homogeneous groups of people. Bonding social capital may, according to Putnam, for instance exist within "ethnic fraternal organizations, church-based women's reading groups, and fashionable country clubs." *Bridging* is social capital associated with groups or networks which include people from diverse social cleavages. Examples, according to Putnam, are civil rights movements, many youth service groups, and ecumenical religious organizations. Bonding social capital may manifest as cohesion, solidarity, and high levels of emotional support. Bridging social capital typically means exchange of information, diffusion of information, and access to external assets. A choir can host both forms of social capital. A choir with members who are all from a small countryside village or neighborhood, and know each other well already, can strengthen bonding social capital and represent an important source of emotional social support and friendship. A multi-ethnic city choir with members from different neighborhoods, with different educational backgrounds, different kinds of jobs, lays the ground for higher levels of bridging social capital. In Chapter 8 we will discuss bonding and bridging as two different "shifts" in community music therapy processes.

Social capital can be used to describe geographical areas such as states and countries. Putnam (2000) attempted to estimate levels of social capital across states in the US. The highest scores on social capital were found in mid-western/northern states like North Dakota, South Dakota, Minnesota and Montana. Lower scores were obtained in southern states such as Alabama, Georgia and Mississippi, with the very lowest scores found for Nevada.[11]

According to Putnam (2000) social capital in the United States decreased during the last three decades of the twentieth century. Civic and political engagement decreased markedly. Informal social ties were weakened and less time was spent with friends. Americans trusted one another less than they used to, and distrust became more widespread. Putnam documented these changes empirically. He also examined possible factors that may have contributed to the decline in social capital: a) pressures of time and money (including the special pressures on two-career families), b) suburbanization, commuting and sprawl, c) modern electronic entertainment media such as TV and computer games, and d) generational change—new generations being less involved in community issues. Putnam's analyses are primarily based on data from the United States. Levels of social capital may vary from country to country and even across regions within countries, and the changes in social capital that take place over time may also differ. The importance of such aspects of life as interpersonal trust, norms of reciprocity and mutual aid is, however, likely to constitute an important prerequisite for good health and a high quality of life in any country or culture. Further research on the relationship between social capital and health is likely to contribute to a more precise and nuanced understanding of the underlying processes and mechanisms.

In a review of studies on the relationship between social capital and health from 2005, De Silva and associates (2005) distinguished between individual and ecological social capital. They found strong evidence for an inverse relationship between common mental disorders and what they call cognitive social capital at the individual level, but few consistent results for ecological level social capital. They concluded that the evidence was inadequate to inform the development of specific social capital interventions to combat mental illness. More recent studies have confirmed that there are inverse associations between indicators of social capital and indicators of health (Åslund, Starrin & Nilsson, 2010). McKenzie (2006) argues against the idea that there are two distinctly different forms of social capital; the individual and the ecological. There are several ecological levels, and lumping together family-level social capital with social capital measured at the level of a whole country does not make much sense. An important challenge in future research on the relationship between social capital and health is to define clearly how and at what level social capital is measured, and to systematically examine associations with specific aspects of health.

Studies on the relationship between social capital and health have been reviewed by Kim, Subramanian, and Kawachi (2010). They found fairly consistent associations between trust as an indicator of social cohesion and better physical health. They add that

104

*Basic
Concepts of
Community
Music
Therapy*

FIGURE 4.6 | Moment of concentration. "Rock am Ring" in Krefeld, Germany.
Photo: Peter Neumann.

"the evidence for trust was stronger for self-rated health than for physical health outcomes, and stronger for individual-level perceptions than for area-level trust." Membership in associations, as an indicator of cohesion, was also associated with better self-rated health at an individual level. Kim, Subramanian, and Kawachi call for stronger study designs.

Box 4.4 | THE THERAPEUTIC REDISTRIBUTION OF SOCIAL–MUSICAL CAPITAL FOR MENTAL HEALTH

Social capital evolves as a shared resource of trust and reciprocity when people listen to each other, work or play together, and care about each other. British music therapist Simon Procter has described how accumulation and distribution of social capital in a community is an issue of outmost theoretical and practical interest for music therapy. In a chapter with the playful title "Playing Politics," Procter (2004) starts the discussion of community music therapy and social capital with a critical appraisal of the contemporary psychiatric system:

Box 4.4

> The psychiatric system prescribes drugs developed, produced and marketed by a small group of multinational corporations. Even non-pharmaceutical interventions for mental health (such as music therapy) are now required to demonstrate their ability to produce drug-comparable results in drug-comparable terms. In essence, the notion of health has been changed away from one focusing on how people *are* within a social *context*, in relation to other people, towards one which sees people as discrete bundles of physiological and psychological functions which can be assessed and treated *in isolation*. This seems particularly absurd in mental health, where so much of the pathology is described diagnostically in terms of the difficulties people encounter in relating to others. The consequence is that little room (or money) is left for non-prescribing practice which has to do with the well-being of community, or of individuals within community. Thus the role of community in health and well-being—and the empowerment of the individual—is forced out (Procter, 2004, p. 215).

Since the mid-1990s community has become a word "back in vogue" in the politics of social work and health care in the UK. Government policy has proclaimed the benefits of care in the community but the word is highly ambivalent in mental health circles, Procter argues. It might be associated with forward thinking but also with retrograde steps where people who previously lived in institutions now are displaced into "isolated, poorly resourced mini-institutions 'in the community'" (Procter, 2004, p. 217). Nevertheless, the shift towards community care has created a space for new possibilities and initiatives, and Procter argues that the many new user-led organizations with at least some state funding are among these. His own practice as a music therapist is in *Way Ahead,* a non-medical community resource center for people with experience of mental health problems. Procter argues that music therapy can fit very well in places like this but that this is not always obvious.

> Places like this are often suspicious of 'therapies'. Therapists are seen as aloof people who do not roll their sleeves up, but instead import their own agendas, their own ideas of what is good and bad. They are middle class and fail to see the world from any other angle (Procter, 2004, pp. 218–219).

The ideal Procter describes is a practice where music therapists do not override community values with "therapeutic values." Music therapists should be "of their communities," he suggests.

> Way Ahead has something very specific to teach me as a music therapist. Its description of itself as a community resource centre has two implications, one of place and the other of ethos. The place is 'community' in that it is not medical, even though it is concerned with people's mental health. But the ethos is also community in that it is not concerned simply with processing individuals through a system, but actively promotes a model of well-being which recognises the value of the communal and the contributions of each individual within the communal (Procter, 2004, p. 219).

Box 4.4 |

Procter links the value of the communal to Putnam's (2000) notion of social capital and he stresses the connection between musical participation and social capital:

> Social capital is accrued through musical participation. Perhaps then we could even talk of musical capital: inherently social in that it is of and between people and increases the chances of positive change within society, but also inherently musical in that it carries opportunities for aesthetic self-realisation and self-experience. It can be both public and private, communal and personal. It is about self-identity but also about being heard by others. It is above all about living performance, about grasping opportunities that promote well-being, as an individual but also as a member of communities. The role of the music therapist, then, must include offering people opportunities to steer a healthy musical course, to renew and develop their health-promoting relationship with music within communities (Procter, 2004, p. 228).

This work explicitly links music therapy practice to research that reveals relationships between social capital and people's health and wellbeing. In later publications, Procter (2006, 2011) further develops the idea of community music therapy as accumulation and distribution of social capital.

SOCIAL EXCLUSION AND MARGINALIZATION

Social exclusion can be defined as a process by which individuals or groups are detached from other people, groups, organizations, or institutions, or more generally excluded from social relationships and participation in activities on the various arenas of social life. The converse of social exclusion is social inclusion. Social inclusion means action to reverse processes which lead to social exclusion or action in order to include individuals or groups that have previously been excluded.

Exclusion can take place at different levels (Abrams, Hogg & Marques, 2005). When one person rejects another person, this is social exclusion at an interpersonal level. When a group of people define criteria for membership, and some individuals do not meet these criteria, this may result in intra-group exclusion. Intergroup exclusion takes place between groups, such as when members in one group develop boundaries that define members in the in-group as different from members in other groups. Institutional exclusion takes place when institutions within society establish their own criteria for inclusion and exclusion. When particular categories of people within a particular society are excluded from social relationships and participation in activities, this is exclusion at the societal level. Psychologists have even defined what they call intrapersonal exclusion. This refers to "a cognitive and emotional frame that prevents a person from considering opportunities for inclusion in the first place" (Abrams, Hogg & Marques, 2005, p. 18).

There are several answers to the question of why social exclusion takes place. One level of explanation refers to the individual person. Humans have a tendency to categorize. This includes categorization of other people and it serves an important function in the lives of people. As described by Hogg and Terry (2001), categorization is a basic cognitive process which operates on social as well as non-social stimuli. Categorization helps us bring into focus those aspects of our experiences which are subjectively meaningful in a particular context (Hogg, 2001). Social categorization is the cognitive basis of group behavior. When we perceive ourselves as members of particular groups (in-groups) and not members of other groups (out-groups), we tend to maximize similarities within groups and to accentuate differences between groups. Important dimensions of such differences are beliefs, attitudes, feelings, and behavior. Prototypes are cognitive representations of the attributes of groups and include all attributes that characterize groups and distinguish them from other groups.

Exclusion may serve other purposes than making our surroundings and our world easier to understand. Human beings strive for a positive self esteem, and our self esteem is to a large extent formed by our perceptions of the groups that we belong to. A positive social identity depends on membership in groups that we find attractive. By joining groups we find attractive (or groups which are highly esteemed) and keeping distance from groups of people that we perceive as less attractive, we may improve our self esteem. Exclusion of individuals, groups, or categories of people from membership in groups, networks or organizations may also contribute to preserving privileges and socioeconomic inequalities and inequities in society.

What then if we experience exclusion from groups we would like to belong to? Twenge and Baumeister (2005) summarize their findings from more than 20 experimental studies on the effects of social exclusion. The outcomes are almost uniformly negative. Social exclusion leads to more aggression, reduced willingness to cooperate with others, and an increased tendency to engage in self-defeating behaviors such as risk-taking and procrastination. Another effect of exclusion is reduced ability to perform well on analytical reasoning tasks. Rejected people may also engage in defensive denial of emotion, a cognitive state, which according to Twenge and Baumeister may explain a number of negative consequences of social exclusion.

A concept that is useful when describing some aspects of social exclusion processes is **stigmatization**. The word *stigma* is Greek, and originally referred to marks that were cut or burned into the skin of slaves or criminals in order to make them easy to recognize or identify. According to the sociologist Erving Goffman, stigma is an attribute that extensively discredits an individual by reducing him or her from a "whole person" to a "tainted, discounted one" (Goffman, 1963, p. 3). According to Goffman, there are three kinds of stigmatizing conditions. *Blemishes of individual character* are stigmas that are understood as reflecting immoral or deviant behavior. According to Major and Eccleston (2005), people with mental health problems and people who have been involved in criminality are categories of people who experience this kind of stigmatization in contemporary American society. *Abominations of the body* refer to stigmas that stem from physical deviations from what is perceived to be "normal." People who are obese might experience this, for instance. *Tribal stigmas* are attributed to people who belong to groups based on, for instance, ethnicity, nationality, or religion. African Americans in the United States and Jews in most of the European countries are examples of groups who have experienced this. Irrespective of reason, social exclusion due to stigmatization is a source of social stress which may make life more difficult for anyone experiencing it. When stigmatization happens to people with mental health problems, the social exclusion that usually follows adds to their burdens and may reduce their chances of recovery and rehabilitation.

Social exclusion might also take place in situations where no stigmatization is involved. Rejection and exclusion are frequently occurring phenomena and an inevitable part of our social life. People have only a limited amount of time and energy to spend on social relationships. Each individual has to choose those with whom they want to develop a friendship or relationship. Social exclusion cannot be eliminated from social life. What is important to eliminate is systematic exclusion of some individuals leading to social isolation, loneliness, reduced quality of life, and negative health consequences. To the extent that community music therapy contributes to inclusion and prevents exclusion, this probably contributes to positive mental health among those involved (Curtis & Mercado, 2004).

Marginalization can be defined as a process of separation from society, resulting in involuntary disconnection with the mainstream of productive activity and/or social reproductive activity. The process is usually associated with material disadvantage (Kagan & Burton, 2005). In countries with less well developed health care systems, marginalization is usually also associated with reduced access to health care. Marginalization is in many respects similar to social exclusion. It refers to processes at different levels, but is perhaps most commonly used at higher levels of analysis. Marginalization at the individual level corresponds to individual level social exclusion. Marginalization at community level happens, for instance, when ethnic minorities or immigrants experience unemployment, poverty, lack of political power, and lack of influence on processes of decision.

Newman (1999) performed an ethnographic study on downward mobility in affluent American communities: Thousands of middle-class families "plunge down" America's social ladder every year, as a result of downsizing, plant closing, and mergers in the industry or because of divorce or other debilitating experiences in people's life. Her study reveals how people experiencing downward mobility find themselves in situations where they have little control and reduced access to resources. Often they are stigmatized. Their social networks are challenged and they often receive less social support in times when the need for support increases. Newman (1999, p. x) underlines that people react differently to this situation. "Some are heroes who find ways to rise above their circumstances; others are lost souls, wandering the social landscape without direction." She warns, however, against the idea of thinking about unfortunates as oddities, whether they are heroes or lost souls. We need to acknowledge the role of the social, political, and economic processes that put people in unfortunate situations:

> Feelings of anger or dismay, a sense of injustice—these are the responses to downward mobility shared by most of its victims. They worked hard for what they had, deferred gratification when necessary, and sacrificed when called upon by their country or their families. But the experience of downward mobility makes it

abundantly clear that this is not enough. Attaining a responsible white-collar job, a skilled blue-collar job, or a stable marriage is no key to a lifetime of security. One can play by the rules, pay one's dues, and still be evicted from the American dream. There simply is no guarantee that one's best efforts will be rewarded in the end.

(Newman, 1999, p. 229)

Newman's study focused on people who had lost their occupational security and experienced economic dislocation. There are millions of people who never experience economic security and access to valued social resources. Inequalities are reproduced over generations and one important reason for marginalization is lack of adequate education. According to UNESCO (United Nations Educational, Scientific and Cultural Organization, 2010), at least 72 million children are excluded from their right to education worldwide. Seven out of ten live in sub-Saharan Africa or South and West Asia. The main reasons for exclusion from education are poverty, gender inequity, disability, child labor, speaking a minority language, belonging to an indigenous population, and living a nomadic or rural kind of life. A huge number of children thus have their life chances irreparably damaged by a failure to protect their right to education.

Improving quality of life and health among marginalized groups is also important in order to reduce inequalities and inequities in society. Access to health care for disadvantaged groups is an important step towards that goal. Even more important are the prerequisites for health that were listed in the Ottawa charter on health promotion (World Health Organization, 1986): peace, shelter, education, food, income, a stable eco-system, sustainable resources, social justice, and equity. This requires political action and collaboration across all sectors of society. Movement towards equality and equity in society also requires the mobilization of the marginalized groups themselves. If music therapists want to contribute towards the mobilization of marginalized groups and beyond, involvement in community music therapy in the service of social justice and equity and other prerequisites for health may be inevitable. The following chapters of the book include many examples of community music therapy practices that take these social realities and challenges seriously. A few examples can be mentioned here, to illuminate the range of issues and practices.

Tait and Murrungun (2010) describe the ArtStories initiative in the Northern Territory in Australia, where music therapy is one component and early childhood learning in remote Indigenous communities one central objective. Many music therapists have been engaged in relation to the educational rights of disabled people (Ely & McMahon, 1990; Ely & Scott, 1994; Stige, 1995; Uricoechea, 2003; Kern, 2005). Marginalization in relation to health and welfare has been addressed by some music therapists (Pavlicevic, 2004; Barcellos, 2005; Oosthuizen, 2006; Chagas, 2007; Tuastad & Finsås, 2008; O'Grady, 2009). Procter's (2004, 2006, 2011) work on social–musical capital and Krüger's (2004, 2007) work on supportive trajectories of community participation challenge inequalities of social support. Marginalization and inequalities in access to music have also been addressed in several community music therapy projects (Kleive & Stige, 1988; Curtis & Mercado, 2004). Vaillancourt's (2009) work focuses on relationships between social justice and peace.

FIGURE 4.7 | Moment of celebration. "Rock am Ring" in Krefeld, Germany.
Photo: Peter Neumann.

CONCLUSION

Reciprocity, cooperation, and sharing are important characteristics of human lives and in this chapter we have explored various notions for description of human connectivity. The ecological model developed by Bronfenbrenner and others illustrates how our lives are formed by the circumstances of our aspirations, actions, and relationships. Several key concepts are needed in order to describe relevant features of these contexts.

A community is generally defined as a group of individuals who are interacting over time in a specific location. The individuals of a community are linked by social ties, whether the community is defined by location or relations. Well functioning communities lead to a *sense of community* characterized by membership, influence, integration and fulfillment of needs, and shared emotional connection. In late modern societies there has been a diversification of communities with complex patterns of connectivity. Communities, whether they are traditional or late modern, also have negative properties and can be characterized by, for instance, repression and exploitation.

Social networks refer to the web of contacts between people in their daily lives. Within social networks there are several possible kinds of relationships and connections among people. To be socially integrated means to participate in a broad range of social relationships. Social support involves the process of one person helping another. All forms of social support might contribute to better health and wellbeing. People's relationships to each other are not only a source of wellbeing and good health, however. At times other people also represent a source of frustration, perhaps even a burden, a fact which has led social epidemiologists to develop a notion of social stress.

Concepts like social networks, social support, and social stress all describe phenomena and processes taking place at the personal and interpersonal levels. The term social capital can be used to add to this picture by describing characteristics of trust and reciprocity at larger units, such as local communities, municipalities, counties, and countries. Scales for measuring social capital have been developed and much research is being performed to evaluate associations between social capital and health and wellbeing. Bonding and bridging are two important forms of social capital, the first term associated with the social capital of networks of homogeneous groups of people and the second with social capital associated with groups or networks which include people from diverse social backgrounds.

Bonding and bridging are processes of social inclusion which are thrown into sharp relief by the processes of social exclusion and marginalization. The latter terms refer to processes where people are involuntarily separated from various areas of participation in society. These processes are harmful to the unfortunate individuals and their networks. This is exemplified by the fact that more than 72 million children around the world are currently excluded from their right to education and therefore have their life chances irreparably damaged. The role of the social, political, and economic processes that put people in unfortunate situations should be acknowledged and counteractions such as education for all initiated.

Community music therapy and other initiatives that are characterized by a focus on *community participation* can be seen in relation to the fields of public health and health promotion, where community participation has become a central concept. Community participation refers to the involvement of individual community members in activities such as identification of community needs, setting priorities, and action for improving the health and wellbeing of those belonging to the community. People can be encouraged to participate in community activities to the extent that they feel their contributions are valued and to the extent that there is a balance between what they give and what they gain (Wagemakers, 2010). Community participation is not only good for the community in general, but may also be important for the person who is involved. Participation in the work of community organizations is associated with improved quality of life (Veenhoven, 2004).

Health promotion has been defined as the process of enabling individuals and communities to gain control over factors that influence health and use this control to improve health. Empowerment is a concept which denotes this process of winning control. Community participation is one example of a practice which contributes to empowerment. Communities such as neighborhoods, teams working together in workplaces, and local members of a voluntary organization are important arenas for health promotion. Community music therapy practices can be seen as one contribution to the promotion of community health. In Chapter 5 we will discuss notions of music that resonate with the social perspectives developed in this chapter. In Chapter 6, 7, and 8 we will describe the issues, values, and processes that characterize practice compatible with these perspectives.

KEY TERMS, DISCUSSION TOPICS, AND NOTES

Key Terms

Key terms in order of appearance:

Ecological model
Community
Geographical notion of community
Relational notion of community
Sense of community
Community of practice
Social support
Direct effect hypothesis of social support
Buffer effect hypothesis of social support
Social stress
Positive stress
Negative stress
Social capital
Social cohesion
Bonding
Bridging
Social exclusion
Stigmatization
Marginalization

Discussion Topics

The following critical thinking questions can be discussed in class or in groups or used by the individual student for critical reflection on topics discussed in the chapter. Extra resources can be found on the website of the book.

1. Communities change, and new forms of communities develop. How are the communities that you are a member of today different from the communities your parents belonged to when they were the same age as you are now?
2. Putnam has provided evidence suggesting that social capital decreased in America during the last three decades of the twentieth century. Do you think that social capital is increasing or decreasing in the country or state where you live?
3. Social exclusion and marginalization exist in all parts of the world. What can be done to reduce exclusion and marginalization in the community or municipality where you live? What kind of action would be needed?

Notes

1   The concept of *context* is a major concept in theories about culture and human development but the meaning of the term is not always clear. In relation to human interaction, context usually refers to the milieu or environment of the activity. The relationships between persons and activities on one side and contexts on the other are conceived in different ways; sometimes the context is understood as given (coloring the persons and activities), at other times the relationships are conceived of as more reciprocal and constitutive. In both cases, context is conceived of as the *surrounding* situation or structure (in time and/or space). Cultural psychologist Cole (1996, p. 135) clarifies that this is only one possible conception. Context can also be seen as "that which weaves together," or "the connected whole that gives coherence to its parts." This interpretation calls less on the image of a "surrounding circle" and more on that of a "link," or maybe a web of links. Social networks, which we will discuss later in the chapter, fit this image of context as a connected whole that gives coherence to its parts.

2   It can be argued that to some degree Redfield's (1953/1963) text also hinted at ways out of the somewhat biased treatment of the stable little community as prototype. In his book he explored various means by which scientists have tried to understand human communities; for instance as ecological systems and as social structures. He explored biographical and historical approaches to the study of traditional human communities as well. In doing so, he challenged some assumptions that have been common among anthropologists, namely that individuality and history is irrelevant for the understanding of traditional communities. This enabled Redfield to link the study of traditional communities to that of modern communities.

3   This one-sided use of the notion of community has been integrated into some influential work on contemporary culture. The value of community has then been seen in relation to society at large as a counterforce to developments in the direction of, say, individualism and fragmented relationships. Consider for instance the work of the British cultural theorist Raymond Williams, who mainly focused on communities as vehicles for human agency in relation to authorities and centers of power (Williams, 1961/1971).

4   Cohen and Wills (1985) summarize research which could throw light on these two models and conclude that they are both supported: "evidence for a buffering model is found when the social support measure assesses the perceived availability of interpersonal resources that are responsive to the needs elicited by stressful events. Evidence for a main effect model is found when the support measure assesses a person's degree of integration in a social network." In other words, direct effects are typically found for structural measures of support (such as network size) while buffer effects are found for functional measures, particularly emotional support (Wills & Ainette, 2007).

5   In more conventional forms of music therapy, multiple relationships are often seen as an ethical problem and a hazard to the therapeutic process (Dileo, 2000). In the perspective described here, where community music therapy contributes to the development of social networks, multiplexity is typically a positive resource, although the complexities of managing shifting roles should not be ignored.

6   Stress was originally defined by Hans Selye (1956) as a physiological response to physical and mental strain.

7   In spite of the seemingly trivial nature of daily hassles (as opposed to stressful life events or sudden traumas, for instance), the impact on health and wellbeing is strong and has probably been underestimated. One possible explanation of the association between socioeconomic status and health is higher levels of daily hassles among less educated and low-income sectors of populations.

8   The researchers who originally developed scales for the measurement of stressful life events (Holmes & Rahe, 1967) even included Christmas celebrations and vacations as events which potentially could threaten health and wellbeing (but these events came out rather low on the list as potential stressors).

9   There is no clear consensus in the scientific literature as to how social capital should be defined. Some researchers would even prefer to get rid of the concept, claiming that it only represents old ideas dressed

up in fancy economic language, representing a dangerous distraction from more important public health agendas such as the political struggle for justice and equality (Kawachi, Subramanian, and Kim, 2010).

10 See the discussion in Chapter 7 on possible tensions between the values of freedom, equality, and solidarity.

11 In Europe there is no similar comparison available for all countries, but as part of the *European Social Survey* a question was asked regarding trust in other people. There were two alternative response categories: "You can not be too careful when you deal with other people" and "Most people can be trusted." It turns out that the highest levels of trust in others are found in the Nordic countries (Norway, Denmark, Finland, and Sweden). The lowest levels were found in Portugal, Russia, Poland, and Bulgaria. The north–south dimension is not as obvious as for the social capital differences found in the United States. Three of the four countries which obtained low scores on trust were former communist countries which have been through a painful process of transition to capitalism. Their welfare systems, which were rather well developed under the communist regime, were replaced by a primitive kind of capitalism where the situation of less well-off groups worsened considerably and social inequities increased sharply. This is in contrast to the Nordic countries which are characterized by high income, moderate levels of socioeconomic inequality, and well developed welfare systems (Source: European Social Survey/NSD).

Chapter 5

Music, Health, and Community

After studying Chapter 5, you will be able to discuss questions such as:

■ What is the relationship between music therapy and other music disciplines?

■ How can relationships between musical and paramusical processes be conceptualized?

■ How does musicianship relate to human musicality and the musics of various cultures?

■ What does the term "musicking" suggest?

■ How can communal musicking cultivate unity and diversity?

■ How can links between music, health, and community be conceptualized?

WHAT MUSIC COULD BE

MUSIC is a hook; it pulls people into a social space. Or perhaps social space is what music is; it is a world where people can act and interact through sound and movement. We use various metaphors when talking about music and might for instance think about an object (such as a song), an event (such as a concert), or an activity (such as singing). What we consider to be musical is linked to available discourses on music, some valuing tradition and others innovation, some valuing perfection and others participation, and so on (Keil & Feld, 1994). Music therapy can offer inclusive activities, partly because musical participation is possible without mastery of language. It is still important to remember that musical activities and experiences are not separated from language and culture: They are embedded in culturally informed assumptions and values, to the degree that the notion of music is variable between cultural contexts and within any given cultural context over time (Korsyn, 2003).

The word we use in English when talking about melodies and rhythms and some elements and activities that go with, is *music*. The word originated from the Greek word *mousiké.* In early antiquity this was a very broad term, referring to singing and dancing and the performance of lyrics and drama. The modern more narrow meaning of the word music in the English language is therefore not universal. It is the result of social and cultural developments over centuries, where practices and institutions have become more specialized. Not all languages have a specific term corresponding to the English term music, except perhaps as a loan word. The term *ngoma,* common in several Bantu languages, is an often-mentioned example of a notion that is related to the term music but clearly different. In Chapter 2 we encountered ngoma as a tradition of healing, where dance, drama, song, and drumming are central and inseparable components.

Some have argued that holistic notions such as ngoma represent important corrective perspectives compared to the specialized notion of music that has been established in modern Western countries (e.g. Bjørkvold, 1989/1992). This argument has been linked to contemporary research on mother–infant interaction, which reveals that sound, movement

FIGURE 5.1 | What music can be. Music-making in an inclusive summer workshop. Kublank, Germany.
Photo: Kristin Richter.

and (proto)narrative are closely related in human sensitivity (see below). This is interesting, but there is no type of music that is not colored by culture.

> Music may be what we think it is; it may not be. Music may be feeling or sensuality, but it may also have nothing to do with emotion or physical sensation. Music may be that to which some dance or pray or make love; but it's not necessarily the case. In some cultures there are complex categories for thinking about music; in others there seems to be no need whatsoever to contemplate music. What music is remains open to question at all times and all places. This being the case, any metaphysics of music must perforce cordon off the rest of the world from a privileged time and place, a time and place thought to be one's own. Thinking—or even rethinking—music, it follows, is at base an attempt to claim and control music as one's own.
>
> (Bohlman, 1999, p. 17)

Bohlman's conclusion could of course be examined in its own critical light. In the context of this chapter, we can use his argument as a call for self-critical reflection. A brief excursion to the first hundred years of musicology as a modern university discipline illustrates the relevance of this for any discipline studying music, including music therapy.

Williams (2001) explains how the Austrian scholar Guido Adler, one of the pioneers of musicology in the late nineteenth century, divided the study of music into two main areas; historical musicology and systematic musicology. The latter area should include the study of subjects such as acoustics, the psychology of music, and comparative musicology. The first area should focus on Western art music, which was considered the only music tradition worthy of historical study. The assumption was not only that this music was unique and superior. It was considered a source of standards. This way of thinking became influential in musicology, not only in Europe. Until the mid-1980s it would be reasonably correct to describe musicology as a discipline concerned mainly with the musical structures of a canon of master works in Western art music, with less interest in other genres such as popular music or in performances and other situations of use and action. This has changed considerably; a cultural and performative turn has brought the discipline in closer contact with ethnomusicology, popular music studies, and music sociology. In all of these fields there has been an increasing interest in music as a social phenomenon. This has opened up a space of interdisciplinary music studies, with an interest in how people use and experience music in various situations.[1]

Contemporary music therapy is part of the current rethinking of music studies, as Ruud (1987/1990, 1998, 2000), Ansdell (1997, 2001), Stige (2002, 2003), and several others have argued. Musical processes and outcomes are central in music therapy, but to suggest this might require a rethinking of what "musical" means. The following sections explore this through discussion of the musical and the paramusical in light of the interplay between biological, psychological, and sociocultural processes. The changes in disciplinary thinking described above suggest that the links between music therapy and other music disciplines are much more significant than many textbooks on music therapy have suggested. There is currently a rethinking of music in parts of the music therapy literature that might resemble developments within sister disciplines such as music education, where there has also been a growing interdisciplinary orientation, for instance in the examination of how knowledge about popular musicians' learning strategies has substantial implications for contemporary classroom pedagogy (Green, 2002, 2008).

Bohlman's controversial conclusion is still a pertinent reminder. Even when we think we rethink music we do run the risk of attempting to claim and control music as our own. There is a need to stay open for critique and alternative perspectives.

THE MUSICAL AND THE PARAMUSICAL

One of the questions music therapists have to address is how music is related to emotion, cognition, and behavior. These processes—which we often consider extramusical—are of interest because changes in them are typically thought of in terms of therapeutic outcome. If we focus on music as stimulus and the change in how a person feels, thinks, or behaves as response, we conceptualize **music as means**. This has been an established way of thinking about music in music therapy (Gaston, 1968). Figure 5.2 illustrates this conception (note the one-way arrow between music and client).

The established notion of music as means focuses on the direct effect of music on the organism. This concept has been important especially in medical and behavioral practices of music therapy and it suggests a focus on the client's *reactions* to music. Music therapists informed by other theories and areas of practice have been concerned about what they consider limitations of this idea. For instance, Aigen (1995, 2005) and Garred (2002, 2006) have argued that the notion of **music as medium** is more relevant in practices with a focus on human communication and relationship. Instead of focusing on the client's reactions to music, the notion of medium highlights *interactions* in and through music. Figure 5.3 illustrates how each person's relationship to music is mediated by the

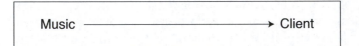

FIGURE 5.2 | Illustration of music as means.

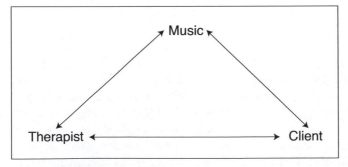

FIGURE 5.3 | Illustration of music as medium.

relationship to the other person, and also how the interpersonal relationships are mediated by the participants' relationship to music (note the two-way arrows).

The notions of music as means and music as medium reflect certain clinical realities as well as some basic assumptions about music and health in the music therapy literature. There are clear differences between the two notions, but also some similarities. For instance, in most of the literature using these notions there is implicitly or explicitly a focus on change and development at the level of the individual, with less concern about community and context. This suggests that for community music therapy it is necessary to explore broader ideas about what music could be. If we take interest in context and community, the traditional music therapy question about how music works should be supplemented by questions on where, when, and with whom (Stige et al., 2010a). We could perhaps describe this as focusing on **music as milieu** rather than as means or medium, but this would be accurate only if we think in "dramaturgical" terms where a milieu is a setting that includes actors engaged in performance and participation. An ecological metaphor supports this conception of music as milieu, not as surroundings separate from the individual but as a "scene" where we take part in the drama of performing relationships (Small, 1998).

Box 5.1 | FINDING OURSELVES WITHIN THAT WHICH IS OUTSIDE OURSELVES

In an essay on self-expression in music-centered music therapy, Erinn Epp (2007) discusses notions of relevance for community music therapy theory. Epp suggests that most people find the idea that music communicates reasonable; we tend to think of music as emotional expression and perhaps as a way of making the internal external. She claims, however, that the topic of musical self-expression has rarely been rigorously investigated in the music therapy literature. She therefore offers a presentation of various theories of musical expression and then relates them to different ideas of the self. One of her concerns is the continuing influence in contemporary music therapy of the romantic trope of music as direct expression of one's core self. She starts the essay with the following vignette:

> I am mid-way through a music therapy session at a nursing home with a group of 3 elderly women with dementia. After a few attempts at improvisation, I begin to sing "Let Me Call You Sweetheart." One of the women, who has advanced Alzheimer's, immediately sits up straight and sings out strongly. "She's so expressive now," I think to myself, "but what is it she's expressing now that she wasn't expressing in our improvisations?" (Epp, 2007).

The path Epp takes in responding to her own question goes via an examination of basic assumptions on music and expression among pioneers of music therapy. This includes a discussion of key themes such as whether or not psychological realities can be heard in the client's music. The idea of music as a direct expression of one's core self leads to an artificial separation of the individual and the sociocultural, Epp claims, and she exemplifies this in the following appraisal of one of Priestley's statements on music:

Box 5.1 |

Priestley, from the perspective of an improvisational model, also emphasized music's direct, singular effect: "Part of the joy of free expression is that it has only the aim the client herself likes to put into it. As no purpose is being pushed in from outside, it is easier for some purpose to emerge from within" [Priestley] (1975, p. 221). It can be inferred from such statements that authentic musical expression springs from a place within the self that is free from all external influence. One can accurately represent one's private, idiosyncratic inner states through the private, idiosyncratic use of music (Epp, 2007).

A more contemporary understanding of musical expression, according to Epp, would be developed if we challenge the romantic idea of the self having an inner core and explore the possibility of a de-centered self, continuously emerging through the development of new relationships:

Following the shift from the unified to the differentiated self, we may then ask ourselves in the music therapy context: Do we view our clients' music as projective of a single (i.e., psychological) reality? What levels of experience does the music therapy session address? Which are we overlooking? (Epp, 2007).

Two of the ideas that Epp suggests need to be reconsidered in music therapy theory are: First, the idea that music departing from stylistic conventions is the most authentic and directly expressive (with the implication that use of familiar musical form is less expressive). Second, the idea that musical expression could be found in the sound-structure itself (with the implication that performance and context is neglected in the analysis of music therapy sessions).

In Epp's view, a theory of self-expression for a music-centered music therapy must embrace an exploration of the paradoxical and reciprocal relationship between the musical and the extramusical and it cannot detach expressive content from the live performance of music.

Can we, then, still conceive of self-expression in music in terms of an inner reality manifested in a musical experience? The answer is both yes and no, or rather, the answer is—we're asking the wrong question! To begin with, and as we saw previously, our inner lives are not contained, private states of being. What is personally significant for us is, in part, what has been given to us. To manifest the inner life in music may be to articulate one's position—to articulate the many levels one lives on and create relationships between them (not necessarily integrate them) in the act of performance. Yes, there is a subjective position we can express in music, but that subjectivity is not completely "inner": it is thoroughly embedded, thoroughly worlded, and thoroughly irreducible (Epp, 2007).

Music sociologist DeNora (2000; 2003; 2007) explores the question of how music works by studying concrete situations of use. Her work illuminates the *complementarity* between individual, music, and environment. This does not imply that use is all there is or that any music could be used for anything. Various musical pieces and practices afford different possibilities for action. Usually they lend themselves more to some action possibilities than to others. Musical structure matters, then, as **affordances** allowing for the development of relationships between person, music, and environment through **appropriation** in a given situation.[2] Complementarity between individual, music, and environment implies something different from the idea that the musical reflects or affects the extramusical. In this perspective it is more helpful to explore the circularity involved. There is mutuality between those phenomena that we perceive as musical and the processes and activities that go with it (DeNora, 2003).

Stige and associates (2010, p. 298) have explored this claim in relation to several community music therapy case studies. To highlight the idea of reciprocity they used the term paramusical instead of extramusical. As discussed previously in this chapter; what humans consider musical is linked to convention and the available discursive resources. The term **paramusical** is therefore used to avoid a rigid impression of processes as either musical or not musical. Figure 5.4 illustrates this argument.

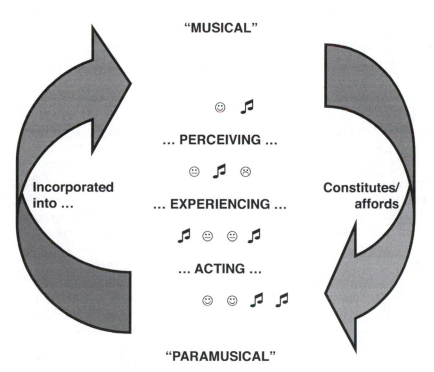

FIGURE 5.4 | The co-construction of the musical and the paramusical.
Source: (Stige et al., 2010b, p. 299). Reprinted with permission from Ashgate Publishing.

The idea of a circular relationship between the musical and the paramusical suggests that community music therapy is music-centered (see Aigen, 2005) through use of a de-centered notion of music. Community music therapy does not go well together with the idea of "music itself." The focus is on music in context, action, and interaction. Epp (2007) has developed a discussion of musical expression that embraces such a de-centered perspective on music. She argues that traditional notions of music in music therapy have often included the idea of music as a direct expression of one's individuality or core self, which she claims is an idea that leads to an artificial separation of the individual and the sociocultural (see Box 5.1).

MUSICALITY, MUSICS, AND MUSICIANSHIP

In order to understand the dynamics between the musical and the paramusical in any given situation, it is helpful to understand the interplay between the human protomusicality in the cultural context and the individual's personal history. We will clarify these notions through use of the terms musicality, musics, and musicianship.

Musicality traditionally refers to an individual's sensitivity to and talent for music, such as receptiveness when listening to music and resourcefulness when reproducing or creating music. People are obviously different concerning their receptiveness and resourcefulness, and the term musicality is therefore sometimes used to discriminate those who know music from those who do not. In contrast, musicality is increasingly also used as a notion to denote a shared human capacity for relating to and through sound and movement. The more specific terms *protomusicality* and *communicative musicality* are sometimes used to communicate this perspective.

The term protomusicality suggests that our capacity to make music developed during the evolution of the human species (phylogeny).[3] Cross and Morley (2009, p. 77) argue that it "would be impossible to do away with music without removing many of the abilities of social cognition that are fundamental to being human." This view has been strengthened lately, but when it comes to specific arguments about the involved mechanisms of evolution, there is still disagreement. For instance, Miller (2000; 2001) proposed that sexual selection was the main mechanism. According to Miller, music evolved as male competitive sexual display, comparable to the peacock's tail; not very practical except when you try to convince females that you carry superior genes. In contrast, Dissanayake (1992/1995, 2000a, 2000b, 2001, 2009) has argued that music evolved because of the survival value of the communal instances it enabled. The latter view has been influential in music therapy and we will concentrate on this perspective in the following pages.

Malloch and Trevarthen use the term *communicative musicality* to indicate that human protomusicality is the basis of human companionship. In an article specifically relating their theory to music therapy, Trevarthen and Malloch (2000) describe how all humans have the capacity to sympathize with the rhythmic and melodic movements of body and voice. Newborn infants demonstrate this when they communicate with adults. Adults demonstrate this when they communicate with infants or when they are able to recognize and sympathize with the humanly organized sounds of other cultures. According to these authors, children are born with a uniquely human motivation for gestural communication, a talent that later in life may be cultivated into general communication skills as well as conventional musical abilities.

According to Trevarthen and Malloch (2000) humans have an innate capacity to relate to pulse, quality, and (proto)narrative. *Pulse* refers to the succession of regular and predictable discrete events. *Quality* relates especially to pitch and intonation and refers to contours of expression moving through time. *Narrative* refers to the shaping of sequenced units of pulse and quality, as found in jointly created "phrases" or protonarratives of gestures. Communicative musicality is not just a capacity for relating to sound and movement, then, but also a capacity for relating to other people. Emotionally satisfying communication is established through the creation of a coordinated relationship through time. In a more recent publication, Malloch and Trevarthen (2009) have elaborated on their theory of musical expression in human interaction, in an anthology that also includes contributions from neuroscience, evolutionary studies, psychology, music therapy, music education, and performance. Along with the work of Daniel Stern (1985/1998, 1995, 2004, 2010) and others, Malloch and Trevarthen's theory of communicative musicality has contributed to a renewed interest in the relationship between the musical and the interpersonal relationships in music therapy practice. Human protomusicality is also a resource for cultural learning. It enables and requires communication in cultural context.

Musics (music as a noun in plural) refers to the existing musical-cultural realities that a person encounters. The concept has been central in ethnomusicology (May, 1983) and it serves to demonstrate that the tendency to talk about music in the abstract and in general is grounded in an ethnocentric bias. It is a sensitizing notion that reminds us about the multiplicity of musical traditions and practices that surround a person, as more or less accessible cultural resources. Music and music's function and meaning must be examined in concrete situations of practice, where actions, words, and musical elements elucidate each other.[4] This does not mean that certain musics necessarily belong to certain situations. An important characteristic of contemporary societies is that technology enables people to decontextualize and recontextualize music in many ways. This gives us a high degree of flexibility in musical meaning–making. One individual can relate to a range of different musics, sometimes by mixing elements from several traditions.

Musics exist as resources for individual and community. For instance, musics provide people with various *artifacts*, such as musical vocabularies and formulas, works, instruments, and techniques. Such artifacts are tools that people can use in processes of cultural learning and identity development. All resources are not available for everybody, however. Musics are inclusive and exclusive in various ways. In an ethnomusicology of disability, Lubet (2004) discussed the tradition of Western classical music as an exclusive institution. It is a tradition driven by a search for perfection to a degree that excludes many people from musical participation. To be left-handed could be enough to be left out of a symphony orchestra, Lubet asserts, as the direction of your violin would not match that of the others. Other genres, such as rock music, would by many be considered more inclusive. But we all know that not everybody is allowed into every band. Your opportunities are linked to the values and attitudes of the community that you want to be part of and the match between these and your musicianship.

Musicianship, as used here, refers to the skills, attitudes, and personal resources that the individual has developed in relation to music. Musicianship is a product of the history and development of the individual, which obviously is related to what kind of interconnections have emerged between the innate musicality of the person and the available musics of the environment. The mastery of one or more musics is the result of cultivated human capacities, or what Dissanayake (2001) has called "artification of human protomusicality." Pavlicevic and Ansdell underscore the importance of musicianship in community music therapy and describe it in the following way:

Musicianship is a cultivated facility of musicality-in-action within sociocultural contexts. It involves the skillful coupling of musicality to specific musical cultures, traditions, games, techniques, and artefacts. This happens through the affordances offered by situated musics, and its skilled musicers, and the appropriation of these by individuals (in short, the process of communicating and generating musical knowing through musical doing).

(Pavlicevic & Ansdell, 2009, p. 362)

FIGURE 5.5 | The recording of "I am who I am." Community music therapy project in a town in the bush north of Melbourne, Australia.

Photo: Kate Teggelove.

The notion of musicianship sheds light on the notion of affordances that we encountered above. Affordance is a *relationship* between person and music situation. What various musics have to offer depends on how affordances are perceived by the individual in the situation, which depends on the "rules of the game" but also on the match between the involved music(s) and the musicianship of the individual. Some people, including participants in community music therapy practices, develop their musicianship to levels that could be described as expertise and dexterity. Whether or not aptitudes would be considered prowess is less central, however, than the quality of the relationship between musicianship, musics, and the musicking of a situation. These relationships are not just musical, but paramusical as well. How we are able to act and react emotionally, relate to other people, think and talk about music is therefore part of our musicianship.

MUSICKING AS PERFORMANCE OF RELATIONSHIPS

The notion of *musicality* (as applied here) suggests that we all have a universal capacity for engagement in music. The notion of *musics* suggests that the conditions of this engagement are relative to a group or community. The notion of *musicianship* suggests that the skills and attitudes of the individual evolve as relationships between musicality and musics. Musicking brings these levels together:

> [I]n studying music in music therapy, *musicking* is an inevitable perspective, that is, music as performed relationships. This contention would be rather empty, though, if not for human protomusicality and for the cultures of music. Protomusicality provides humans with capacities for engaging with expression and communication through sounds, and cultural history provides humans with artifacts that afford, including symbolic tools for communication and for the construction of one's life history.
>
> (Stige, 2002, p. 84)

We encountered the term musicking in Chapter 1, where we explained that we can think of music not just as an object (e.g. song or work of music) but also as an activity that people take part in. An activity is always linked to a situation, so the notion of musicking also invites us to think about the relationships between sounds, those who make sounds, and those who make sounds possible. Small's book *Musicking* (1998) is central for this ecologically oriented understanding of the term.[5] Musicking refers to our participation in music and to how music is enacted and experienced as the performance of various relationships in a situation. The term performance, as used here, has a broad meaning; it involves action and interaction in a social and cultural situation.[6] The relationships that are established exemplify the interaction of the musical and the paramusical that we discussed previously in the chapter. Pavlicevic and Ansdell (2009) describe musicking as "musicianship-in-action."

Musical meanings and effects are due to interactions between musical and paramusical processes and they are performed in acts of musicking within historically

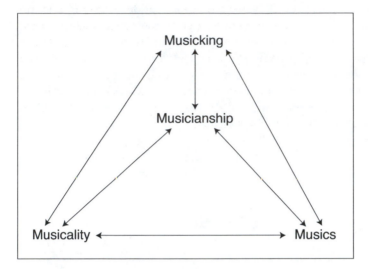

FIGURE 5.6 | Relationships between Musicality (shared human capacity), Musics (cultural resources), Musicianship (personal facility), and Musicking (social activity).
Source: Revised after (Stige, 2002, p. 107). Reprinted with permission from Barcelona Publishers.

created conditions and constraints. These conditions and constraints have been described above as musicality, musics, and musicianship. In acts of musicking, participants encounter a range of resources, including the musicality and musicianship of other participants and the musics of the community. Each participant's musicality and musicianship constitute personal resources that enable engagement with the social resources of musics and musicking. Figure 5.6 illustrates these relationships.

Another way of describing the interactions demonstrated in Figure 5.6 is to think of the processes that lead to musicality, musics, and musicianship (human evolution, cultural history, and personal development respectively) as processes that build affordances. Musicking is then the appropriation of such affordances. The two-way arrows between musicality, musics, musicianship, and musicking should remind us about the possibility that appropriation not only involves the use of affordances but also produces affordances. When we participate in music we are influenced by our personal history (as expressed in our musicianship) but this history is recreated in every moment as new encounters enable us to be creative and do something new.

THE UNITY AND DIVERSITY OF COMMUNAL MUSICKING

Musicking, as discussed above, involves social action and interaction. Small (1998) argues that even when we relate to music alone, such as when we listen to music in solitude, social relationships are implied and involved. For community music therapy it is of specific interest to examine music activities which involve the *communal* musicking of a group of people. Communal musicking is an eminent vehicle for collective action, collaboration, and group cohesion. The links between music, time, and movement enable groups to use music to structure time, synchronize body movements, and pace collaborative work. Music also allows for social bonding and the expression of traditions and values. These and other social uses give music an important role in practices as diverse as commerce and advertising, film, social control, and therapy (Clarke, Dibben, & Pitts, 2010, pp. 101–124).

Box 5.2 | COMMUNITAS IN RITUALS, JAZZ, AND MUSIC THERAPY

In introducing the term **communitas** to music therapy theory, Even Ruud (1991, 1992a, 1995, 1998) has developed a tool for reflection on the experience of unity in musical community.[7] Ruud appropriates Turner's notion of communitas[8] to describe the strong experiences of equality and togetherness that characterize some music therapy processes. Taking improvisational music therapy as his example, he describes improvisation as an experience that affords a "joint project" of closeness and mutuality, sometimes through a temporal leveling-out of all social roles:

> Instead of "aesthetic refinement," improvisations in music therapy seek to build a community ("communitas") through a temporary leveling-out of all social roles. During improvisations, all traditional expectations regarding the role of the therapist do not apply: music therapists try to build a spontaneous, immediate community through "free collective improvisations," in which complementary symmetrical forms of social interaction originate spontaneously out of musical interaction. Improvisation becomes a joint project in which emotion is the main measure of the credibility of the experience (Ruud, 1998, pp. 131–132).

Ruud's description of improvisation as liminal experience includes a discussion of terms such as flow and fluidity, the spontaneous and the immediate, as well as peak experiences, trance, and the transcendent. Ruud argues that practices of music therapy often value such experiences and that they share this with ancient rituals as well as some contemporary art forms such as jazz.

A central theme when considering communal musicking in relation to community music therapy is how this activity affords experiences of both unity and diversity. To make music together creates many possibilities for shared focus of expression and experience. Each member still participates in his or her own way. Our (proto)musicality is a shared human capacity but it is cultivated into musicianship through different life histories and different encounters with various musics. Consequently, the experience of communal musicking will differ from participant to participant. Each participant contributes with his or her musicianship, as cultivated musicality and appropriation of the perceived affordance of various musics. Communal musicking is at once private and public, personal and social, centered and de-centered. To create unity beyond uniformity is therefore one of the possibilities of communal musicking. This is often considered a community ideal:

> The "*common*ality" which is found in community need not be a uniformity. It does not clone behaviour or ideas. It is a commonality of *forms* (ways of behaving) whose content (meanings) may vary considerably among its members. The triumph of community is to so contain this variety that its inherent discordance does not subvert the apparent coherence which is expressed by its boundaries.
>
> (Cohen, 1985/1993, p. 20)

Unity beyond uniformity could also be described as unity that embraces diversity. In Chapter 7 we will discuss how this relates to some of the central values of community music therapy; respect, freedom, equality, and solidarity. Unity embracing diversity is of course somewhat of a utopian idea; in real world processes there will at times be conflicts which require careful navigation and negotiation. If communal musicking links to the history and aspirations of individuals and groups, the evolving story will include dispute and dissension. Possibilities of controversy in and through communal

FIGURE 5.7 | Get-up-and-go. "Rock am Ring" in Krefeld, Germany.
Photo: Peter Neumann.

musicking are many. Consider the clashes that noisy music-making could create. In many cases such disputes materialize various social conflicts (Frith, 2004). There is a need to take both accord and discord into consideration when studying communal musicking.

In a chapter on *collaborative musicking*, Pavlicevic and Ansdell (2009) develop a perspective on communal musicking through a critique of how the notion of communicative musicality in music therapy mainly has been used to explore dyadic relationships, with less awareness about experiences of musical community. According to these authors, the emergence of community music therapy has led to a shift towards a more culture-centered, context-sensitive, and reflexive orientation:

> We suggest that for this new approach, communicative musicality provides a necessary, but not sufficient, theoretical platform. What further theory is necessary for accounting for how music therapy works in broader contexts, and at a more social and cultural level beyond dyadic forms of relatedness? We suggest—as the beginning of an answer to this question—a model for coupling such subsequent musical and social development, by way of cultural learning (musicianship) and direct social participations (musicing). We call this further function of music 'collaborative musicing'.
>
> (Pavlicevic & Ansdell, 2009, p. 358)

The basic claim in Pavlicevic and Ansdell's argument is that musicking as active musical participation requires social development and that we need to study this not only in relation to dyadic communication but also in relation to collaboration in broader contexts. Their hypothesis is that there is a naturally incremental relationship between musical and social experiences (Pavlicevic & Ansdell, 2009, p. 364). The authors suggest that collaborative musicking is the outward and audible sign of musical community and that collaborative musicking builds community. This argument includes a description of how the function of communication transforms into collaboration.

Pavlicevic and Ansdell present several arguments to back up their hypothesis, for instance by describing how human (proto)musicality enhances communicative interaction and how musical companionship facilitates musicianship. They exemplify this through description of three musical events and through discussion of links to theories within fields such as biomusicology, cognitive neuroscience, sociology of music, and musicology (Pavlicevic & Ansdell, 2009, pp. 363–373). The hypothesis about a naturally incremental relationship between social and musical experiences deserves further examination. It contradicts some established assumptions about social–musical relationships. The amateur musical life of a community is for instance often described as a "social outlet," and this description does not usually suggest incremental relationships between musical and social experiences. Correspondingly, perfectionist professional music traditions are sometimes described as "conspiracies" to shut ordinary people up (Keil & Feld, 1994). Research also suggests that professional musicians score high on introversion, which could be explained by the fact that many forms of musicianship require much time practicing alone (Clarke, Dibben, & Pitts, 2010, p. 107). There is probably a need to qualify Pavlicevic and Ansdell's hypothesis, then, and to examine it in relation to various practices and value contexts.

In the following we will elaborate on the ecology of music's help through explication of the notion of *health musicking* followed by a discussion of two relevant notions of social collaboration in community music therapy; *interaction rituals* and *communities of practice*.

HEALTH MUSICKING

The field of community music therapy has a unique identity but is also part of a larger interdisciplinary field of music, health, and wellbeing (MacDonald, Kreutz & Mitchell, in press). Fields such as music psychology, music sociology, music education, ethnomusicology, community music, and music therapy are involved in studying how music and music-making afford health benefits in various situations. Some researchers have started to articulate theories describing the generative mechanisms by which musicking impact on health and wellbeing. For instance, in a study of choral singing and psychological wellbeing, Clift and associates (2010) proposed six generative mechanisms that link singing with wellbeing: First, choral singing engenders happiness and raised spirits, which counteract feelings of sadness and depression. Second, singing involves focused concentration, which blocks preoccupation with sources of worry. Third, singing involves deep controlled breathing, which counteracts anxiety. Fourth, singing offers a sense of social support and friendship, which mitigates against feelings of isolation and loneliness. Fifth, choral singing involves education and learning, which keeps the mind active and counteracts the decline of cognitive functions. Sixth, choral singing involves a regular commitment to attend rehearsal, which motivates people to avoid being physically inactive (Clift et al., 2010, pp. 29–31).

Related discussions are found in the community music therapy literature on choir participation. Zanini and Leao (2006) focus on singing as self-expression and self-fulfillment, with implications for the participants' self-confidence and expectations about the future. Knardal (2007) describes senior choir singing as a resource for memory maintenance, the monitoring of body functions, emotional work, and the experience of community. Future research will qualify and supplement these suggestions. Studies from other fields also inform our understanding of generative mechanisms. Research in neurology, for instance, suggests that music activity affects the brain's plasticity and that this could have prophylactic functions in relation to disease and illness (Cohen, 2009).

In the present section we will illuminate the need to supplement any generalized account of generative mechanisms with an understanding of how the effects of musicking are relative to person and situation. Health benefits are not decontextualized effects. This contention does not imply a rejection of systematic investigation but suggests a serious consideration of how processes are embedded in social and cultural contexts. In Chapter 3 we discussed three aspects of health; one of them clarifying that health is not only a property of the individual. Health is a relational concept and thus links to possibilities of participation. A person's ability to master the challenges in daily life is relative to demands and challenges of a situation and to organizational, cultural, and societal contexts. In order to understand health fully, it is important to understand the relationship between personal resources and available social resources (see Chapter 4). If we take these notions seriously, we realize that general accounts of the effects of music must be supplemented by an examination of musicking in specific contexts. It is crucial to understand the ecology of how music helps.

Box 5.3 | THE GRIEG EFFECT

In a tongue-in-cheek allusion to the more famous Mozart Effect, Brynjulf Stige (2007, 2011) plays with the idea of a Grieg Effect, in an account of music as a tool people can use in the process of handling the challenges of everyday life. The account exemplifies how musicality, musics, and musicianship interact in acts of musicking, ideally in ways that are meaningful for participants and afford new possibilities of participation. The idea of a Grieg Effect is elaborated through the unfolding of Upbeat's encounter with Grieg and his music. Upbeat was a group of six adults with Down's Syndrome who in the 1980s were participants in a community music therapy project in Western Norway, focusing on inclusion and cultural participation:

> The six heroes of the story that I will tell are Gunnar, Knut, Reidar, Jon Reidar, Solbjørg, and Solveig. I call them heroes because they are the main characters of the story, they had to travel a long way before they could come home, and they demonstrated lots of courage and curiosity. Most of them were born in the 1940s, in Sogn og Fjordane, a rural county north of Bergen. In this county there is no big town and when people talk about "going to town" they actually mean "going to Bergen." Our six heroes did go to Bergen and for quite a long time too. In the 1950s, when they grew up, very few people considered the possibility of letting children and adolescents with Down's Syndrome grow up in their own community. They were sent to institutions, and the central institution for people from the county of our heroes was located in the "capital" of Western Norway; Bergen. So they had to leave their families; they had to go the six or eight or ten hours or whatever it would take to go to Bergen, where they would live in this institution, in principle for the rest of their lives (Stige, 2007).

Principles tend to change. After many years the people that would form the group Upbeat moved back to a small rural town close to where they came from. Two music therapists worked in this town, trying to establish music activities that could be inclusive and allow for community participation (see Box 2.5). Upbeat's encounter with Grieg's music happened by chance. The effects of this encounter could be related to the relationships that were developed between the biography of the musicians, the musical material, the performative practice of the group of musicians, and the cultural history of the community they belonged to. The biography came into play because Grieg was from Bergen too; the shared connection to this city instigated an immediate interest among the group members. Selected pieces of Grieg's music worked well for these musicians, because of the simplicity of the music with many short phrases and repetitions. Specific ways of performing the

Box 5.3 |

music were essential, in order to attune to the tempi and the gestures of the group members. Upbeat played Grieg's music in their own way, with unusual instruments, a slower tempo, lots of rubato, and a very special seriousness with an expression of pride and pleasure. When the group went public with their idiosyncratic version of Grieg, how would the community react? They reacted with enthusiasm, possibly because Grieg's music had already been appropriated as an emblem of identity in this community.

> The above description of the contextualized effects of music can be summarised by creating an acronym based upon Grieg's name. The central letter, *I*, can be used to refer to *interaction*, as this is the main claim made in this argument: effects are the result of interactions. The preceding letters, *G* and *R*, may be used to refer to the interaction between an individual's protomusical capacity for participation through *gestures* and the available cultural *resources* in a given context. The two letters following *I*, namely *E* and *G*, can be used to refer to the interactions between personal *experiences* and *group* processes. The entire acronym GRIEG reminds us of the continuous contextualised interactions on several levels, between biologically evolved human capacities, psychological tendencies and preferences, and social and cultural realities (Stige, 2011, p. 135).

Not all composers have names that are equally suitable for the construction of acronyms communicating a contextualized understanding of the effects of music. But Grieg is of course not unique in that his music enables the performance of transforming relationships in a situation. If there is a Grieg Effect there could be a Glinka Effect, or a Madonna Effect, or indeed a Mozart Effect. The list could be made longer but could hardly be created by consulting experts in the library or laboratory. It would grow out of the study of musical practice in cultural context.

Stige (2002, p. 211) conceptualized **health musicking** as the appraisal and appropriation of the health affordances of arena, agenda, agents, activities, and artifacts of a music practice.[9] Musicking requires space and place, that is; an *arena* where artifacts, agendas, and agents can be located and activities unfold. Musicking is also grounded in an *agenda*; there are some goals and issues that are conceived consciously and unconsciously by the participants. These goals and issues focus on the immediate situation (e.g. "let's have some fun") or more long-term objectives (e.g. "let's practice for the next community concert"). Furthermore, musicking involves participation and collaboration between *agents*. Individual agents can form alliances, such as dyad, group, or community, which then also become agents in a process. Musicking necessarily requires *activity*, and allows for action over a long period of time, as well as momentary acts. Musicking also involves the use of several types of *artifacts*, such as instruments, songs, and lyrics. The affordances of artifacts are manifold; instruments can invite playing and participation, songs and lyrics can invite involvement and reflection, and so on.

These dimensions of musicking are connected in various ways and form complex webs of relationships. In considering health musicking as the performance of such relationships in ways that promote health and wellbeing it is significant to remember that human relationships to resources are characterized by ambivalence. Any arena or agenda produce possibilities for inclusion or exclusion, depending on the objectives and traditions they are connected to. Similarly, activities and artifacts encourage or discourage participation, for instance because of the skill levels they require or the values they are connected to. The agents that take part in communal musicking therefore usually need to negotiate on choice of arena, agenda, activities, and artifacts.

The temporal dimension is an important aspect of health musicking. Music unfolds over time and cannot be compressed or reordered in any other way without changing properties. Music therefore not only enables (and requires) musical activity; it can happen alongside other activities (Clarke, Dibben & Pitts, 2010). As discussed previously in this chapter; activities and behavior that go with musical activity can be considered paramusical. The interaction of musical and paramusical processes could happen at several levels of social organization; in a dyad, in a group, or in a broader community.

When people make or use music, they do not necessarily reflect deliberately about the possibilities of all the musical and paramusical components involved. Usually they engage in a "forgetful" pleasurable activity without too much of a controlling focus on over-conscious goals. They are often searching for an optimal experience of *flow*

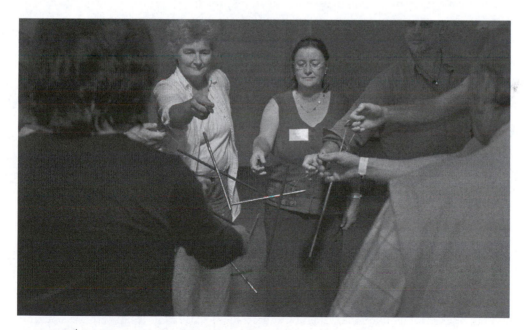

FIGURE 5.8 | Performance of sound relationships. A music and art festival for people with and without disabilities in Sondershausen, Germany.
Photo: Wanda Möller.

(Csikszentmihalyi, 1990). Nevertheless, scholars such as DeNora (2000), Ruud (2002), and Batt-Rawden (2007) have been able to demonstrate that music as a health resource depends on ways and contexts of use. We need to develop an understanding of how resources are mobilized in the service of health and wellbeing. Two possibilities (that are not mutually exclusive) in community music therapy are engagement in *interaction rituals* and participation in *communities of practice.*

INTERACTION RITUALS

An **interaction ritual** is what happens when people come together, if they start interacting in ways that create shared attention and increased emotional energy. Formalized procedures can be one element but can also be absent; they are not what define these rituals. Interaction rituals can be spontaneous and improvised. The vital ingredients are bodily co-presence, mutual focus of attention, and shared mood (Collins, 2004, pp. 47–101).[10] Interaction rituals with these ingredients lead to increased emotional energy and the construction of a sense of community. Religious ceremonies and sporting events are examples of the range of situations that could be examined through the lens of the theory of interaction rituals. Music is a powerful tool in the making of interaction rituals, not least because of the rhythmically coordinated quality that typically characterizes musicking.

In a case study of a community music therapy project, Stige (2010a) used the theory of interaction rituals to analyze and interpret social–musical interactions in a group of participants with intellectual disabilities. A simple greeting song served as example. The participants were seated in a semicircle and therefore visibly present for each other. Also, the song was arranged so that each person was given a separate "verse of attention." In these verses, the therapist intensified the ingredient of bodily co-presence by approaching one person at a time. Consequently, the group's attention was drawn to the person "owning" the verse in question, as this person got involved and engaged in the musical activity. In this structured yet flexible way, mutual foci of attention were established through musical interaction. This led directly to another ingredient of interaction rituals; the establishment of a shared mood. Part of this process was the way the various participants chose to present themselves for the group during the interaction. Stige developed a description of five different styles of self-presentation, the three most common being *Silent participation* (being there but not joining in), *Conventional participation* (joining in but not standing out), and *Adventurous participation* (standing out but not going across) (see Box 7.1).

> The broad range of possible styles of self-presentations in music . . . does not necessarily imply fragmented situations with a series of individual foci so that things fall apart. If integrated in interaction rituals, these various styles of self-presentation may become part of the co-creation of a more inclusive social space. *Participatory spaciousness* implies that there is room for unity beyond uniformity.
>
> (Stige, 2010a, p. 138)

The notion of interaction rituals illuminates how communal musicking can be carefully tailored in order to meet the specific needs of each participant *and* the group as a whole. This is not always as simple as it sounds, of course, but the biological foundation of human musicality as well as the wide range of musics available makes music an extremely versatile tool for maintaining human interaction even when the resources of each participant are limited. The benefits, such as increased emotional energy and the construction of a sense of community, could be considered therapeutic or health-promoting (Stige 2010a).

If an interaction ritual works well, participants build positive emotional energy, enjoy the situation and usually want to come back for more.[11] As Collins (2004) explains; the emotional energy and sense of community produced by interaction rituals is not unremitting. After some time, usually a few days, the effects vanish gradually, even after the most intensive interaction ritual. Various symbols and emblems (such as a group name or a badge) contribute to the perpetuation of the consciousness developed in the interaction ritual. The value of such symbols notwithstanding, interaction rituals must be repeated

FIGURE 5.9 | Music as dance as human interaction. Ngoma in the Kamba tradition in Kenya. Photo: Muriithi Kigunda.

in order to have a maintained effect. This is probably one of the reasons why amateur choirs and other musical ensembles come together regularly. There is a skill component involved, of course, but there are emotional and social motives involved also. After some days, people feel that it is time to make music again, in order to renew the emotional bonds that musicking can create.

This is one of the reasons why community music therapy practice is not necessarily designed as a time-limited intervention (see Chapter 8). The dose-effect logic of the health care sector, where therapy is offered in a certain number of sessions in order to produce intended effects on the individual, does not usually apply. Instead, community music therapy practices often establish interaction rituals that become an integrated element of community life, as a multifaceted everyday resource that when mobilized seems to be good at mobilizing other resources.

COMMUNITIES OF PRACTICE

When people repeatedly come together for a purpose, relationships evolve and a **community of practice** might be established. Wenger, McDermott, and Snyder (2002, p. 4) define communities of practice broadly as "groups of people who share a concern, a set of problems, or a passion about a topic, and who deepen their knowledge and expertise in this area by interacting on an ongoing basis." Communities of practice develop shared engagement for a purpose and thus build sustained mutual relationships. There is overlap in the members' appraisal of who takes part and who does not in the endeavor of the community. Similarly, the role of each participant in relation to the shared undertaking is identified and the members are able to assess each others' contributions. Often, the community members also share tools and technology and/or specific ways of representing or understanding a phenomenon or process (Wenger, 1998).

The notion of community of practice has been used in various academic contexts. Wenger's approach builds on the usage that Lave and Wenger (1991) proposed in their theory of learning as a social activity. Learning has traditionally been studied as the individual's acquisition of knowledge but Lave and Wenger suggest that participation in a social practice is a fundamental form of learning. According to this view, learning involves increased participation in a community of practice. Effects of participation therefore include changes both in personal and in communal identity. For each individual the value of participation is not restricted to the acquisition of knowledge and skills but also includes membership and valued social participation.[12]

In the community music therapy literature, several authors have used the notion of community of practice in order to describe the affordances of the roles and relationships that evolve over time when people come together in order to make music. Stige (2002) used this notion to clarify how formats of practice that go beyond the dyad include many new possibilities for music therapy, as the range of possible roles and relationships increases. Krüger (2004) drew on the notion of community of practice in his study of learning in a rock band, focusing specifically on Lave and Wenger's (1991) concept of "trajectories of participation." Ansdell (2010a) has explored the relevance of

FIGURE 5.10 | In performance. Glorious MUD Singers Choir in the Making Music Being Well
program, New South Wales, Australia.

Photo: Lily Richardson.

the notion of community of practice in a case study of *Musical Minds*, a group in East
London supported by an organization for adults with long-term mental health problems
(see Boxes 4.2 and 7.3). Ansdell describes *Musical Minds* as a community of practice
by focusing on how membership affords belonging and learning and allows for the
balancing of identity and difference. He suggests that a prime function of community
music therapy is to cultivate, nurture and sustain communities of musical practice in
challenging circumstances where they are otherwise difficult. Similarly, Ruud has used
the term when describing a music project in a Palestinian refugee camp (Ruud, 2011, in
press; Storsve, Westby & Ruud, 2010).[13]

Communities of practice allow for **participation** and depend on participation.
Participation could be understood as a process of collaborative action and mutual
recognition, which implies that individuals collaborate in a socially and culturally
organized structure (a community) and create goods indigenous to this structure (Stige,
2006). When it comes to community music therapy, the goods produced can include
health, music, and social resources. This, then, suggests a notion of participation that goes
beyond joining in. In the German language, there are two different words for participation,
namely *Teilnahme* and *Teilhabe*, and these words illuminate an important distinction. The
first refers to the act of entering into something predefined, while the latter refers to the

action of being part of a whole where you have some influence (Völker, 2004). Metell (2011) explains the difference in the following way: "Teilnahme means joining in, taking part in something, while Teilhabe addresses more the political dimension of taking part in society. . . . The main difference . . . is the dimension of power. Teilhaben, taking part, requires a mutual relationship, while teilnehmen is possible in any hierarchical or nonhierarchical constellation."

As musical and paramusical processes interact, more than music is made when music is made (Clarke, Dibben & Pitts, 2010). Participation in a community of musical practice can be of existential, educational, and social value for each person and of transformative value for the community.

CONCLUSION

Humans share a biologically evolved sensitivity and interest for sound, a fact that to some degree supports the idea of using music as *means;* a pleasurable stimulus that could lead to relaxation and lower blood pressure, for instance. The effects of music as means are always mediated by cultural experience, however. The organism's reactions to music in clinical or quasi-clinical settings seem to be linked to the individual's musical actions in everyday life (Mitchell, MacDonald & Knussen, 2008). This research finding is congruent with the theories of human (proto)musicality referred to in this chapter. Humans' sensitivity and interest for sound and movement is linked to their capacity for communication and cultural learning. This suggests the relevance of a quite different notion of music in therapy, namely music as communicative *medium.* The focus shifts from how people *react* to music to how they *interact* through music. These two notions of music complement each other in music therapy.

The argument developed in this chapter has been that notions of music as means and medium are necessary but insufficient for community music therapy. The term *musicking* (Small, 1998) has been used to elaborate a broader perspective. Implications go beyond seeing music as a verb and include the study of music as *situated activity.* Musicking as situated activity must be understood ecologically, in relation to a situation where relationships are performed and perceived. Music, then, is more than a stimulus to which humans react or a vehicle for action and interaction; it is a multidimensional and continuously changing *milieu* where an aggregate of biological, psychological, and sociocultural processes interact. This interaction has a transactional character, that is; agents, activities, and artifacts change and develop over time through processes of mutual influence.

The complexity of the above description suggests that no single metaphor can capture the range that is adequate to describe music in community music therapy, but the idea of *music as ecology* becomes central. Two caveats to consider are: First, no ecology of performed relationships could develop if music did not operate as mediated means and medium, that is, if there were no stimulation or communication. Second, the notion of music as ecology is of course not relevant for community music therapy only.[14]

In music therapy, differences of application will relate to the scope of the use of the metaphor, that is, whether one is focusing on the ecology of the microsystem within the boundaries of a more conventional music therapy approach or whether one also includes the other levels of analysis that are central in community music therapy practices (see Chapter 4).

A basic argument in this chapter has been that music originates from a shared human *musicality* developed in human phylogeny. Protomusicality (or communicative musicality) is then considered a basic element in humans' capacity for nonverbal communication (Malloch & Trevarthen, 2009). Such interaction is not necessarily music, however. The capacity for music evolves into *musicianship,* as expressions become culturally informed by a cultural plurality of *musics. Musicking*, then, is the performed establishment of relationships between sounds, people, and values. The notions of affordance and appropriation (DeNora, 2000) are conceptual tools for the study of such relationships and suggest that it is possible to treat music as situated event and activity without overlooking the potential of the musical material as based in human biology and developed in cultural history.

Music's help in community music therapy could be described as health musicking, perhaps even *collaborative health musicking*; it is usually produced through joint action and activity in a situation. It is "co-produced," so to say, as it emerges from within interaction rituals and communities of practice.[15] Music as means and health as end is therefore a very inaccurate description in community music therapy. To focus on changes in health and wellbeing is only one of several possible ways of framing the outcomes of initiatives. There will be musical and social changes too, in circular processes where health and wellbeing depends on and leads to social resources and exciting music.

KEY TERMS, DISCUSSION TOPICS, AND NOTES

Key Terms

Key terms in order of appearance:

Music as Means, Medium, and Milieu
Affordance and Appropriation
Musical and Paramusical Processes
Musicality, Musics, and Musicianship
Musicking
Communal musicking
Communitas
Community of practice
Health musicking
Interaction rituals
Participation

Discussion Topics

The following critical thinking questions can be discussed in class or in groups or used by the individual student for critical reflection on topics discussed in the chapter. Extra resources can be found on the website of the book.

1. People come to community music therapy with assumptions, attitudes, and expectations shaped by their previous experiences with music and music-making. Some are occupied with the idea that they are not musicians, while others are eager to engage with the music and worry less about their competence. Some feel liberated by the idea of free improvisation, while others feel that a conventional song gives them the structure and space they need in order to engage with the music. If invited to sing in the microphone, some would feel nervous about the risk of being evaluated, while others would perhaps start dreaming about their musical possibilities. Present some similar examples from your own practical experience and discuss implications for practice.

2. Lullabies can soothe a child but the effects are relative to the way we sing and to other aspects of the situation, such as the child's condition and the amount of noise in the environment. Discuss how this observation could be linked to the notions of music as means, music as medium, and music as milieu.

3. The notion of musicking suggests that music is something people do. Describe and discuss the various forms that music as action and activity could have in community music therapy. In your appraisal, what are the most important advantages and limitations of this way of thinking about music?

Notes

1   For overviews and discussions of these interdisciplinary shifts, see e.g. (Leppert & McClary, 1987; Cook, 1998; Cook & Everist, 1999; Scott, 2000; Clayton, Herbert & Middleton, 2003; Martin, 1995, 2006).

2   The concept of *affordance* is now well established in music sociology and community music therapy. It was originally developed by James J. Gibson in the study of visual perception. Gibson used the notion to describe the *complementarity* between environment and organism, especially in relation to action possibilities: "The *affordances* of the environment are what it *offers* the animal, what it *provides* or furnishes, either for good or ill" (Gibson, 1979/1986, p. 127).

3   The literature used in this chapter suggests that (proto)musicality evolved as a biological characteristic of our species (see e.g. Wallin, 1991; Wallin, Merker & Brown, 2000; Cross, 2003, 2005, 2009). This view is gaining increasing support, but contrasting views exist. One established view in evolutionary theory has been that music is an offspring of more basic evolutionary processes (Pinker, 1997). According to this way of thinking, music is not a biological trait that promoted survival or reproduction in the evolution of the species.

4   As discussed by Stige (2002) and several other authors, meaning in music could not be linked to the musical object only but emerges as people and musics interact in specific situations. This perspective is related to Wittgenstein's (1953/1967) influential discussion of meaning in language. According to Wittgenstein, local contexts are not arbitrary sources of variation and distortion. Meaning emerges from interaction and use of signs in social situations. Wittgenstein introduced the metaphor of *language game* to explain how language operates as part of social practices embedded in forms of life.

5   Ruud's (1987/1990, 1998) discussion of the concept of music as action and interaction in context could be considered one precursor (not using the specific term musicking, however).

6   This reflects the discussion in Chapter 1 of the performative quality of community music therapy.

7   Ruud first presented the concept of communitas in a paper at the 1st Nordic Conference in Music Therapy in Sandane in 1991 and has later published different versions of the paper.

8   Turner (1969) used the term communitas in his elaboration on van Gennep's (1909/1999) seminal work on *rites de passage* (rituals that mark our movement from one status to another). Van Gennep was interested in rituals as they proceed in time and proposed that all rites of passage can be described as transitions through three phases; the phase of separation, the threshold phase, and the phase of (re)integration. By using the Latin word for threshold, van Gennep called these three phases for preliminal, liminal, and postliminal. Turner took special interest in the liminal phase, a phase that could lead to communitas and which usually includes considerable alteration of the customs and habits that characterize everyday life. The notion of communitas should therefore be seen in relation to Turner's notions of *humanitas* and *societas*. He used the term humanitas to denote a shared "pre-social" human identity and the term societas to denote the social conventions and cultural regulations that separate humans into classes, sub-cultures, and so forth. According to Turner, communitas could occur in situations where the contradictions between humanitas and societas are temporarily reduced or experienced as nullified (Berkaak, 1993, pp. 25–26).

9   Stige (forthcoming) elaborates on the notion of health musicking and its relationship to Vygotsky's (1978) cultural psychology, Burke's (1945/1969) notion of literature as equipment for living, Wittgenstein's (1953/1967) perspective on meaning, DeNora's (2000) discussion of affordance and appropriation, and Small's (1998) concept of music.

10 Randall Collins (2004) has expanded a tradition of ritual studies that originates from the sociologists Emile Durkheim (1912/1995) and Erving Goffman (1967). In this tradition, formal procedure and stereotyped actions are not what constitute rituals. Mutual focus of attention and emotional entrainment is much more central.

11 Interaction rituals sometimes go wrong. Some people could for instance put themselves at the center of action in ways that others experience as debilitating.

12 The original context for the development of Lave and Wenger's (1991) theory of situated learning was the anthropological study of traditional apprenticeship. Later, the notion of community of practice has been explored in many other contexts that do not involve any established institution of apprenticeship (Wenger, 1998).

13 The specific project is a community music project, but the implications for community music therapy are obvious.

14 Interestingly, the ecological metaphor has been applied by several music scholars lately. Eric Clarke (2005), for instance, uses it in his exploration of "ways of listening."

15 This description in no way suggests that individual use of music from say portable MP3 players in everyday life is without interest in community music therapy. In various traditions of music studies there is a growing research literature on this, see e.g. (Bull, 2000, 2007; Saarikallio, 2007; Skånland, 2007, forthcoming).

Community Music Therapy in Practice

IN Part III we examine the practice dimension of community music therapy. The main idea that guides the development of the three chapters that follow is that practice can neither be derived directly from theories or research nor be based on a prescriptive model. A main characteristic of community music therapy practice is that it is responsive and responsible in relation to a social situation. Responsiveness and responsibility can be nurtured by local knowledge in interaction with theory and research, in combination with the sensitivities that values-informed human interaction instigate.

Chapter 6 focuses on the issues that community music therapy practices relate to. This will be described with reference to the individual–communal continuum and the seven qualities of the PREPARE acronym that we introduced in Chapter 1.

Chapter 7 elaborates on the values that inform the identification of issues and connect these values to human rights facilitation.

Chapter 8 describes a flexible model for participatory processes, with regard to the values and issues discussed in the two previous chapters.

Issues

After studying Chapter 6, you will be able to discuss questions such as:

■ How does community music therapy practice involve work across the individual–communal continuum?

■ What issues relate to the participatory quality of community music therapy?

■ What issues relate to the resource-oriented quality of community music therapy?

■ What issues relate to the ecological quality of community music therapy?

■ What issues relate to the performative quality of community music therapy?

■ What issues relate to the activist quality of community music therapy?

■ What issues relate to the reflective quality of community music therapy?

■ What issues relate to the ethics-driven quality of community music therapy?

■ What does it mean to suggest that community music therapy is a non-medical or extra-medical but not necessarily anti-medical practice?

BETWEEN PRIVATE TROUBLES AND PUBLIC CONCERNS

Participants drawn and attracted to community music therapy practices often live troubled lives. Their health could be frail, they might live in hardship, or perhaps they are in the midst of a difficult transition in life. A general idea of community music therapy is that such troubles are not treated as individual pathology but acknowledged and worked with in relation to broader issues. In other words, the practical work is not restricted to individuals. Neither is it restricted to working with communities. Community music therapy practices involve working across the individual–communal continuum. To explore the communal possibilities of musicking entails, for example, addressing the isolation that some people experience within society. Linkages between micro- and macrosystems are explored; the personal, musical, and political are seen in relation to each other. Community music therapy thus involves issues that are simultaneously private and public. This suggests the development of a broader practice, closer to self-help, community development, and social action than to individual treatment and rehabilitation.

Community music therapy practice usually involves a focus on transformation that includes both personal and social change, at the level of personal growth and empowerment as well as community development and revitalization. Practice addresses problems such as isolation and marginalization, which are often relevant for vulnerable groups such as immigrants, refugees, elderly people, and disabled people. These issues all go beyond problems defined at the level of the individual, although individuals experience them. The suffering of individuals—as well as their hopes and dreams, resources and possibilities—must be recognized and seen in relation to broader agendas:

> The social and political upheavals of our time, the refugee crisis, the stress to urban environments are forcing us all to reframe what it means to belong to a social group, and what it means to communicate and collaborate with one another. Many music therapists now work not only with the ill, but also those whose 'problem' is social, cultural and political—those exiled from their cultures, their musics, and their homes. More than ever, musicing needs to be in the service of generating communities, addressing social fragmentation, rebuilding trust and social bonding.
>
> (Pavlicevic & Ansdell, 2009, p. 373)

To work with relationships between individuals and communities, helping people to mobilize resources and instigate social change, could be viewed as an acknowledgement of their right to a life in dignity and equity. In this chapter we will illuminate pertinent practice issues for community music therapy. In doing this we will not develop any taxonomy of practice since this would be hard to defend, given the situated and emerging character of community music therapy practice. Instead we will exemplify relevant issues by elaborating on the qualities suggested by the acronym PREPARE.

As explained in Chapter 1, community music therapy practice is typically participatory, resource-oriented, ecological, performative, activist, reflective, and ethics-driven. In the present chapter we will use these seven qualities as tools to identify significant practice issues. If people are marginalized in society, for instance due to prejudice and inequality, their right to participation in society is challenged. The participatory quality of community music therapy touches upon this, but if the other six qualities are not involved the result would again be individualization of problems since marginalization is also related to access to resources; it evolves and must be challenged ecologically and it might require performative, activist, and reflective efforts, all which would be guided by an ethics-driven process where values such as respect and equality are central. In the examples that follow, the quality that is highlighted could therefore be thought of as a "handle" for each case, while the other qualities could be thought of as the bottom, top, and sides of the "package" that frames it. The handle alone could not handle the whole case. If the situation and process is dealt with in an adequate way it is because of the whole package. Each of the highlighted qualities could only handle a case in the sense of "touching upon" it then, not in the sense of "dealing with" it. Even though the constellation of qualities varies, their **interdependence** in practice needs to be acknowledged.

FIGURE 6.1 | Listen to my drum! An ArtStories student from Henbury School participates in Making Music Being Well, Northern Territory, Australia.

Photo: Christine Carrigg.

PARTICIPATORY ISSUES: INCLUSION AND CITIZEN PARTICIPATION

A participatory approach involves willingness to listen to all voices involved. Community music therapy practices build on the idea of partnership and value the input and contributions of all participants. This means that a democratic ethos is central to community music therapy, so that there could be several legitimate leaders in a process of change.

The participatory quality of community music therapy touches upon issues such as **inclusion** and **citizen participation**, with the negative counterparts of exclusion and marginalization. The experience of being excluded or marginalized is psychologically stressful for most people and it reduces access to social support and social capital. The theme of inclusion applies to all groups of people. In music therapy it has often been discussed in the field of disabilities (Ely & McMahon, 1990; Ely & Scott, 1994; Stige, 1995; Uricoechea, 2003; Kern, 2005).

Processes of inclusion and exclusion can be understood at various levels of analysis. At the level of the individual, inclusion includes the experience of being acknowledged, and supports the development of a positive personal identity. At aggregated relational levels such as groups, organizations, and localities, inclusion involves supportive relationships, well functioning social networks, and welcoming attitudes and actions. At these levels, and not least at the macrosystem level, inclusion also involves equity and

FIGURE 6.2 | Playing for the folks. A client of music therapy services in a community mental health agency entertaining a group of elders at a care facility in Vancouver, Canada.
Photo: Chialing Chen.

access to valued social resources. These processes are reciprocal. Inclusion in short involves a culture of connectedness, tolerance for diversity, and the recognition of human interdependence (Nelson & Prilleltensky, 2005, pp. 126–127).

The various aggregated levels illuminate how community music therapy practices can build cultures of connectedness. Each musical situation is an opportunity for building participatory spaciousness where there is room for different styles of self-presentation, including peripheral and silent forms of participation as well as conventional and more adventurous forms (Stige, 2010a). Beyond the microlevel, intergroup relationships are crucial when it comes to inclusion (Elefant, 2010a). Work with intergroup relationships usually moves in the direction of community engagement and social action (Curtis & Mercado, 2004). A possible bias can emerge when the work reflects the values of the majority of society, and at worst, practice turns into a request for social conformity (Miyake, 2008). Values and processes that nurture participation will be discussed in more detail in Chapters 7 and 8.

Box 6.1 | INCLUSION, FRIENDSHIPS, AND COMMUNITY ENGAGEMENT

Sandra Curtis and Chesley S. Mercado (2004) in the USA developed a community music therapy practice for citizens with developmental disabilities that illuminated several aspects of the issues of inclusion and participation. The authors relate their work to community engagement, a movement that criticizes the tendency to assess community integration in relation only to physical presence and community tolerance. They argue that the significance of social context and belonging has not been given enough attention within community integration efforts. To belong to a community means to be able to share experiences, participate in activities, and contribute to the development and maintenance of that community. A consequence of true participation is a focus on friendship, learning experiences, and collaborative action (Curtis & Mercado, 2004).

Friendship is characterized by acceptance, communication, and reciprocation. People with developmental disabilities often do not have many contacts that could be characterized as true friendships. Frequently their main social contacts are the helpers of various sorts who can offer friendly experiences but only within the boundaries of a formal structure. Curtis and Mercado (2004) examine the barriers that hinder people with disabilities in developing friendships and community engagement. Besides a range of practical and attitudinal barriers, the authors suggest that agencies of human services often make community engagement and friendship-building difficult by providing little free time for the consumers and little support for the pursuit of these experiences. The fostering of friendships that transcend the formal structure of professional help should therefore be part of the professional support people with disabilities receive.

Box 6.1 |

Curtis and Mercado developed a broad music therapy program to increase opportunities for community engagement. During the five semester period of the program the participants gave very positive evaluations, with responses focusing on the joy of making music together. The caregivers and guardians that completed the evaluation also gave mostly positive evaluations, while suggesting some specific improvements. Comments from the public included several statements suggesting that established attitudes and expectations had been challenged: "It is wonderful what you have done;" "They can do so much more than expected;" and "This is testimony that people will achieve when given the opportunity" (Curtis & Mercado, 2004).

RESOURCE-ORIENTED ISSUES: WELFARE AND EQUALITY

Mobilization of resources is central in community music therapy practices. Resources exist at several levels, such as personal strengths (musicianship, skills, interests, etc.), relational resources (trust, hope, emotional support, etc.), and community resources (arenas, artifacts, traditions, organizations, institutions, etc.). Resources can be appropriated by members of a community but there is often inequity in the distribution of access.

The resource-oriented quality of community music therapy relates specifically to issues such as **welfare** and **equality**, with the negative counterparts of deprivation, poverty, and inequality. This could be considered in relation to tangible and intangible resources. For instance, material poverty is a major problem in many developing countries and one to which music therapists must relate (Pavlicevic, 2003). Music therapists might have to think through how their own resources are best utilized. It is not necessarily those that can pay for music therapy who are most in need. Sometimes the opposite is closer to the truth (Oosthuizen, 2006). Music therapists of course also encounter problems of poverty in wealthier countries (MacDonald & Viega, 2011) and some music therapists have started to explore the degree to which community music therapy could be activist and contribute to social change and more equitable distributions of resources.

Music is a central intangible resource. In this respect, the possibility of resource orientation is a central theme for music therapy more generally, as Aigen (2005) and Garred (2006) have argued. Schwabe (2005) has demonstrated that resource orientation could be considered an alternative to more pathology oriented approaches in music therapy. In a theoretical and empirical investigation of music therapy in mental health institutions, Rolvsjord (2010) has made a similar argument and detailed the implications for practice, such as an interest in the client's contribution to the process and in contextual factors, empowerment, and collaboration. Her work clarifies the relationship between resource orientation and current developments within salutogenic thinking, positive psychology, and theory on resilience and recovery. In short, Rolvsjord suggests that

FIGURE 6.3 | Creating the beat for the next song. Two members of "The Little Saints," with music therapist Mike Viega. Philadelphia, USA.

Photo: Ryan Brandenberg.

resource orientation implies a change from a model-driven to a client-directed approach to psychosocial therapy.

Solli (2006) has argued that human protomusicality is a basic resource for participation and development in music therapy. As outlined in Chapter 5, this is a resource that enables creative interaction with others and therefore increases possibilities for accessing resources that are socially and culturally produced. It is thus a resource that could give access to other resources and open up opportunities for participation in new contexts. In a study more specifically linked to community music therapy, O'Grady (2009) explored the therapeutic potential of creating and performing music with women in prison. Music-making and performance served the participating women as a "bridge" between inside and outside places, between privacy and the public, between self-focus and a focus on others, between solitude and togetherness, and between subjective and objective thought processes. The study also revealed that these potentials needed to be enacted and that there were five personal and relational resources that helped in that process (see Box 6.2).

Procter (2001, 2004, 2006) has used the terms *social capital* and *musical capital* to discuss how collaborative musical activity requires and generates resources such as trust and support. Several music therapists have used the notion of *community of practice* to illuminate how various resources are manufactured and shared among participants in a group (see e.g. Stige, 2002; Krüger, 2004; Ansdell, 2010a; Ruud, 2011, in press; Storsve, Westby & Ruud, 2010).[1]

As with tangible resources, access to intangible resources is usually not distributed justly. The resource-oriented quality of community music therapy therefore involves performative and activist efforts to change this situation (see below).

Box 6.2 | CREST: PERSONAL AND RELATIONAL RESOURCES FOR ENACTMENT OF THERAPEUTIC POTENTIALS

Lucy O'Grady (2009) examined the therapeutic potentials of making and performing music in a maximum-security women's prison in Australia. The study focused on a creative process involving seven women who worked in collaboration with artists from a theatre company to create a musical together. O'Grady describes the process as a "Collective Creative Journey" of five phases: Creating the foundations for the performance, Consolidating and fleshing out the foundations, Bringing it all together, Performing the show to an audience, and Winding-down. Each phase was colored by the emergence of themes and events, as this description illuminates:

> Throughout the first phase, the ideas surrounding the theme of 'Moving forward the hard way' were subjected to a continual process of *play, transformation, reflection, negotiation* and *collaboration* ... *Play* involved drama improvisations, musical improvisations, creative writing and verbal discussions. The musical director or participants *transformed* this play material into song or script form and *reflected* it back to the group. The participants then *negotiated* any changes with each other and with the musical director. They then *collaborated* as a group to complete lyrics and script or to orchestrate and arrange the songs. Emerging from this process were five original songs related to the theme of 'Moving forward the hard way' as well as script ideas for how each song could be introduced (O'Grady, 2009, p. 103).

O'Grady uses the term "therapeutic potentials" to communicate that music is not intrinsically therapeutic; the capacity for change needs to be enacted. Her analysis of the case she studied suggests that music-making had the potential to serve as a "bridge" for these women:

> [C]reating and performing music ... served as a *one-way* bridge ... towards outside realms under the assumption that this was the direction forward. ... As each woman moved in this outward direction, albeit in her own individual way and with her own individual struggles, she experienced a sense of it all 'coming together'. Many women in the group also experienced a feeling of having come back to a love of music, of returning 'home' (O'Grady, 2009, pp. 117–118).

O'Grady adopts the acronym CREST to communicate the personal and relational resources required to enact the therapeutic potentials in this case; courage, readiness, exchange,

Box 6.2 |

support, and trust. She suggests that each resource could radiate out and interact with other resources, which this description of "exchange" illuminates:

> Exchange not only occurred between group members or between performer and audience but also between the women and the spaces to which they were confined. For example, Sarah reported that the joy she experienced along the journey "radiated out" to her unit and to the compound in general. She was also particularly "rapt" (thrilled) that a fellow prisoner with a severe mental illness had seemed to share her joy during the performance, as seen by her clapping and smiling. These actions, according to Sarah, were unusual for this particular audience member and fuelled Sarah's joy even more (O'Grady, 2009, p. 137).

ECOLOGICAL ISSUES: RELATIONSHIPS AND TRANSITIONS

The ecological metaphor suggests that there are several interacting levels of activity in human life, such as individual, group, organization, locality, and various macrosystems. Community music therapy practices actively explore the socio-cultural ecology created by reciprocal relationships between these levels of organization. The levels can be understood as nested; lower levels are embedded in higher levels. For instance, a microsystem is a group of individuals that relate to each other in a setting, while an organization encompasses many microsystems.

The ecological quality of community music therapy touches on issues such as **ecological relationships** and **transitions**, which could be productive or challenging in various ways. Which systems and ecological levels are involved can vary considerably, depending on the needs and resources in each situation. We will present examples illuminating each of these two types of issues.

One implication of socioecological thinking in community music therapy is that not only relationships between individuals but also relationships between various systems come into consideration. Kleive and Stige (1988) demonstrated how community inclusion involves individual change and community change but also change in the relationships between various microsystems. This involved altering attitudes and communication patterns between a community music school, several cultural organizations, and a community home for people with intellectual disabilities. The community music therapy process involved much more than music therapy sessions; it also included public communication and negotiations between various microsystems and organizations. In a similar vein, Elefant (2010a) explored intergroup relationships in a project on the inclusion of children with special needs into a mainstream school setting.

FIGURE 6.4 | In concert. Music education in a Palestinian refugee camp in Lebanon.
Photo: Vegard Storsve.

Ecological transitions usually refer to phases of change when individuals or groups move from a well-known to an unknown context. For instance, when a young person moves from the status of a student to that of a worker this could be considered an ecological transition. A transition involves new possibilities, such as access to new resources and relationships, but it can also be challenging to a degree that is difficult to manage. Examples of work with ecological transitions in community music therapy include Stige's (2002) work on the transition from kindergarten to school, Krüger's (2007) work with adolescents in transition from children's welfare to responsibility in society, and the work of Tuastad and Finsås (2008) on the transition from prison to community.

Many music therapists have developed community music therapy practices that are mobile in order to relate to various ecological challenges. One example is the Music Therapy Community Clinic within the Greater Cape Town area in South Africa, a traveling service to disadvantaged people from poorer communities (Fouché & Torrance, 2005; Oosthuizen, Fouché, & Torrance, 2007). In Germany, examples of mobile services include the "Hausmusik" of Muthesius in Berlin, working in the homes of people with dementia together with their relatives and the out-patient-care-service. "Musik auf Raedern" (music on the wheels) in Muenster is another example (Wosch, 2011).

The public or semi-public character of many community music therapy practices contributes to the possibility of having **ripple effects** in various systems: "the idea that the impact of music therapy can work 'outwards' for an isolated person towards community, and it can also bring the community in" (Pavlicevic & Ansdell, 2004, p. 16). To suggest that community music therapy practices go public should not be understood as an absolute rule, then. The point is not that things need to happen in the street or on the stage but that they could, and that music therapy always takes place in contexts that are nested in other contexts (see the discussion of ecological models in Chapter 4). There is flexibility concerning choice of context and linking of contexts, depending on what the participants, their musicking, and their situation call for.

Box 6.3 | THE GEOGRAPHY OF SONGS

Norwegian music therapist Trygve Aasgaard (1998, 1999, 2000, 2002, 2004) has developed perspectives on the ecological qualities of music therapy. In discussing music therapy in hospital settings, Aasgaard has gone beyond an individualized focus and instead examined how music therapy may contribute to the *milieu* or *environment*. The wards, Aasgaard claims, could be transformed by public musicking, including activities such as community singing, improvisation, and performance of songs composed by the children in collaboration with the music therapist. Aasgaard (1998, 1999) argues that the role of music therapy in relation to the task of creating favorable environments should continue to be examined:

> A modern paediatric oncology ward is . . . permanently struggling between providing a milieu that facilitates the most effective, life saving, but very uncomfortable medical treatment and providing conditions for the best possible good life for patients/relatives during hospitalization. If the ultimate goals of any treatment are set with the patient's *quality of life* in mind, it might be wise to assess the realities of the environmental aspects of treatment and care, and not just consider each service or profession as an isolated entity (Aasgaard, 1999, p. 31).

Goals of music environmental therapy should, according to Aasgaard, encompass all people present. In outlining therapeutic strategies he focuses on three levels:

First, strategies may relate to the *physical environment,* which for some clients and in some cases may create sensory deprivation, in others overload. This is a matter of relationship and it depends on the properties of the physical environment and the sensory needs and capacities of the client. The task of the music therapist is to assess this relationship and suggest suitable possibilities.

Second, strategies may relate to the *social environment,* through activities such as community singing, collective improvisation, or concerts and performances. Aasgaard underlines the importance of establishing socially stimulating but secure environments where music therapy could create open meeting-points for social interaction.

Box 6.3 |

Third, strategies may relate to the *symbolic* (or *cultural*) *environment*. Aasgaard argues that many clients are concerned about being looked upon merely as patients (and not as persons) and suggests that opportunities for conventional social roles to be overturned should be sought. Examples include medical doctors who get involved in a musical improvisation and try out roles outside their expert domain, or young clients who gain recognition through the performance of songs they have written.

Aasgaard has given special attention to songs that the children write together with the music therapist. Songs can transcend the intimate situation at the hospital bed where they perhaps were produced and be appropriated in a range of other settings, such as the open wardrooms, the family home, and the child's school. Aasgaard (2000, 2002) talks of the "*geography of songs*" and has examined the range of contexts in which songs have been used and links established. This work therefore throws light on the ecology of contexts at the mesosystem level.

PERFORMATIVE ISSUES: HEALTH AND IDENTITY

Community music therapy practice is performative; it focuses on human development through action and the performance of relationships. The implication is not that reflection is made subsidiary but that it is related to performances of self and social systems.

The performative quality clarifies how community music therapy practices primarily take proactive roles in relation to health and development, usually with a focus on the **promotion of health** and **prevention of problems** rather than cure and treatment. The question of how persons, groups, or communities live with and deal with health problems becomes central and this illuminates how issues of health are related to issues of **identity** (Ruud, 1997a b; McFerran, in press). Ansdell describes this through reference to Aldridge's work on health as performance:

Aldridge (1996, 2004) has outlined a performative concept for music therapy, suggesting the motto "*argo ergo sum*—I perform therefore I am" (instead of the Cartesian "cogito ergo sum") (1996, p. 27). "Performing the self" is here not just a psychological or sociological concept, but a physiological one too (the performance, for example, of our immune system or motor coordination). This becomes clearer when such performance "fails" or is severely restricted through acute or chronic illness—at a physical, cognitive, expressive, or social level. At a more existential level we can also see how our illness–health and our identity are performative. So when patients play in music therapy with us they "perform their lives before us" (p. 27)—who they are now (their illness *and* their health) and who they *can* be. Their musicing is thus a "health performance." Aldridge also suggests how music therapy

Box 6.4 | HEALTH PROMOTION IN A PARTNERED PRACTICE

Susan Baines (2000/2003) developed and documented a consumer-directed and partnered community mental health music therapy program in Canada. She situates the program with reference to the substantial changes in the nation's health care system:

> A consumer-initiated and informed model would primarily incorporate consumer values, skills, initiatives and priorities into the team approach already in existence in much of our health care system in Canada today. Secondly, the awareness of families and community care-givers would be explored and synthesized. In this way, the expertise of people living with various health conditions followed by the expertise of those most directly care-giving would be integrated into the overall process of health delivery in the community, including treatment and prevention programs (Baines, 2000/2003).

An eight-week music group was piloted as part of the social program of a clubhouse and the therapist took the role of a *facilitator*. Instead of applying a more conventional psychotherapy group model—which would have been inappropriate to the setting—she saw her role as that of giving professional support to a self-help group. The development of this role was inspired by the literature of community psychology, concerning concepts such as *mutual help, helping transactions,* and *empowering community narratives.*

All attendance in the program was voluntary. Participants were self-referred, the sessions were held in an open space, and there was an open in-and-out policy during sessions. In each session, participants would choose and sing familiar songs of personal significance, selected from a community book developed and maintained by the participants. The songs addressed a wide spectrum of themes and emotional needs. While singing, the participants would accompany themselves on various percussion instruments, whereas the music therapist usually played the guitar. In addition to accompanied community singing, sometimes participants would spontaneously dance or there would be a short instrumental improvisation. Poetry and personal compositions would also occur.

Baines explains how she found the emerging format to be in keeping with an empowerment approach, well-matched with a consumer-initiated ethic. Individual goals were managed personally by the participants but could be discussed with other group members or the facilitator, both in the group and outside of sessions. Peer support was an essential element of the process, and the facilitator's role was to support the group in processing and managing experiences and negotiating group goals and norms.

The goals for the music program focused on general needs such as "decreased isolation, increased community development, increased empowerment and communication skills, enhanced creativity and quality of life, and fulfilling consumer driven initiatives" (Baines, 2000/2003). When the initial pilot program was completed the consumers requested its extension and the service provider both extended and increased it by establishing new groups on other sites.

can offer a form of help or "repair," with the music therapist's job being to provide
sites for performance such that the performance of the self can continue and elaborate.

(Ansdell, 2010b, p. 171)

This also suggests that early intervention (Williams & Abad, 2005), the enacting of
potentials (O'Grady, 2009), and empowerment (Procter, 2001; Rolvsjord, 2004) are
important strategies. The performative quality of community music therapy practice
should be seen in light of the fact that the majority of factors influencing health and
wellbeing in a society are localized outside the health care services. Activities and
structures in other sectors, such as education and cultural life, are vital (see Chapter 3).
Even though community music therapy sometimes grows out of health care settings,
practices are linked to the challenges of everyday life. The question of how persons,
groups, or communities live with and deal with health problems comes into focus and
the promotion of positive health and quality of life is vital (Ruud, 2002). This is especially
relevant for vulnerable groups such as people with chronic health problems (Aasgaard,
2002), people in custody (O'Grady, 2009), and people who experience multidimensional
problems such as HIV/AIDS where a medical problem is only one dimension.

The enacting of potential requires some kind of collaborative effort and ritual, in
order to mobilize resources, create support, and handle challenges. This ritual can be
improvised and informal, as long as it creates a shared focus of attention and mobilizes
the participants emotionally (Stige, 2010a; in press). Community music therapy as
performative practice suggests a broad notion of performance, including the performance
of self and social systems. In the words of Halstead (2010); to participate in a community
of musical practice enables the production of sounds, self, and society.

The performative quality of community music therapy indicates a broad perspective
on human life, then, far beyond the debates on when, why, and how musical performances
could be helpful in music therapy. Still, the performance of music in a social situation
could be one natural implication, if handled sensitively and responsibly concerning the
preparation and processing for performers and audience. The care for person, place, and
process that this practice requires is discussed in different ways by authors from different
traditions of music therapy (Aigen, 2004; Maratos, 2004; Powell, 2004; Zharinova-
Sanderson, 2004; Ansdell, 2005b, 2010b; Turry, 2005; Dahle & Slettebakk, 2006; Jampel,
2006, 2011; O'Grady, 2009; McFerran, 2010).

ACTIVIST ISSUES: AWARENESS AND SOCIAL CHANGE

While the performative quality of community music therapy highlights human agency, the
activist quality of community music therapy takes this one step further by acknowledging
how people's problems and challenges are related to structural limitations in society, such
as repression and discrimination, injustice and unequal access to resources. Social change
is therefore an important part of the community music therapy agenda. The activist quality
is perhaps more controversial and less documented in the literature than other qualities
discussed in this chapter, but logically goes together with all the other qualities.

FIGURE 6.5 | George rehearsing. Baltic Street Clinic, New York.
Photo: South Beach Psychiatric Center.

The activist quality of community music therapy relates to issues such as **awareness** and **social change**. Many scholars focusing on social change insist on the importance of relationships between inward and outward awareness-raising, leading to a "transformational activism" where personal and social change are two sides of the same coin and liberation considered neither a "gift" nor a self-achievement but a mutual process (Freire, 1970/2000). Actions intended to bring about social change inevitably involve confrontation. Possibilities for deliberation and pragmatic forms of "acting in concert" are also sought out (Mattern, 1998). Community music therapy as activism is related to the idea of working with the relatively disadvantaged and also to the metaphor of attending to unheard voices. In the following we will illuminate implications for practice by presenting community music therapy examples from the area of community work and community engagement and the area of peace and conflict transformation.

In a project on cultural inclusion in a community in Western Norway, the music therapists realized that this goal required community work and cultural engagement, since barriers to participation were not only located at the level of the individual but also in community attitudes and practices (Kleive & Stige, 1988). No change was conceivable before a new critical awareness could be established in the local community. The communication developed could be described as "call for action" based on the message that segregation involves violation of the rights of people with disabilities. Written and verbal reference to principles of national policies and international declarations of human rights were made, together with performative demonstration of the resources and aspirations of disabled people in relation to musical participation (Stige, 1993, 2002).

FIGURE 6.6 | What do you think? A Children's Welfare Musical, Bergen, Norway.
Photo: Astrid Merete Nordhaug.

In America, music therapists Curtis and Mercado (2004) also worked with community inclusion of people with developmental disabilities, with inspiration from the tradition of community engagement (see Box 6.1). The authors highlighted that strategies for change could not be described in any context-independent way. Some strategies have been found useful across several contexts, however, and they include *matching, self-advocating, social networking,* and *bridging.* Matching refers to the connection of persons with and without disabilities, self-advocating to possibilities for people with disabilities to educate other community members, social networking to the linking of people with disabilities with existing social networks, and bridging to the introduction of persons with disability to their local community (Curtis & Mercado, 2004).

Peace work and conflict resolution is another area which has inspired music therapy activism, with pioneering efforts by Boxill (1988, 1997a), Kenny (1988), Moreno (2003) and others. Contemporary contributions sometimes advocate a two-sided approach with therapeutic services for individuals suffering from the consequences of conflict and violence supplemented with peace advocacy (Amir, 2002; Stewart, 2004; Ng, 2005; Vaillancourt, 2007, 2009).

Some contemporary contributions in the music therapy literature concentrate on the promotion of tolerance and mutual respect through musicking in non-clinical settings (Krüger, 2007; Dunn, 2008, see also Box 6.5). Smyth (2002) presents an example from the troubles in Northern Ireland. There is a culture of denial and silence in this context, she argues, and musical instruments have taken on political identities. The Lambeg drum, for instance, is associated to Orangeism and Unionism, while the Bodhran drum is linked to a traditional Irish identity. Music is part of the conflict, then, but could still contribute to reconciliation, according to Smyth. Initiatives such as "Different Drums" have put the above-mentioned drums to use, together. On this basis Smyth suggests that music therapy could play on a broader scale:

> Music therapy as a whole-school activity in divided societies might use such approaches to contribute to the reconstruction of our society after a period of devastating destruction and division, such as we have lived through. Music therapy in Northern Ireland and other divided societies could well provide an opportunity for creatively exploring our divisions and contribute to our capacity to understand and transform those divisions into harmonious rather than dissonant diversities.
>
> (Smyth, 2002, p. 79)

Box 6.5 | TRANSFORMING CONFLICT THROUGH MUSIC

American music therapist Barbara Dunn (2008) studied how music could be added to a facilitated process of addressing conflict with adults. The theoretical orientation selected was *conflict transformation,* as opposed to conflict resolution. With reference to John Paul Lederach, one of the pioneers of conflict transformation, she explains the difference in the following way:

Box 6.5 |

If only the identified problem is addressed (as is standard practice for conflict resolution), once it is resolved, the conditions that allowed the problem to develop may still be present. These conditions can set the stage for the problem to re-emerge or for new problems to develop. Thus, the operative word is *transformation* of the situation that created the conflict in the first place (Dunn, 2008, pp. 2–3).

In Dunn's study, 18 experienced conflict mediators participated in a researcher-designed workshop in order to explore the use of music to transform conflicts. In addition Dunn gathered information from three international professionals with experience in using music in conflict intervention strategies. Conflicts exist in many areas of life, from neighborhood disputes to contentious international relations. One of the participants described the possible role of music in the mediation of conflicts in the following way:

[T]hey come into a dispute, they are really very hard, they're very focused on themselves and how they've been wronged. It's kind of all about "me" at that point. . . . there's a sort of shift that has to happen internally in each person before there can be a resolution. And for that person, there's several things that have to happen: they have to soften, they have to be able to get outside of themselves a bit so they can see the other person's point of view . . . Once a person gets into a certain space they can have more compassion for themselves, which we do by validating their feelings. Having compassion for them, we're modeling that behavior as mediators. Those are the kinds of things that are going to help them move. . . . If we can get them in a state where they are more receptive, less fixed in a stance, then that's where we're going to see the movement that's going to lead to the resolution or the possible resolution of the conflict. I believe that music can really help in that because they've proved that it can change your brain state, your brain waves can actually switch. I don't know all the scientific, technical—beta, alpha, gamma—but it can actually switch those and put you in a place where you are more receptive. It can get you out of yourself. I think music can tap something deep within all of us that reminds us of our connection to larger, universal connectedness (participant in Dunn, 2008, pp. 62–63).

Conflict transformation implies the challenge of engaging with relationships, interests, discourses, and structures in a community. In her summary of the possibilities of music, Dunn (2008, p. 66) stated, "music transforms conflict by creating common ground, eliciting psychological change, addressing feelings and thoughts, and improving communication." This is articulated as one of the three main themes that emerged from the research; the effects of music that are relevant in relation to conflict transformation are physiological as well as personal, communicative, and social. The two other main themes that emerged from the analysis suggested that these effects depend on certain conditions and considerations. The importance of conditions was articulated in the theme "antecedent experiences with music affect the ability to use it to address conflict" (Dunn, 2008, p. 66). This theme involves awareness of cultural context:

Box 6.5 |

In the United States, it is more common to find music in performance halls than in places that are actively addressing conflict. The reservations expressed by participants are fully understandable when placed within this cultural context. Again, in my experiences with music therapy, clients and colleagues do not seem to fully understand or support the use of music to address nonmusical goals until they have a positive experience with the music as an intervention, either personally or observed with a client (Dunn, 2008, p. 77).

The third theme that emerged was that "musical exercises require careful consideration when used to address conflict" (Dunn, 2008, p. 69). The results of Dunn's study suggest that it is potentially helpful to use music in conflict transformation, as music can tap into different levels of human functioning better than the more conventional verbal strategies. Dunn maintains, however, that the practical application of music requires careful consideration of how to present musical exercises or activities, of what music and instruments to select, and of how the selected activities, music, and instruments relate to the participants' culture. The study thus invites mediators to include music in their repertoire and music therapists to use their skills in nonclinical settings.

REFLECTIVE ISSUES: RECOGNITION AND CRITIQUE

Community music therapy practices deal with real world challenges in ways that require active reflection. Such processes of reflection are research-informed but the participatory ethos opposes the idea of the music therapist as the sole or central expert. Reflection therefore always involves dyadic as well as collective processes, situated in the context of practice.

The reflective quality is linked to issues such as **recognition** and **critique**. Without mutual respect and acknowledgement it is impossible to create a space or climate for shared reflection. Reflection, understood in this way, is a dialogic enterprise that involves affirmation of someone else's consciousness, as suggested by Bakhtin (see Stige, 2002). Within critical theory, Honneth's (2003) work examines recognition both at the level of the individual and at various aggregated levels (Ruud, 2010). Without parity and solidarity, a climate where everybody has a voice is unattainable. The reflective quality is therefore pertinent in a special way when comprehension is distorted by silencing or other mechanisms of repression. Community music therapy practices encourage people to collaborate in creating a climate for enhanced reflection in ways that affirm diverse voices.

In community music therapy it is also significant to acknowledge an inclusive notion of reflection, beyond the use of language. The activity of reflecting entails putting human ways and activities in perspective. We often do this through verbal processing, but the

FIGURE 6.7 | Discussing the facts—and a vision. Brain Day presentations from the Centre for Brain Research at the University of Auckland.

Photo: Godfrey Boehnke.

option of using other modalities to perform this function is highly relevant when working with music (Stige, 1995). Warner (2005) and several other music therapists have explored this through use of participatory action research (see Box 6.6 and Chapter 9).

Even when reflection involves the modality of language it does not necessarily involve a conventional approach to verbal processing as performed in contexts of psychotherapy. Two individuals sitting down to talk things through is not the only possible model of how verbal reflections can be cultivated in community music therapy (Krüger, 2007). McFerran describes this feature of verbal reflection in community music therapy in a vignette on a community-based program with young men with emotional and behavioral problems:

'So what are you up to this weekend, Simon?' the music therapist asks as the other boys disappear from the room on some urgent mission. 'Uhhh, I've just gotta make a phone call,' Simon responds, pulling out his mobile phone and beginning to look through it. 'No worries,' replies the music therapist, standing up to reorganize the equipment. Intimate face to face attention is often too strong for these young men, who quickly feel awkward without their peers around. She knows that he is more likely to talk if the situation is casual.

(McFerran, 2010, p. 196)

McFerran (2010) argues that telling the story can be more important than the content of it and continues to explain how she works to encourage the participants' capacity for reflection in relation to their situation, for instance concerning relationships between family and school.[2]

Music therapy may be able to provide him with enjoyable experiences that connect him into networks of peers who are also striving to move beyond their failure with the school system. Making music with other people may not directly build a bridge between family and school, but it can offer an experience of bridging that fans the flames of Simon's intentions.

(McFerran, 2010, p. 198)

When it comes to research as a source of shared reflection in community music therapy, this suggests that reflexivity—the capacity to critically examine one's own position and perspective—is essential (Stige, 2002). There is need for research-informed knowledge that can enable music therapists to take an active musical and social role in a community, but the relationships between this knowledge and other relevant forms of knowledge in a given situation must be acknowledged.

Box 6.6 | AN ACTION RESEARCH INQUIRY INTO GROUP MUSIC THERAPY WITHIN A COMMUNITY HOME

English music therapist Catherine Warner (2005) initiated an action research project to investigate group music therapy within a community home. The project tracked one year of a group music therapy process with adult residents who had severe learning difficulties and challenging behavior. Two music therapists were involved in the project, together with the staff and the residents of the community home. According to the ethos of participatory action research, they all worked as co-researchers and collaborated in the process of developing research questions, design, and interpretations of results.

One of the challenges Warner and her co-researchers faced was that several of the residents were not able to use language. How could they then be involved as co-researchers? The group innovatively worked out visual and audio materials that became central in the research process, as empirical sources and tools for reflection. In spite of the fact that they lacked language for expression of their concerns, the residents were able to make some changes to the design and delivery of the project. Contributing with "reflection through action" the residents initiated changes in musical interaction as well as in use of instruments and equipment and in the layout of the room:

> In this inquiry, one difficulty was how to know whether some participants were intentionally taking a stance in order to change a situation, or whether their actions were primarily reactive and expressive. For example, in the course of the community

Box 6.6 |

home inquiry, one participant, Ralph, hit the video camera many times over the course of the year. When the camera was not there, Ralph stayed in the room for longer than usual. As a result the therapist and day care worker agreed to stop using the camera at the end of the year. Furthermore, the therapist reflected on his general use of video in his work, did not subject the original participant to any more video and reduced his reliance on video in his normal working practice. As participants we were not certain whether Ralph was intentionally objecting to the camera, or whether he just liked thumping the object. We had to acknowledge that although we could not always know, our interpretation of the intentionality was as important a factor as the action itself, and these interpretations must be part of our critical reflection (Warner, 2005, p. 18).

All participants reflected on their difficulty in hearing some of the resident's less welcome communications and raised their expectations of what the residents were capable of. "Less welcome communications" could include aggressive episodes or acts. One of the challenging questions that evolved through the research process was whether these behaviors should be considered *actions,* that is behaviors that reflect intentions. In other words; should they merely be considered incidents of negative behaviors to be worked with or should they be acknowledged as legitimate expressions of the residents' concerns? As the project evolved through use of various modes of expressions and repeated cycles of reflections, the tendency was that the staff and the music therapists increasingly developed their willingness to acknowledge "less welcome communications" as legitimate expressions of concerns. This also led to increasing recognition of individual differences between residents.

This specific project exemplifies more general challenges when doing research with vulnerable people. Together with other scholars, Warner has developed a perspective on good practice and a cyclical consent process in such research (Norman, Sellman & Warner, 2006).

ETHICS-DRIVEN ISSUES: RESPONSIVENESS AND RESPONSIBILITY

Expert decisions informed by diagnostic information about the pathology of the individual do not drive community music therapy practices. Negotiated visions of music, health, and community do. Such visions are necessarily values-informed, as we will discuss in the next chapter. The ethics-driven quality of community music therapy touches on issues such as **responsiveness** and **responsibility**. Responsiveness could be thought of as a musical quality but involves interpersonal relationships as well, as explicated by Aigen in this description:

> The creation of vital, alive, quality music does not derive from the ability of musicians to link with each other around perfect tunings and precise co-temporal musical

events, merging their identities into some perfect unity. Instead, music is created by an ability to connect with others in unique ways that preserve our separateness . . . Hence groove is a necessarily social activity. It requires an awareness of and responsiveness to the present moment in time and to the musical contributions of other people in that moment. Thus, the establishment of groove requires moving past barriers that frequently bring clients to music therapy, particularly those which reinforce social isolation.

(Aigen, 2002, p. 35)

Musical and social responsiveness are linked. This is acknowledged in much of the music therapy literature, where musical interaction is often seen in light of the theory of communicative musicality and human companionship (Malloch & Trevarthen, 2009). In community music therapy communicative musicality provides a necessary but not sufficient theoretical platform, as Pavlicevic and Ansdell (2009) have demonstrated in their discussion of a model for coupling musical and social development. In community music therapy, responsiveness includes but goes beyond a focus on individuals and dyadic relatedness.

Responsiveness is inevitably linked to responsibility. Community music therapy practices work with people in relation to their situation and offer support and help in a context-sensitive way. Since community music therapy does not focus specifically on pathology, there is less of a possibility for focusing one-sidedly on the shortcomings of the individual and overlooking the inadequacy of the system. The risk of "blaming the victim" (Ryan, 1971) is considerably reduced. It should not be replaced with a tendency of "blaming the system." Even though the defects of the system are at times glaringly obvious, it is always relevant to explore issues of individual responsibility.

Rio (2005) examined the therapeutic process of a group of people who were homeless or had recently moved out of a homeless shelter into a private home. The participants were involved in a church gospel choir and agreed to participate in a music therapy program and research project to explore issues of homelessness, substance abuse, interpersonal relationships, music, creativity, and spirituality. Rio argued that the development of greater insight into personal issues was central for these participants and would aid in their recovery from addiction and life on the street.

Exploration of personal responsibility is necessary but not sufficient in community music therapy, since it addresses only one dimension of reflection. The activist quality of community music therapy suggests that it is also necessary to explore how material and social inequalities and lack of recognition at personal and aggregated levels contribute to the problems people experience (Ruud, 1987/1990; Storsve, Westby & Ruud, 2010).

The participatory quality of community music therapy indicates that the relationship between responsiveness and responsibility is a burning issue not only for music therapists but also for all participants. In a study of a senior choir, Stige (2010b) discussed the problem of the potentially limitless responsibility that responsiveness to other people's needs could involve. Some choir members expressed concerns about this but they also proposed that collaborative singing contributed positively because people were responsive to each other and responsibilities became distributed. Stige called this a *culture of mutual care*.[3]

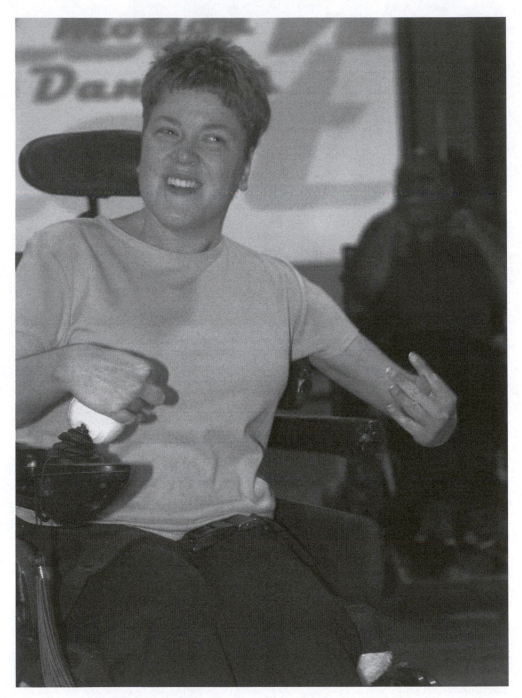

FIGURE 6.8 | Circular Motion Dancer Torie. Creative Expressions Studio and Gallery, Milledgeville, GA, USA.

Photo: Scott Kitchens.

Box 6.7 | AFTER THE BLACK SATURDAY BUSH FIRES

Australian music therapist Katrina McFerran (2009) described one example of a community music therapy project developed in response to a community contingency, in this case the destructive fires in the state of Victoria in February 2009. Almost 200 people died in the fires and many families lost their homes:

> I have been traveling to this small country town for seven weeks now, working alongside my colleague Kate Teggelove, who organised the project. Kate was contacted by a local Mathematics Teacher who was desperate to find some way to support the teenagers in her school. Kate wanted to help, and sent out an email to music therapists she knew that worked with teenagers, myself amongst them. This did not happen as immediately or independently as the response of our New York colleagues after September 11th (as described by Amir, 2002). To some degree, bushfires are an expected part of the Australian summer, so they did not elicit emergency responses from the music therapy community. But these fires were particularly devastating . . . and I recall thinking that I would love to make a contribution some time down the track, when all the support began to wane, as it inevitably did. So when Kate emailed with the project my response was immediate, and I continue to be grateful for this opportunity to "do something."

> My experience of working with these young people as they grapple with the repercussions of surviving the fires has been heart-warming at many levels. It strikes me as the kind of work that makes theory truly come alive as a reflection of practice. Before beginning I had absorbed myself in Julie Sutton's book on music therapy and trauma (2002) and worried about the possibility of re-traumatisation. I had contemplated the relevance of community music therapy theory (Pavlicevic & Ansdell, 2004; Stige, 2003) and considered how this work might be different to conventional music therapy, with its treatment plans and anticipated outcomes. I had revisited my favourite influences in the form of Irvin Yalom (2005) for his advice on working with groups as well as Andy Malekoff's (1997) approach to the whole teenager, positioning myself as an adult who is open to having some fun, as well as being able to hang in there and not lose hope (McFerran, 2009).

The music therapists decided to take a gentle approach, allowing the adolescents to direct the pace at which to approach the topic of grief after the fires (it varied between groups). They also took an ecological perspective and focused on the young people as located in their contexts, as teenagers, living in the countryside, part of a community that was trying to rebuild after the fires, but also part of the futures they were trying to create. The authors (McFerran & Teggelove, 2011) describe group dynamics and group developments and the involved activities of group improvisations, playing, and song-writing. Ultimately the adolescents decided that they wanted to create a recording. A CD labeled "I Am Who I Am" was produced in collaboration with a local community musician and then launched in a local pub; a public event where family and friends could witness the groups perform and celebrate the work that had been done.

FROM BELOW, OUTWARDS, AND AROUND

Two of the meanings we assign to the term *issue* in everyday life are "a matter of concern" and "a topic of discussion." Both meanings are of relevance here and the latter dimension is crucial, because issues in community music therapy cannot be defined by music therapists or other experts. They often emerge "from below" and usually materialize through dialogue and negotiation. In the next chapter we will explore the values that support this concept of practice as emerging "from below." The examples presented in this chapter demonstrate that the course of community music therapy practice could be said to be "outwards and around" too. In summarizing a series of case studies of community music therapy practice, Stige and associates argue that:

> The overall orientation of the work described in this book is often "outwards-and-around" (in contrast to conventional music therapy's typical concentration on working "down-and-within"). We have chosen to label this feature as performative, in the broad sociological meaning of that term. While concerts and gigs at times may be important, the performative character of Community Music Therapy suggests something much broader than this. It is based upon a *relational perspective* on human development and it also emphasizes the music-centered nature of Community Music Therapy in a way that suggests a concept of music which emphasizes its social character.
>
> (Stige et al., 2010b, p. 282)

From below, outwards, and around recapitulates the participatory, relational, and ecological characteristics of community music therapy practice. These characteristics are thrown into sharp relief by a comparison with the **medical model**. As a decision-making process, the medical model implies that the professional investigates the problems of an individual, identifies a diagnosis, prescribes an intervention, and evaluates the effect of the prescribed treatment. At a more abstract level, the medical model is informed by several interconnected assumptions; the individual presents with a disorder or condition for which there is a scientific explanation, while the intervention is defined by specific remedial ingredients.

The assumptions of the medical model differ substantially from the participatory, relational, and ecological foundations of community music therapy. Because the medical model is an influential model, not only in medicine, this is worth noting.[4] In the music therapy literature, concerns about the dominance of the medical model have been articulated by, for instance, Rolvsjord (2010) in her development of a resource-oriented approach to music therapy in mental health. This approach stresses resources rather than pathology and aims at mutual empowerment through collaboration rather than symptom relief through interventions initiated by the therapist. Similar directions are common in the community music therapy literature. A few examples illustrate this. Baines (2000/2003) and Procter (2001, 2004) have described user-led mental health services which are explicitly non-medical. Stige (2002, 2003) has argued that community music therapy represents a reorientation of music therapy in the direction of democratic collaboration and citizen participation. Ansdell (2002, 2003) has critically examined assumptions in contemporary music therapy and has argued for more communal and context-inclusive approaches. Ruud (2010) has proposed that the emergence of community music therapy involves the development of a new language for music therapy, where words such as "action," "participation," "marginalized," and "health" substitute for words such as "behavior," "conflict," "handicap," and "illness."

The above arguments do not amount to a general anti-medical argument. The medical model has its own strengths and limitations which should be assessed in the contexts it is designed for. The main concern here is the expansion of the assumptions of the medical model to other areas and sectors. **Medicalization** is a process where an increasing range of human problems and processes are defined as medical, usually in terms of illness and disorder (Conrad, 2007, p. 49). Medicalized problems come under the jurisdiction of doctors and other health professions, for observation, diagnosis, treatment, and prevention. Medicalization is not a negative development in every respect. Many people applaud the possibility of developing effective treatment of an increasing number of disorders. Others are more concerned, for instance about the financial, personal, social, and cultural costs involved. The financial costs obviously include expenditure on professional salaries, medical equipment, medicines, and so forth. The personal, social, and cultural costs are more difficult to analyze but include the perceived problem of an expanding "therapy culture" (Furedi, 2004) that cultivates people's vulnerabilities rather than their strengths. People grow dependent upon professional help. The sociological literature on medicalization is therefore to a large extent a critical literature.

Medicalization is not a process driven or initiated by the medical profession only. The dynamics are complex and shaped by general processes of modernization (such as specialization and commercialization) and by processes specific to medicalization (linked to the interests and initiatives of the health professions, authorities, industries, and patient organizations). So, medicalization cannot be thought of in terms of "medical imperialism" only (Conrad, 2007). Several processes are interacting at various levels and all professions working with health need to consider their role in relation to medicalization. If community music therapy practices are based on assumptions informed by the medical model, such as a focus on diagnosis, pathology, and treatment, these practices contribute to the medicalization of community life. Community music therapy engages in processes and events close to the everyday life of participants and consequently requires a high level of self-critical awareness in relation to the risk of contributing to medicalization. We therefore argue that an explicit non-medical or extra-medical foundation should be the basis of community music therapy.[5]

CONCLUSION

The qualities and issues that we have discussed in this chapter show how community music therapy practices involve working musically with people in context. Community music therapy practices therefore involve issues that are simultaneously private and public. This typically requires transformation that includes both personal and social change. Practice issues in community music therapy may have individual components but can not be reduced to the level of the individual. Issues such as inclusion, social justice, and peace exemplify this. Community music therapy also increases the focus on health promotion work that includes positive and growth-oriented goals such as friendship, social networks, music creativity, spirituality, and aesthetic dimensions. The issues are not just framed as problems, but also as possibilities for the mobilization of resources, and they are not only framed at the individual or dyadic level, but also at group, institution, and community levels. Needs at various levels of analysis are seen in relation to each other; personal needs are defined in relation to groups, organizations, and localities. This demands that community problems are taken seriously. Problems include homelessness, crime and violence, prejudice and exclusion, poverty and unemployment, drug and alcohol abuse, and epidemics of illness and disease.

We have identified some practice issues by elaborating on qualities suggested by the acronym PREPARE. The *Participatory* quality of community music therapy touches upon issues such as inclusion and citizen participation, which are obviously significant to people who have experienced exclusion and marginalization. The *Resource-oriented* quality of community music therapy relates to issues such as welfare and equality, which again have obvious significance to people who have experienced deprivation, poverty, and inequality in relation to tangible and intangible resources. The *Ecological* quality of community music therapy touches upon issues such as relationships between systems and people's transitions from one system to another, both of which could be productive or destructive in various ways. The *Performative* quality illuminates how community music therapy practices primarily take proactive roles in relation to health and development, usually with a focus on the promotion of health and prevention of problems. The *Activist* quality of community music therapy relates to issues such as awareness and social change, often with a focus on "transformational activism" where personal change and social change are seen in relation to each other. The *Reflective* quality touches upon issues such as recognition and critique, where recognition is sought for at the level of the individual and at aggregated levels and where critique is considered central when comprehension is distorted by silencing or other mechanisms of repression. The *Ethics-driven* quality of community music therapy touches upon issues such as responsiveness and responsibility, which are expressed as collaborative efforts for dignity and a decent life, in response to challenging contingencies at a personal and communal level.

In the examples given, the highlighted quality in relation to the various issues has been used as a "handle" to lift up and illustrate challenges and possibilities. As we clarified in the introduction to the chapter, to deal with the complex situations and processes that each issue reflects requires an approach where the various qualities are seen in relation to each other. One consequence of not including the ecological, activist, and reflective qualities, for instance, could be the individualization of problems or even "blaming the victim" (Ryan, 1971). The issues related to the ethics-driven quality sum up a central point: To work with relationships between individuals and communities, helping people to mobilize resources and instigate social change, could be viewed as an acknowledgement of their right to a life with dignity and equality.

The issues discussed in this chapter reveal that community music therapy is a participatory, relational, and ecologically oriented practice. The phrase "from below, outwards, and around" captures these characteristics, which we contrasted to the medical model. If the practice of community music therapy is based on medical assumptions—with a focus on diagnosis, pathology, and treatment—it will add to the tendency towards medicalization in late modern societies. We have therefore argued that community music therapy must be based on non-medical or extra-medical foundations.

In Chapter 2 the term *multiple healing systems* was used in relation to the contemporary context of traditional practices. With reference to several African examples, we described how traditional healers, community initiatives, and medical services co-exist and supplement each other. The situation for community music therapy practices is perhaps similar. In contemporary societies there are multiple practices—based on a range of rituals and rationales—that promote health. If we acknowledge the dimension of health promotion and the importance of people's active participation, we can speak of multiple health action systems or health action fields (Stige, 2003, p. 208). In other words; in contemporary societies there are *multiple health action systems* where the services of the health sector and a range of other health promoting initiatives—including community music therapy—co-exist and supplement each other (see also Chapter 10).

KEY TERMS, DISCUSSION TOPICS, AND NOTES

Key Terms

Key terms in order of appearance:

PREPARE
Inclusion
Citizen participation
Welfare
Equality
Ecological relationships
Ecological transitions
Ripple effects
Promotion of health
Prevention of problems
Identity
Awareness
Social change
Recognition
Critique
Responsiveness
Responsibility
From below, outwards, and around
Medical model
Medicalization
Multiple health action systems

Discussion Topics

The following critical thinking questions could be discussed in class or in groups. They could also be used by the individual for critical reflection on topics discussed in the chapter. Extra resources can be found on the website of the book.

1. It has been argued in this chapter that community music therapy is about working with the relationships between people and their communities. Present some examples of how and why it could be fruitful for the music therapist to work with an individual or group *and* a broader community of some sort.
2. Issues addressed in community music therapy usually go beyond the amelioration of problems to encompass the mobilization of resources. Resources may exist at the individual as well as at the interpersonal and institutional levels. Discuss how the resource-oriented quality can be linked to other qualities of community music therapy practice, such as the ecological, activist, and reflective qualities.
3. Music therapists who have worked with issues such as social justice and conflict transformation have argued that there is a need to prepare music therapy students for this kind of work. Discuss how your own training has prepared you for these issues. What competencies would be essential for music therapists to develop?

Notes

1   These issues are discussed in more detail in Chapters 4 and 5.
2   This dynamic of inward–outward movement in reflection echoes Freire's (1970/2000) insight that social critique requires self-critique and vice versa.
3   Mutual care, as distributed responsiveness and responsibility, could be seen as a process of community development. Responsiveness and responsibility are expressed, then, as collaborative efforts for human rights, in response to challenging contingencies at a personal and communal level. This theme will be explored in the next chapter on values in community music therapy.
4   The medical model has been a significant influence on other health care professions. In a critical review of psychotherapy research, Wampold (2001) claimed that the prevailing traditions of psychotherapy have been informed by assumptions congruent with the medical model. His review of the research suggested that a more holistic and contextual understanding of psychotherapy is more adequate.
5   Community music therapy can be extra-medical; there are many examples in the literature illustrating how community music therapy practices collaborate with or grow out of medical contexts (Aasgaard, 2002, 2004; Maratos, 2004; Wood, Verney & Atkinson, 2004; Helle-Valle, 2011).

Chapter 7

Values

After studying Chapter 7, you will be able to discuss questions such as:

- What are the similarities and differences between attitudes and values?
- What is the relationship between human needs and human rights?
- Could community music therapy be developed as rights-based practice?
- Is there a set of values that can be articulated as a basis for community music therapy practice?
- How can conflicting values be dealt with?

ATTITUDES AND VALUES IN PRACTICE

IN the previous chapter we concluded that a non-medical or extra-medical foundation is necessary for community music therapy; practices involve issues that are simultaneously private and public and which typically require transformation that includes both personal and social change. One implication is that community music therapy involves working with **attitudes** and assumptions in order to increase people's prospects for social participation. Ruud (1980, 1998) presented a similar argument, when he linked music therapy to efforts for increased possibilities for action. Such possibilities are not solely defined by the individual's preferences and performances but by the relationships between individual and community, including the material, psychological, and socio-cultural forces that keep some people in marginalized roles.

> In traditional medical thinking, therapy is connected to some kind of disease or illness, often related, in Western medicine, to our biology. In addition, there is also a tendency in our culture to regard disease as something that strikes the individual independent of society and culture. . . .

Because music therapists work with a broad range of life problems and handicaps, this way of thinking about therapy is not adequate, of course, in many instances. Sometimes we work with clients whose problems may be deeply interwoven with the material and economic structure of society, or whose problems are shaped more by their own attitudes and reflections, as well as by the attitudes of others, rather than by their individual or objective biological constitution.

(Ruud, 1998, p. 51)

This broader way of thinking about problems and possibilities is typical in community music therapy, most explicitly perhaps in practices oriented towards inclusion and citizen participation. Several authors describe practices that are geared towards challenging established views and attitudes, in the service of reducing social and cultural barriers to participation (Kleive & Stige, 1988; Bowers, 1998; Maratos, 2004; Curtis & Mercado, 2004; Krüger, 2007; Pavlicevic, 2010b).

Attitudes and **values** are central rather than peripheral elements in community music therapy practice. This chapter seeks to outline some principal values for community music therapy. A first step in this direction must be to clarify the relationship between attitudes and values. A classic text in social psychology compares and distinguishes the two in the following way:

While it has been traditional to treat attitudes and values as distinctive, they do share certain common qualities. They both are motivational–perceptual states which define what an individual *expects* and *desires,* and they therefore affect behavior. They both are acquired from contact with others.

Attitudes differ from values in several ways. An *attitude* refers to a set of beliefs about a given object or situation; a *value* represents an end-state or goal. A value goes beyond the specific things and conditions to a long-range concern with standards of conduct and the ends to be served. Examples of values are truth, freedom, cleanliness, and justice. Furthermore, individuals hold many more attitudes than values. As Rokeach (1968) has noted, we may have thousands of attitudes, but only dozens of values.

(Hollander, 1976, pp. 138–139)

Values reflect one's judgments or beliefs about what is important and valuable in life. Rokeach (1968) made an influential distinction between terminal and instrumental values. Terminal values refer to the end-states mentioned by Hollander; goals that are personally or socially worth striving for. These vary among cultures. Working in an American context, Rokeach studied terminal values such as friendship, self-respect, happiness, equality, freedom, pleasure, social recognition, wisdom, family security, a sense of accomplishment, a world at peace, and a comfortable life. Instrumental values refer to preferable modes of behavior. Rokeach's examples include values such as cheerfulness, ambition, love, self-control, courage, honesty, imagination, independence, broad-mindedness, helpfulness, responsibility, and forgiveness.

According to Rokeach (1968), beliefs, attitudes, and values are all parts of a functionally integrated cognitive system, so that change in any part of the system will affect other parts, and may culminate in behavioral change (p. ix). This is so even though we at times experience conspicuous gaps between actions and expressed values:

> We cannot safely underrate any value merely because it seems characterized by lip-service, or more honored in the breach than in the observance, or is advocated primarily by hypocrites. For all these activities serve to maintain the value as valid currency or acknowledged benchmark—whereupon it can be used at any time to praise or blame, to honor or bring into disrepute. We must never lose sight of the fact that values continually are used as weapons in social struggles.
>
> (Williams, 1979, p. 29)

Unlike attitudes, values can be analyzed at all ecological levels. A cultural community can be seen to possess certain values (rather than attitudes) and this value system has a significant effect on the individual's judgments and actions. At the same time, differences in value systems also exist within and between groups. Values are not nice ideas that everybody subscribes to; they are the tools people use when negotiating goals and priorities. Values illuminate and activate intersections between individual and community and between various practices in a society. Articulations of a values-base for community music therapy must therefore incorporate reflections on the relationships between the various agents of a practice (Stige, 2003).

The descriptive phrase "from below, outwards, and around" was used in the previous chapter to summarize qualities of community music therapy practice. Community music therapy is driven by broader questions on the values of empowerment rather than by specific questions on the ingredients of treatment. The contrast between the two ways of thinking can playfully be illuminated by comparing what has been established in the psychotherapy literature as "Paul's question" with what we could call "Knut's question." Paul, a psychotherapy researcher, articulated his question in 1969 to address how treatment can be purposefully tailored: "What treatment, by whom, is most effective for this individual with that specific problem, under which set of circumstances, and how does it come about?" (Paul, 1969, cited in Wampold, 2001, p. 21). Some 14 years later, Knut, a member of a group of musicians with intellectual disabilities, asked a very different question: "May we too play in the [marching] band?" (Knut as cited in Stige, 2003, p. 4, see also Box 2.5). Paul's question was raised within the context of specialized practice. Knut's question was raised within the context of a participatory process. It emerged from a desire to be part of a community. It addressed attitudes in the community and values related to inclusion and citizen participation. Basically, Knut asked a question about his rights as a human being.

HUMAN NEEDS AND HUMAN RIGHTS

In the previous chapter, human needs were described in terms that linked private troubles with public concerns. Community music therapy is informed by awareness of the value of human connectedness rather than by assessment of individual pathology. The argument that we will develop is that human needs can be fruitfully examined in light of human rights.

People in need usually experience challenges to their dignity; their freedom to have a voice is often threatened, and access to resources such as education, health services, and cultural participation is frequently hindered. In short, the issues that request involvement are situations where human rights are violated or not realized. It is also true that many of the contexts in which music therapists work are contexts of rights restrictions. Hospitals and prisons exemplify institutions where human rights restrictions are considered legitimate by the authorities. Patients and inmates do not have the opportunity to exercise basic freedoms and they are sometimes denied cultural and social rights, such as the right to education. We often think of these rights restrictions as necessary, but community music therapy practices may evolve in these milieus because restrictions are disputed or because they are acknowledged as problematic and problem-producing. Other community music therapy practices address injustice and various human rights violations in disadvantaged communities. In this light, a key value underpinning community music therapy practice is the realization of human rights.

FIGURE 7.1 | That's right! A Children's Welfare Musical, Bergen, Norway.
Photo: Astrid Merete Nordhaug.

Our argument is that community music therapy practice evolves in the intersection of human rights challenges and social–musical possibilities. This description of practice involves defining and approaching problems as residing in the relationships between individuals and communities instead of localizing them as individual pathology. To define human needs in terms of human rights contributes to the development of a relational and contextual foundation for community music therapy. There are of course limitations in adopting this perspective as in adopting any other perspective. But it offers another angle to the work, with increased focus on the transformations that the mobilization of resources through musical collaboration in context can instigate.

Some might counter that human rights is too grand a vision and too heavy a burden for a small profession. Typical human rights professions include lawyers and politicians, and characteristic human rights instruments are declarations and conventions. So when did the guitar become a human rights instrument and music therapy a human rights profession? Our argument is that community music therapy can take action and contribute as **rights-based practice** and that the idea that human rights belong to a higher sphere than collaborative music-making is not well grounded. The efforts of lawyers and politicians working for human rights are highly valuable but limited. Many of the social and cultural rights, for instance, cannot be achieved by laws and regulations only. They must be actively provided for. It is therefore important that a range of professions see their obligations in relation to the human rights (Centre for Human Rights, 1994).

Traditionally, fundamental freedoms (civil and political rights) have dominated public discourse on human rights. These rights need protection by law, which makes the legal profession essential. As economic, social, cultural, and environmental rights win recognition, professions that can contribute to the active realization of positive rights grow increasingly important (Galtung, 1994). The social work profession is one of these professions (Ife, 2008). Community music therapy can also make a significant contribution, not least in relation to social and cultural rights.

While the idea of rights-based practice may appear somewhat overwhelming at first, it would be highly problematic to avoid the integration of a human rights perspective in community music therapy practice. Far too often this mounts to uncritical support of the status quo concerning oppression of vulnerable groups. In order to integrate a rights-based perspective in community music therapy, we must move beyond thinking of human rights as part of abstract treatises only and embrace them as part of our everyday lives:

'Doing' human rights traverses the mundane and dramatic. It is close to home, as well as in faraway places. It requires creativity and courage. But it is not always serious and difficult—human rights work is often fun, sometimes hilarious, and time and again involves forging the most extraordinary friendships.

(Ball & Gready, 2007, pp. 8–9)

The proposal that community music therapy could be understood as human rights practice has several precursors. If we revisit Chapter 2, we will see that a focus on human rights is integrated in the systemic and sociocultural turn and the expansion of agendas that started to emerge in music therapy in the 1980s. In Ruud's (1980, 1992b) work we find references to human rights, for instance in his discussion of the right to musical and cultural participation. Kleive and Stige (1988) focused on the social and cultural rights of people with disabilities. Kenny (1982, 1988, 1989) embraced music and the arts in work for the rights of indigenous people. Boxill (1988, 1997a) stressed music therapy's responsibility in relation to human rights issues such as peace and justice.

A focus on human rights is implicit in much of the contemporary literature of community music therapy. Ansdell (2002, 2004, 2010a, 2010b) and Pavlicevic (2004, 2010a, 2010b) stress the centrality of themes such as equality, collaboration, and social change in community music therapy. In a discussion of how community music therapy is informed by values such as justice and equity, Stige (2003) advocated that practice must include a focus on social change. Procter's (2001) and Rolvsjord's (2004) discussion of empowerment is related to human rights issues such as equality and dignity, as is Ruud's (2010, 2011) focus on recognition at societal levels, and O'Grady and McFerran's (2006) discussion of community music therapy in relation to feminism and civil rights. Other contributions which have illuminated the relevance of human rights for community music therapy include Baines's (2000/2003) and Solli's (2010) work on consumer advocacy and recovery, Dunn's (2008) and Vaillancourt's (2009) discussion of social justice and peace, and Krüger's (forthcoming) linking of his work to the UN Convention on the Rights of the Child.

In various situations people make claims for rights that cannot be justified on the grounds of human rights, so the above argument requests a clarification of the criteria that must be met for **claims based in human rights**. In a discussion of social work as rights-based practice, Jim Ife proposes a list of criteria that is also relevant in the context of community music therapy:

- Realisation of the claimed right is necessary for a person or group to be able to achieve their full humanity, in common with others.
- The claimed right is seen *either* as applying to all of humanity, and is something that the person or group claiming the right wishes to apply to all people anywhere, *or* as applying to people from specific disadvantaged or marginalized groups for whom realisation of that right is essential to their achieving their full human potential.
- There is substantial universal consensus on the legitimacy of the claimed right; it cannot be called a 'human right' unless there is widespread support for it across cultural and other divides.
- It is possible for the claimed right to be effectively realised for all legitimate claimants. This excludes rights to things that are limited in supply, for example the right to housing with a panoramic view, the right to own a TV channel, or the right to 'own' large tracts of land.
- The claimed right does not contradict other human rights. This would disallow as human rights the 'right' to bear arms, the 'right' to hold other people in slavery, a man's 'right' to beat his wife and children, the 'right' to excessive profits resulting in poverty for others, and so on (Ife, 2008, p. 14).

Rights do not happen; they are achieved because people are ready to take respons-ibility and build structures and practices that support the rights of every human being, not just the powerful and privileged; in other words human rights rather than some humans' rights (Ishay, 2004). This is perhaps especially clear in relation to the fourth point above: Realization of rights requires resources and it is necessary to discriminate between claims that are legitimate as human rights claims and claims that are not attainable for everybody. In most societies even legitimate claims, such as the right to decent education and health care, are challenged for many people because of an uneven distribution of resources. This demonstrates that human rights do not address the rights of individuals only; they represent a call for social justice and solidarity.

CONTESTED AND TESTED VALUES

The Universal Declaration of Human Rights was passed by the UN General Assembly in 1948. As Ife (2008) explains, it represents a remarkable global consensus on human rights, even though its articles have not universally been adopted in practice. In examining the declaration, it is common to talk of several "generations" of human rights. The first generation is often labeled **civil and political rights**. These include the right to citizenship and equality before the law, the right to free assembly, the right to freedom of religion, the right to self-expression, the right to vote, and the right to free participation in the society. The second generation is often called **economic, social, and cultural rights**. These include the right to employment and an adequate wage, the right to housing and sufficient food and clothing, the right to education and health care, the right to social security, the right to recreation and leisure, and the right to be treated with dignity in old age.

The first generation of rights focuses on individual liberty. The initial 22 articles of the Universal Declaration of Human Rights focus mainly on this type of rights. In the present articulation, central intellectual origins could be traced back to the Enlightenment of the eighteenth century. The second generation of rights focuses on welfare. In the Universal Declaration, articles 23 (starting with "Everyone has the right to work . . .") to 29 (starting with "Everyone has duties to the community . . .") focus on these rights. Origins of this generation include nineteenth- and twentieth-century social democracy and socialism, also the philosophies of care and justice implied in most major religions and cultural traditions. The rights of the second generation are sometimes called positive rights, because they involve an active role for the public in the provision of adequate conditions and services for everyone. The first generation of rights requires protection by law. These rights are therefore sometimes called negative rights; the role of the state is to guarantee the legal mechanisms that protect them from being violated. The two categories of rights are reflected in the UN's approach to human rights work through the two international covenants adopted by the UN General Assembly in 1966 (in force from 1976): The International Covenant of Civil and Political Rights and The International Covenant of Economic, Social and Cultural Rights (Centre for Human Rights, 1994).

There is now talk of a third generation of human rights. In the Universal Declaration of Human Rights there are the seeds of this generation, but only in the last two or three decades of the twentieth century did a strong international discourse on these rights emerge. Unlike the two other generations they do not have a corresponding UN covenant.

The articulation of these rights developed as a response to a critique of UN's discourse on human rights, suggesting that it had been based on a Western focus on the individual and would therefore be of somewhat less relevance to cultures, such as many Asian cultures, with more collective norms. A third generation of collective or **solidarity rights** was then proposed, such as the right to live in a peaceful society. Various **environmental rights**, such as the rights to unpolluted air, clean water, and access to nature also belong to the third generation of rights.[1]

The articulation of the second and third generation of human rights suggests that a discursive approach to human rights is necessary. The political disputes around rights that are expensive—such as decent health services to all—and that challenge asymmetries in power and privilege demonstrate this clearly. The Universal Declaration of Human Rights and other UN treaties are important contributions to the international discourse on human rights but should be examined critically and discussed in relation to real world challenges in various contexts (Ife, 2008). This illustrates that the (relative) consensus that has been established on the legitimacy of human rights does not result in a list of unproblematic entitlements. Human rights reflect values that have been contested in debates and tested in practice. No simple recipes for rights-based practice are available. Such practice will always require negotiation and there will probably never be full agreement about the interpretation and implementation of rights.

The initial responses to Knut's question about playing in the marching band (see above) exemplify this. His question was voiced at a time where policies of cultural inclusion had been established in Norway but with a sizeable gap between principles and practice. At first, very few members of the local marching band had much support to offer. This was a prestigious ensemble in the rural town where Knut lived and his question challenged values of both convention and perfection. To include people with intellectual disabilities in the marching band was against customary practice and the idea instigated worries about what would happen to the quality of the marching band's music. The situation needed to be negotiated over a period of almost three years. As Knut's group went public in musical performances that highlighted his dreams and illuminated the group's potential, attitudes in the marching band as well as in the broader community gradually changed. It was possible to find a compromise between values. The legitimacy of Knut's claim for the right to cultural participation was acknowledged, while the marching band's concerns about conventional musical quality led to a flexible approach of time-limited collaborative projects concluded by public performances. Knut never became a permanent member of the marching band but his group was still welcomed and included in a new way in the local community (Kleive & Stige, 1988; Stige, 2002, pp. 113–134).

Community music therapy as a rights-based practice involves an acknowledgement of universal challenges in local contexts. In a community there might be resistance to change and controversy about priorities, since values are disputed, almost by definition. The idea of human rights suggests that injustice and repressive discourses and practices should be challenged. This claim leads to the conclusion that the central **values that underpin the human rights** have universal relevance, even though they are disputed and interpreted differently in various contexts. In our appraisal, the first article of The

Universal Declaration of Human Rights functions as a précis that reveals the most relevant values:

> All human beings are born free and equal in dignity and rights. They are endowed with reason and conscience and should act towards one another in a spirit of brotherhood.
> (Universal Declaration of Human Rights, United Nations, 1948)

Four values that are central to the Universal Declaration of Human Rights can be recognized in this article. We could say that the perhaps contrasting values of **freedom** and **equality** are framed by the values of **respect** and **solidarity**. In the following we will explore how these values have been articulated in relation to community music therapy practice. Each one of these four values is multifaceted. The purpose here is not to explicate all of the complexities but to illuminate dimensions and dilemmas that can instigate reflections on the role of these values in community music therapy.

FREEDOM

We associate freedom with openness, inventiveness, and nonconformity as well as with liberty, autonomy, and independence. The idea of freedom can be expressed in negative and positive terms, as *freedom from* (lack of restrictions and regulations) and as *freedom to* (access to choice and opportunity). It is a multifaceted notion that might be integrated in a range of contrasting worldviews.

John Stuart Mill's (1859/2003) *On Liberty* is a classic text on human freedom. Mill was interested in civil and social liberty and consequently in the nature and limits of the power that can legitimately be exercised by society over the individual. Main chapters in his work focused on the liberty of thought and discussion, on individuality as an element of wellbeing, and on the limits to the authority of society. Mill's work attempts to define and defend the appropriate region for human liberty. He divides this region into three domains which we could call consciousness and communication, occupation, and collaboration. The first domain involves freedom of opinion and sentiment on absolutely any subject, including the right to express these thoughts and feelings. The second domain involves liberty of tastes and pursuits. Other people might find our activities and preferences foolish, perverse, or wrong, but Mill argues that if we do not harm others this does not give them a right to limit our freedom. The third domain involves the liberty of combination of individuals; the freedom to unite for any purpose, again so long as we do not harm others.

> No society in which these liberties are not, on the whole, respected, is free, whatever may be its form of government; and none is completely free in which they do not exist absolute and unqualified. The only freedom which deserves the name, is that of pursuing our own good in our own way, so long as we do not attempt to deprive others of theirs, or impede their efforts to obtain it.
> (Mill, 1859/2003, p. 83)

FIGURE 7.2 | Freedom to move. Bergen Red Cross Nursing Home, Bergen, Norway. Photo: Thor Brødreskift.

Continuing this argument, Mill suggests that each person is "the proper guardian of his (*sic*) own health, whether bodily, or mental, or spiritual." His essay is very clear in its critique of tyranny and oppression but when it comes to the theme of human relatedness it has lent itself to various interpretations (within conservative, liberal, and radical politics, for instance). In the context of community music therapy, an interpretation stressing an individualistic framework would have limited bearing. Reflections on human freedom in the context of the individual–communal continuum invite a range of questions. What is the link between independence and interdependence? How could agency and control be combined with relationships and sensitivity to others? The existing community music therapy literature suggests that we can think of autonomy as a relational accomplishment.[2]

Freedom as openness and inventiveness is often hindered by subscription to conventions and interpersonal pressures for conformity. To reclaim freedom of consciousness and communication is a relational accomplishment that music therapy is well positioned to promote, as Procter (2004) demonstrates in a vignette describing his work with Josie, a client who at first was very dismissive of her own playing. This extinguished any possibility for playful interaction, but over time this gradually changed:

As I listen back each week to the recordings of our sessions, I note the development of her spontaneity, her expressiveness, her sheer reveling in music-making. One day, after a lively and protracted improvisation in which both of us move freely between many instruments and she also sings, she spontaneously exclaims, 'Wow, that was amazing!' This feels like a real change: Josie is beginning to be able to take pleasure in our music-making. This pleasure encourages greater freedom, which in turn leads to greater pleasure. The role of music in Josie's life, formerly a force for failure, seems to be changing and allowing her to be more fully herself. She is taking pleasure in being herself, and in being herself with me.

(Procter, 2004, pp. 223–224)

This vignette describes work in one-to-one sessions, but Procter (2004) thinks of the work as related to community music therapy, since the process allowed Josie to rediscover a healthy relationship with music in ways that enabled her to "perform herself" more fully and share with others.

The community music therapy literature includes several examples of practices that stress the participants' freedom to choose whether or not to participate, for instance through open in-and-out policy (Baines, 2000/2003; Warner, 2005). A variant of this is to highlight the participants' freedom to join in or go across within group sessions. Stige's (2010a) study of various strategies of participation and the rituals that allow for participatory spaciousness and tolerance exemplifies this (see Box 7.1).

In Japanese community music therapy, a group of authors have discussed freedom in relation to music, with a specific focus on the affordances of free improvisation (Wakao, 2002) and new musical forms (Numata, 2009). A critical perspective is added by Miyake (2008), who warns against the risk that music therapy might operate as a "normalizing discipline," socializing clients to cultural conformity in the name of community participation.

Freedom involves complex processes at several levels. Even when restrictions are substantial, as when someone is in prison, islands of freedom might emerge and allow for hope and inspiration (Tuastad & Finsås, 2008; O'Grady, 2009; Tuastad & O'Grady, forthcoming). The critical and liberating potential of community music therapy is explored by authors who describe processes where participants go public with performances that challenge established views and attitudes, see e.g. (Kleive & Stige, 1988; Maratos, 2004; Krüger, 2007, Pavlicevic, 2010b).

Box 7.1 | ACTION, SOCIAL SPACE, AND FREEDOM OF EXPRESSION

Norwegian music therapist Brynjulf Stige (2010a) studied a Cultural Festival for people with intellectual disabilities in order to explore how participants chose to participate in this context. The choice of focus was informed by the values of the Non-Governmental Organization (NGO) organizing the festival, which stressed that it should be about participation and respect for every participant so that the idea of perfection would not exclude anybody.

Box 7.1 |

The vision of the festival as an inclusive space inspired Stige to investigate what freedom the participants would have in the various activities and situations. He related this to a previous literature review that revealed that the notion of participation had been given little conceptual consideration in the music therapy literature. The focus has often been on participation as "joining in" (taking part in a pre-defined activity). Behaving in ways adjusted to a context is valuable in many ways but it is a very limited notion of participation. Joining in might be unachievable or unacceptable for some individuals, due to discrepancies in skills or interests or values (Stige, 2006).

In the case study of the festival, Stige (2010a) noted that unpredicted and discrepant acts were typical. Many of the events were characterized by some "breaking of rules" and "diversification of action." Sometimes there were also tendencies towards "subversive action" where participants would break out from what was going on and lead in different directions from those that the music therapists had proposed. A description of participation in this festival would need to account for these *participatory diversifications,* Stige argued, adding that it would not be possible to understand this without a concept of *conventional participation.* Human interaction is always regulated by some understanding of what is customary, even though this varies from context to context.

> As suggested above, the Cultural Festival is a context where participation is diversified. Unusual and unpredictable contributions are quite common. But conventional participation is not rare in this context either, as when participants try to play the basic beat on a drum or decide to take up the microphone to sing a song. And the fact that participation may be conventional does not mean that it is flat or without engagement or enthusiasm. Participants may well internalize the values and rules of the situation and be expressive through use of the involved conventions (Stige, 2010a, pp. 129–130).

The participants explored different roles and styles of self-presentation, ranging from conventional participation to various diversifications. Based on participant observation, video analysis, and consultation with relevant literature, Stige developed a description of five different styles of self-presentation in the context of this festival: *Non-participation* (not being there), *Silent participation* (being there but not joining in), *Conventional participation* (joining in but not standing out), *Adventurous participation* (standing out but not going across), and *Eccentric participation* (going across). Stige clarified that the five forms of participation were related in multiple ways:

> Non-participation, for instance, may gradually be transformed into silent participation which again may turn into conventional participation. Elaborated conventional participation at some point becomes adventurous, and if escalated further may turn into eccentric participation. The process is not necessarily linear, however. As we have seen, silent participation may at times turn into say adventurous participation. And eccentric participation, at the extreme, may turn into non-participation. Together the forms of participation represent a repertoire of possibilities. . . Stige, 2010a, p. 132).

A repertoire of possibilities concerning participation can be considered a form of *freedom,* expressed as actions in an inclusive and tolerant social space.

EQUALITY

Equality is a relationship between two or more people or groups of people. It can be understood as sameness and similarity but also as fairness and justice, which is more important in the context of this discussion. There are various forms and dimensions of equality to take into consideration. Working in the tradition of equality studies, Baker and associates (2004) have developed a framework that describes three notions of equality; basic equality, liberal egalitarianism, and equality of condition.

Basic equality is the notion that all humans have equal worth and importance. This is the cornerstone of all egalitarian thinking:

> The minimum standards involved in the idea of basic equality are far from trivial. They include prohibitions against inhuman and degrading treatment, protection against blatant violence and at least some commitment to satisfying people's most basic needs. . . . In a world in which rape, torture and other crimes against humanity are a daily occurrence, and in which millions of people die every year from want of the most basic necessities, the idea of basic equality remains a powerful force for action and for change.
>
> (Baker et al., 2004, p. 23)

Liberal egalitarianism is a broad family of views that go beyond basic equality. In relation to distribution of resources, for instance, the liberal egalitarian view involves an anti-poverty focus, not just the view that subsistence needs should be met. The basic assumption is nevertheless that inequalities are inevitable. The idea of equality in this tradition means to strengthen the minimum to which everyone is entitled and to regulate the competition for advantage according to the principle of equality of opportunity (Baker et al., 2004, p. 25).

Equality of condition is a more ambitious approach based in the assumption that inequalities could be eliminated or at least substantially reduced. Baker and associates (2004) argue that the key to this view is the recognition of inequalities as rooted in social structures that could be changed deliberately. These social structures include systems of oppression. Like liberal egalitarianism, equality of condition is a broad family of views. Various systems of oppression have thus been identified, with capitalism, patriarchy, and racism as three of the most established candidates. Marginalization of various groups, such as disabled people, can also be examined in this light.

This emphasis on social structures in explaining inequality affects the way equality of condition should be understood. In contrast to the tendency of liberal egalitarians to focus on the rights and advantages of individuals, equality of condition also pays attention to the rights and advantages of groups. In contrast to liberal egalitarians' tendency to concentrate on how things are distributed, equality of condition pays more attention to how people are related, particularly through power relations. In contrast to the tendency of liberal egalitarians to treat individuals as responsible for their successes and failures, equality of condition emphasizes the influence of social factors on people's choices and actions (Baker et al., 2004, p. 33).

In the field of community psychology, Dalton, Elias, and Wandersman (2007, pp. 60–61) have elaborated on the notion of equality by referring to the work of William Ryan. They make a distinction which is similar to the one between liberal egalitarianism and equality of condition, namely the distinction between *fair play* and *fair share*. In the fair play notion of equality, the basic metaphor is that of a race. There will be winners and losers but this is accepted if rules of fairness in competition can be assured. In the fair share notion of equality, the basic metaphor is that of a family or community where people collaborate and share in order to take care of its members. Supporters of fair share tend to suggest that the idea of fairness in competition is often an illusion. Inequalities due to class, ethnicity, gender, and so on are reproduced over generations, so it is hard to imagine that people begin at the same starting line. In order to achieve fair share it might be necessary to compensate for limitations and discrimination of individuals and groups.

Chapters 3 to 5 demonstrated that inequalities in health and welfare, social support, and access to music are real challenges that are central to community music therapy. This was also demonstrated by the issues discussed in Chapter 6. There is therefore no need to go into more detail here, but some illustrative examples from the literature can be mentioned. Inequalities in health and welfare have been addressed by music therapists working in countries where disparities are blatant, such as South Africa (Pavlicevic, 2004;

FIGURE 7.3 | Group work. Music education in a Palestinian refugee camp in Lebanon.
Photo: Even Ruud.

Oosthuizen, 2006) and Brazil (Barcellos, 2005; Chagas, 2007). They have also been addressed by music therapists working in more affluent countries with somewhat less grave inequalities generally but with substantial challenges in relation to marginalized groups (Tuastad & Finsås, 2008; O'Grady, 2009). Inequalities of social support have been addressed in Procter's (2004, 2006) work on social–musical capital and in Krüger's (2004, 2007) work on supportive trajectories of community participation. Inequalities in access to music have been addressed in various projects supporting disabled people's right to cultural participation (Kleive & Stige, 1988; Curtis & Mercado, 2004) and in practices in hospitals and other restrictive settings where the right to music has often been neglected (Aasgaard, 2002; Maratos, 2004). Addressing inequality amounts to active support of social justice, which Box 7.2 exemplifies.

Box 7.2 | MENTORING FOR SOCIAL JUSTICE AND PEACE

Canadian music therapist Guylaine Vaillancourt (2009) investigated possibilities for mentoring apprentice music therapists for social justice and peace through community music therapy. Five apprentice music therapists came together for a series of five co-researchers' group experiences, using an approach informed by arts-based research and participatory action research.

The apprentice music therapists' appraisal of community music therapy included statements such as: "It is a coming together for a cause," "It creates solidarity," "It makes people proud," "It raises social consciousness," "It is creativity, freedom, and democracy" (Vaillancourt, 2009, p. 191). In relation to social justice and peace, the co-researchers were concerned about the risk of expressing idealistic and utopian visions. They considered the two notions to be linked and claimed that social justice contributes to peace. They also considered social justice to be extremely hard to achieve and even conceive, but several of the co-researchers nevertheless explored possibilities for working with social justice and peace in their own practice. As apprentice music therapists they argued that their main possibilities for action would be at the local level, such as when working in a small town school with discord and tension between students:

> When I get the children in their respective classes, it is the 'little choir train.' We go from class to class and . . . we end up with 20 children going to the same room. You know that in their regular classes they are no more than 10 because of their behavior problems. But when they come with me, they know very well that the goal of the choir is not to have inappropriate behaviors . . . They know this is a place of respect and right there it creates a 'bubble of peace' (co-researcher Anna, in Vaillancourt, 2009, p. 154).

Vaillancourt (2009) argues for the relevance of a multilayered concept of peace, ranging from personal, group, and community levels to national and international levels. In contexts such as schools, where bullying and conflicts between children often create trouble, the co-researchers stressed the importance of working with respect and trust as

> **Box 7.2** |
>
> conditions for the development of a culture of peace. They also proposed that music therapists might take on roles as mentors for the children and as leaders in the development of a culture of peace. With support and encouragement, some of the children might also develop into "little mentors" and "little leaders," which Vaillancourt relates to the positive ripple effect that mentoring for social justice and peace might instigate.

RESPECT

Like equality, respect is a relationship. In our everyday lives we might develop reverence for people who live up to standards we have been taught to regard highly. Some people, then, lose some of our evaluative respect because of their behavior or performance. If we take a different perspective, we may think that all people are worthy of respect in their capacity as human beings (Dillon, 2010). This notion of respect, focusing on the intrinsic and incomparable worth of each person, can be thought of as a meta-value, namely as the honoring of the dignity and the human rights of the other.[3]

There is more than one dimension of respect to consider, such as self-respect, respect for the other, and mutual respect. It is also a common assumption that self-respect and mutual respect are deeply connected (Dillon, 2010). Mutual respect—which opens up for closeness and friendship—is especially pertinent for community music therapy. Acknowledgement is a typical expression of respect for the other. Some cultures stress respect as awe and admiration. The degree to which these expressions are compatible with mutual respect and self-respect vary and should be open for critical examination.

There is a strong tradition within music therapy to work with musical and interpersonal relationships in ways that nurture self-respect and mutual respect. This attitude has for instance been linked to the notion of *personhood,* "the idea that each of us is unique and deserving of recognition, respect and trust in relationships with others" (Procter, 2001). Dorit Amir refers to the Israeli music therapist Michal Zilbermintz's description of community music therapy performances in a multicultural setting, and illuminates the relationship between mutual respect and self-respect:

> [T]he end-of-year show has definite benefits for all of the people involved. The show brings out the students' (clients') inner, sometimes hidden creativity and talent. Performing in front of an audience connects them to a 'healthy place' within. Suddenly, staff and parents see them differently, more like regular human beings. The students gain self-respect, they have increased respect for their friends and receive respect from others.
>
> (Amir, 2004, p. 263)

It is easy to assume that the audience in the kinds of public performances that may emerge in community music therapy practice will be respectful of the performers' capabilities and effort. However, this is not an expectation that should be taken for granted. The ability and willingness of the audience to show respect for the participants in a performance is critical to its success (Baines, 2000/2003; Turry, 2005; McFerran, 2010). It is crucial to select and educate audiences carefully and to respect audience members as participants whose needs are also worthy of consideration.

In the community music therapy literature, several qualifications concerning respect have been proposed, such as the qualification that respect must be performed and that it includes not only persons but culture and community also. With reference to Sennett's (2004) work, Ansdell (2005b, 2010a) has explored the assumption that respect includes but goes beyond feeling and intention; it must also be enacted (see Box 7.1). Several music therapists have proposed the extension of respect to include culture and community (Brown, 2001/2002; Stige & Kenny, 2002; Chase, 2003; Stige, 2004b; Shapiro, 2005). Attempts at showing empathy and respect could fail if they are not culturally informed,

FIGURE 7.4 | Listening and creating: A multi-cultural resource-oriented music therapy group in Berlin, Germany.

Photo: Teresa Samulewicz.

since respect has different forms of expression and meaning in different cultures. This means that it is often vital to be able to work with the musical values and idioms that are significant for the participants (MacDonald & Viega, 2011).

Respect can therefore be thought of as dialogue informed by inter-cultural sensitivity and reflexivity. Pavlicevic exemplifies this in a study of a South African music therapist working in a neighborhood in Eersterust close to Pretoria. The music therapist's attempts at learning culture and assigning respect to the knowledge of "folk-in-the-street" are described in the following way:

> [S]he decides to attend the local arts festival over a weekend . . . in order to get a direct experience of the musical events, to listen to what people in the street say about the various musical performances. She chats with folk wherever she is. Their opinions and descriptions, she hopes, will educate her. From this experience she describes gaining a sense of local music *in situ*, learning about local opinions (of which there are plenty), local attitudes and norms. It is her engagement within this social event that affords her a direct, experience-based "knowing" of what musicing goes on where and how and with whom . . . They are the experts in Eersterust's musical happenings, and she is there to learn from them.
>
> (Pavlicevic, 2010b, pp. 228–229)

To respect involves recognition of the other, with social and cultural implications. Ruud (2010) builds on Axel Honneth's (2003) "philosophy of recognition" when he elaborates on this point. Ruud argues that we must broaden our understanding of recognition and operate not only at an interpersonal level but also at a societal level. Recognition is not only fundamental to our primary relationships but can be included in broader, critical perspectives where social inclusion and human rights play an important role (Ruud, 2010, p. 35).

Box 7.3 | MUSICAL MINDS AND MUTUAL RESPECT

English music therapist Gary Ansdell (2005b, 2010b) argues that respect must be performed; you cannot respect without showing it. With reference to Richard Sennett, Ansdell reflects on how performing arts reveal the collaborative elements of expressing respect:

> Where inequality (of health, money, opportunity) is unavoidable, how can people retain their self-respect? When well-meaning social and health workers give aid, therapy and advice, is mutual respect ever possible? The sociologist and amateur musician Richard Sennett (2004) suggests that practicing and performing music may be a paradigm for thinking about mutual respect in these situations. Respect, Sennett suggests, cannot just be intended, it must be *performed*: 'Respect is an expressive performance. That is, treating others with respect doesn't just happen, even with the best will in

Box 7.3 |

the world' (p. 207). What people want, suggests Sennett, is usually something more collaborative and less personal. Musicing is exemplary here of collaborative 'respect-in-action', of 'taking the other seriously' (p. 52) (Ansdell, 2005b).

Ansdell uses Sennett's argument as a resource in his case study of Musical Minds, a music group sponsored by an organization that helps adults with long-term mental health problems (see Box 4.2). For the members of Musical Minds, the skills and craft element of learning music nurtures self-respect. The members of the group engage with the music to make their shared performance a quality event, which cultivates what Sennett calls "secure self-respect." This work builds a feeling of dignity and *self-respect*. Ansdell also argues that musical collaboration nurtures *mutual respect*:

[E]nsemble work requires collaboration. Unless the musicians are playing in unison, they have to sort out differences and inequalities, loud against soft parts, or soloists and accompanists working together [. . .] This is mutual respect as musicians perform it, a matter of recognizing someone else who is doing something different (Sennett, 2004, quoted in Ansdell, 2005b).

This description of the enactment of mutual respect matches Ansdell's experience of the rehearsals and performances of Musical Minds. Mutual respect characterizes the participants' balancing of autonomy with community and also the interplay when the music therapist sensitively shifts her role as situations change (see also Box 4.2).

SOLIDARITY

Solidarity is associated with ideas such as unity and cohesion, shared aims, and readiness for concerted action. Solidarity as experience of group cohesion and shared identity is a common outcome of interaction in groups (Collins, 2004). This form of solidarity is legitimate but also limited, since it is exclusive. People are ready to support their own group, not others. In a society, broader forms of solidarity are necessary.

In an outline of the sociological tradition, Nisbet (1966/2002) explains that cohesion and community were among the key ideas explored by the emerging discipline of sociology in the nineteenth century. Sociologists of this period realized that the birth of modern societies led to the effect that traditional bonds were torn apart. Pioneers of sociology, such as Comte, Tönnies, and Durkheim, consequently examined these processes and theorized on the (changing) foundations and objectives of social cohesion. In an exploration of the idea of solidarity in the European context, Stjernø (2004) adds to this picture by exploring how this idea has been central to two of the main political traditions within European politics, namely social democracy and Christian democracy. Origins and traditions of solidarity obviously differ from continent to continent but the above examples illuminate some typical connections; solidarity as rooted in traditional communities and transformed by modern societies, solidarity as rooted in the struggles of underprivileged groups, and solidarity as rooted in religious and philosophical traditions stressing altruism and humanity.

There is a range of notions of solidarity and not all of them are compatible in every respect. Stjernø (2004) discusses the aspects of foundation, objective, inclusiveness, and collective orientation. Some traditions focus on common interests as the foundation of solidarity, while others identify the basis in a universal concept of humanity. Consequently, objectives range from the realization of common interests to the realization of a good society or world. Ideas of inclusiveness also vary, ranging from a restricted number of people with shared interests to all human beings. Collective orientation also seems to vary with these other dimensions. If solidarity is based in common interests, the collective orientation tends to be strong; individual autonomy is submitted to the shared cause. If solidarity has broader objectives, with the aim of achieving a better society for all people, there is space for individuals to preserve their autonomy (in the interrelated sense that we discussed in the section on freedom).

In community music therapy, feelings of belonging and solidarity usually emerge from interaction in groups. This has been explored and described in various ways, such as in Ramsey's (2002) discussion of unified group responses rather than individual differences, in Pavlicevic and Ansdell's (2009) discussion of collaborative musicking, in

FIGURE 7.5 | Together. Improvisation in an inclusive summer workshop. Kublank, Germany. Photo: Kristin Richter.

Ansdell's (2010a) discussion of hospitality and belonging in communities of practice, and in Stige's (2010a) discussion of interaction rituals that create shared moods and strong feelings of community and solidarity. The human value of these experiences might be assessed in relation to people's need for companionship in individualized societies. As discussed in Chapter 4, it might also be assessed in relation to processes of exclusion and marginalization, which give some people and groups limited access to social support.

For community music therapy, solidarity as rooted in the struggles of underprivileged groups is therefore of clear relevance. Generally, this leads to a focus on music therapy as empowerment (Ruud, 1998, Rolvsjord, 2004). Examples include community music therapy practices challenging the exclusion of disabled people (Kleive & Stige, 1988; Elefant, 2010a), practices advocating people's equality concerning friendship (Curtis & Mercado, 2004), and practices serving underprivileged communities (Fouché & Torrance, 2005; Oosthuizen, 2006). Solidarity rooted in the struggles of underprivileged groups requires that music therapists are "of their communities," as Procter (2004) argued (see Box 4.4).

Taken together, this suggests a more political role for music therapy. Music therapists might decide to engage with repressive practice and social structures and for instance advocate for more inclusive music practices in society and for a general concern for welfare (Stige, 2004a). This expanded agenda requires reflexivity and critical thinking. Frohne-Hagemann (2001) argues that ignorant "fixers" of the world are at best ineffective and at worst detrimental in relation to processes of social change (see Box 7.4).

Box 7.4 | SOLIDARITY AND OTHER ROADS TO GROWTH AND HEALTH

German music therapist Isabelle Frohne-Hagemann has developed several theoretical ideas that are relevant for an understanding of community music therapy, including a discussion of solidarity as an element of growth and health. Her work is integral in relation to psychotherapeutic and sociotherapeutic perspectives (Frohne, 1986; Frohne-Hagemann, 1998). In this respect her work has been informed by Gestalt principles as developed within the school of *Integrative Therapy*, with Hilarion Petzold as the leading figure. A basic idea in Frohne-Hagemann's work has been the "rhythmic" principle (dialectic movement between polarities), which she has discussed in relation to music and movement and also more metaphorically as the balancing of processes such as creation and integration, impression and expression, contact and withdrawal, and symbiosis and individuality (Frohne-Hagemann, 2001).

According to Frohne-Hagemann, music therapy should go beyond conventional *treatment* to include the enabling of human beings in relation to sociocultural and political processes. The argument is based on a conception of humans as fundamentally *creative beings* (Frohne-Hagemann, 2001, p. 98 ff.). In this perspective it is not enough to treat or heal,

Box 7.4

it is also necessary to help the client to grow and develop. Based on this premise, Frohne-Hagemann (with reference to Petzold) describes four roads to growth, health, and healing: 1) Work with consciousness and the exploration of meaning, 2) Work with re-socialization and basic trust, 3) Activation of experience and work with personality development, and 4) Experience of solidarity, metaperspective, and engagement.

The first road, work with consciousness and the exploration of meaning, is psychotherapy as originally and commonly conceptualized. The second road, which is linked to the first and the third, is work with re-socialization and basic trust. The third road is grounded in the growth potentials linked to positive emotions and experiences, as explored by, for instance, self-help groups and self-experience groups. She advocates that the importance of music for this way of working is related to its potential as *communal and pleasurable activity and experience*, and that this potential should be used much more actively among music therapists (Frohne-Hagemann, 2001, pp. 109–111).

The fourth road described by Frohne-Hagemann is the experience of *solidarity*, metaperspective, and engagement. She relates solidarity with engagement and responsibility for the interests of the other and sees this in contrast to narcissistic and self-absorbed strategies of interaction as well as to self- effacing strategies. The fourth road is therefore not independent of the three others. Self-awareness, tolerance, dignity, and identity are considered pre-requisites of true solidarity. Frohne-Hagemann (2001, pp. 112–113) underlines quite clearly the danger of becoming "ignoranten Weltverbesserer" (ignorant menders of the world) and advocates that determined attempts of developing metaperspectives are necessary in order to counteract this. Metaperspectives in this context means theories about society and about the cultural and social factors that lead to health problems in individuals, groups, and communities. In music as *experience and expression of solidarity*, Frohne-Hagemann suggests that possibilities for acknowledgment of oneself as a *historically situated* human being exist and thus also possibilities for intercultural solidarity.

DEALING WITH CONFLICTING VALUES

Freedom, equality, respect, and solidarity are central values informing the Universal Declaration of Human Rights. Awareness of these values can inform community music therapy as rights-based practice but does not provide the music therapist with a specific tool for ethical navigation. Each value is complex and disputed. Also, in a concrete situation various values might be experienced as contradictory. The possibility for conflicts between freedom and equality is a classic example. Also, the four values discussed above might be in conflict with more local values. Some norms for handling value conflicts can be helpful, and we propose three such norms. First, values should be articulated in relation to various levels of analysis. Second, values should be checked and balanced. Third, values should be negotiated locally.[4]

Values should be articulated in relation to various levels of analysis: Since community music therapy is an ecological practice, values should be considered in relation to different levels of analysis (individuals, microsystems, organizations, localities, and macrosystems, see Chapter 4). If freedom, for instance, is analyzed at the level of the individual only, implications for the freedom of others, and thus for equality, respect, and solidarity might be neglected.

Values should be checked and balanced: In human history there are plenty of examples of repression performed in the name of equality and injustice in the name of freedom. Similarly, solidarity that is not balanced with the values of freedom, respect, and equality could degenerate to in-group cohesion endangering the rights of others. This shows how a certain value can be misused in the service of powerful individuals and interest groups. This does not imply that there is anything "wrong" with the value in question but that there has not been a process allowing for values to be checked and balanced.

Values should be negotiated locally: There are always tensions between general values-based visions and the reality of needs, resources, traditions, and possibilities in a given context. Therefore, one will need to explore the meanings of freedom, equality, respect, and solidarity in each situation. This is not to say that music therapists should be chameleons but that they need to reconsider their values in context. *Respect* can be used as an example here: The music therapist may think of it as a moral obligation to treat all people as ends in themselves and to acknowledge their dignity. In certain contexts, however, respect might be enacted more in the direction of honor and esteem of people in power. These notions of respect are not necessarily compatible and in a given situation there might be a conflict of values that needs to be negotiated. Judgments will have to be made in the tension between the universalism of the human rights and the specificity of cultural traditions.

Note that the three norms we have proposed here are guidelines for negotiations, not for rational decision making. There is no logical procedure for resolving value conflicts. For community music therapy we will argue that there must be a commitment to achieving human rights "from below" in processes where means and ends are not separated.[5] In other words; the practical work itself must be in line with the values that inform the human rights. This suggests that the norms should be interpreted in the context of democratic negotiations.

Democracy is a tested way of balancing views and values. It is an egalitarian tradition, allowing for freedom and requesting respect and solidarity (Baker et al., 2004). As we will discuss in the next chapter, community music therapy processes should therefore allow for maximum participation in the decision-making processes. The rationale for this could be compared with the rationale for peace negotiations: There is not only need for answers to complex dilemmas but for processes that acknowledge this complexity. Every voice and the legitimacy of different perspectives should be attended to (Galtung, 1999, 2008).

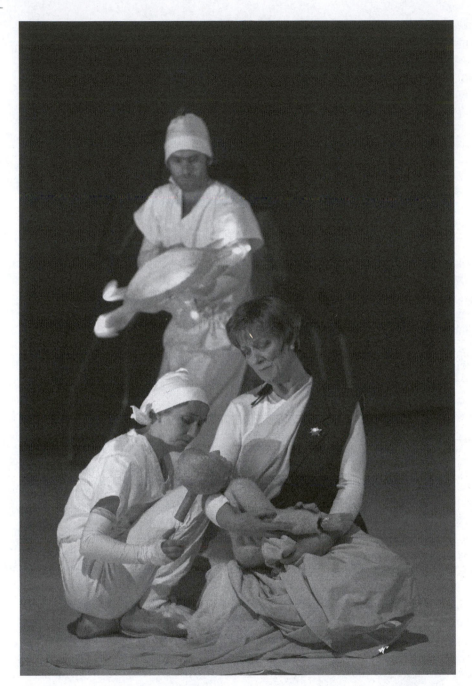

FIGURE 7.6 | Facing the music. From an opera written with cancer patients and O'Brien, Melbourne, Australia. Soprano Merlyn Quaife and puppeteers Sarah Kriegler and Jacob Williams.

Photo: Jeff Busby.

CONCLUSION

Attitudes and values are central elements in community music therapy and we have in this chapter argued that practice can be developed as rights-based practice. The issues that request involvement are situations where human rights are violated or not realized and many of the contexts where music therapists work are contexts of rights restrictions.

Community music therapy practice evolves where human rights challenges and social–musical possibilities meet. This way of conceptualizing practice involves a focus on how problems reside in the relationships between individuals and communities. According to a medical perspective, there might be individual pathology involved, but community music therapy focuses on participation, resource mobilization, and social change.

Rights-based practice requires knowledge and understanding of human rights. Some criteria for assessing claims based on human rights were proposed before we discussed the Universal Declaration of Human Rights and the three generations of rights that have been articulated. In practice, rights are disputed. Knowledge about the values that underpin human rights does not resolve such disputes but provides the music therapist with a tool for qualified participation in negotiations on rights. Four values were discussed and seen in relation to each other; freedom, equality, respect, and solidarity.

The discussion of these values revealed that each one of them is disputed, and in acknowledgment of these complexities we proposed three norms for the handling of value conflicts. These norms were not considered guidelines for logical decision-making but rather as the basis for negotiations. Community music therapy as a rights-based practice that takes place "from below" suggests that means and ends cannot be separated; processes (and not only outcomes) must be related to the values that inform the human rights. This suggests that community music therapy processes resemble a form of participatory democracy, a contention that we will discuss in detail in the next chapter.

KEY TERMS, DISCUSSION TOPICS, AND NOTES

Key Terms

Key terms in order of appearance:

Attitudes
Values
Rights-based practice
Civil and political rights
Economic, social, and cultural rights
Solidarity rights
Environmental rights
Values that underpin the human rights
Freedom

Equality
Respect
Solidarity
Democracy

Discussion Topics

The following critical thinking questions can be discussed in class or in groups or used by the individual student for critical reflection on topics discussed in the chapter. Extra resources can be found on the website of the book.

1. Several authors have described community music therapy processes geared at changing attitudes in a community, through song-writing and performances, advocacy and public communication, and so forth. Describe a case example where attitudes constitute barriers to participation and discuss feasible strategies for change in the given context.

2. All of the four values discussed in this chapter are complex and disputed. Select one of the values, outline various positions (such as basic equality, liberal egalitarianism, and equality of condition) and discuss the strengths and limitations of each position.

3. The conclusion of this chapter is that community music therapy processes resemble a form of participatory democracy. Processes of participatory democracy are hardly easy. Sometimes consensus is difficult to achieve, and this might block development and create frustrations among participants. If majority decisions are made, there is a risk of neglecting the needs and rights of the minority. Discuss how the values presented in this chapter might inform the development of a participatory democracy that can handle these kinds of challenges.

Notes

1   The notion of three generations of rights is well established in the literature but could be criticized for being somewhat ethnocentric, as it to a large degree reflects the sequence by which various types of rights have been acknowledged within Western societies (Ife, 2008).

2   For a discussion of a dialogical framework for self-determination, with a specific focus on the rights of people with intellectual disabilities, see (Tarulli & Sales, 2009). For more general, philosophical discussions of freedom and its relationship to other values such as equality, see (Berlin, 1969/2002; Skinner, 1998).

3   Respect is also a central value in the definition of peace that the United Nations General Assembly subscribed to in a resolution adopted in 1999: ". . . a set of values, attitudes, traditions and modes of behavior, and ways of life based on: respect for life; respect for all human rights and freedoms; commitment to nonviolence in settling conflicts; commitment to meet development and environmental need of present and future generations; respect for equal rights and opportunities for women and men; respect for freedom of expression, opinion and information; and adherence to the principles of justice, democracy, and tolerance" (United Nations as quoted in Vaillancourt, 2009, pp. 34–35).

4   For similar discussions in relation to community psychology, see e.g. (Nelson & Prilleltensky, 2005). Note that these norms could be said to be informed by values also. If asked to articulate these values we would be led into an endless cycle of qualifying statements that would also need to be qualified (an

endless regress). There is no generally accepted and context-independent priority rule (no value always has priority over other values).

5   Inspired by a Ghandhian perspective, Ife (2010) has developed an argument for why means and ends cannot be separated in democratic human rights work: "if a community is able to embark on a process of self-determination in which people are actively involved in determining the direction they wish to go, and involving the genuine participation of all, there is no need for predetermined goals, objectives, targets, or outcomes. These will emerge naturally from the process and, if the process is sound, the outcomes will also be sound" (Ife, 2010, p. 37).

Processes

After studying Chapter 8, you will be able to discuss questions such as:

■ When is community music therapy relevant?

■ What does a participatory orientation look like?

■ How can community music therapy build critical awareness and build on this?

■ What are the aspects involved in planning community music therapy?

■ How can processes of bonding and bridging through music mobilize resources?

■ What kinds of predicaments are typical in community music therapy processes?

■ What are the different forms of evaluation in community music therapy practice?

■ How and why are communicating and celebrating central dimensions of practice?

■ How does community music therapy request rethinking of time and place in music therapy?

PRE-ENTRY CONSIDERATIONS

QUESTIONS about what to do in health promotion and therapeutic practice can be surprisingly difficult to answer. Every initiative is complex and contextualized and invites the examination of a chain of questions about how to do things, with whom, where, and for what reason. To develop and qualify our questions is important, but does not take the challenge of decision-making away. Paul's question, which we encountered at the beginning of Chapter 7, apparently addressed every relevant dimension: "What treatment, by whom, is most effective for this individual with that specific problem, under which set of circumstances, and how does it come about?" Still, Knut's simple question—"May we too play in the [marching] band?"—opens up a completely different way of thinking about practice. Paul's question was based on certain premises, such as the idea that problems belong to individual clients and solutions to professional experts. Knut's question was based on premises pointing in more collaborative and community-oriented directions.

When is community music therapy relevant? The theory, research, and practical examples presented in this book give some answers to this question. A myriad of questions remain unanswered however, and it is critical to stimulate more research in this direction. In our appraisal it is equally crucial to consider how we address the question of relevance in the context of practice. One seemingly waterproof approach will be to assess what the best approach would be in every unique case. The challenge is that when we examine this we are necessarily positioned within a social, cultural, and professional context. If we assess the needs in every case we encounter, it makes a difference whether we do this from a clinical position within a hospital or from a position in a community music school, for instance. Similarly, it makes a difference whether we start with examining problems or resources, or whether we start with individuals or communities, or some combination of these. Our appraisal is always colored by our position and informed by certain perspectives. This is part of the human condition. We can acknowledge this and try and improve our judgment by searching out more than one perspective on practice.

The question about when community music therapy is relevant could therefore not be answered through examination of needs of participants only, crucial as this is. The music therapist must also examine his or her own reasons for becoming involved and the social and cultural context in which the question is embedded. The previous chapters outline some of the perspectives we can take when examining the question. Theory and research about health and wellbeing, including research on inequities, is one source of knowledge (Chapter 3). Theory and research about the importance of social resources and the affordances of collaborative musicking is another (Chapters 4 and 5). These sources of knowledge can be related to real world issues such as marginalization (Chapter 6). Our appraisal of all of this information will be colored by how we relate to the values linked to the idea of universal human rights (Chapter 7).

Sometimes music therapists are made aware of the possibilities of community music therapy by client initiatives. Alan Turry's (2005) work with his client Maria Logis exemplifies this. This woman had found that performing for others and creating a musical product helped her to stand up to the voice of the critic inside that would silence her if left unchallenged (see Box 1.4). Turry was willing to listen and to collaborate in adjusting the music therapy process. This led to what we can call boundary crossings (in contrast to boundary violations, see Chapter 10); the therapy process was opened up and processes and products made more public. In this respect, conventional music therapy and community music therapy could reciprocally support and challenge each other in ways that acknowledge the continued relevance of established insights in the discipline but also challenge dogmas or assumptions about the way music therapy should be.

Valuable as the idea of working from therapy to community is, community music therapy does not always grow out of individual therapy or traditional group therapy. It might grow out of an observed and values-informed appraisal of inequities at a societal level and it might grow out of public health or health promotion initiatives as well as out of musical and cultural initiatives. In the model of participatory processes that we will

FIGURE 8.1 | Joy with a bell. A music therapy session in British Columbia, Canada.
Photo: Randolph Parker.

develop in this chapter, creating critical awareness about needs and rights violations at different levels of analysis is considered to be one of the important shifts in community music therapy processes (in the model we describe below, process will be described as movement shaped by interacting shifts).

The fact that community music therapy processes have various origins suggests that there are necessarily different types of practices. In reviewing the literature, we propose to describe at least three different types of practice: The first type we will call **particular routes**; trajectories of community-oriented development that emerge from the specific needs and initiatives of individuals or groups. The above-mentioned expansion of contexts for Maria's music therapy process (Logis & Turry, 1999; Turry, 2005) exemplifies this. The second type we will call **projects**; collaborative endeavors whereby a range of agents go together (usually for a limited time period) with the aim of establishing new practices and inducing social change to the benefit of a location or a group of people. The context of Knut's question was a project on cultural inclusion, initiated at government level and performed in collaboration with local agents, the municipality, and the county (Kleive & Stige, 1988). The third type we will call **programs**; practices that have been established with a recognizable structure, agenda, and approach. The partnered community mental health music therapy program that Baines (2000/2003) developed as part of the social program of a clubhouse in Canada, exemplifies this type (see Box 6.4).[1]

The three types are in no way mutually exclusive. The terms are launched here only to sensitize to differences, not to establish any strict categorization. Particular routes can grow out of conventional music therapy practices as well as community music therapy projects and programs. Similarly, projects might develop into programs, while experiences with programs might necessitate new projects, and so on. Any variation of the theme is considered worthy as we will now propose a model that characterizes processes in community music therapy.

A MODEL OF PARTICIPATORY PROCESSES IN COMMUNITY MUSIC THERAPY

In many ways, change and transformation is what music therapy is about, and the word **process**—referring to a course of development leading to change—is prominent in the music therapy literature. The word is derived from the Latin *processus,* meaning "a going forward." In the context of community music therapy practice, we could think of process as movement in the direction of health, wellbeing, and social–musical change. These are interrelated areas, as we discussed in Chapter 5.

The values of freedom, equality, respect, and solidarity, linked to the notion of community music therapy as a rights-based practice (see Chapter 7), suggest that community music therapy processes should be democratic and participatory. What does a participatory orientation look like? In a description of a community music therapy project with adolescents, Australian music therapist McFerran suggests that the invitation to participate does not come with any qualifications:

> A participatory orientation looks like the people who are participating. This music therapy group is a direct reflection of the young people in it. At this early stage in the process, this group is much more closely linked to street life and family life than it is to the structure and responsibility of school and adulthood. The chaos that marks the group is comfortable for the young people and for the music therapist who is willing to sit with it. Nobody is giving directions and nobody is being told what to do. Moments of joy and laughter mark the sessions, as do moments of confusion and frustration. The instruments are provided and a warm welcome is offered. The invitation to participate does not come with any qualifications; it simply is.
>
> (McFerran, 2010, p. 203)

The lesson to learn is hardly that chaos is a necessary ingredient in all community music therapy processes but that it could be, depending on its compatibility with the lives of the participants. Some teenagers are more comfortable freestyling and might resist structured activity (McFerran, 2010). Other community music therapy practices are collaboratively structured, such as the activities of the Senior Choir studied by Stige

(2010b). These participants were comfortable with order and were happy to let the music therapist lead the musical activities. The participatory components of the process were taken care of through establishment of a board of management where the singers were in charge. In addition, there were plenty of plenary discussions of priorities and directions in the development of the choir activities. Structure is not the main question here, then, but power.

Community music therapy practice therefore requires awareness of the various forms participatory democracy can take. It does not necessarily involve the establishment of a board and specific democratic procedures, like those the Senior Choir found preferable. It does involve looking for ways that enable participants to be as free and equal as possible, within a culture of mutual respect and solidarity (Baker et al., 2004). Attending to voices that have particular difficulties in making themselves heard is therefore crucial. The community music therapy literature includes several important studies demonstrating how participatory action research can contribute in this direction (see e.g. Elefant, 2010b), even more dramatically when participants lack verbal skills and other resources that we usually rely on in democratic negotiations (Warner, 2005).

The model that we will propose for characterization of **participatory processes** in community music therapy takes inspiration from models of process in participatory action research, often described as steps towards social change through a series of collaborative action–reflection cycles. We find action research a suitable inspiration for a description of community music therapy processes, since the action research tradition is very close to practice and allows for the integration of practice, knowledge development, empowerment, and social change.

> The process starts with some regulating values and ideas that give direction to the work, while the concrete steps in the process could be depicted as recurring cycles of assessment, planning, action, evaluation, and reflection. The objectives and plans for action are based on the original values and ideas, but through assessments of the situation the available means to reach the objective are examined. The making of plans goes beyond concrete action planning to include necessary modifications of the original ideas. The action may then be seen as the first step of an overall plan and leads to the next step, evaluation, which could serve multiple functions: to learn, to gain information for planning the next step, and to create a basis for future modifications of the overall plan. All this is achieved through various forms of collective discussion and reflection.
>
> (Stige, 2005b, p. 409)

Collaboration in **action–reflection cycles** in the service of social change is a helpful guideline for the development of community music therapy practice and reflects several of the qualities of the PREPARE acronym we discussed in Chapters 1 and 6. The acronym also emphasizes other principles that inform practice, such as orientation towards resources and ecological contexts and awareness about the performative possibilities of music. These principles suggest that process in community music therapy cannot be

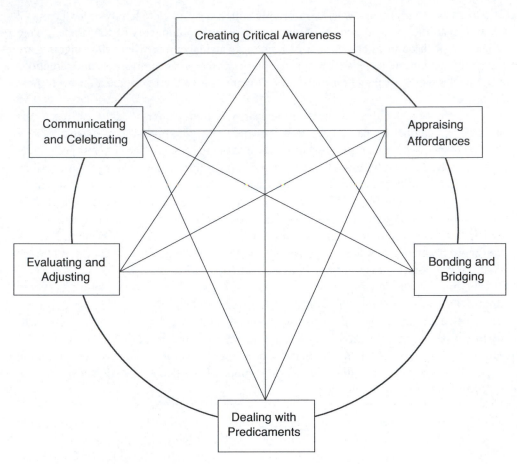

FIGURE 8.2 │ A model of participatory processes in community music therapy.

described in terms of a predefined sequence of steps. A flexible matrix with a range of interacting shifts is a more illustrative representation of the relational realities of practice (Stige, 1995, pp.104–147; Wood, 2006). In reviewing the ideas and descriptions of process in the community music therapy literature and then linking this to a) the notion of process in participatory action research, b) the qualities of community music therapy suggested by the PREPARE acronym, and c) relevant theory on social resources, we will propose that community music therapy processes can be described as movement in the direction of health, wellbeing, and social–musical change through the interaction of six different shifts: Creating critical awareness, Appraising affordances, Bonding and bridging, Dealing with predicaments, Evaluating and adjusting, and Communicating and celebrating. Figure 8.2 illustrates the relationships between the various shifts. In the following we will describe each one of the shifts.

CREATING CRITICAL AWARENESS

Creating critical awareness is crucial since needs in community music therapy are examined beyond the level of the individual and are seen in relation to rights violations and social and cultural contexts. This creates at least two challenges for community music therapy practice; the request for information about broader contexts, and the challenge of ideology. The request for information about broader contexts constitutes mainly a methodological challenge; what are the best procedures for gathering this information at both the introductory and evaluative stages of therapy? Ethnographic fieldwork and surveys are two helpful approaches, as we will discuss in the next chapter. The challenge of ideology is complex and important when detailed within the tradition of critical theory. As we will discuss in relation to action research in Chapter 9, ideology functions as repressive trains of thought that induce people to accept the current situation as natural. If we think of inequalities as inevitable, for instance, is that because we have analyzed the situation and the possibilities carefully, or is it because we have been taught to think this way? If the latter is the case, in whose interest is it to think of inequalities in this way? These questions exemplify how ideology is a challenge and can be challenged in community music therapy practice.

It is usually neither possible nor helpful to create critical awareness on behalf of participants. Again we can take inspiration from the tradition of action research, where the first step in the direction of critical awareness is made through the establishment of an arena where agents can interact and an agenda evolve (Reason & Bradbury, 2006). The performative nature of music creates some very special possibilities both in relation to arena and agenda: Music often brings people together and helps them interact, and

FIGURE 8.3 | Sharing your view. A Children's Welfare Musical, Bergen, Norway.
Photo: Astrid Merete Nordhaug.

music also allows for a combination of verbal and nonverbal communication in relation to evolving agendas.

We can once more use Knut's question as an example: His question about playing in the marching band was verbally simple but gained weight through the interaction of several other actions and expressions. The enthusiasm he and the other members of his group communicated through gestures when they observed photos of the marching band was one part of this. The musical actions some of the group members had performed previously, such as marching close to the marching band with a little flute ready, just in case possibilities for participation would emerge, was another (see Stige, 2002, pp. 113–134). Perhaps these actions and expressions would still have been neglected if not for the fact that the music therapists and members of the broader community acknowledged them in the context of the issue of rights of people with intellectual disabilities concerning community participation. In other words; critical awareness in community music therapy is a collaborative process where values and visions are negotiated through use of music, gestures, and words. It is often a process where the personal and the political interact and illuminate each other.

APPRAISING AFFORDANCES

While creating critical awareness is about values and visions and the articulation of what changes should be made, appraising affordances is about planning; what is possible to

---

Box 8.1 | THE MESSAGE OF THE LITTLE SAINTS

American music therapists Scott MacDonald and Michael Viega (2011) work in a program called Hear Our Voices, under the auspices of the Arts and Quality of Life Research Center at Temple University in Philadelphia. Hear Our Voices is a music therapy songwriting program, part of a larger initiative by the Arts and Quality of Life Research Center called Arts at Your Side. In a column called "Hope is Change," Joke Bradt (2009) describes the Hear Our Voices program in the following way:

> This is a 14-week songwriting program for at-risk youth who live in a section of Philadelphia that is marked by great poverty and high crime rates. Each week, elementary school aged children from diverse cultural backgrounds come together and create, under guidance of two excellent music therapists, Mike Viega and Scott MacDonald, songs about their lives and their community. In their songs, they explore issues of poverty, violence, lack of education, as well as emphasize the importance of love, community, hope, and the need for change. Their songs contain the complexity of their daily experiences while, at the same time, express rather straight forward but insightful messages to the world. Just a couple of weeks ago, a group of 1st and 2nd graders wrote a song to President Obama:

Box 8.1 |

> Mr. President
> we've got something to say
> We want change in the world
> Please help us bring change to the world
> We can change bad things
> into good things
> so all those bad people
> can change to good people
> And no one will steal anymore
> [. . .]

The song starts in a slow gospel style but then transitions into a faster tempo with lots of percussive energy. I see in these children . . . determination and hope . . . They know what changes are needed in their community and believe that, if we all work together, change is possible. . . . Whereas one could view the children's messages as idealistic and naïve, I like to think of them as messages of belief, hope and empowerment (Bradt, 2009).

In describing their own work in the program, MacDonald and Viega (2011) discuss the relevance of Hip-Hop culture and the musical framework it offers to the music therapy process and the success of the program. The songwriting program uses a theme-centered approach with the goal of providing children with a creative outlet for both the exploration and expression of issues that are relevant to their lives, such as violence, gangsterism, family situation, drug use, anger management, school, and peer pressure. The program also offers opportunities to collaboratively create strategies for personal safety and success.

The Little Saints was one of the first groups in the Hear Our Voices program. There were seven girls and six boys in the group, ages 9–12, predominantly with an African American and Latino background. Several of the members of the group had previous musical experience, both formal and informal, and MacDonald and Viega explain that an important factor in determining the direction to take in song writing with this group was to find out what they listened to. The music they preferred ranged from rap and Hip-Hop, to reggaeton, American R&B, and pop. The music therapists comment that the musical tastes of the children seemed to teeter between childhood and adolescence, which perhaps is illustrative of the transitional phase of development that they find themselves in:

> Although as children they continued to exhibit such behaviors as teasing, competitive-ness, occasional disputes, and mischief, what comes through in their words and music are beliefs concerning humanity, social consciousness, and spirituality, even though the surrounding milieu included the specter of drugs and violence (MacDonald & Viega, 2011, p. 156).

do with this community in this context? The phrase "appraising affordances" is appropriate because planning in community music therapy involves appraisal of resources and challenges in relation to several dimensions of practice and at several levels of analysis.

Dimensions of practice can for instance be examined by focusing on the affordances of arena, agenda, agents, activities, and artifacts (Stige, 2002, pp. 210–230, see also the discussion of health musicking in Chapter 5). Relationships between arena and agenda were discussed in the previous section. The dimension of the participating agents has been used throughout this book to illustrate how several levels of analysis are relevant; such as individual, group, organization, and broader community. In the next paragraph we will give a few examples from the community music therapy literature illustrating how the affordances of activities and artifacts can be appraised and appropriated.

The community music therapy literature naturally focuses on various forms of collaborative music-making, such as group improvisations, community singing, and ensemble playing (Kleive & Stige, 1988; Scheiby, 2002; Numata, 2009). Specific forms include drum circles (Boxill & Roberts, 2003), rock bands (Roer, 2001; Aigen, 2002; Krüger, 2004; Jampel, 2006, 2011; Tuastad & Finsås, 2008), and choirs (Zanini & Leao, 2006; Knardal, 2007). Several of these activities also include the possibility of communicating to broader audiences, which is also stressed in the literature on songwriting (Aasgaard, 2002; McFerran, 2010; O'Grady, 2009) and performance (Kleive & Stige, 1988; Ansdell, 2005b; Jampel, 2006, 2011). In communicating with an audience,

FIGURE 8.4 | Rehearsing a public performance. A choir for disadvantaged children in Singapore. Photo: Beyond Social Services.

the affordances of artifacts are usually crucial; what are the cultural connotations of the instruments, songs, and lyrics we use, and what are the possibilities for action that correspond to or contrast with the established conventions? In Chapter 6 this was exemplified in relation to the bridging affordances of "Different Drums," bringing together the Lambeg drum associated with Unionism and the Bodhran drum linked to a traditional Irish identity (Smyth, 2002).[2]

Wood (2006) has developed a way of appraising affordances through the use of what he calls the "community music therapy matrix." The matrix describes various interrelated formats which integrate several of the dimensions of practice described above (see Box 8.2).

Procedures and functions of planning can vary considerably among practices. Planning in relation to particular routes is often informal and linked to an appraisal of what to do next (When? How? and Where?), whereas planning in relation to projects might involve the development of comprehensive written documents. Within programs, planning is constrained and enabled by the structures, the agenda, and the approach that has been established for the program.

Box 8.2 | A COMMUNITY MUSIC THERAPY MATRIX

In Southern England, music therapist Stuart Wood and colleagues have performed a number of consecutive community music therapy projects, the starting point being a project called "From Therapy to Community'" (Wood, Verney & Atkinson, 2004; Wood, 2006). The original project was based on a neurological rehabilitation unit in Aylesbury, South East England, and set up to provide a music therapy program that was structured in three stages: individual music therapy in acute and in-patient medical settings; group music therapy in community medical settings; and workshops in arts and other community venues in the town. Wood explains how this initial project challenged him to change his ways of working and thinking as a music therapist:

> I felt a commitment to follow where music led each participant in the programme, and a duty to ensure that each step was safe. I was challenged to conceive of a way in which the vast range of musical experience could fit together, creating a 'joined-up' system that was flexible and responsive to the needs of participants. I came to see that the agencies and disciplines surrounding this work also had to integrate in order to keep the process moving. Theory too needed to provide a meaningful system for reflection. On each level I was tending towards a view that allowed difference *and* unity, was non-hierarchical, networked and ensured an optimum connectedness. In searching for a model for this view I found that the 'matrix' formation allowed a new way of thinking. "The matrix" is proposed as my response to the challenges of planning, practising and evaluating community music therapy. It is offered in the hope that it may help other music therapists facing similar challenges (Wood, 2006).

Box 8.2 |

The community music therapy matrix that Wood developed consists of interrelated formats of practice, such as individual music therapy, group music therapy, workshops, ensembles, concert trips, performance projects, tuition, and music for special occasions. After presenting this concrete matrix of interrelated formats, Wood (2006) then brings in theoretical perspectives from neuromusicology and music sociology in an attempt to illuminate how and why music could mediate the relationship between individuals and communities.

Wood (2006) argues that community music therapy practices are *ecological* and situated, so that processes in one node of the matrix influence processes in other nodes. The systemic approach taken by Wood does not suggest that individual initiatives are less important. On the contrary, he exemplifies the model by telling the story of Pam, a lady in her mid-fifties who had developed unusual neurological phenomena that remained a puzzle to her neurologists. In contrast with her medical status, Pam achieved a personal transformation from being a patient in the hospital into being a creative musical participant in the local community.

BONDING AND BRIDGING

The terms bonding and bridging were introduced in Chapter 4, with reference to Putnam's (2000, p. 22) distinction between two forms of social capital. In the context of this model, we will use the terms somewhat freely to describe various social–musical processes in community music therapy. Bridging refers to processes that connect people *within* a homogeneous community and bonding refers to social–musical processes that connect people *within* a heterogeneous community or *between* communities (Stige et al., 2010). Both bonding and bridging build and mobilize social resources.

The interaction rituals and communities of practice described in Chapter 5 exemplify how shared music-making builds and mobilizes social resources. *Interaction rituals* are characterized by bodily co-presence, mutual focus of attention, and shared mood and they lead to increased emotional energy and the construction of a sense of community (Collins, 2004). An interaction ritual could be repeated in an "interaction ritual chain" but could also be a one-off event. A *community of practice* is created when people repeatedly come together for a purpose (Wenger, 1998). Interaction rituals often involve bonding but do not exclude the possibility of bridging. Communities of practice also often involve bonding and are usually strengthened if they also include bridging.

The music therapy literature is rich in references to the use of music as bonding, focusing on group coherence and solidarity within group processes. References to bridging (or related metaphors and processes) are not equally represented in the literature but are central in community music therapy. Examples include music therapists who focus on performance (Ansdell, 2005b, 2010b; Jampel, 2006, 2011), inclusion of groups that have been marginalized in society (Broucek, 1987; Kleive & Stige, 1988; Curtis & Mercado, 2004; Elefant, 2010a), and on peace and conflict transformation (Dunn, 2008; Vaillancourt, 2009; Katz, 2011).

Stige and associates (2010, p. 286) argue that community music therapy practices cultivate interplay between bonding and bridging. Bridging builds space for diversity, which is a point stressed by Jampel in his discussion of performance in community music therapy:

> Stronger communities are established when lines of ethnicity, gender, and age are crossed. Performing music that reflects diversity can bring not only the performers together but their audiences as well. In Bowers' (1998) tale of the performance experience of a multi-generational choir composed of troubled teenagers and the well elderly, the bonds that they ultimately formed helped to bridge the gap of misunderstanding and antagonism that had originally existed. They learnt to appreciate each other through performing music. Through the intervention of the music therapist, both generations eventually became willing to open themselves up to musical idioms that were initially perceived by each as something alien. The resolution of this intergenerational conflict was critical in promoting understanding. I had experienced similar effects in working with performance. At any given time, I have worked with people in the band who were as young as nineteen and as old as their late seventies. Despite differing initial preferences for certain styles of music, the performers eventually learnt to at least tolerate if not come to appreciate each other's musical choices.
>
> (Jampel, 2006, p. 17)[3]

FIGURE 8.5 | Bonding and bridging. Children of the staff kindergarten, performing for the residents of Bergen Red Cross Nursing Home, Norway.
Photo: Tove Gulbrandsen.

Bridging also allows for work within broader alliances, as we will discuss in Chapter 10 with reference to partnerships. The community music therapy literature is rich in references to such work, including collaboration with local amateur musicians (Kleive & Stige, 1988), with community musicians (McFerran & Teggelove, 2011), and with other sectors, such as the police (Fouché & Torrance, 2005). Another form of bridging is cultivated through collaborative practices such as consultation, where the music therapist encourages others (professionals or community members) to use music as a resource for health and development (Stige, 2002, pp. 135–153; Rickson, 2008, 2010). In a different but related vein, Vaillancourt (2009) describes how music therapists in a school setting can operate as mentors and leaders supporting and encouraging some of the children to develop into "little mentors" and "little leaders" in ways that instigate positive social change. Vaillancourt relates this possibility to an awareness of the ripple effect that community music therapy can kindle.

Box 8.3 | UNITED BY MUSIC

Gerd Rieger in Krefeld in Germany is a music therapist who is also trained in social education. For many years he worked with immigrants from Eastern Europe, using rock bands as a vehicle for work with creativity, identity, and connectivity (Rieger, 1992, 2006). Since 2003 he has worked with a band project called Rock am Ring, where he has experimented with creative collaborative processes leading to bridging across socially constructed divides (Rieger, 2008).

Rieger's work with Rock am Ring (Rock at the Ring) is part of his job as a music therapist working with people with intellectual disabilities. Once a week 15 musicians with various disabilities come together in order to practice. They use rock band instruments such as bass, guitars, keyboard, and drums, as well as djembes and congas and various other percussion instruments. Rieger explains that for many of the musicians in this band, the rehearsal is the highlight of the week.

Rieger is the leader of a jazz workshop in Krefeld as well, where musicians come together on a weekly basis to improvise over jazz standards. Rieger introduced the jazz musicians to the idea of also improvising over rock themes, and the musicians agreed to experiment with themes that Rock am Ring had developed in their processes of song writing. It turned out that the jazz musicians appreciated this variation in their musical practice. The rock themes were harmonically simple and offered possibilities for groovy and powerful sounds.

In a chance meeting, two of the musicians of Rock am Ring listened to one of the concerts of the jazz band. As the jazz musicians started to play one of their own songs, they spontaneously joined in and ended up improvising together with the jazz band. The contributions of the two rock musicians invited respect; the sincerity, energy, and ingenuity of their playing were much applauded by the audience. The idea of further collaboration between Rock am Ring and the jazz band was born.

Box **8.3** |

This was explored one Saturday when the two groups decided to meet and spend the day together under the auspices of a local church. Space was created for practice and performance, as musical instruments were carried in and set up in a way that allowed for collaborative music-making on a provisional stage close to the altar. Rieger (2008) describes how the jazz musicians were cautious at the beginning, some on the verge of refusing to participate. This was a new and different experience, so a process of loosening-up was needed. Some warm-up exercises were used in an attempt to achieve this. What seemed to break the ice was a combination of humor and serious musicianship. The musicians in Rock am Ring did not intend to let this possibility go; they wanted to play and they wanted to play with the jazz musicians.

The first song they practiced together had been selected carefully. It was a powerful yet simple tune which the musicians in Rock am Ring knew very well. They felt safe and participated with vigor and confidence. After the first round of the tune the wind players of the jazz band came in with their powerful sound, first in one voice, then multi-voiced. Things started to happen. A groove was established and musical space was created for solo sections. Philipp, a percussionist from Rock am Ring, had the first solo. The vibraphonist from the jazz band made the next contribution, followed by many others from both groups.

A rewarding rehearsal was in process. While the musicians practiced, volunteers and family members started to make a grand lunch table. They felt that hard-working musicians deserved excellent food and drink. The shared lunch then afforded conversation, so that the two groups of musicians could start to learn more about each other.

The day this happened was not just any Saturday in town. It was market day and the streets were filled. As the musicians started to play again they left the door of the church open. People outside were attracted by the sound and some came to the door to steal a look. They were then informed of the performance event that was planned in the afternoon. When the concert started the little church was packed with people; family, friends, nurses, and social workers were there, but also quite a few people who had come in from the street, invited by the energy of the music and the enthusiasm of the musicians (Rieger, 2008).

DEALING WITH PREDICAMENTS

The processes of bonding and bridging are not always smooth and easy, and the same can be said for all the different shifts in the model of participatory processes that we are discussing in this chapter. Music therapists must be prepared to deal with unexpected events and conflicts of various sorts. In community music therapy, predicaments are encountered at all levels of analysis.

FIGURE 8.6 | Jennie singing the blues, with Victor Washington on the piano. Baltic Street Clinic, New York.

Photo: South Beach Psychiatric Center.

At a personal level, participants might experience processes as too challenging or products as unsatisfactory. Participation in music might also trigger personal problems and challenging memories. Dunn (2008) gives one example from a community sing-along situation:

> In my combined experiences in music therapy, musical performing, and community music, I have been humbled by the effect a simple song can have on an individual. I recall leading a community sing-along when a woman burst into tears with the song "You are My Sunshine." It was the song her father used to sing to her mother who had recently passed away. The facilitator needs to be aware that music can have a strong effect on people.
>
> (Dunn, 2008, p. 89)

Dunn argues that situations where there is an intense reaction to music might create a need for follow-up, including referrals to support services. In most cases, immediate support in the social situation or a follow-up by the music therapist will suffice. One of the assets music therapists bring to work with inclusive (and sometimes public) music practices is that they have training in dealing with emotionally challenging situations. In Chapter 6 we discussed the perceived problem of an expanding "therapy culture" (Furedi, 2004) that cultivates people's vulnerabilities rather than their strengths in late modern societies. To deal with challenging emotions in a community music therapy context is a different phenomenon. It involves building an emotional community characterized by freedom and solidarity, so that there is tolerance for a range of emotional expressions (Rosenwein, 2006).

In groups there is plentiful space for conflicts and difficult communication, as participants have different values and attitudes and different experiences of processes and outcomes. Conflicts of interest are also common. Ansdell (2010a) describes how the music therapist Sarah works with this in Musical Minds, a group in East London supported by an organization for adults with long-term mental health problems (see Boxes 4.2 and 7.3):

> There's a week-by-week process which is at once both a musical and a social one. When Sarah first came to the group people would simply want do their own thing ("be a soloist"), could hardly listen to each other, and then would argue about not respecting each other, or being unable to practically coordinate the concerts they wanted to do together. The group often split up temporarily, unable to negotiate their differences. But there had been a gradual shift in the group. Sarah had used her skills as a mental health advocate to negotiate with the group, and to get them to negotiate their needs with each other. Gradually there has been more collaboration—both musically and socially. . . . Sarah puts it this way:
>
>> What a lot of the members of the group seem anxious about is maintaining their own identity . . . and of course that's exactly what it's most difficult to do with a mental health difficulty—you're labeled, and you're living in this traumatic community. So it's an irony really that as I'm pushing them together musically they're becoming better at feeling individuals! . . .
>
> As I watch Sarah more with the group I'm increasingly fascinated by her shifting role and responsibility throughout the different occasions (it's certainly not static). Sometimes in the group she's more like a conventional therapist: helping the group understand their conflicts, mediating, helping them negotiate, and supporting them. Then, as the preparation of the show gets underway she's treated more like a coach, helping the members get their solo and group numbers as good as possible. Then . . . something else happens in performance—she's an accompanist (be it one with unusual demands!).
>
> (Ansdell, 2010a, p. 36)

Conflicts are also probable at higher levels of analysis, beyond the group. Working with conflict resolution as her main theme, Dunn (2008) argues that it is potentially helpful to use music in attempts at transforming conflicts, since music can tap into different levels of human functioning compared to more conventional and exclusively verbal strategies.

Elefant (2010a) documented how important the work with intergroup relationships can be in relation to integration and inclusion. Kleive and Stige (1988) discussed how disabled people's attempts at realizing their rights to citizen participation not only instigated support and sympathy in the broader community, but also fear and resistance.

The ecological ripple effect often referred to in community music therapy might also involve some challenging consequences. If central values such as basic equality and respect are shared across groups, situations are usually manageable (although they might require systematic and long-term work towards attitudinal change in the broader community, for instance). If central values are not shared or the process challenges power or privilege in ways that are not welcomed, the situation can be much more difficult, perhaps even dangerous (as when efforts to help homeless children provoke drug syndicates that exploit these children). In these cases, partnerships in broad alliances for positive social change are absolutely necessary.

Box 8.4 | RESILIENCE IN THE FACE OF A DISRESPECTFUL AUDIENCE

In Norway, Kathrine Dahle and Veronica Slettebakk (2006) studied the roles and relationships in a community music therapy performance. The focal point in the study was a performance event at a leisure club. An unexpected situation evolved that required action and reflection. The club in question was located in a small town in a rural municipality. It was open for all adolescents of the municipality and especially designed to be inclusive to people with disabilities. Some of the members of the club had established a band with support from the local community music school. Dahle and Slettebakk, who were Masters students in music therapy at the time, were engaged to lead the band in rehearsals and performances.

It was a small band. At the particular performance there were only two participants in addition to the two music therapy students; a drummer and a bass player. The students therefore joined in on piano and guitar. Both the drummer and the bass player were musicians with intellectual disabilities, limitations in language, and some challenges in relation to coordination and rhythm.

The band did not take performances lightly. In the weeks before the event they carefully selected songs they liked and felt they could do well. Each song was rehearsed thoroughly and the four band members prepared for performance by discussing roles, arrangements, and announcements. The drummer and bass player were both quite nervous about the event and such rituals of preparation were one way of reducing stage fright.

Finally the night of the gig arrived. The musicians set up their instruments, the audience arrived, and the band was welcomed by the leader of the leisure club. The drummer proudly announced the first song and the band started to play. Things went reasonably well. In the beginning the rhythm was not too steady but soon the drummer felt more relaxed and

Box 8.4 |

the music gradually grew more solid. The musicians started to enjoy themselves. It seemed like the audience did fine too, but suddenly five persons decided to stand up and walk out. What was going on? The bass player and the drummer exchanged confused gazes. What did we do wrong? They looked at the music therapy students. What should we do? No words had been uttered but in a split second this was the students' interpretation of what the two other band members communicated through face expressions and body language.

In the case study, Dahle and Slettebakk (2006) explored aspects of the strategies they used in order to deal with this difficult and unexpected situation. The performance situation itself was analyzed with focus on affect attunement and social referencing (Stern, 1985/1998). Then they analyzed how as leaders of the band verbally they had processed the incident with the participants afterwards, trying to clarify what had happened and talk through the event so that continued and mutual emotional support could be offered. After this, Dahle and Slettebakk decided they had to look at the mesosystem dimensions of the incident (Bronfenbrenner, 1979). Since this happened in a small town, it was possible to find the audience members that had left and to talk with them. Who were they and why did they leave? It turned out that they were nurses working in assisted apartments for disabled people. They had left the concert because their working hours were over at that time. The music therapy students were taken aback by what they considered lack of consideration for the needs of the performers, while they also realized that the time selected for the event was not ideal, given that nurses on duty would be part of the audience.

So, what was the lesson to be learnt from this incident? The problem was not that the two music therapy students had neglected the broader context and relied entirely on the assumption that preparing and processing within the microsystem of the band would ensure that performances were safe for the band members. The time of the event had been chosen in dialogue with the leader of the leisure club. It turned out that this leader was less informed about the working hours of the nurses than they assumed and the value of communicating directly within broad social networks is important to acknowledge. For Dahle and Slettebakk (2006) the recognition of performance as a risky business was highlighted in their analysis. There are processes at many ecological layers going on at the same time and all agents involved must prepare themselves for unexpected incidents.

EVALUATING AND ADJUSTING

Evaluation is central to professional practice, as a tool enabling the music therapist to learn from experience and the collaborators to enhance and develop practices. The formal requirements for evaluation in community music therapy vary because practice might take place in systems that have less formal and systematic evaluation expectations. In a study of how apprentice music therapists can be mentored for work with social justice and peace, one informant describes the encounter with community music therapy practice in the following way: "there is less paperwork, evaluations, interventions, evolution notes, and all. This [CoMT] is a process that is really different" (Vaillancourt, 2009, p. 145). This informant obviously enjoyed the reduced bureaucracy that some community music therapy practices entail. Nonetheless, the argument that evaluation allows for learning is still valid and it is important for evaluation to be integrated into working processes whether or not there is a system that formally calls for evaluation reports.

As with the other shifts in the model we are describing, evaluation needs to be a collaborative process. Several characteristics of evaluation in action research are relevant for community music therapy, such as evaluation through collective discussion and reflection, evaluation as mutual empowerment, evaluation as a continuous or cyclical process, and evaluation informed by an extended epistemology (Stige, 2005b). To evaluate and document can go beyond the production of verbal and written reports to include artistic aspects, for instance. Several authors in the community music therapy literature have described the production of CDs as one way of documenting and evaluating a process (Aasgaard, 2002; Rieger, 2008; McFerran & Teggelove, 2011; MacDonald & Viega, 2011).

One helpful way of thinking about evaluation is to use it as a possibility to examine strengths and weaknesses in the particular shifts and the concrete relationships that evolve in each case. Evaluation then examines questions about what degree of critical

FIGURE 8.7 | A break is a meeting too. The CeleBRation Choir, Auckland, New Zealand. Photo: Jeff Brass.

awareness is developed, how well the affordances in various dimensions and at different levels are examined, how the balance between bonding and bridging is managed, and how communication and celebration is performed. Such evaluation focuses on processes and outcomes and requires considerable reflexivity, as differences in values, positions, and perspectives among participants may create discrepancies in judgment.

The function of evaluation varies between practices established as particular routes, projects, and programs. In the first case, evaluation is mainly a tool for enhancement of the work and for clarification of the collaboration between music therapist and participants. In the two latter cases there is at least one third party involved who is interested in the results of the evaluation. When it comes to projects, the quality of the evaluation performed (and not only the quality of the project itself) might be decisive in deliberations about whether the project should be continued, discontinued, or transformed to a program. When it comes to the evaluation of programs, it is common to talk of formative evaluation (to inform decision making on how programs can be improved) and summative evaluation (to inform decision making about whether or not the program is to be continued) (Nelson & Prilleltensky, 2005, p. 261). Different evaluation methods (qualitative and quantitative) lend themselves to different purposes of evaluation (see Chapter 9). To include stakeholders and participants in the evaluation process is crucial in community music therapy, for instance through use of structured interviews or focus groups (Baines, 2000/2003; Schwantes, forthcoming).

Box 8.5 | WHAT MUSIC THERAPY COULD MEAN TO THE COMMUNITY

With reference to her work in Berlin in Germany, Oksana Zharinova-Sanderson (2004) explains how European countries have changed during the last few decades. Societies are much less monocultural and music therapists increasingly meet clients from different cultural backgrounds. She argues that this challenges established music therapy theory and practice in fundamental ways. One of the questions Zharinova-Sanderson considers is what music therapy could mean to the community.

In addressing this question, Zharinova-Sanderson examines the contexts of her own work as a music therapist at the Treatment Centre for Torture Victims in Berlin. One context is the city where she operates. Berlin is at the heart of the German integration process but Zharinova-Sanderson claims it is also a difficult city for refugees. There is a lack of cohesion in the city's social structure and heavy bureaucracy in the social and legal systems. In parts of the city foreigners could feel unwelcome. Another context is the institution where she works: How does music therapy fit in an institution where trauma treatment based on a medical model dominates? Zharinova-Sanderson concludes that music therapy in this context should not try to fit with the medical model but to complement it by focusing on the whole person, taking the individual's cultural resources and own potential for healing into consideration, as well as challenges concerning access

Box 8.5 |

to resources in community and society. The patients[4] who come to music therapy are different in very many respects, but some things are shared:

> All of them are either survivors of torture and/or political persecution or traumatic events during wars. I came across people from a huge variety of backgrounds—from a Kurdish political activist to an African woman who lost her husband and children, from a bank manager from Chechnya to a Kosovo orphan. It may seem surprising that torture and traumatic experiences are generally not their biggest concern. Instead, their insecure residential status and unhappy life in exile without money, freedom of movement and employment, and fear of East German neo-Nazis—these are the most burning issues that are shared by every patient. Because of their refugee status there is very little help available for them in the German health and social services, so they flood into our privately run centre for all the help that they can get (Zharinova-Sanderson, 2004, p. 236).

The realization that insecure residential status and an unhappy life in their new country were the biggest concerns for refugees led Zharinova-Sanderson to reevaluate her own practice and to develop a project that emphasized integration and community.

For the individual who has experienced torture and trauma it is difficult to renew trust in humanity. For a community to thrive, trust is a requirement. Zharinova-Sanderson argues that individuals who are victimized cannot recover in isolation; they need to recover a sense of belonging. The space that music therapy occupies in the treatment model of the Treatment Centre for Torture Victims in Berlin has thus expanded over time, from the private space of the therapy room to include other settings that allow for broader engagements connecting people. This has required an expansion of the role of the music therapist as well. In the process the music therapist acts as a "musician-ethnographer" who learns to access the therapeutic value of non-Western clients' musical traditions and also as a "campaigner" for music as a force for change in the community.

COMMUNICATING AND CELEBRATING

Community music therapy involves aesthetic processes which usually are not complete without communication to broader audiences and celebration of processes and outcomes. This shift is obviously related to the processes of bridging and bonding and it illuminates how the shifts described in this model are not to be interpreted as sequences (e.g. bonding before bridging before evaluating before communicating). Communication to broader audiences may stimulate bonding and bridging in ways that instigate further creative and musical development in the direction of new presentations. The interplay and interaction of shifts is often central.

Communicating and celebrating links with the performative quality of community music therapy and integrates aesthetic and social processes. Often, though not necessarily, this involves gigs or concerts. In modern societies, performances have often functioned to drive music in more perfectionist and commercialized directions (Keil & Feld, 1994). Use of performances in community music therapy therefore requires awareness and reflection (Ansdell, 2005b; 2010b) and it does, by definition, involve risks (McFerran, 2010, see also Box 8.4).

What is nurtured in community music therapy is a participatory notion of performance, where the interaction between performer(s) and audience is acknowledged as an important aspect of the process. When this works, a musical performance is not only a personal performance, but a performance of community. In a column on the performance of community, Stige (2004b) refers to the anthropologist Askew (2002), one of many social scientists who follow Goffman (1959/1990) and Turner (1967, 1969) in exploring human life through the lens of a notion of performance:

> It is probably not obvious for all readers if and how a theory and practice of performance may be relevant for music therapy. Communication in music therapy is often described as (preferably) authentic and dialogic, while performances may be viewed as less authentic and as one-way communication; that is, merely as transmissions of pre-defined texts, plots, or products. . . . [A] different and richer conception of performance is possible and could be explored by music therapists. . . . Askew (2002, p. 291) argues that performance is emergent, interactive, and contingent. Performance, like power, is not just a product that is given; it is also a process subject to the vagaries of history and context and on-the-spot improvisation.
>
> (Stige, 2004b)

If performances are conceived as interactive events, the role of the audience goes beyond that of evaluating the quality of the performance and the competency of the performers. Similarly, performers are not reduced to transmitters of predefined structures. The values, choices, and powers of each attendant and group of attendants come into play and interplay:

> Paraphrasing Berthold Brecht we may then argue that music and art is not only a mirror held up to reality; it may also be a hammer with which to shape it. When working with the empowerment of clients, performance then obviously may be one of the tools we would want to use. Since empowerment is about the relationship between individual and community, this also illuminates how communities may be viewed as works in progress, maintained and developed by performances.
>
> (Stige, 2004b)

Practical implications involve working carefully with selection of, and communication with, audiences (Turry, 2005; O'Grady, 2009; McFerran, 2010). Another more far-ranging implication is that it becomes relevant for music therapists and their collaborators to engage in broader discussions in society about aesthetics, aesthetic quality, and notions

FIGURE 8.8 | In deed. Glorious MUD Singers Choir in the Making Music Being Well program, New South Wales, Australia.

Photo: Lily Richardson.

of music and performance (Ruud, 1980; Kleive & Stige, 1988). When certain musical expressions are marginalized, people are marginalized too, so a notion of aesthetics that acknowledges multiple practices—multiple aesthetics so to say—seems pertinent for community music therapy (Stige, 1998, 2008a).[5]

The performative quality of community music therapy involves celebrating, not just communicating, and this dimension is crucial in the performance of community. Several music therapists describing performative events have highlighted this dimension (e.g. Aasgaard, 2002; Maratos, 2004). In a dialogue on conviviality and hospitality in community music therapy, Pavlicevic communicates her view on this dimension in the following way:

> Could we see, then, that the kind of musicing promoted by Community Music Therapy is in some ways an alibi that enables people—in challenging and unlikely places—to get together, sing and dance and make friends and have fun together? As the sociologist Richard Sennett comments, you can't just respect people by saying "I respect you." You have to *perform* respect—and you have then to have some medium through which you do this performance of respect. Could it be the same for hospitality, for conviviality: You can't welcome people without a place and a genuine

activity to welcome them *into; y*ou can't be together creatively without something genuine to do—something you want to do, something that's good to do. Music and musicing affords such hospitality, as welcoming in, such conviviality, as creating collective joy.

(Pavlicevic in Stige et al., 2010b, pp. 307–308)

Box 8.6 | RESTORING PRIDE, TALENT, AND ACCOMPLISHMENT

Peter Jampel, a music therapist in New York, worked with music therapy performance at a community mental health center in this city for several years. In a qualitative study of this practice, Jampel (2006) focuses on the experience of music performance for ten people living with chronic mental illness. As an introduction to the topic, Jampel presents the story of Maxwell; a middle-aged African American man that he worked with in the early 1990s.

> His talent as a musician became apparent to me during the music therapy groups in which he participated. Though he talked in a monotone, mumbled, repeated statements echolalically, talked to himself at times, dressed in wrinkled garments, was usually unshaven, and displayed the blunted affect that is characteristic of people who are diagnosed with schizophrenia, there was a remarkable vitality about the way that he played music. He revealed that he was a performing musician with a rhythm and blues band from his late teens to his early twenties but at age 22, he was unable to resume his career due to the onset of his mental illness. He has been in and out of inpatient psychiatric facilities since that time. Though he has maintained an interest in music, he had not had the opportunity to perform since he became ill (Jampel, 2006, p. 1).

After a few months, Maxwell began to participate in a performing band that Jampel was directing in the clinic. Maxwell sang and played the piano. When he performed, he sang with feeling and displayed a considerable amount of dexterity on the piano. Jampel also felt that Maxwell used his voice much more clearly when he sang than when he spoke. After the performances he seemed to carry himself in a more upright way. His appearance and the way he dressed started to improve also.

> After a couple of months, the band was invited to perform on a cable television show that was being broadcast to the very psychiatric inpatient unit that had discharged him just six months earlier. On the day of the show, he came dressed in a dark suit and tie, and was clean-shaven. He sang and accompanied himself on the song *Groovin'* and I remember thinking how well he was playing and vocalizing. I looked up at the monitor and saw a long close-up that they were taking of him and thought how impressive he appeared. He seemed to be an almost entirely different person from the one that I had first met several months before.

Box **8.6** |

When we exited the TV studio about forty-five minutes later, we were walking back to our vehicle across the campus of this inpatient facility. Maxwell was carrying the keyboard. He was stopped by a young man who recognized him and the two of them embraced. They talked briefly and it became apparent that they had been on the same psychiatric unit six months before. The young man had just heard him play on the TV show and complimented Maxwell on his performance. Maxwell smiled and then beamed a huge grin when he was asked if he wouldn't mind signing an autograph for him. He complied willingly. I produced a pen and the flier of the show on which he then signed the autograph. They shook hands, Maxwell wished him luck, and he said that he hoped that he too would soon be leaving the hospital. They waved to one another as they parted.

Maxwell's TV performance seemed to complete his transformation from inpatient to touring artist. Though his illness would persist five years after that performance, he continued to play with the band and had not had a return admission to the hospital. He left the band after he decided to move to an adult home that was too far from the clinic for him to be able to travel to band rehearsals. He did however continue to perform in his new residence. . . . It seemed as though his transformation had become a lasting one (Jampel, 2006, pp. 1–3).

Maxwell's musical talent was extraordinary but Jampel's (2006) research suggests that he was not alone in his ability to use the music therapy performance group as a vehicle for restoring pride, talent, and accomplishment. Jampel relates this to the current direction of community mental health in the USA, which points towards the fullest restoration of the person with mental health problems into the fabric of society (see also Jampel, 2011).

A NOTE ON TIME AND PLACE IN COMMUNITY MUSIC THERAPY PROCESSES

The examples presented throughout this book suggest that community music therapy is practiced with considerable flexibility. The course of processes may depart from the conventional boundaries and frames usually suggested for music therapy practice. In a music therapy textbook, such conventional frameworks are presented in the following way:

In the same way that a picture frame creates a boundary round the art work and contains it, so the therapeutic framework contains the work of the therapist and client.

The therapeutic framework calls for regular sessions, as well as consistency of time and place. This regularity establishes a vital rhythm to the work, which further contributes to the client experiencing the therapy setting as being safe.

(Darnley-Smith & Patey, 2003, p. 49)

If we allow ourselves to play with the metaphor employed by Darnley-Smith and Patey, we could say that community music therapy is more related to relational art, conceptual art, and performance art than to the notion of art as an object (not to mention that music is usually considered part of the performing arts). In community music therapy, there is much less of a request for regularity of sessions, time boundaries, privacy of the music therapy room, and planned beginnings and endings of the process. Consistency in place is neither necessary nor helpful in all cases and the same can be said about consistency in time. It is established when it is in accordance with the needs of participants and abandoned when it is not. In community music therapy processes, needs concerning frames typically change considerably over time and are flexible and evolving.[6]

A review of the literature reveals some vital characteristics of time and place in community music therapy processes:

Time is often conceptualized in non-linear or multiple terms: Community music therapy processes are often linked to practices of health promotion, which suggests that continuous activity gains importance, often in cyclical terms. People come to a band or choir, week after week; they do not leave because they feel better but stay because they feel good. In interaction ritual chains and communities of practice, outcomes of processes go beyond individual change to include the continuous recreation of community and social resources (Stige et al., 2010a). At other times, community music therapy involves one-off events, such as a large collaborative concert (Katz, 2011) or an improvised performative event (Aasgaard, 2002; Stewart, 2004). While one-off events perhaps are not standard practice, the ripple effects in the social networks of participants (including the audience) can make them valuable and important. The point here is not that linear conceptions of processes in time are made irrelevant, but that multiple and interacting processes gain importance. Some processes may have linear aspects (such as when participants develop skills gradually), others involve non-linear shifts (when social barriers to participation are overcome), others are cyclical (when a group continues to work together, with no clear beginning or ending), and others may have spiral-like qualities (such as the reflection–action process in participatory action research).

Place is considered a prominent element in the processes of change: Some descriptions of conventional music therapy suggest that what matters concerning place is consistency, regularity, and protection, not the place itself. In reality, place is often much more important, as when the music therapist adjusts practice to various sites and situations in a hospital, such as the bedside and the open ward setting. The ecological quality of community music therapy increases the prominence of place in the development of practice. Processes often evolve from one place to another, sometimes with sessions and events taking place in unexpected venues, such as an arts centre or a parish church (Wood, Verney & Atkinson, 2004; Wood, 2006). The appraisal and appropriation of the affordances of each arena (and its artifacts, activities, relationships, and audiences) become crucial. In community music therapy it is not possible to explore the question of how music helps independently of the question of where music helps (Stige et al., 2010a).

Time and place often intertwine in ways that are highly descriptive of community music therapy processes: From the fact that place gains importance in community music therapy, it follows that the interaction of time and place also is significant. One way of describing this is to say that processes are situated. In the community music therapy literature, this is sometimes described as convergences; people come together in certain places at certain points in time (Oddy, 2001/2005). At other times the metaphor of trajectory is employed; people finding their way from legitimate peripheral participation to fuller participation in the community (Krüger, 2004)). The idea of the ripple effect (Pavlicevic & Ansdell, 2004), or music's emerging geography (Aasgaard, 2002), also illuminates this aspect. The intertwining of time and place happens in particular ways in each case. There might be some recognizable patterns but there are also many unique aspects to each process. This is one of the reasons why qualitative research in the tradition of ethnography is important in community music therapy (see Chapter 9).

CONCLUSION

Community music therapy processes have various origins and consequently there will be different types of practices, such as *particular routes* (community-oriented development that emerges from the specific needs and initiatives of individuals or groups), *projects* (collaborative endeavors with the ambition of establishing new practices and inducing social change), and *programs* (practices that have been established with a recognizable structure, agenda, and approach).

In the context of community music therapy practice, we think of *process* as movement in the direction of health, wellbeing, and social–musical change. These are interrelated areas. The values of freedom, equality, respect, and solidarity, linked to the notion of community music therapy as rights-based practice, suggest that community music therapy processes should be *democratic* and *participatory*. What this entails might vary considerably, as different groups have very different histories, notions of democracy, and qualifications for participation. The model that we have proposed for characterization of participatory processes in community music therapy in this chapter must therefore be interpreted as a simplified representation of a complex reality, not as a standard intended to regulate practice.

The model we have presented was developed through a review of ideas and descriptions of process in the community music therapy literature and the connection of these ideas to a) the notion of process in participatory action research, b) the qualities of community music therapy suggested by the PREPARE acronym, and c) relevant theory on social resources. The model suggests that community music therapy processes can be described as movement in the direction of health, wellbeing, and social–musical change through the interaction of six different shifts: *Creating critical awareness* (developing information about broader contexts and challenging ideology); *Appraising affordances* (planning what is possible to do in a given context, through appraisal of problems and resources in relation to several dimensions of practice and at several levels of analysis); *Bonding and bridging* (supporting social–musical processes that connect people within homogeneous and heterogeneous communities); *Dealing with predicaments* (transforming conflicts at various level of analysis, ranging from person to group to broader communities), *Evaluating and adjusting* (examining strengths and weaknesses in all of the shifts made within the participatory process, with the aim of improving practice), and *Communicating and celebrating* (performing for broader audiences and creating and welcoming collective joy).

In the final section of the chapter, three characteristics of time and place in community music therapy processes were described. First, time is often conceptualized in non-linear or multiple terms. Second, place is considered a prominent element in the processes of change. Third, time and place often intertwine in ways that are highly descriptive of community music therapy processes.

In the last two chapters of the book we will proceed to discuss developments in discipline and profession, with a special focus on research in Chapter 9 and on professionalization in Chapter 10. Some of the questions that emerge are: What are the pertinent premises and purposes of research? What are the contexts for development of critical and constructive reflection about the music therapy profession in late modern societies? and: What are the relationships between music therapy and other professional and lay practices? The issues, values, and processes that we have discussed in Chapters 6 to 8 influence how we relate to these questions.

KEY TERMS, DISCUSSION TOPICS, AND NOTES

Key Terms

Key terms in order of appearance:

> Particular routes
> Projects
> Programs
> Process
> Participatory processes
> Action–reflection cycles
> Creating critical awareness
> Appraising affordances
> Bonding and bridging
> Dealing with predicaments
> Evaluating and adjusting
> Communicating and celebrating
> Time
> Place

Discussion Topics

The following critical thinking questions can be discussed in class or in groups or used by the individual student for critical reflection on topics discussed in the chapter. Extra resources can be found on the website of the book.

1. Participatory processes can take very different forms, depending on the needs, resources, and values of participants. In this chapter we described discrepancies between participation in a group of adolescents and in a senior choir. Choose one context of practice and discuss how voices can be attended to, negotiations performed, and decisions made in this context.
2. Working with (collaborative) consultation involves enabling others to use music as a resource. Discuss implications for the role and required competencies of the music therapist and what the advantages and disadvantages of this form of practice can be.
3. The inclusion of performances as one component of music therapy practice has been controversial in some circles. Define a group of participants and discuss what the possibilities and pitfalls of performance would be in this specific case.

Notes

1   In some countries community music therapy programs are funded by "soft money" from charities or organizations, while in other countries they are sometimes established as permanent components of the public welfare system. Publicly funded music programs in Norwegian prisons involving professional support from music therapists and music educators exemplify the latter possibility, see Box 10.1.

2   The references given in this paragraph and in the next sections are illustrative and not comprehensive.

3   The relevance of cultivating the interplay of bonding and bridging can also be seen in relation to the value of aspects such as size, inclusiveness, and multiplexity in human social networks, as discussed in Chapter 4.

4   Zharinova-Sanderson (2004) uses the term "patient" as it dominates the discourse of the medically oriented center where she works, while she acknowledges that the term could be awkward in the context of the broader practice that she has developed.

5   For a criticism of this view, see Aigen (2008).

6   When comparing practices, as is done here, there is always the risk of making things look more different than they are. We are not proposing that there is never any flexibility in frames in conventional music therapy, but that such flexibility is more characteristic in community music therapy, and usually considered helpful. See also the discussion in Chapter 10 on the difference between boundary violations and boundary crossings.

Part IV

Community Music Therapy as Development of Discipline and Profession

PART IV examines how community music therapy can develop as discipline and profession and how this is related to the development of music therapy more generally. Community music therapy instigates reflections on the relationships as well as the differences between discipline, profession, and practice. We remember from Part III that the term therapy is used with parsimony in any description of community music therapy practices. The music therapists working in these practices still typically identify themselves as *music therapists* (and not as community music therapists or musicians, for instance). The professional role is extended rather than abandoned.

Chapter 9 discusses the specific challenges of community music therapy research. Our goal is to provide an overall picture of some central premises, purposes, and procedures in community music therapy research, with a specific discussion of the relevance of four different research traditions. In light of the values of participatory practices discussed in Part III, it is germane to examine how research, which requires expertise and skills, could be combined with participatory values such as equality and solidarity.

Chapter 10, the final chapter of the book, sums up some current challenges for the music therapy profession. Professionalization, the process by which labor is differentiated and particular responsibilities delegated to specialized vocations, has often been considered an antagonist to popular participation. If popular participation is to be valued, as we have argued throughout the book, what are the implications for the music therapy profession? Does community music therapy challenge the profession or could it be understood as an invitation to reprofessionalization? If so, what alternatives exist for the music therapy profession in late modern societies?

■■■■ | *Chapter 9*

Purposes and Practices of Research

After studying Chapter 9, you will be able to discuss answers to questions such as:

- What premises and purposes characterize research efforts?
- How could the processes and products of research be described?
- How and why is action research central to community music therapy research?
- What is the relevance of ethnographic research to community music therapy research?
- How could survey research contribute in community music therapy research?
- In what ways could experimental research be used in community music therapy research?
- What would be the arguments for the claim that community music therapy requires practical and pluralistic research?

PREMISES AND PURPOSES

RESEARCH is one of the foundations of professional practice and plays an important part in the shaping of relationships between professionals, participants, and the public. Choosing to ignore the contribution of research increases the risk of less than optimal practice. Theories, as tools of reflection, enhance our capacity to reflect when we relate to research. Consequently, the integration of empirical grounding and theory development is central to the strengthening of community music therapy as a disciplinary field.

Even though research can be seen to provide a foundation for professional practice it is more precise to think of "research-related practice" than of "research-based practice." Empirical grounding and theory development are vital factors influencing community music therapy practice, but not the only ones. Practice evolves locally, informed by values, local knowledge, and social–musical processes. Obviously, practice cannot be reduced to the technical application of knowledge previously generated by researchers. Instead of envisioning a unidirectional flow of information from research to theory to practice, we can think of the relationships between practice, theory, and research as reciprocal, keeping in mind that these relationships are also influenced by metatheory (Stige, 2002).

Research is informed by basic assumptions about the world (ontology) and about knowledge (epistemology). Such assumptions could be called **premises** since it is not possible to objectively appraise the validity of these assumptions. For instance, some researchers subscribe to a notion of "truth" that refers to *correspondence* between statements and a given reality, while others focus more on interpretive *coherence* or on *consequences* of knowledge as a form of action. Premises are often grouped in clusters that have been labeled as *paradigms* or *worldviews,* such as postpositivist, constructivist, participatory, and pragmatist worldviews.[1]

Differences in basic assumptions (premises) are relevant for understanding the distinction between **qualitative** and **quantitative research**. Some would argue that quantitative researchers focus on the discovery of facts while qualitative researchers describe people's multiple constructions of phenomena and processes. Such a dichotomy might give us some initial ideas about differences but is actually misleading. There is, for instance, more to quantitative research than discovering facts; it can be used to develop theory and to test out sophisticated models.

FIGURE 9.1 | Ready to explore the possibilities of music. The Little Saints with music therapists Mike Viega and Scott MacDonald, Philadelphia, USA.

Photo: Ryan Brandenberg.

At a concrete level, differences between qualitative and quantitative research simply influence the choice of procedures and type of data collected. Qualitative researchers tend to interpret experiences and situations, while quantitative researchers tend to collect data that can be transformed to numbers and then analyzed. Even though there is no general consensus on how to conceptualize similarities and differences between quantitative and qualitative research, most researchers would agree that different research questions are asked in the two traditions, that the roles of researchers and participants are defined differently, and that the process of inquiry is understood in diverse ways. **Objectivity** or reduction of bias is often an ideal in quantitative research. **Reflexivity**, the process of articulating and evaluating questions underlying and motivating a study, is usually a more prominent ideal in qualitative research (Finlay & Gough, 2003). Both in quantitative and qualitative research it is common to acknowledge that the researcher might influence the research processes. If objectivity is the ideal, this influence should be controlled and reduced as much as possible. If reflexivity is the ideal, this influence (and reactions to it) could also be acknowledged as a resource contributing to understanding. This example illuminates how differences between the two research traditions should be explored from several angles. In some ways it is helpful to think in terms of differences in kind; in others it is fruitful to think in terms of differences in degree.

Why do we do research? We can carry out studies because we want to describe something (*descriptive studies*), because we want to identify and examine important processes and causal factors (*explanatory studies*), or because we want to learn something about the outcomes or effects of interventions and policies (*evaluation studies*). Similar ways of systematizing research **purposes** can be observed across sciences and disciplines.[2] The participatory and activist quality of community music therapy suggests that we also do research because we want to change a situation, not only because we want to describe, explain, or evaluate it. Research is linked to the accountability of a profession, and in community music therapy this is interpreted in a broad way to include and emphasize accountability to participants and community members.

PROCESSES AND PRODUCTS

The **research process** often starts with the articulation of one or more research questions. These questions are grounded in a situation and in the foundation of existing knowledge. Previous research is reviewed, a study is designed, and the researchers engage with a number of tasks in order to be able to collect data, analyze and interpret the material and communicate the results. In Figure 9.2 the process of doing research is depicted as a circle consisting of distinctive tasks or procedures.

In practice the research process is seldom as well-ordered as suggested in Figure 9.2. Reviewing previous studies can be an ongoing process and new research questions might emerge during the process. In some cases additional data collection can take place after periods of data analysis. All approaches to research require some adaptations to the real world process. In qualitative research there is considerable elasticity in the process. Robson (2002) uses the term *flexible designs* to describe this attribute. Bruscia (1995)

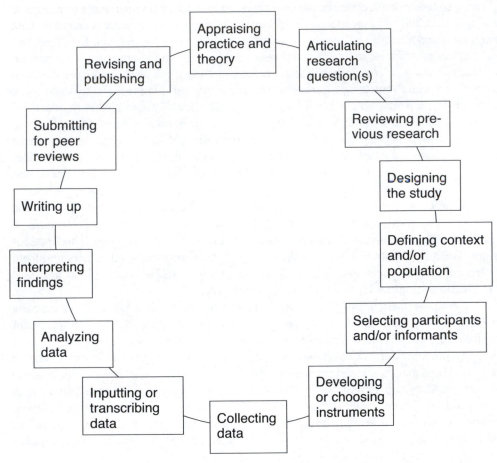

FIGURE 9.2 │ A circle of research procedures.

and others have characterized the qualitative research process as nonlinear, personal and interpersonal. Instead of a sequence of steps, the qualitative research process often consists of movements back and forth between the various procedural steps suggested by the circle of research procedures. As we will see later in this chapter, the idea of action research can challenge the research procedures outlined in Figure 9.2 even further, as the process grows more participatory over time. In addition, the **products** of the research are not necessarily publications and presentations only. The understanding of research is expanded to include empowerment and social change.

Despite the disparities between various research methods, there are certain shared **values** that tend to influence the choices that researchers make.[3] Two of these values are *communalism* and *skepticism* (Ziman, 2000). In trying to understand the role of these values in research, it is helpful to take notice of the final steps of the circle in Figure 9.2: the sub-practices of submitting for peer reviews, revising, and publishing. These steps reflect the value of both communalism and skepticism. Communalism implies that knowledge is produced for the broader community. Without publication or other forms of sharing there is no research, no matter what effort has been put into the process. Skepticism guarantees that new findings and insights are never taken at face value; they are critically examined to ensure that the quality of research processes and products is satisfactory. Depending on the fit between the premises of the researchers and the reviewers, this process can be either straightforward or complex (Stige, Malterud, & Midtgarden, 2009).

Two other values that are considered central in research are *disinterestedness* and *originality* (Ziman, 2000). The value of disinterestedness does not exclude engagement and commitment but is related to the ideas of objectivity (reduction of bias) and reflexivity (articulation of premises) that we discussed above. The value of originality implies that researchers should not merely confirm what we already know but also search for new ways of describing and understanding things. Creativity is therefore highly valued in most, perhaps all types of research. Originality is not only a product of creativity, however. In research, originality needs to be founded on what is already known. Reviewing previous research on the topic is therefore one of the essential steps in the research process and should prevent researchers from "reinventing the wheel." More importantly it is also a way of learning from others. Research can therefore be thought of as innovation within tradition.

In the following sections we will describe four traditions of research practice; action research, ethnographic research, survey research, and experimental research. This is of course not a comprehensive list but represents a wide range of approaches relevant to community music therapy. Details about procedures are not included in order to explain how to do research, but rather to illuminate the characteristics of each tradition that are uniquely influenced by their own history of development. New and improved procedures have evolved over time and the premises and purposes ascribed to each tradition have also evolved. A historical perspective is therefore a resource for deliberating on what the premises and purposes of community music therapy research are and what the implications might be.

In the context of community music therapy there are different ways of understanding the relationships between the four traditions of research that we will describe. It is not uncommon to think of the traditions as separate. The researcher chooses one of them, according to the purpose of the study. Alternatively it is also possible to think of action research as primary in community music therapy and the three other traditions as "reservoirs of tools." This interpretation opens up for mixed methods research (Creswell & Clark, 2011) but requires in our appraisal awareness about relationships between various levels of abstraction—ranging from worldviews to methods—in the development of research studies. We will first present the four research traditions separately and then discuss such relationships in some more detail.[4]

ACTION RESEARCH

Action research is an umbrella term covering a continuum of collaborative research practices with goals ranging from practical problem-solving to societal transformation.

Origins of this research tradition are manifold and include the pragmatist philosophy of John Dewey from the early twentieth century, the social psychology of Kurt Lewin from the 1930s and 40s, the critical theory of Jürgen Habermas beginning in the 1960s, and emancipatory research practices as initiated by Paulo Freire and others in the 1960s and 1970s (Reason & Bradbury, 2006).

Participatory action research is part of the broad family of action research that is of special relevance to community music therapy. Participatory action research goes beyond the practice of studying others to include collaborative research; it aims at solving problems as they are experienced by a given group or community. Four elements are central to this tradition of research: "a) active lay participation in the research process; b) empowerment of participants and sociocultural change as part of the research agenda; c) linkage of theory, practice, and research; and d) application of a broad conception of knowledge when evaluating research processes and outcomes" (Stige, 2005b, p. 405).

Many participatory action researchers explicitly elaborate different ways of knowing. Knowledge is not considered in cognitive and theoretical terms only, but as emerging and embodied processes and practices in context. There is an interest in local knowledge (Geertz, 1983) and also in social critique and social change, as discussed in the critical theory of the Frankfurt School (see Habermas, 1968/1971). The critical theorists emphasize the value of human agency but also consider agency as conditioned by restraints of the natural and the sociocultural world. Of specific importance to critical theory are the restraints created by *ideology*. In this tradition of thinking, ideology functions as repressive trains of thought that induce people in subordinate positions to accept their situation as natural. If and when they do, they accept the worldview of the privileged. Ideology is produced and reproduced continuously, as people in dominating roles communicate that inequality is necessary and normal. Suggesting that people are poor because they are lazy is an example of a statement that might have ideological origins and functions. By "blaming the victim" (Ryan, 1971), the statement not only oversimplifies but also conceals how power and privilege is involved in the construction of the current situation. Critical theorists advocate that analysis and critique of ideology is central in social research.

In participatory action research the use of specific research methods is a secondary consideration to the emerging processes of collaboration and communication. A participatory action research project could involve the use of diverse and mixed methods, depending on the needs in each situation. While methods are often qualitative, quantitative methods can also be highly relevant, for instance in assessing the needs and attitudes in a community. In other words, participatory action research cannot be described as a specific methodology or set of methods. Choice of specific methods grows out of the collaborative process, with communal action–reflection cycles functioning as central elements. In a participatory action research process it is crucial to give marginalized people voice and to listen to the voices of others. The process may thus be described as a self-reflective spiral through the building of creative and self-critical communities (Stige, 2005b).

Participatory action research stresses the values of participation and social change in and through research. These values suggest that various forms of knowledge, including tacit and artistic forms, become intrinsic to the research process. In traditional research, peer reviews and publishing are usually considered the final steps of the research process, and the product is a written text communicating new information and insight in language, numbers, and figures (see Figure 9.2). In participatory action research, the concept of products is expanded beyond published texts to include any actions that empower participants and promote social change in a given context. This does not suggest that production of cognitive knowledge is ignored, but that it is also seen in direct relation to other forms of knowledge.

Since action research involves collaboration, a negotiated appraisal of the participants' situation guides the research process. This does require a great deal of openness as to what research traditions and methods are of relevance. Research questions emerge from practical circumstances, and the significance of the research depends not only on the validity and sophistication of research publications produced but also the relevance and usefulness of outcomes for those involved. Practices embracing participatory perspectives therefore invite research that takes an interest in pragmatic outcomes. In fact, action research not only suggests that the origins and outcomes of research are practical; processes are practical too, evolving around the participants' mutual efforts at understanding each other (Gustavsen, 2006). Such a practical ethos requires an expanded epistemology; there are different kinds of knowledge to be acknowledged.

Traditionally there is focus in research on propositional and representational knowledge. In action research, other forms of knowledge are equally important. Many of these forms express themselves in action, as *knowing;* the practical knowing of how to do things, the experiential knowing of face-to-face encounters, and the presentational knowing as expressed in music and other arts forms (Heron, 1992). An expanded epistemology incorporates methodologies such as arts-based research, where music is accepted and employed as a form of knowledge (Vaillancourt, 2009).

Action research should not be treated as a solution searching for problems. Some participants are less interested in a focus on social change, leaving an action researcher at risk of probing for answers to questions never asked by the participants (McFerran & Hunt, 2008). As a participatory process, action research requires openness and flexibility in the definitions of objectives as well as outcomes.

Box 9.1 | WHOSE VOICE IS BEING HEARD? PARTICIPATORY ACTION RESEARCH IN ACTION

As part of an international collaboration on community music therapy research, Cochavit Elefant (2010b) intended to do a qualitative case study of two collaborating Israeli choirs: Idud and Renanim. The Idud group was made of about 45 adults with intellectual and developmental disabilities at a mild to moderate level, while the Renanim group consisted of about 20 singers with quadriplegia, a paralysis affecting all four limbs. All singers were between 30 and 50 years old. The members of the choirs were living in the same town and worked with the same music therapist. With "giving voice through collaboration" as the leading idea, the music therapist initiated a performance allowing the two choirs to

Box 9.1 |

collaborate. This gave a contradictory outcome. The members of Renanim felt that their performance was overshadowed by the larger sized choir of Idud. The Renanim singers' experience was that they were not heard, in spite of the good intentions of the music therapist. In studying this process, Elefant realized that action research might contribute to positive change:

> My original thought was that it would be interesting to understand the two choirs' interest and perception towards music and performance in the community and to observe intergroup relations between the two choirs. It turned out that the choir members had questions, concerns, and goals that they wanted to pursue too. This resulted in the development of our collaboration inspired by the tradition of Participatory Action Research (Elefant, 2010b, p. 189).

The Renanim group, the music therapist, and Elefant decided to collaborate in order to see whether a process of change could be achieved. The research questions and the approach taken were determined through discussion among participants. Gradually the theme of "Whose voice is being heard?" (socially and musically) emerged as the main research focus. The process was not easy; there were tensions, disappointments, and diverging interests to deal with. For a period, Renanim made the choice not to collaborate with Idud, but gradually a new and more empowering approach to collaboration developed:

> There were many different voices that were expressed and the discussions were at times heated and loud. . . . My role was that of a group facilitator during this process. Individuals learnt to listen while others dared to speak. The group learnt to negotiate and compromises were made. . . . "Idud can amplify our voices," said Dorit [a choir member]. These were the exact words Rina [the music therapist] also had used two years earlier when she first had tried to merge the two groups during performance. So what was the difference? This time the words were said by Renanim after a long process of evaluating, reflecting, acting, and reflecting again. Rina's attempt then in merging the groups gave them an opportunity to build something new all by themselves. "We were heard!" they declared in the second performance (Elefant, 2010b, p. 197).

ETHNOGRAPHIC RESEARCH

Ethnography is the study of cultures and contexts where people communicate and collaborate in groups and communities. The history of ethnography goes back to the European colonial powers' attempts of describing and understanding the natives of their colonies. In consequence, ethnographers at this time were criticized for serving colonial powers. The late nineteenth- and early twentieth-century pioneers of modern ethnography tried to break the servile tradition of earlier ethnography with pioneers such as Bronislaw Malinowski advocating that the ethnographer's main task is to understand the world as seen by local people. The goal of ethnography, according to this view, is to grasp the native's point of view (Eriksen, 2010). This ideal of giving primacy to insider perspectives is not unproblematic, however. Theories of knowledge and interpretation, such as hermeneutics (Gadamer, 1960/1999), propose that pre-understanding inescapably influences understanding. For an ethnographer to grasp the native's point of view is not fully attainable, then. Reflexivity—reflection on one's own role and contribution in interaction with other people—is therefore central in ethnographic research (Finlay & Gough, 2003; Hammersley & Atkinson, 2007). Among contemporary ethnographers, criticisms of ethnocentric perspectives have flourished, and feminist and third world ethnographers in particular have carefully examined the relationships between insider perspectives and outsider perspectives (Naples, 2003).

FIGURE 9.3 | Social–musical situation. Ngoma in the Kamba tradition in Kenya.
Photo: Kigunda Mulundi.

Ethnography has evolved to become an interdisciplinary research tradition relevant for the study of any setting where people interact and are embedded in culture. Ethnographers focus on how knowledge, artifacts, values, and ideas are constructed and communicated in a given context, and they explore the roles, rituals, rationales, and relationships that support these habits and practices. Researchers often concentrate on what it means to be human in a specific social and cultural context, but ethnographic research is still usually comparative. Possibilities for transferring findings and insights to other contexts are considered. As one anthropologist explains: "If, say, one chooses to write a monograph about a people in the New Guinea highlands, one will always choose to describe it with at least some concepts (such as kinship, gender, and power) that render it comparable with aspects of other societies" (Eriksen, 2010, p. 4).

Fieldwork, the gathering of empirical material through prolonged presence in the field, is central to the ethnographic research process. The techniques of fieldwork are used flexibly, as fixed procedures would be counterproductive to the sensitivity for context that good ethnography requires (Atkinson et al., 2001). Central techniques include participant observation, interviews, and the interpretation of texts and artifacts.

Participant observation through prolonged and/or repeated presence in the setting of interest is the main approach to doing ethnography. Prolonged presence involves activities such as "hanging around" and "joining in." Alternations between peripheral participation and full participation in the activities of the setting are often helpful in attempts at understanding its culture. An ethnographic account includes concrete observations as well as appropriate quotations of spontaneous dialogues in relevant situations. A community music therapy researcher could use participant observation to study music activities over time and also by following participants in other situations, such as in daily life activities. Each setting is distinctive and regulates the possible roles a researcher can take in different ways. Usually, researchers need to negotiate this with the local people of the setting, according to the limitations set by the specific activity and cultural tradition.

Interviews are helpful in soliciting the accounts of participants. Some interviews are conducted in separate and protected settings while others are not much different from any spontaneous conversation and therefore come close to participant observation. Interviews give information about phenomena under scrutiny and also about the person(s) presenting the accounts. Community music therapy researchers have an interest in learning from the accounts of participants in music activities, as well as from peers and community members and other professionals working in and with the community.

Interpretation of texts and artifacts focuses on those objects that are crucial for an understanding of the activity and context studied. Texts and artifacts must be understood in the context of their social use and in light of the researcher's own pre-understanding. These issues illuminate how ethnographic interpretation in many ways is related to the tradition of hermeneutics (Geertz, 1973/1993; Alvesson & Sköldberg, 2009). In community music therapy research interpretation of texts and artifacts includes the study of, for instance, lyrics, recordings, and other artifacts used or produced in music activities.

Use of the techniques described here is usually supplemented with *field notes* where the researcher's impressions, ideas, and provisional interpretations are outlined. Field notes can be viewed as a fourth central technique and also as a major strategy for the integration and interpretation of information. The techniques mentioned above are the most common in ethnography. Other techniques, such as questionnaires or polls, are less typical but sometimes relevant.

The use of several techniques when conducting ethnography encourages the researcher to develop multiple perspectives on the empirical material (Hammersley & Atkinson, 2007, pp. 230–232). The research process usually leads to a "heap" of empirical material that is experienced as quite messy; it does not present itself in ready-made concepts. Some kind of order must then be developed from the field notes, interview transcripts, and recordings that have been compiled. Geertz's (1973/1993) concept of *thick description* illuminates the relationship between description and interpretation in ethnographic studies. Imagine you observe a male participant who is not playing at the same tempo as other participants in a musical activity. How should you interpret this? It could be that he has minimal musical experience and is not aware of the discrepancy. He could be distracted by something. Or he might be trying to tease or distract some of the others. Possibilities are manifold. When doing ethnography it is not enough to describe what is seen or heard. You need to thicken the description by putting it in relation to other observations and the knowledge you are able to gain about the persons, activities, cultural norms, and social structures involved: How does this person act in similar or related musical and non-musical situations? How do the other participants react to him? What are the values and attitudes guiding these actions? Thick description is an approach to interpretation of meaning.

Box 9.2 | AN ETHNOGRAPHIC STUDY OF AN UNSCHEDULED EVENT

Mercédès Pavlicevic (2010a) performed an ethnographic case study of the Music Therapy Community Clinic in Heideveld, outside Cape Town in South Africa. This is an area challenged by gang wars, drug syndicates, and a high incidence of alcoholism and other problems (see also Box 1.2). One of the projects that Pavlicevic tracked was called Music for Life and included a choir, a marimba band, a drumming group, and a rap group. It also included an annual weekend music camp in preparation for the Heideveld Community Concert.

On the basis of participatory observation, field notes were documented, interviews transcribed, and musical events captured on video. In studying the recordings, Pavlicevic noted that "music's power" in the various events was not "given" but needed to be invoked, shared, and worked with in particular ways. She became increasingly interested in this and selected for detailed study what she termed "magic moments" of collaborative musicking:

> At these moments, each group was in optimal flow: in other words, they were "peak" moments when the groups seemed propelled within highly fluid musical groove; moments that—frankly—electrified me. The nearest analogy being moments in a live

Box 9.2 |

jazz concert when the improvisation "takes off," with corresponding whooping, cheering, whistling, and clapping by the audience. At such moments in group music therapy, the (socially assigned) identities and roles of therapist and clients seemed to meld: all became people doing "magic" music (Pavlicevic, 2010a, pp. 99–100).

In focusing her study on such magic moments—using moments of low level collaboration and musical incoherence as a useful backdrop—Pavlicevic took inspiration from the ethnographic approach of music sociologist Tia DeNora (2003). In her study, Pavlicevic undertook a detailed analysis of one video excerpt, seen in the context of the broader field work. The selected moment happened while she was filming the Heideveld Children's Choir in preparation for the Heideveld Community Concert. The choir had just been rehearsing a song, the two music therapists conferred for a few moments, and there was general chatter and disarray in the room. As Pavlicevic was about to switch off the camera, she discovered an unscheduled happening in the back-row. She zoomed in:

> Seven children are clustered around the table, facing one another with heads lowered as they spontaneously sing the last line of "Kan'n man dan nie" and move their hips. Half the group taps the song's rhythm on the table, which tapping anchors and drives the continuing crescendo and tightening of the singing, towards a sudden sforzando of vocal and physical energy with exclamations of Ya-Ya-Ya!. Simultaneously, all jump backwards, away from the table, laughing, and almost immediately forming various looser pairs (Pavlicevic, 2010a, p. 101).[5]

In a general comment to the event, Pavlicevic states:

> What emerged during micro-analytic study of this (and other excerpts) is the effortless synchronic musicing within and between each of the young folk. To think in terms of a number of youngsters singing and dancing "together as one" falls qualitatively short of explaining the supra-individual choreographed elegance. It is as though, during optimal moments, there is no phenomenological distinction between the group's musical sounds, movements, and use of space (Pavlicevic, 2010a, p. 102).

On the basis of this specific observation, several research questions emerged and Pavlicevic got involved in a focused investigation of collective and complex group musicking events, of how collaborative musicking is regulated by the participants, and of what strategies music therapists use to generate optimal collaborative musicking (Pavlicevic, 2010a, p. 103).

SURVEY RESEARCH

In **survey research** information is gathered from a selection of individuals through asking (verbally or in writing) a set of pre-formulated questions in a given sequence. The earliest type of survey is the census, often used by governments. The idea of studying representative samples instead of whole populations was first coined by the Norwegian statistician Anders Nikolai Kiær. In 1895 he presented a report on what he called "the method of representativity." His point was that if you can select a sample in such a way that its distributions on key variables corresponded to those of the population as a whole, you can assume that statistics based on the sample will fairly well describe the population. By 1903 his approach was more or less accepted by the international community of statisticians. Kiær did not, however, suggest that representative samples could be obtained by selecting randomly. This was suggested by Arthur Lyon Bowley in 1906 (Bethlehem, 1999). Modern sampling techniques were developed much later, mainly after 1950.

An important reason for doing surveys is to gain understanding of social problems. This can be traced back to Charles Booth (1840–1916) who carried out a pioneer study titled *Inquiry into the Life and Labor of the People of London*, between 1886 and 1903. He did not use standard survey methods as we know them today with well-defined sampling techniques and standardized questions. He did, however, use quantitative summaries from systematic measurements to describe and analyze an important societal problem (Groves et al., 2004). He started a tradition that has been labeled *social surveys*, where the focus is to document material problems and health challenges amongst various disadvantaged groups. In the British context such surveys were often followed by political initiatives to improve the life conditions of those concerned and can be considered an early example of action-oriented research. Social surveys have not always led to action to improve lives of disadvantaged groups, however. Abrams (1951) maintained that in the United States similar surveys were carried out, documenting results that were not less shocking than the findings from British surveys, but with no action for improvements. After briefly describing the Pittsburgh survey he says "The main result of the survey was merely to stimulate a widening flow of further studies which fed a more or less academic appetite for facts" (p. 115).

A separate tradition of survey research has grown out of journalism and marketing, where surveys are used to describe changes in political preferences, and attitudes among the general public, and to evaluate the marketing success of commercial products. The purpose of doing surveys in this tradition is quite different from the action-oriented social surveys described above: to influence the public politically or simply to encourage increased purchasing of a product. While one could say that opinion polls are carried out in order to improve services and products and to help politicians adjust their policy to the views of the population, such surveys are also instruments in the hands of people with power and privilege.

Various types of survey are used by researchers, either individually or in combination. These types include *single cross-sectional surveys*, *repeated cross-sectional surveys* (same study population, but new samples covering the same age groups repeatedly), *panel studies* (same sample of informants surveyed two or more times), and *studies covering more than one population* (for instance community music therapy participants in two different countries)

The purpose of surveys can be either descriptive (to describe prevalence, means and variation) or analytical (to identify factors which can predict a dependent variable or a set of dependent variables). Surveys can also be used for the purpose of evaluating interventions. For instance, surveys can be employed in large-scale field experiments with intervention groups and control groups in order to evaluate effects of psychosocial interventions and to identify important elements of such interventions. Statistical procedures for handling and analyzing data have become increasingly sophisticated and complex and require considerable statistical skills to be adequately utilized (Bijleveld, van der Kamp & Mooijaart, 1998; Harkness, van de Vijver & Mohler, 2003).

A typical survey is based on self-completion questionnaires or structured interviews as the methods for collecting data. The questions usually solicit information about demography (i.e. gender, age, education), behavior, opinions and attitudes, subjective health experiences, or aspects of the social or cultural context. Answers are usually coded with numbers and entered into a large matrix with one row per informant (subjects) and one column per questionnaire interview or item (variables). Not all questions are necessarily relevant to all informants. The data matrix might therefore have empty fields. Statistical software is used for the analysis of data.

Questionnaire items must be constructed according to sound principles and piloted before being used for research purposes (Presser et al., 2004). Good questions are relevant to informants, unambiguous, and easy to understand. Questions should be phrased in such a way that social desirability is avoided. Response categories should be mutually exclusive and cover all relevant alternatives. An important challenge in surveys covering different cultural and social groups is the comparability of questions across these categories. Ideally each item and response category should have the same meaning for all informants. If the same questionnaire is used in different languages, the translation must be followed by a re-translation and careful examination of discrepancies. Equivalence of scales across groups is a prerequisite for the analysis of inter-group differences. An important innovation in the testing of instruments is *item response theory analysis* (Embretson & Reise, 2000).

Representative samples are obtained by selecting informants according to specific rules. A sampling frame is a list of members of the study population. Ideally such a list should be as complete as possible. In a survey among music therapists, a possible sampling frame would be all members of a music therapy association. The higher the membership rates, the better this list would serve as a sampling frame. A representative sample is drawn up in such a way that all persons have some probability but no certainty of being selected. As an alternative to the sampling of individuals, it is also possible to sample clusters of individuals. This is called *cluster sampling*. When analyzing data based on cluster sampling or any other procedure deviating from simple random sampling, statistical techniques specifically developed for such designs must be applied.

The variety of tools available for *statistical analysis of data* has grown enormously since the introduction of personal computers. Univariate statistics is used to describe properties of single variables, bivariate statistics for describing associations between two variables, and multivariate statistics for describing associations between three or more variables. Some researchers would define multivariate statistical techniques as analyses where there are two or more dependent variables. The choice of statistical techniques depends on the measurement level of each variable, distributions, the number and specification of variables, and the nature of the associations among them. *Descriptive statistics* is used to describe the estimated properties of the population (percentages, measures of central tendency or dispersion, etc.), while *inferential statistics* is used for making inferences from sample to population (e.g. significance testing and confidence intervals).

Survey research has developed from being a method of describing populations by analyzing samples with simple statistical techniques to becoming an area of research where complex causal models can be tested. The development of statistical techniques is still ongoing. Areas of relevance to community music therapy include *multilevel analysis* and *analysis of latent variables*. Multilevel analysis involves the combination of data at the level of individuals and the level of groups in the same statistical models (Heck & Thomas, 2008). Latent variables are factors (for instance attitudes or personality traits) that cannot be directly observed but may be inferred from series of manifest variables (Brown, 2006). *Structural equation modeling* can be used to analyze patterns of associations among latent and observed variables (Hancock & Mueller, 2006).

Box 9.3 | SURVIVING BY SINGING? A SURVEY ON THE BENEFITS OF CULTURAL PARTICIPATION

In Sweden, Lars Olov Bygren and associates (1996) wanted to examine the possible effects of activities such as attendance at cultural events, reading books or periodicals, and making music or singing in a choir as determinants of survival. The researchers carried out interviews on involvement in cultural activities with 12,982 Swedes (aged 16 to 74 years). Attrition was 15% only. The interviews took place in 1982 and 83. Survival was registered until end of 1991. During that period, 847 died.

Statistical analyses were carried out with survival as the dependent variable and involvement in the various cultural activities (rarely, occasionally, or often) as the predictor. After having controlled for several confounders such as age, sex, education level, income, and health situation, the adjusted odds ratio for surviving among those who often attended cultural events compared with those who never did was 1.57 (95% confidence interval: 1.18 to 2.09). An odds ratio of 1.00 would mean that there was no association. An odds ratio higher than 1.00 means that survival was higher among those who often attended cultural activities. A confidence interval not covering the value 1.00 would mean that the finding was statistically significant. The researchers concluded that attendance at cultural events *may* have a positive effect on survival. The reason for their modesty is probably that you can never be sure that you have carried out a complete control for all

FIGURE 9.4 | Singers in flow and glow. Førde Senior Choir at The Music Therapy Center
of the County of Sogn og Fjordane, Norway.

Photo: Bent Are Iversen.

Box 9.3 |

possible confounders. Still, the results of such a large and well-designed study provide some evidence in favor of the assumption that involvement in cultural activities is healthy. The authors suggest a number of possible physiological mechanisms that can explain the positive effects on survival of involvement in cultural activities.

Surveys can of course be carried out for a number of other reasons than predicting survival, for instance to find out to what extent people living in a town would be interested in joining a new choir, to examine variations in musical preferences across gender or other demographic variables, to examine changes in involvement in musical activities over time, or to study prospectively associations between involvement in music and quality of life.

EXPERIMENTAL RESEARCH

In an **experiment** a hypothesis is tested systematically, with as much control over influences (independent variables) and confounding factors as possible. The development and refinement of the experiment was central to the scientific revolution of the natural sciences of the sixteenth to eighteenth centuries. Its use has later been extended to fields such as medicine, psychology, and social sciences. In experimental research on humans, the point is to influence some study participants systematically in order to examine the possible effects of such influences. There are different forms of experimental research. *Laboratory experiments* are characterized by rigorous control over environmental influences (physical and social). In social psychology one of the classic experiments on norm formation was carried out in a laboratory setting. Study participants had to sit on a chair in a room which was totally dark. At regular intervals a small light was made visible just in front of them and their task was to try to estimate how far the light moved in the short time it was visible. The light, in fact, never moved, but since they were sitting in a totally dark room with no visual reference points, they tended to perceive that the light moved. It turned out that when participants could hear what other participants answered, their own answers were influenced and their perceptions tended to converge. A "norm" for their perception of the movement of the light had emerged (Sherif, 1935).

When an experimental study is carried out under circumstances where the context and influences cannot be well controlled, it is usually called a *field experiment*. An example would be a study where a number of clubs for the elderly were randomly allocated to two groups: an intervention group and a comparison group. A data collection was carried out, and among the instruments used there was a scale for the measurement of quality of life. In the intervention group, a series of afternoon musical events were held by music therapists. After a specific number of such events, a new data collection was carried out among the members in both the intervention group and the comparison group. The researchers would want to find out to what extent participation in musical events had led to a higher level of quality of life among the residents in the intervention group. In a field experiment a number of factors that influence the participants' quality of life are hard to control. One obvious problem with such an experiment is that it would be difficult (and probably not desirable) to stop musical activities from taking place in the comparison clubs.

A distinction is made between *internal* and *external validity* in experimental research. If we have reason to believe that it was the intervention that led to a particular outcome, the internal validity of the experiment is high. If we believe that it is safe to conclude that the findings from the study can be generalized to other similar settings in the whole region or country, the external validity is high. Internal validity is about the causal relationship between intervention and outcomes. External validity is about generalizing the findings beyond those settings and the people who participated in the study.

An important precaution to increase the internal validity of an experiment is *randomization*. Random allocation should eliminate any systematic differences between intervention group(s) and comparison group(s). Random allocation does not eliminate all possible differences between groups, but remaining differences are random, not systematic. This means that they are under statistical control. If the number of units allocated is not too small, the differences between groups will usually be negligible. One way to improve a field experiment is to use *matching*. In our example with clubs for the elderly this could mean that clubs which were similar in terms of location (e.g. urban vs. rural), size, and age and background of members could be arranged in pairs. Within each pair, one would then be randomly allocated to the intervention group and the other to the control group. Such matching has implications for the statistical analysis of data.

One of the main challenges in studies that examine the effects of therapeutic interventions is *regression towards the mean effect*. Regression effects occur when a group of people are selected because they have particularly low or high scores, for instance on scales measuring psychological complaints. If measured again, this group will tend to obtain less extreme scores. It is probable that clients entering music therapy would obtain rather high scores on scales for psychological complaints. If tested again, their mean level of complaints would tend to be lower. Without a control group, it would be rather difficult to find out how much of the reduction was due to the regression effect and how much was caused by music therapy. The regression effect easily becomes a bias in therapists' understanding of their own practice. If they regularly observe that clients get better, it is easy to attribute all improvements as the outcome of their own therapeutic activities without taking into account that much (if not all) of the positive change might have taken place anyway (Barnett, van der Pols & Dobson, 2005).

Randomized controlled trials (RCTs) are often considered the "gold standard" for research on effects of therapeutic interventions. In the field of community music therapy, where units of allocation would be clusters rather than individuals, such studies easily become quite large and expensive and the possibilities of actually randomizing units might be limited. Under such circumstances, it can be necessary to find other research designs that will provide at least some evidence of the effectiveness of interventions.[6] One option would be to explore single case experimental designs. These are experiments in which one entity is observed repeatedly during a certain period of time, under the influence of at least one independent variable (Onghena, 2005).[7]

The independent variable is usually some condition that is manipulated (for instance involvement in community music therapy activities). Since there is only one single case involved, this case has to be exposed to various levels of the independent variable (no influence versus influence). The entity that is studied is not necessarily an individual person but could also be an aggregate of individuals, for instance a community choir. There are a number of possible designs in single-case experiments (Bordens & Abbott, 2008). Levels would, for instance, be baseline observations (denoted A) and observations after intervention or exposure (denoted B), with designs such as ABAB. There can be multiple interventions or exposures (denoted C, D etc.) and simultaneous combinations of exposures (denoted BC, BD etc). Multiple measurements over time (within each level or in combinations of levels) are also possible.

A major challenge in single case experimental designs is generalization. If you carry out a study which involves only one entity (for instance one group of adolescents who play together in a band under the supervision of a music therapist), how can you be sure

FIGURE 9.5 | Singing vivacity in rehearsal. The CeleBRation Choir in Auckland, New Zealand. Photo: Neil Shepherd.

that your findings are relevant also to other entities? If variability across entities is negligible, generalization is not a big problem. Or, if demonstration in one single case is enough to verify the existence of a phenomenon, generalization is also not an important issue. But if you, for instance, work with a group of young people and want to develop practices which can be applicable in other groups of young people, you need to know to what extent your results are of relevance to these other groups. The obvious answer to the challenge of generalization is *replication*. If you succeed in reproducing your findings when repeating the study in new contexts, you have substantiated the claim that your results could be of relevance to community music practices across several groups and contexts.

Box 9.4 | AN RCT ON RESOURCE-ORIENTED MUSIC THERAPY FOR CLIENTS WITH MENTAL HEALTH PROBLEMS

In Norway, Christian Gold and collaborators have performed a number of studies on the effects of music therapy in mental health care, including systematic reviews (Gold, Heldal et al., 2005; Gold et al., 2009). From 2004 to 2011 Gold was the principal researcher in a randomized controlled trial (RCT) on resource-oriented music therapy for clients with mental health problems and low therapy motivation. The study was developed in the Norwegian context (Gold, Rolvsjord et al., 2005) and since 2008 extended to a multicenter study involving collaborators in Austria and Australia.

The purpose of the study was to examine the effects of resource-oriented music therapy with clients with severe mental health problems. The rationale was based on the fact that traditional treatments such as medication and verbal psychotherapy have limited effects on some of the most severely affected clients. Clinical experience has suggested that music therapy can help these marginalized groups to bring forth hidden resources and build social competencies, and a theoretical foundation stressing empowerment, collaboration, and music as a personal and social resource was developed (Rolvsjord, 2004, 2007, 2010).

RCTs are designed to investigate effects of initiatives, in this case a complex intervention. What was studied was not the effect of musical stimulation but the effect of the whole "music therapy package" of interpersonal and musical relationships, activities, rituals, rationales, and reflections. The study was therefore linked to a contextual model rather than a medical model of therapy (Frank & Frank, 1991; Wampold, 2001). This choice created tensions between research rigor and therapeutic flexibility, for instance when it came to definition of the therapeutic intervention. In the medical tradition, RCTs should specify the intervention in detail, to ensure the validity and replicability of the study. Therapy manuals are often used to ensure this, but manuals with fixed sequences of techniques are clearly at odds with the most basic principles of any therapeutic endeavor that tries to understand and relate to the individual client. The solution developed for the RCT on resource-oriented music therapy was to establish guidelines of therapeutic principles

Box 9.4 |

rather than of specific techniques. Some of the central principles proposed were: Focusing on the client's strengths and potential, recognizing the client's competence related to her/his therapeutic process, fostering positive emotions, and acknowledging and encouraging musical skills and potentials. Proscribed principles were: Neglecting the client's strengths and potential, having a strong focus on pathology, avoiding emerging problems and negative emotions, and directing in a non-collaborative style (Rolvsjord, Gold & Stige, 2005).

Having defined the intervention in a way that allowed for therapeutic flexibility, Gold and collaborators could design a study that took criteria for solid outcome research into consideration, including the use of effect sizes (Gold, 2004). Based on calculations of effect sizes, the RCT was designed with 144 participants who were randomly selected to either an intervention group or comparison group. Interventions were provided and monitored over the course of three months from randomization. Outcomes were assessed at pre-test (before randomization), an early intermediate time point (1 month after randomization), post-test (3 months after randomization), and six-month follow-up (9 months after randomization). Informed by previous systematic reviews, a central objective was to determine whether resource-oriented music therapy helps clients with severe mental health problems reduce their level of negative symptoms (such as affective flattening, poor social relationships, and a general loss of interest and motivation). Secondary outcomes such as general functioning, interest in music, motivation for change, affect regulation, relational competence, and actual social relationships were also investigated. Another objective for the study was to determine whether general outcomes are mediated by specific outcomes, provided that significant effects are found (Gold, Rolvsjord et al., 2005).

At the time of writing, the results of this RCT are in the process of being analyzed, with several promising findings. Preliminary results suggest that music therapy was superior to standard care, independently of participants' age, sex, type of diagnosis (psychotic vs. non-psychotic disorder) or the specific hospital in which music therapy was offered. Drop-out rates were lower in music therapy, indicating that music therapy encouraged sustained engagement with services. In addition to documenting the effects of music therapy, results of the study also include the development of a new measurement instrument linked to assumed mechanisms of resource-oriented music therapy, namely an "interest in music scale" (Gold et al., forthcoming).

This study was performed in institutions of mental health care but illuminates some of the issues that need to be taken into consideration in future developments of RCTs for community music therapy. Definition of interventions in ways that allow for flexibility in practice is one such issue, the choice and development of relevant instruments of measurement is another (with outcome measures for individuals as well as for communities). In addition there will be issues such as the integration of RCTs and participatory designs and challenges linked to cluster sampling and randomization.

PREMISES AND PURPOSES REQUESTING PRACTICAL AND PLURALISTIC RESEARCH

Several authors have argued that action research is especially pertinent to community music therapy, due to its participatory nature and the affinity in values (e.g. Kleive & Stige, 1988; Stige, 2002, 2005; Hunt, 2005; Warner, 2005; McFerran & Hunt, 2008; Vaillancourt, 2009; Elefant, 2010b). Ethnographic fieldwork has also been established as a relevant approach to the study of community music therapy (see Stige et al., 2010a). Very little survey and experimental research has been documented, as is evident from the examples we have chosen for Boxes 9.3 and 9.4. Does this situation reflect the premises and purposes of community music therapy research or is there a need to broaden the bandwidth of research? In our judgment this is a question that requires careful consideration. A few suggestions for further deliberation will be presented here.

The qualities communicated by the acronym PREPARE discussed in Chapters 1 and 6 and the values discussed in Chapter 7 suggest that community music therapy is compatible with participatory, relational, and ecological premises. This does indeed suggest that the tradition of action research is central to community music therapy. We would still warn against the temptation to elevate this fit to generalized claims about the relevance of specific research methods or methodologies. Two of the characteristics of action research are that it is **practical** and **pluralistic** (Reason & Bradbury, 2006). In our view this suggests that the relevance and usefulness of surveys and experimental research should be recognized. This argument inevitably leads to acknowledgement of mixed methods in community music therapy. At the beginning of this chapter, we explained how there are tensions and contradictions between qualitative and quantitative methods of research. How then is the idea of mixed methods helpful?

Creswell and Clark (2011, pp. 38–51) appropriate a framework proposed by Crotty and suggest that it is useful to distinguish between worldviews, theoretical lenses, methodological approaches, and methods of data collection and analysis when designing studies. Worldviews differ when it comes to claims for knowledge; the post-positivist worldview focuses on cause and effect, the constructivist on meaning, the participatory on political concerns, and the pragmatist on consequences of action. These worldviews might be mutually exclusive in some respects, but not all. Few people would for instance support the case that political realities should be discussed in neglect of research on causes and effects. Similarly, research on the outcomes of initiatives which neglects political realities is also potentially problematic and might end up supporting the status quo when it comes to power and privilege.

As researchers we might need to relate to more than one worldview, then; there is no unified or total portrayal to rely on. Different ways of knowing supplement each other but do not replace each other. In our view this leads to a pluralistic stance that acknowledges action research as prominent in community music therapy, in a way that includes ethnography, survey research, and experimental research. Ethnography and surveys could be used in combination to gather information about everyday uses of music among various groups of people. Similarly, solid field experiments could give vital information about the outcomes and benefits of community music therapy activities.

It could be countered that experimental research, which is based on the premise that results can be generalized from one context to another, is difficult to combine with ecologically oriented practices (DeNora, 2006). The expertise and rigor required for RCTs might also constitute challenges for the development of participatory and collaborative approaches. These challenges are substantial but should be examined in the context of practical concerns. In many contexts, experimental research will be valued by lay and professional participants as one way of describing and analyzing the practice situation. The weight of the ecological criticism of experimental research, for instance, depends on the practice in question. In Chapter 8 we distinguished between particular routes, projects, and programs. RCTs are usually more relevant for the evaluation of programs than of particular processes and projects. The challenge of combining experimental designs with participatory processes in the context of a program has been explored by Schwantes (forthcoming), who engaged participants in the development of both study and program through use of focus groups.

Sometimes a qualitative study is what is needed, at other times a quantitative or a mixed methods study. In other words; the relevance of research methods can not be defined once and for all by reference to theoretical and philosophical criticism.

FIGURE 9.6 | Knowledge performed. Opera created with cancer patients and O'Brien in Melbourne, Australia. Performers Emma O'Brien, Merlyn Quaife, Michael Bishop and Judith Dodsworth.

Photo: Jeff Busby.

Negotiations on relevance and usefulness in a given social and historical context are always useful (see Nerheim, 1995; Ziman, 2000). Instead of treating action research as a specific research approach it is more helpful to think of it as a broad umbrella embracing various approaches to research, depending on the needs of each situation. It might hinder the flexible development of the field to define or ground this "umbrella" in a specific methodology. Premises and purposes should be explored and negotiated in social contexts. If a foundation is needed, the values that inform democratic practice (see Chapter 7) would serve researchers and participants better than any given research methodology.

CONCLUSION

To learn from research is central to a profession such as music therapy. Research is not the only factor that shapes community music therapy practice, however. Practice evolves in social contexts and is therefore also informed by values and local knowledge and by various musical and interpersonal events and processes.

The articulation of one or more research questions is usually central in the early phases of the research process. Research questions are usually informed by concerns that grow out of a situation or tradition of practice. This then leads to a review of the existing literature, in order to learn about the status of current knowledge, to refine the initial research question, and to develop the methods and design that could be used for exploration of it. Before data is collected, it is usually necessary to define populations and sites, select informants and other elements to study, and to develop and pilot instruments. After the data is collected it is time for transcription and analysis, which usually leads directly into the phase of interpreting findings and discussing them in relation to existing theory and knowledge. When a research paper has been carefully crafted on the basis of this, then it is time for submission to a journal or publisher, which leads to a process of peer review and revision before publication. This description illuminates some of the steps in a research project, but the process is seldom completely linear. In qualitative research especially there is room for movement back and forth between the various procedural steps. In action research the process and products of research are extended to include participatory and practical dimensions.

One way of conceptualizing differences between traditions of research is to focus on various paradigms or worldviews. Some of these differences are expressed in the debates between the traditions of quantitative and qualitative research. The differences between traditions notwithstanding, many values are shared among researchers, such as the values of communalism and skepticism. Communalism implies that knowledge is shared with the public, while skepticism implies that all new ideas and proposals are examined and evaluated critically.

Differences among research traditions could also be articulated in relation to different purposes, such as the intention to describe something, to explain something, or to evaluate something. Action researchers stress that research should contribute towards social change, and we have argued that this is a relevant view in community music therapy.

There are several traditions of research of potential relevance for community music therapy. We have discussed four approaches, namely action research, ethnographic research, survey research, and experimental research. Action research allows for focus on the integration of research activities, social change, and theory development. Ethnographic research enables the exploration of community music therapy as cultural practice in a given context. Survey research usually involves the use of self-completion questionnaires or structured interviews and is helpful for the exploration of how problems, resources, and attitudes are distributed in larger populations. Experimental research involves influencing some study participants (or groups) systematically in order to examine the possible effects of such influences.

The current literature on community music therapy research primarily consists of action research and ethnographic studies. Whilst the participatory, relational, ecological, and activist qualities of community music therapy practice resonate especially well with the tradition of action research, this should not dominate in ways that hinder the development of other research traditions. Surveys and experimental research do have a place within community music therapy. A general hierarchy of research methodology, with systematic reviews and RCTs at the top and qualitative studies at the bottom (see Kristiansen & Mooney, 2004) does not. Participatory perspectives invite practical and pluralistic research, not singular worldviews or prescriptive methodological beliefs.

Community music therapy researchers should take interest in expanded epistemologies in a radical yet cautious way; radical in its willingness to accept different ways of knowing (including experiential and presentational knowing) and yet cautious so that established values of research (such as communalism and skepticism) are not violated. The future development of community music therapy depends on the creation of high quality research studies. Fixed criteria of evaluation would not be successful in evaluating the social and situated character of community music therapy research, however. A dialogic approach to research evaluation, embracing practical and pluralistic assets might be more helpful (Stige, Malterud, & Midtgarden, 2009).[8]

KEY TERMS, DISCUSSION TOPICS, AND NOTES

Key Terms

Key terms in order of appearance:

Premises
Qualitative research
Quantitative research
Objectivity
Reflexivity
Purposes
Research processes
Research products

Research values
Action research
Ethnographic research
Survey research
Experimental research
Participatory worldview
Pluralism

Discussion Topics

The following critical thinking questions could be discussed in class or in groups. They could also be used by the individual for critical reflection on topics discussed in the chapter. Extra resources and self-correcting "skill-drill" questions could be found on the website of the book.

1. Research needs might vary from context to context, depending on the status of knowledge and the social situation at hand. Think of one context you know of where community music therapy is relevant and suggest some possible research questions. What research traditions and methods could be relevant for the exploration of these questions?
2. Participatory action research is developed from the concerns and visions people have in relation to the contexts in which they live and work. Some researchers report on the challenges of situations where participants have not articulated concerns and visions. Discuss different ways of dealing with such a situation.
3. Not all researchers would agree that experimental research is compatible with the practice of community music therapy. In this chapter we have argued that relevance can not be evaluated in abstract terms but needs to be negotiated in context. Imagine a situation where this is negotiated and develop pro and contra arguments of relevance for this situation.

Notes

1   Inspired by Kuhn's (1962/1996) well-known sociology of science (but given a much more philosophical interpretation), the discussion of paradigms has been common in the literature on qualitative research (see Guba & Lincoln, 2005). This discussion has been helpful in clarifying that philosophical assumptions influence our conceptions of research but it has also highlighted abstract distinctions in ways that are not always helpful in pragmatic adjustment to real world research needs.

2   Epidemiologists (who study the occurrence and causes of diseases and death) distinguish between descriptive epidemiology, analytic epidemiology, and experimental epidemiology. In the social sciences, a similar distinction is established between research that aims at bringing about three kinds of information: *problem information* (how large or widespread is the problem), *causal information* (what are the factors or processes behind the problem), and *action information* (what can be done to reduce or eliminate the problem).

3   It is not uncommon to talk of two cultures of research (Snow, 1959/1998) but Ziman (2000) argues that there are enough similarities across the range of research practices to suggest that they are

influenced by a shared set of values. Ziman's argument is developed from Merton's (1942/1973) famous work on this theme.

4   The presentation of action research and ethnography in this chapter is based on a rethinking of arguments developed in two previously published book chapters in *Music Therapy Research* (see Stige 2005a, b).

5   Pavlicevic describes seven sequences of this event in detail, of which we have included the first.

6   The strengths and weaknesses of different designs for field experiments have been carefully described and discussed in the literature (Shadish, Cook & Campbell, 2002).

7   Single case experimental designs is one sub-category of the broader field of single-case research (Yin, 2008).

8   Stige, Malterud and Midtgarden (2009) argue that the diversity of traditions that characterize qualitative research suggest that any set of shared criteria for evaluation would be problematic. The authors then propose an approach to research evaluation that encourages reflexive dialogue through use of an evaluation agenda. Unlike criteria, an agenda could embrace pluralism; it does not request consensus on philosophical or methodological issues, only on what themes warrant discussion. The specific evaluation agenda proposed by the authors—EPICURE—consists of two dimensions communicated through use of two acronyms. The first, EPIC, refers to the challenge of producing rich and substantive accounts (based on Engagement, Processing, Interpretation, and (Self)-Critique). The second, CURE, refers to the challenge of dealing with preconditions and consequences of research (with a focus on (Social) Critique, Usefulness, Relevance, and Ethics). The arguments for the EPICURE agenda could perhaps be extended to the evaluation of community music therapy research more generally, since requests for pluralism and practical relevance will be similar.

Professionalization for Participatory Practice

After studying Chapter 10, you will be able to discuss questions such as:

- How does community music therapy influence the profession of music therapy?
- What characterizes the landscape of professions in late modernity?
- Is a strong professional identity a hindrance in the development of adaptable practice?
- How are the ideas of partnership and leadership relevant for community music therapy?
- How will community music therapy affect training and supervision in music therapy?
- What distinguishes the ethics of an ethics-driven practice?

THE POLITICS OF PROFESSIONALIZATION

In an essay on past and present in music therapy, historian Peregrine Horden (2000) argues that contemporary professional music therapy is remarkably hard to specify. He finds the official definitions of the field rather open-ended and suggests that criteria of success will be as elusive as definitions. In a similar vein, Ruud (2010) suggests that the diversity of contemporary music therapy makes it very challenging for clients, workplaces, and the public to relate to the profession. In the light of these concerns, community music therapy makes a bad situation worse, as its development leads to a further extension and diversification of contemporary music therapy. This is perhaps part of the explanation why the emergence of an international discourse of community music therapy after 2000 not only instigated interest and enthusiasm but also disapproval and criticism, ranging from the proposal that community music therapy is redundant (Edwards, 2002) to the appraisal that its non-medical profile is professional suicide (Erkkilä, 2003). In 2008 the *British Journal of Music Therapy* devoted a special issue to the question whether community music therapy challenges the profession or expands it more positively (Barrington, 2008;

FIGURE 10.1 | Three hands on a keyboard. Music education in a Palestinian refugee
camp in Lebanon.

Photo: Even Ruud.

Ansdell & Pavlicevic, 2008; Procter, 2008). One of the themes explored in this chapter is whether the identity of the profession is best nurtured through specialization within a prescribed territory or through involvement in contingent and collaborative relationships.

There are several ways of describing **professions** and degrees of **professionalization**. Hernes (2002) summarizes the literature by focusing on three sets of criteria: One set focuses on the recognized value of the work done and the type of knowledge required. Physicians who work with life and death and base their work in the science of medicine are a group with a very high degree of professionalization according to this frame. A different set of criteria is linked to professional education and training. A high degree of professionalization implies that the training is long and demanding and that nobody could enter the vocation without this training. A third set of criteria is related to the authority, autonomy, and responsibility of the practitioner. A high degree of professionalization implies authority and autonomy in the process of assessing, working with, and evaluating a case, with ethical and juridical responsibility for the results.

Such "check-list" descriptions of what characterizes professions have been challenged as being too simplistic, but the above suffices to illuminate an important dilemma. Professions legitimate themselves by referring to the service they offer for clients and by claiming that their practice affords the safety of expert help. These claims are not necessarily wrong, but they reveal only one side of the coin. To work for your profession is also self-promotion; it leads to increased status and job protection. It might even at times disempower clients. Professionalization is integral to the increasing division of labor in modern societies and it makes sense to suggest that the ambiguity that characterizes modernization also is typical of professionalization; the process solves some problems and creates some new ones (Fornäs, 1995).

The debates we referred to in the *British Journal of Music Therapy* throw light on this dilemma. Barrington (2008) argues that the success of British music therapy in gaining legal registration (in 1997) has not only allowed the profession to grow but has also been beneficial to clients. The Health Professions Council (HPC) is the regulatory body in the UK and its prime role, Barrington explains, is to protect clients and the public. The standards established by the profession under HPC supervision therefore represent expert advice that it would be irresponsible to neglect. The critique within the British community music therapy literature of how music therapy has progressed as a discipline and profession is therefore potentially destructive, in Barrington's view. Procter's interpretation of the situation is quite different:

> Regulatory standards, such as those imposed by the HPC, are not written by clients: they are a means of ensuring "professionalism" by ensuring that registered professionals behave like "professionals". "Protecting the clients" is unquestionably important: here, however, it may be argued to be little more than a cover story for elitism. As a music therapist, I would like to believe that Barrington's supposition is true. As a sociologist, I remain to be convinced.
>
> (Procter, 2008, p. 80)

Responding to Barrington, in Ansdell and Pavlicevic (2008, p. 73) they suggest that her analysis perhaps uses community music therapy "as a straw man for a more general anxiety about recent unexpected twists in the professional story of music therapy." Community music therapy does not challenge the profession in a negative way, these authors argue; it could instead be understood as a symptom of a more general transformation on its way, instigated by social and cultural change in society at large. "Times change; needs change, professions change!" Ansdell and Pavlicevic (2008, p. 74) assert, in an argument that echoes a point made very clear by Freidson (1970/1988) in his study of the profession of medicine. He underlined that *profession* is not a generic concept; it is a changing historic notion with particular roots in each national context. Freidson also claimed that professionalism—understood as the struggle for increased professional status and autonomy—is especially prominent in countries influenced by Anglo-American culture. He went as far as calling it an "Anglo-American disease." If this is accurate, it is probable that not every aspect of the heated British music therapy debate is recognizable in other countries. The more general theme of how and why the profession develops in various directions would be recognizable.

This is the theme of this chapter and we will also look at how the emergence of community music therapy might influence the music therapy profession at large. The latter focus is relevant because the community music therapy literature has avoided the title "community music therapist." The professional title "music therapist" has been maintained, while the term community music therapy has been used to describe developments in discipline and practice. No new professional group has been established. As many of the debates about the professions are concerned with the issue of whether or not (and when and how) the role of the professional disempowers clients, the question that guides the elaborations in this chapter is how professionalization could become compatible with the values and principles of participatory practice that we outlined in Chapters 6 to 8.

Box 10.1 | PROFESSIONALIZATION OF MUSIC THERAPY IN NORWEGIAN PRISONS

Music therapy has established itself as a professional practice in Norwegian prisons, after idealistic pioneering work in the 1990s. What did the encounter between a small and unconventional profession and an established and bounded institution lead to? How has the institution influenced the profession and the profession influenced the institution? These questions were asked in a study of the music therapy profession in Norwegian prisons (Pettersen, 2008).

In the framework for the investigation, the researcher utilized Abbott's (1988) theory of "the system of professions." Abbott used the term *jurisdiction* to describe the link between profession and practice. Jurisdiction describes the "territory" that is under each profession's authority. Traditionally, professionalism has been understood as the fight for monopoly but Abbot underlined that there are several types of jurisdiction. Full jurisdiction involves control over a territory, but there are supplementing strategies such as subordination, division of labor (according to specific competencies), and intellectual jurisdiction (superior knowledge in a field of competition).

Box 10.1 |

In investigating how profession and institution had influenced each other, Pettersen (2008) also sought to find out what kind of "jurisdictional practice" characterized Norwegian music therapists in this context. He made a case study of three prisons which had all introduced musical activities as part of the rehabilitation programs offered to inmates. Two of the prisons had engaged music therapists to do the work, while one prison had engaged music teachers instead. One of Pettersen's conclusions was that the Norwegian music therapists working in these prisons had not prioritized attempts at establishing formal jurisdiction, such as requests for authorization or other formal regulations. This is not to say that there had been no struggles involved, only that the music therapists' appeal for recognition had been performed in more informal ways. Interest and demand for music therapy had been established through high quality work, research, and media coverage.

Before the late 1990s, only one prison in Norway used music systematically. This prison had employed a music therapist (Nilsen, 2007). At the beginning of the new millennium this pioneering work was recognized at national level and the ambition of establishing music activities in all Norwegian prisons was supported by parliament. This remarkable increase in interest and support did not automatically lead to increased professionalization of music therapy, however. The music activities became linked to the school system established in the prisons, and all music workers, including the music therapists, had to accept that the formal title of their job was music teacher. This situation represented a challenge for the identity of the music therapists. One of the informants summarized the situation by suggesting that they were employed as teachers and worked as music therapists but did not do therapy (Pettersen, 2008, p. 74). In other words: The professional identity was that of being a music therapist, and the understanding of discipline and practice was informed by community music therapy, so that practice was defined as empowerment leading to community participation rather than as individualized treatment.

When Pettersen (2008) examined how the music therapists and the music teachers described their work in the prisons, he discovered that the music therapists focused more on personal resources, interpersonal relationships, and social participation than the music teachers, who emphasized high quality musical products and learning according to a curriculum. Pettersen then examined whether administrators would recognize any differences between the two occupational groups. On this point the results were highly disparate. A leading administrator of the prison school system insisted on the formal fact that the music therapists were engaged as teachers, while two of the prison directors were open to the possibility of music therapy as a profession with a new hybrid identity, somewhere in between that of musician, teacher, health worker, and social worker.

Pettersen's (2008) conclusion is that continued professionalization of music therapy in Norwegian prisons is important, not just because it will strengthen the safety and profes- sional identity of music therapists but because it has the potential of influencing the values of rehabilitation activities in prisons in the direction of participation and empowerment.

THE LANDSCAPE OF PROFESSIONS IN LATE MODERNITY

As Freidson (1970/1988) argued, the specifics of social structures and cultural traditions of each nation should be taken into consideration when we examine the development of professions. There are also some developments that seem to characterize all modern societies. In this section we will examine how the notions of **modernity** and **late modernity** can shed light on the processes of professionalization. In sociology, modernity refers to the particular attributes of modern societies, while **modernization** denotes the processes by which traditional societies achieve modernity. The concept of modernization has sometimes been used in a biased way, understood as part of the process of "upgrading" primitive societies. It has thus been used in ways that neglect the positive values of traditional societies and the negative effects of modernity. We use the term more broadly to denote the continuous transformation of industrialized and post-industrialized societies, with ambivalent qualities in the processes and outcomes.[1]

It is beyond the scope of this chapter to go deep into sociological theory, but some reflections will be helpful. Modernity is usually analyzed in several dimensions. *Economic modernization* has been linked to technological development and increased division of labor, while *political modernization* has been linked to the development of political institutions, with the implication that there is some separation of our immediate life context and the power relations of the society. *Social modernization* has brought increased literacy and education, as well as the decline of traditional networks and structures of authority. *Cultural modernization* has been characterized by secularization and rationalization. This is not to say that a rational certainty has been established:

> Modernity is a post-traditional order, but not one in which the sureties of tradition and habit have been replaced by the certitude of rational knowledge. Doubt, a pervasive feature of modern critical reason, permeates into everyday life as well as philosophical consciousness, and forms a general existential dimension of the contemporary social world. Modernity institutionalises the principle of radical doubt and insists that all knowledge takes the form of hypotheses: claims which may very well be true, but which are in principle always open to revision and may have at some point to be abandoned.
>
> (Giddens, 1991, pp. 2–3)

Modern societies are highly complex, with a division of labor characterized by specialization and differentiation. The radical doubt that permeates modern societies might then to some degree explain why modernity has led to the growth of professions; occupational groups claiming expert knowledge in specialized fields can argue that they are able to help client groups in need of their specific expertise. It is important, however, not to think of this as a psychological process only. In a complex and uncertain world we might all feel that we need the help of an expert, but this feeling is not unrelated to how the experts have presented themselves to the public. As part of their competition in a market, the professions tend to underline their altruistic intentions and this rhetoric seeps into the culture.

Abbott (1988) studied professionalization in modern societies by examining the system of professions as a whole, through comparative and historical studies of professions in nineteenth- and twentieth-century England, France, and America. Central to his theory is the notion that professions compete in a market, in a system where directions taken by one profession have effects on the opportunities for others. If one profession feels strong enough to attempt to increase its market value by keeping its numbers relatively low, this might create opportunities for new occupations to enter the segments neglected by the first profession, for instance. According to Abbott, this competition should not solely be understood in the light of power dynamics, however. A complex range of social and cultural processes is involved, so he does not suggest that the naïve assumption that professions are idealistic servants of their clients and society should be replaced by the cynical accusation that they are looking for nothing but money and power.

Complexity has increased as societies the last few decades have been in a process of transformation that some scholars have labeled late modernity. There are several related

FIGURE 10.2 | Open air. Music therapy with hypertensive patients, University Hospital of Goiás, Brazil.

Photo: Lara Silva.

if not completely overlapping ways of describing this shift; it could be understood as a radicalization of modernity, as the emergence of the risk society, as reflexive modernity, or as liquid modernity.[2] Stige (2003) related the emergence of community music therapy to late modern developments, and this point has been illuminated in several of the chapters of this book. Three examples could be given: First, we underlined in Chapter 3 that health is more than absence of disease. To an increasing number of people it is also a personal project of health and wellbeing, which is a development that links to reflexive identity and concerns for risks. Second, as we illuminated in Chapter 4, relationships between individuals and communities are increasingly "liquid" and in flux in contemporary societies. Third, the notion of health musicking discussed in Chapter 5 exemplifies the radicalization of modernity. The enormous contemporary interest for music and health could be taken to embody a radical transformation of the differentiation that characterized modernity. Radicalization has led to a hyper-differentiation in the two areas of music and health in ways that have eventually introduced new hybrids such as medical ethnomusicology, community music therapy, the health psychology of music, and the arts and health movement.

Late modernity transforms the landscape of professions. The idea of expert knowledge is challenged, relationships between professions are destabilized, and the request for flexible and reflexive practices increases. Implications include not only altered relationships to workplaces and regulatory bodies but also to clients and the public (Pettersen, 2008). The degree to which these developments lead to either powerlessness or empowerment of the individual is not possible to decide theoretically or empirically once and for ever. It is a matter of struggle in concrete contexts. Thus it is important to explore questions of how and when professionalization could co-exist with client rights and valued participation (Knorth, Van Den Bergh & Verheij, 2002).

PROFESSIONAL IDENTITY AND REFLEXIVE ADAPTABILITY

Hippocrates is known as a pioneer of medicine in Greek antiquity. He was also a pioneer of reflections on the rights and obligations of the physician and he argued that to practice medicine means to belong to a community where knowledge is developed and contested (Leer-Salvesen, 2002, p. 13). Modern professions including music therapy are also communities of scholar-practitioners. In Chapter 4, we defined community as a group of people who share space and practice and develop a culture of commitment. In the community of a profession, the idea of shared space must be modified to include a series of sites for interaction, such as international conferences, research journals, and electronic forums. As such, there are elements of "imagined community" in a profession, but usually a strong culture of commitment and **professional identity** is developed.

As communities, professions are relative to the societies they belong to. Studies in medical sociology have also revealed that a powerful profession such as medicine has been an influential agent in the development of modern societies (Turner, 2004). According to Turner, medicine's "golden age" of status and authority could be identified as the period between 1910 and 1970. Like any institution with power, medicine has been strong in the construction of its own official history. The dominating history of medicine has been that of progressive development from harmful ignorance to the benign triumph of rational science. This narrative has been challenged more than once, most influentially perhaps in Foucault's (1961/1991) work *Madness and Civilization.* Even though the intention of many individual psychiatrists was to help the insane, Foucault claimed that psychiatric practice could be understood as a way of ruling the population in order to make it more adaptive and productive.

Details of Foucault's argument could be disputed but his work has been recognized as a groundbreaking contribution illuminating the need to think critically in relation to the self-promotion developed by a profession in power. In Turner's (2004) appraisal, the official history of the medical profession tends to neglect the continuous struggle among competing medical systems in a society and also fails to notice the growing complexity and pluralism of modern health care. Developments in late modernity, with globalization and de-regulation of the economy, make these issues acute. Turner therefore suggests that we might need to replace the idea of linear progress with that of endless circular

FIGURE 10.3 | Music in Motion. Creative Expressions Studio and Gallery, Milledgeville, GA, USA. Photo: Field Whipple.

struggles between professional and lay autonomy, individualized and socialized health strategies, technical and political solutions, concerns for risks and rights, and so on.

Music therapy is not a very powerful profession compared to medicine, but music therapists run the risk of neglecting the growing complexity and pluralism of modern health practices, within and without the health care sector. As outlined throughout this book, some of the struggles that have made community music therapy relevant in contemporary societies relate to requests for more participatory and empowering practices focusing on people's resources in everyday contexts. The emergence of community music therapy is one possible response to this, with a particular focus on music's social and communal possibilities. This implies a contextualized transformation of music therapy and it is not possible to identify one specific professional identity that could be said to be essential for community music therapy practices. What seems to be shared is a readiness to negotiate roles and identities. Procter (2008) uses the term **reflexive adaptability**—the willingness to reconsider our professional role in relation to the changing needs of a situation—to describe what he considers a necessity and an ideal. In Chapter 7 we discussed the notion of autonomy as a relational accomplishment. If we use two of the notions we applied in Chapter 8 for description of community music therapy processes, we could say that bonding within the community of the music therapy profession can be supplemented with bridging to other lay and professional communities.

In late modern societies, interest in music and health has increased dramatically. In many contexts where music therapists were previously the only ones to introduce music, community musicians, music educators, and other professional groups now also bring in their experiences and competencies (Edwards, 2007; Hartley, 2008; MacDonald, Kreutz & Mitchell, in press). The emergence of community music therapy indicates that the inverse process also takes place; music therapists bring their experiences and competencies to areas that perhaps used to be conceived as the domain of community musicians (Aigen, in press). Relationships between music education, community music, and community music therapy are therefore important to examine (Veblen, 2007). Relationships to other professions—including medicine—are equally important in many contexts.[3] In this complex landscape of criss-crossing relationships and responsibilities, the question of how to build structures that could nurture a culture of collaboration is pressing, as indicated by the terms *multiple healing systems* (Chapter 2) and *multiple health action systems* (Chapter 6).

Box 10.2 | AMATEUR GROUP SINGING AS THERAPEUTIC EXPERIENCE AND SOLIDARITY IN ACTION

Valuing amateur musicianship is one element of the community music movement. Betty Bailey and Jane Davidson's (2003) article about a Canadian choir for homeless men also illuminates the therapeutic value of music in everyday life and society's increasing interest in this.

Box 10.2 |

> The Homeless Choir was initiated and directed by a soup kitchen volunteer who was not trained as a music specialist or a therapist. After years of service helping to feed the homeless, this young man determined that his efforts were not resulting in observable long-term changes. He began to search for a means to help the homeless men break the cycle of dependence. His own positive experiences as a choral singer led him to believe that some of the homeless men might be inspired through singing and sharing their voices with the larger community (Bailey & Davidson, 2003, p. 20).

After a rather fragile beginning with just a few participants, the size of the choir gradually stabilized with about twenty members. Many of the homeless singers struggled with emotional problems, alcohol problems and drug addictions, and unsuccessful relationships and unfortunate life circumstances were more of a rule than an exception in this group. The process of the choir was never smooth but the choir was able to keep going and started to perform in public. Gradually things started to change. A few years after the choir was established, the members were interviewed by the two researchers referred to above, who describe some remarkable changes:

> The choristers' present situation presents quite a sharp contrast to their previous circumstances. At the time of the interviews all the choir members were in permanent housing and some had part-time employment. During the past five years the choir has performed at over 1,000 concerts, occasionally in the company of notable performers and often in the subway terminals where they first sang for the public. They have appeared on television broadcasts and have made a number of CDs which they sell at performances and distribute to prisoners and others who exist in difficult circumstances (Bailey & Davidson, 2003, pp. 20–21).

The transformation included, in other words, radical personal changes as well as elements of solidarity and social action. The Homeless Choir in fact started a political party—Parti de Rien (Party of Nothing)—which gave the homeless of Canada a representative in the first federal election in which the homeless in this country had been given the right to vote (Bailey & Davidson, 2003, p. 21). The story of this astonishing transformation is balanced, however, by a note the researchers make on what they consider problems with participation:

> It must also be mentioned that although hundreds of patrons eat at the soup kitchen daily, only approximately 20 of these individuals were members of the choir at any given time. Therefore, it is evident that, for the vast majority of disadvantaged people, a barrier exists which dissuades them from participating in a group singing activity even when the activity is situated within the unique cultural framework of the community. Whether the general reluctance to participate is based on notions related to musical ability, the fear of having to stop using drugs and/or alcohol, the effects of mental illness or other unknown factors can only be determined through continued research with marginalized groups (Bailey & Davidson, 2003, pp. 30–31).

Box 10.2

The results for those who did participate suggested that the amateur singers coached by a volunteer in a community setting did experience therapeutic effects. Bailey and Davidson (2003, p. 31) related these effects to Ruud's music therapy theory on music and quality of life (Ruud, 1997a and b; see also Box 4.3).

PARTNERSHIP AS ETHOS AND ORGANIZATION

The literature on professionalization typically describes the relationships between professions as being characterized by domination, subordination, and rivalry, modified by negotiated divisions of responsibilities (Abbott, 1988). These patterns are perhaps especially clear in the hierarchic structures of the health care sector. Many would argue that hierarchy and a clear division of labor is necessary in complex organizations such as hospitals. Critics have argued that it is difficult to develop practices that are participatory and empowering for clients within these structures (Rolvsjord, 2010). It could thus be said that "normal professionalism" creates and reproduces power relations and that it might benefit clients if professions could detach somewhat from the struggles of demarcation. Others argue that the professions increasingly find themselves squeezed in between growing consumer expectations and expanding systems of central government regulation and bureaucratic management.

There is a dearth of studies on community music therapy and professionalization at this point. Barrington's (2005) doctoral thesis on the professionalization of music therapy in the UK included a critique of the community music therapy literature and what she conceived as a lack of recognition of the necessity to adhere to established professional standards. Pettersen's (2008) study of the professionalization of music therapy in Norwegian prisons suggested that the music therapists there—who defined their work in community music therapy terms—did not prioritize the strategies of establishing formalized recognition of rights and responsibilities (jurisdiction). This finding was in conflict with what could be expected according to Abbott's (1988) theory of professionalization. Two diverse studies do not constitute a very solid platform for wide-ranging conclusions, but taken together with the reflections developed previously in this chapter on how late modernity seems to transform the landscape of professions, our interpretation is that community music therapy invites different strategies of professionalization from those that have been used by the established health care professions. In the remainder of this chapter we will examine this interpretation, starting with the proposal that professional community music therapy practice can be developed within **partnerships**.

Ideally, partnership is based on the quality and experience of affiliation and mutual support, compatible with the values we discussed in Chapter 7. Some music therapists have been able to demonstrate that what could be called a **partnership ethos** of equality

FIGURE 10.4 | Drum circle. The Music Therapy Community Clinic in the Greater Cape Town area, South Africa.

Photo: India Baird.

and mutuality at least to some degree (and in some moments) could be cultivated even within the walls of the hierarchic hospital (Aasgaard, 2002, 2004, see also Box 6.3). Partnership also includes the possibility of organization, and we will elaborate this possibility, as one strategy for creating contexts for professionalization in accordance with the idea of reflexive adaptability.

If one accepts the assumption that health problems are not limited to the level of the individual organism, health should not be considered a field for specialists but an area for collaboration. Discussing community music therapy in light of public health, Stige (1996) argued for the relevance of considering professionals and people in need as partners. The notion of partnership involves an alteration of the role of the professional, often changing it from that of an expert to that of a resource person in collaborative processes. This idea is well established within the scope of the therapeutic relationship but Stige's point was to propose broader partnerships. This was exemplified with the presentation of a community music therapy project challenging traditional boundaries and models of professional practice by focusing on participation in a community context.[4]

Partnership is not opposed to professionalism. In fact, one tradition of partnership has been linked to professionalism very closely, namely the tradition of partnership within professional service firms (Empson, 2007). This tradition differs from the one we will elaborate here, as it concentrates on partnership between professionals rather than on collaborative work where lay people are also involved. It does, however, have some of the same characteristics concerning trust, collective decision-making, and dedication to shared goals. Empson claims that these qualities are not created by idealistic individuals but by the way the work is organized; partners have a share of ownership and a say in the management of the firm. Partnership is a way of tempering tensions between individualism and collectivism.

Partnership has been established as a notion referring to a collaborative and inclusive way of working within the field of public health. This is a notion that we find relevant for future explorations of the professional role in community music therapy. Partnership could be understood as committed collaboration between **independent** partners acknowledging that they are also **interdependent**. The causes that bring agents together in a partnership are often complex and multifaceted and require collaboration across traditional boundaries or lines of differentiation. Experts and lay people, local governments and a range of voluntary organizations might for instance collaborate in relation to community problems that affect people's health (Amdam, 2010).

A partnership approach takes into consideration that health involves all sectors and levels of society. Partnerships for health therefore involve a range of sectors, levels, goals, and arrangements. An endless variety is imaginable. The community music therapy literature gives a few examples of partnerships, often without using the term. We will briefly describe four of the possibilities; self-help partnerships, project partnerships, institutional partnerships, and governance partnerships.

A non-governmental agency in East London advertised for a musician to facilitate an ongoing music group who called themselves Musical Minds. The agency, Together Tower Hamlets, is a community project providing a range of self-help, user involvement training, and social opportunities for adults experiencing mental health problems. The organization emphasizes a social model, with user involvement, support, and empowerment as guiding principles. A music therapist took the job of helping Musical Minds to sing together and to put on occasional performances (see Boxes 4.2 and 7.1). A community of practice emerged, where goals and ways of working were negotiated among members (Ansdell, 2010a). Collaboration between professionals and self-help groups is sometimes called "assisted self-help" (Williams & Windebank, 2001). In the context of this discussion, **self-help partnership** is also a relevant term, highlighting that the collaborative relationships are characterized by a democratic process of collective decision-making.

In South Africa, a group of music therapists formed a non-profit organization called the Music Therapy Community Clinic, working with deprived communities within the Greater Cape Town area. Adolescents in these communities face the danger of becoming immersed in gang culture. At one point, the music therapists were approached by the local police who were concerned about the huge number of adolescents at risk in the community. The music therapists and the local police then partnered in an attempt to help the youngsters stay out of the criminal justice system (see Box 1.1). The adolescents themselves appeared skeptical and aloof at the beginning but gradually got involved.

"Music seems to be the magnet. It is a 'cool' thing to do" (Fouché & Torrance, 2005). In the literature on public health, local and informal partnerships geared towards shared goals are often called **project partnerships** (Amdam, 2010). In this case music could be said to be part of the partnership too.

Creative Expressions Studio and Gallery in Milledgeville, the capital of Georgia in the US, is a program that promotes creativity and self-expression for artists with developmental disabilities through the use of music therapy, nature explorers, visual arts, and performing arts. The program was implemented in 2000 with the partnership of the Life Enrichment Center (a non-profit organization) and the Music Therapy Department of Georgia College and State University. To provide performing arts experiences for people with disabilities within intentional communities and the broader community has been an important purpose in the development of the program (see Box 6.1). This purpose is linked to an acknowledgment of the rightful place people with disabilities have as full citizens in the community (Curtis & Mercado, 2004). Over the years the program has expanded and partnered with various schools, hospitals, clubs, and organizations in the community. The program employs professional artists and a music therapist and also utilizes a variety of volunteers. This type of formalized collaboration between institutions could be called **institutional partnerships** (Amdam, 2010). Institutional partnerships are more judicially binding than project partnerships.

In the 1970s, Norwegian cultural politics changed substantially, with much more focus on participation in cultural activities as a human right for all citizens. This change could partly be related to processes in the UN, where The International Covenant of Economic, Social and Cultural Rights had been adopted by the General Assembly in 1966 (see Chapter 7). In the early 1980s, The Norwegian Council for Cultural Affairs realized that the right to musical and cultural participation was not realized for disabled people in most Norwegian communities. The council then funded a project in collaboration with a county and municipality in Western Norway in order to explore ways of changing this situation. Two music therapists were engaged to work on the project and various amateur music associations were also involved in the process (see Box 2.5). The practical work in the project was informed by the principles of participatory action research (Stige, 2002). This project exemplifies what is often called a **governance partnership** (Amdam, 2010), where public interests collaborate innovatively with private interests and/or the third sector and local democratic organizations in order to realize shared goals.

The examples given illuminate that different types of partnerships are not mutually exclusive. A governance partnership could include various institutional partnerships and project partnerships and could also embrace self-help partnerships, for instance. Self-help partnerships, as described above, are almost by definition compatible with the principles of participatory practice that we described in Chapters 6 to 8. The legitimacy of the other forms of partnership in relation to participatory practice depends on the degree of participant influence and democracy in decision-making processes.

Participation in partnerships is offered here as one proposed direction for development of the music therapy profession. Partnerships embody the possibility of combining concerns for participatory practice with concerns for professional development within structures that are adaptable. When partnerships are realized as a way of organizing practice they represent alternatives to vertical hierarchies and horizontal demarcations. But partnership models are not without their own limitations and problems. To overcome power differentials and legacies of mistrust is often challenging. Consequently partnerships are at times unstable and vulnerable (Amdam, 2010). The term "partnership" could also be misused as a euphemism for relationships where power and privilege have not been substantially challenged (Cahill, Sultana, & Pain, 2007). Partnerships do not erase conflict and competition, but usually they do create a different frame for working with these issues, as the legitimacy of partnerships is established through communication and negotiation rather than tradition and authority.

Relationships between professional groups could be compared to the many overlapping social groups that we see in a society. These groups are similar in some respects and different in others, with cross-cutting affiliations. People might for instance be divided from each other by disability or sexuality but be united by class or gender. Similarly, professions might be divided from each other in training and status but could still be united by certain goals and values. Conflicts are always possible along any dividing line, but it is also possible that "groups can retain their distinctive commitments while endorsing a shared egalitarian conception of justice, a conception which itself recognizes and values diversity" (Baker et al., 2004, p. 52). Several music therapists have documented work in this direction. In Australia, Threlfall (1998) has explored possibilities for partnerships between community music and music therapy. In Norway, Aftret (2005) has explored the role of the music therapist in the municipality over a period of 20 years and shown that a community-oriented approach to music therapy allows for respectful collaboration in ways that challenge but also nurture the music therapy identity.

If values, such as respect and equality are central in community music therapy (see Chapter 7), the ambition of contributing to constructive conflict resolution between professional groups should be embraced. This also suggests that the idea of partnership should not exclude **leadership**. Vaillancourt's (2009) research on community music therapy, peace, and social justice explores a notion of leadership as service and trans-formation. The values that characterize participatory practice, action research, and partnership all support a communicative form of leadership, stressing inclusiveness, deliberation, and collective decision-making.

TRAINING AND SUPERVISION

To work professionally with music therapy involves being a **scholar-practitioner**. This double identity of being a scholar and a practitioner is shared with other professions (Støkken, 2002, p, 25). There are features specific to music therapy, for instance the fact that the qualification as practitioner includes artistic aspects as well as communication and therapeutic skills. What features would be specific to community music therapy? A theoretical understanding of the social aspects of health, support, and music could be part of it. Skills in initiating and supporting communal musicking could be another. The discussion we developed in the previous section suggests that the capacity to work flexibly within partnerships would also be vital.

Further development of community music therapy as professional practice requires institutionalization of training that could qualify for such practice. As community music therapy is not just a contrast to, but also a continuation of, established music therapy practices, one could say that this is already partly integrated in many music therapy training courses. Some courses include issues that are relevant even though they might not necessarily be framed as community music therapy issues, such as the issue of social justice. The increasing international interest for community music therapy practices suggests that new steps will be taken concerning the institutionalization of training. At least four alternatives are imaginable: First, community music therapy could be integrated as a topic within various subjects on existing courses. Second, community music therapy could be established as a separate subject within existing courses. Third, separate training courses in community music therapy could be established. Fourth, continuing training courses could be established for scholar-practitioners who already have a degree in music therapy.

There is little research to support a description of what is currently the most common alternative or what the advantages and disadvantages of each alternative

FIGURE 10.5 | A participant and a music therapy intern at Creative Expressions Studio and Gallery, Milledgeville, GA, USA.

Photo: Katie Whipple.

would be. In developing training alternatives, one dimension to consider would be how to ensure sufficient links to established music therapy knowledge and how to open up for new ideas within fields such as community music and community psychology. Another concern should be how to ensure that candidates are offered the satisfactory amount and quality of practical and theoretical training as well as sufficient space for experiential learning and reflection. If this criterion is linked to a consideration of the demanding role of the professional working in partnership, this would suggest that training in community music therapy should be extensive and thorough. Perhaps Masters level of training is required in order to be able to guarantee this. Again there is little research to support reflections on what the requirements should be.

To practice community music therapy involves working with varied situations where the safety and possibilities of both individual and group should be managed. There will be intergroup processes to deal with as well as a broader ecology, including deliberations with the public and/or the involved partnerships. All this should evolve around solid social–musical work, respecting the often diverse cultural backgrounds and preferences of participants. It is not obvious that this practice requires less competency and skills than individualized music therapy where you work with one client at a time or perhaps a small group in the safe environment of the music therapy room. It is a common assumption, however, that individualized music therapy requires more competency than other forms of practice. To our knowledge this assumption is not grounded in research. It is perhaps the offspring of the hierarchy that the professionalization of medicine established where individualized treatment won the status competition over public health strategies and other possible medical systems (Turner, 2004).

Vaillancourt (2009) investigated the mentoring of apprentice music therapists to and through community music therapy (see Box 7.3). Her study suggests that integration of practical and reflective components with the purpose of developing a deeper understanding of processes such as oppression is central. Supervision or mentorship in experiential groups for apprentice music therapists can be one approach to achieve this. In line with the participatory values characterizing community music therapy, Vaillancourt also stressed the importance of students or apprentices having an active role in the shaping and development of their own training.

Box 10.3 | SUPERVISION AS QUALIFYING PARTNERSHIP

In an article on the supervision of music therapy students, Brynjulf Stige (2001) explored supervision as a participatory practice by discussing the mode of being a "not-knowing" listener:

> When I have chosen the term "not-knowing," it is with reference to Anderson and Goolishian's (1992) specific use of that term. They express a criticism of therapy models that define humans as information processing "machines." Instead they focus upon man as a meaning-generating being. The term "not-knowing therapist"

Box 10.3

is then sometimes used within the tradition of narrative therapy, to express the idea of a client-centered therapy that also is willing to question the authority of the therapist. A "not-knowing therapist" respects the client's narrative truth, and enters a dialogue based upon this rather than upon his own pre-defined knowledge (Stige, 2001, p. 174).

Stige argued that taking a "not-knowing" stance is very different from having no expertise or from neglecting the pre-understanding that informs the supervisor. He suggested that a "not-knowing" approach is about openness and reflexivity and should not be an excuse for abdication of responsibility. A "not-knowing" approach should not neglect the value of the supervisor as a *qualified* listener, then, but would stress that the main task is to be a *qualifying* partner. One way of doing this is to try and create a space where both partners can adopt the humility of a "beginner's mind":

When I ask my students to take a not-knowing approach, that of course then is not contradictory to a student's search for knowledge. My experience as a teacher and supervisor has taught me that it takes a lot of knowledge to be able to take a not-knowing approach. Lack of knowledge—of oneself and of the topics covered in a conversation—usually contributes to closing stories instead of opening them. . . . What we are searching for is freedom and openness for new and diverse stories, which is related to the freedom and openness we search for in a musical improvisation (Stige, 2001, p. 174).

With a focus on listening and mutual learning, the use of supervision as a strategy of professional development could be collaborative and made congruent with the values of participatory practice.

PROFESSIONAL CODES AND PARTICIPATORY ETHICS

The characteristics of community music therapy that we have described in this book suggest that activities are inclusive, relationships multiple, and rationales polyphonic, as the process is democratic and aims at attending to a diversity of voices. Consequently, boundaries of time and space are usually flexible. In short; participatory practice is a less boundaried practice. At the beginning of this chapter we related some of these characteristics to current developments in late modern societies, with a sociocultural tendency to challenge established norms (Fornäs, 1995). With Bauman (1993) we could say that as "walls" fall down ethical dilemmas pop up. Deviation and emancipation from established standards does not mean that ethics loses its topicality. What it does suggest is that ethical issues need to be dealt with in new ways.

FIGURE 10.6 | A community of practice. Baltic Street Band in 2005, Baltic Street Clinic, New York. Photo: South Beach Psychiatric Center.

In a chapter presenting and discussing practices of performance in and as community music therapy, Aigen (2004) reflects on ethical aspects:

> It is clear that music therapists are developing their practice in new ways, both because the culture is changing and because new ways of interacting with clients are being identified that are helpful to these clients. The present chapter discussed examples of therapists and clients engaging in activities outside of the therapy sessions that involve the public dissemination of material originating in therapy sessions, ranging from public performances of songs written and improvised in therapy sessions, to public discussions of these materials. Because these practices can be beneficial to clients, it is necessary to supplement existing ethical guidelines to accommodate these beneficial practices.

(Aigen, 2004, p. 212)

Existing ethical guidelines vary from country to country. They are sometimes articulated as standards of proper conduct, at other times as a set of principles to be considered in balance in ethical decision-making. The contextual nature of community music therapy is more compatible with the latter approach. The limitation of one-size-fits-all ethical standards is not of course unique to community music therapy but it is thrown into sharp relief by this emerging practice.

In addition to the challenge of balancing principles in a given situation, the ethos of community music therapy suggests that ethical decisions should be participatory. Principles and standards defined top–down by professional associations and regulatory bodies with the declared intention of protecting clients could be used to affirm asymmetries in the relationships between music therapists and participants. We need to examine if and when this would be beneficial or detrimental to the participants involved in a specific practice situation. In other words, it is necessary to explore relationships between proclaimed ethical reasons and experienced ethical realities.

To examine relationships between proclaimed reasons and experienced realities is essential in community music therapy. The debate within critical geography concerning the possibility of romanticizing a simplified community and the process of participation (Cahill, Sultana, & Pain, 2007) is clearly relevant. A similar reflection within community music therapy is developed by Ansdell (2010a), who warns about the risk of conjuring up a warm, nostalgic coziness contrasting with the liquid modern world. Participation might at times be fun and pleasurable, but it is rarely cozy; it is usually a process full of risks, challenges, and tensions. As such, participation is never harmless or safe in a protected way. The ethical challenge of the music therapist is to collaborate and reflect in ways that ensure that the process is safe enough for participants and still "dangerous" enough to enable transformation of social contexts.

In Chapter 6 we described community music therapy as an ethics-driven practice. It is a practice informed by values and visions of social justice rather than theories of individual pathology. This proactive mode of ethical practice is explored in the community music therapy literature, for instance in Stige's (2003) theoretical discussion of an ethics of care and commitment, in Curtis and Mercado's (2004) concern for the civil rights of disabled people, and in Dunn's (2008) and Vaillancourt's (2009) studies of music therapy and conflict transformation. There is much less literature that explores the risks of community music therapy in relation to the possibility of doing harm. This is perhaps paradoxical, as critiques of community music therapy from more established quarters of the profession often focus on what is conceived as violations of boundaries in community music therapy practices.

Taking inspiration from Richard Sennett's work, Ansdell and Pavlicevic (2008) suggest that the metaphor of guarded boundary should be supplemented with that of ecological border; a site of exchange. It would be possible to find a related, if less radical, argument within the literature on ethics and boundaries in psychotherapy. Gutheil and Brodsky (2008) have demonstrated how the concept of therapeutic boundaries is relatively new in the history of modern psychotherapy. Examples in Freud's practice deviating from the norms established today include the habits of analyzing patients while walking along the river Danube, to give gifts, and to share a meal with patients. A boundary represents the edge of professional conduct at a certain point. Boundaries are relative to historical context and the therapeutic contract.

Therapists who traverse a boundary do risk vitiating the therapy process, harming the client, and violating the standards of the profession, Gutheil and Brodsky (2008) argue. With reference to a previous work by Gutheil and Gabbard (1993), they differentiate between boundary violations and boundary crossings, however. Boundary violations are defined by their exploitative nature and harmful effects on the client. Boundary crossings involve the therapist stepping out of the usual framework in some way but the action does not harm the client. In some cases it could advance the therapeutic alliance and the effect of the therapy process (Gutheil & Brodsky, 2008).

This distinction is highly relevant for community music therapy practices that grow out of psychotherapeutically oriented music therapy, as Turry's (2005) work exemplifies. If we use a game metaphor, we could say that the rules of the game are extended, in order to make it more rewarding (for all players) or to adjust it to changing conditions. Whether this extension is helpful and safe must be monitored carefully. In other situations, the extension of rules is so far-reaching and lasting that it makes sense to suggest that a new game has been established. Much of the community music therapy literature describes practices that could be characterized in this way.

The rules of the "psychotherapy game" are not universal but some of them are based on principles that are rather general, such as the principle that conflicts of interest should be managed carefully. Stige (2003) discussed dilemmas in relation to the dual and multiple relationships that are common in community music therapy. Another theme of consideration might be confidentiality, as Aigen (2004) mentioned. The list could be made much longer. These dilemmas require careful consideration, critical research, and theory development. They are crucial in practice, of course, but it should be noted that issues such as confidentiality change character in participatory practice where having a voice attended to in the broader community is often part of the agenda (Cahill, Sultana, & Pain, 2007).

There might be tensions between professional codes and **participatory ethics**, and these tensions are not necessarily easy to resolve. Clear norms such as *exclusivity* (the avoidance of dual relationships) are not feasible in community music therapy. More adaptable norms, such as *reflexivity* (the willingness to consider one's position and influence carefully) and *expressivity* (the willingness to communicate and share the considerations made) might gain importance (Stige, 2003). If the norm of reflexivity is taken seriously, the music therapist will realize that there are limits to one's own capacity for self-insight and communication. The participatory process, as outlined in Chapter 8, creates possibilities for input from a range of angles. This could open up a space for self-reflection within collective reflections. In many ways it works as a model for collaborative decision-making also in relation to ethical dilemmas. In some cases, both music therapist and participants might need input or help in the process. Participatory action research could be one way of resolving ethical dilemmas where the process is stuck, for instance because agendas have been hidden (Elefant, 2010b).

Participatory ethics involves transformation, not abdication of professional responsibility, then. The question of ethical performance in community music therapy will be closely linked to the practice of establishing avenues for communication and shared reflections in situations of concern. Ethical performance includes a range of actions, from showing respect in interpersonal dialogues to showing engagement in relation to situations of social injustice. If we link this to the values we discussed in Chapter 7, we could say that ethical performance involves showing respect in a context where solidarity is nurtured by the acknowledgement of other people's rights to freedom and equality.

Box 10.4 | ETHICAL THINKING AMONG COMMUNITY MUSICIANS AND MUSIC THERAPISTS IN AUSTRALIA

The Australian music therapist Lucy O'Grady (2005) studied how musicians and music therapists describe and attribute meaning to their work in community contexts. The study was grounded in O'Grady's own practical experience as music therapist cum community musician in a theatre company that creates plays with women in prison. The directors of the theatre company were very critical of the application of the term "therapy" in this context:

> [T]he creative directors of the theatre company have a very strong opposition to the work of their theatre company being labeled therapy because they believe it pathologises and disempowers the women unnecessarily and that it also overrides the creative emphasis they place upon the work (O'Grady, 2005, p. 2).

Was this a concern that belonged mainly to the directors, or was it also shared by the participants? O'Grady found that the concern was, to some degree, shared. Still, she felt that her work was heavily influenced by her music therapy training. The dilemmas of this situation instigated a series of reflections on her professional role. From the literature she learnt that she was not alone having such question, and therefore she formulated the following research question: "What is the relationship between the ways that musicians and music therapists describe and attribute meaning to their work in community contexts?" (O'Grady, 2005, p. 3).

A simplified précis of the results of the study could be that the way community musicians and music therapists talked about their work suggests that the first group tended to go where the music went and the second where the participants went, if and when there would be any conflict between the two processes. O'Grady related this to an understanding of community music and music therapy defined by the health situation of the people involved rather than methods utilized.

In a continuation of this argument, O'Grady explored differences in the ethical consider-ations made by the community musicians and the music therapists. What she found was that music therapists mainly considered ethical dilemmas in light of the codes of conduct defined by their professional association. The community musicians had no such guidelines to relate to and felt free to appraise situations more flexibly, considering the relationship between their own values and those of the participants in various complex circumstances.

This finding raises at least two questions concerning ethics in community music therapy practice: To what degree are existing professional codes of conduct articulated in ways that take into consideration the dilemmas characteristic of community music therapy? And: How flexibly could music therapists relate to existing codes of conduct when they encounter conflicting values in a community setting? O'Grady's (2005) study perhaps indicates that the ethics of community musicians could be more regulated and the ethics of music therapists more situated. The study is located in a specific national context and was made a few years ago, so it also reminds us how ethical practices vary from place to place and evolve over time.

CONCLUSION AND PROSPECTS

We have discussed the emergence of community music therapy in relation to late modern developments and argued for the relevance of reflexive adaptability and the capacity to work in partnerships. This suggests that participatory principles should be prominent in the training and supervision of music therapists and that ethical performance is seen in light of the values of respect, freedom, equality, and solidarity. People's readiness to defend these values is not likely to go away. Their concern for health and wellbeing, their interest in music, and music's capacity to bring people together is not likely to go away either. In this respect, practices resembling community music therapy have a long history (as we saw in Chapter 2) and they are likely to have a future too. The question is whether community music therapy is going to be part of this future. One of the pioneers of American music therapy, Florence Tyson, had great visions for community music therapy: "Community Music Therapy represents an important developmental breakthrough in our field, one which poses stimulating challenges and affords new opportunities for growth and service" (Tyson, 1973, p. 123).

The words were expressed in another historical context and related to a more limited concept of community music therapy than what has been established since 2000. Reinterpreted into the current situation, her statement invites reflections on the prospects for community music therapy. Many music therapists argue that community music therapy represents new opportunities for usefulness for people and that it also represents promising developments of discipline and profession. Others have suggested that community music therapy is closer to professional suicide than to professional renewal.

If we want to polarize the prospects, we could suggest that community music therapy will either damage music therapy as a recognized profession and bring it back to the status of an amateur humanitarian mission or it will bring music therapy from a marginal position to a more central one in late modern societies, transforming a restricted space of specialist service to the enormous sphere of music for community development and public health. In between these extremes, there are other prospects, such as: The field of community music therapy will grow too slowly and will be swallowed by larger disciplines and professions. The interest in community music therapy will last for a while but then gradually fade as the fuss is over and service done. Community music therapy will establish itself as a solid specialty within music therapy, with or without a strong influence on the development of the rest of the discipline. Community music therapy will contribute to a transformation of the discipline and profession of music therapy to a degree that could make its status as an alternative to mainstream music therapy redundant.

Only those who live and participate will know. What seems probable is that future developments will not be characterized by linear progress, however each one of us would define that. It is much more likely that the prospects of community music therapy will be shaped within what Turner (2004) described as endless circular struggles between professional and lay autonomy, individualized and socialized health strategies, technical and political solutions, and concerns for risks and rights.

KEY TERMS, DISCUSSION TOPICS, AND NOTES

Key Terms

Key terms in order of appearance:

Profession
Professionalization
Modernity
Late modernity
Modernization
Professional identity
Reflexive adaptability
Independence
Interdependence
Partnership
Self-help partnership
Project partnership
Institutional partnership
Governance partnership
Partnership ethos
Leadership
Scholar-practitioner
Participatory ethics

Discussion Topics

The following critical thinking questions can be discussed in class or in groups or used by the individual student for critical reflection on topics discussed in the chapter. Extra resources can be found on the website of the book.

1. Since community music therapy has emerged as a new field, implications include an altered professional role and an expanded ethical awareness. If this were portrayed as the music therapist leaving the music therapy room and walking out onto the streets ready to advocate for justice and equality, the picture would be somewhat idealistic. Community music therapy will be impossible to develop without some kind of funding of music therapy posts. The welfare system and the range of sponsors or organizations willing and able to support community music therapy varies from country to country. Examples include:

    a. Some health care institutions support an expansion of the music therapist role.
    b. Several community music therapy practices link to prevention and health promotion within non-clinical contexts such as kindergartens, schools, and music schools.

    c. A number of community music therapy practices are linked to institutions which focus on rehabilitation and qualification for community participation, such as prisons.

    d. Many community music therapy practices have been established by community or self-help organizations.

    e. Some music therapists have established community music therapy non-profit organizations that receive support from a variety of sources.

    f. A number of community music therapy practices have been established as projects, for instance those linked to governance partnerships.

In the context of where you live, what do you think would be the most realistic options for the funding of community music therapy practice?

2. Relationships between professions could be characterized by competition or collaboration. In your context, what are the professions that music therapists in community music therapy practices are likely to encounter? What conditions will advance competition and what will advance collaboration?

3. The codes of ethics for professional practice developed by music therapy associations in various countries have not always taken into consideration the possibilities and challenges of community music therapy. Do you deem the codes and standards in your country to be compatible with community music therapy practice? If not, what changes would you suggest?

Notes

1 The Swedish cultural theorist Johan Fornäs clarifies the term ambivalence in the following way: "While 'equi-valence' refers to two things of equal value, the prefix *ambi-* means 'both,' so that the ambivalent has two (opposite) values simultaneously. It does not denote a general vagueness, but rather that one singular force has two precise but contradictory implications" (Fornäs, 1995, p. 29).

2 The idea of radicalization of modernity is exemplified by Crook, Pakulski and Waters (1992), who argue that tendencies are accentuated and then transformed. The idea of late modernity as the emergence of a risk society was made famous by Beck (1986/1992). The idea of reflexive modernity is especially linked to the work of Giddens (1991), while the term "liquid modernity" has been appropriated by Bauman (2000/2001).

3 In Chapters 3 to 5 we outlined various theoretical perspectives that demonstrate that biomedical knowledge is far from sufficient for an understanding of the health potential of music and community. In Chapters 6 to 8 we emphasized that the medical model of practice—with its focus on assessment, diagnosis, treatment, and evaluation—is not adequate for community music therapy practice. In the current chapter we argue that it is not relevant for music therapy to emulate every aspect of the model of professionalization that has characterized medicine. This suggests that community music therapy is non-medical or extra-medical in nature but it does *not* come to the conclusion that collaboration with medical doctors is irrelevant. Some community music therapy practices have been nurtured by hospital doctors willing to try on new roles (Aasgaard, 2002; Maratos, 2004). In some countries, the general practitioner of primary health care systems could be one important collaborator for music therapists working with health promotion and prevention of problems (Helle-Valle, 2011).

4 Stige and associates (2010) elaborated on the need to rethink the role of the professional, also embracing the idea of partnership.

Photo Credits

WE want to express our appreciation to the many colleagues who have contributed with photographs for this book. These photos bring the reality (and the wonders) of the work itself closer. Thanks to:

Susan Baines, Capilano University, Vancouver, Canada, for sharing a photo from the German Canadian Care Home, linked with your work in a community mental health center (Figure 6.2).

Johanne Brodeur, Victoria Conservatory of Music, BC, Canada, for sharing a photo from a music therapy session with children (Figure 8.1).

Ingunn Byrkjedal, Grethe Brustad, Mette Kleive, and Brynjulf Stige, previously connected to the music therapy team in Sandane, Western Norway, for sharing a photo from a community music therapy project in the 1980s (Figure 2.3).

Sandra Curtis and Chesley Sigmon Mercado, Concordia University, QC, Canada and Georgia College & State University, GA, USA respectively, for sharing a photo from your previous work with Signed Song music performers at Georgia College & State University in Milledgeville, GA, USA (Figure 2.2).

Cheryl Dileo, Joke Bradt, Scott MacDonald, and Mike Viega, The Arts and Quality of Life Research Center, Boyer College of Music and Dance, Temple University, Philadelphia, USA, for sharing photos from the music therapy community programs of the center (Figures 1.2, 6.3, and 9.1).

Laura Fogg and Alison Talmage, the Centre for Brain Research at The University of Auckland, New Zealand, for sharing photos from the CeleBRation Choir (Figures 3.1, 6.7, 8.7, and 9.5).

Sunelle Fouché and Kerryn Torrance, the Music Therapy Community Clinic, greater Cape Town area, South Africa, for sharing photos from the organization's work in disadvantaged communities (Figures 1.1, 3.4, and 10.4).

Ulrike Haase and Christoph Schwabe, Musiktherapie Crossen, Dresden, Germany, for sharing photos from the institute's social and inclusive music therapy programs (Figures 4.3, 5.1, 5.8, and 7.5).

Andrea Intveen and Susanne Bauer, Berlin University of the Arts, for sharing a photo from a multi-cultural resource-oriented music therapy group (Figure 7.4).

Peter Jampel, Brooklyn, New York, for sharing photos from your previous work with the Baltic Street Band of the Baltic Street Clinic, South Beach Psychiatric Center (Figures 3.5, 6.5, 8.6, and 10.6).

Muriithi Kigunda, Upland, CA, USA, for sharing photos of ngoma rituals in the Kamba tradition in Kenya (Figures 2.1, 5.9, and 9.3).

Solgunn Knardal, Bergen Red Cross Nursing Home, Norway, for sharing photos from the inclusive music therapy activities developed at this institution (Figures 7.2 and 8.5).

Viggo Krüger, Aleris Ungplan and University of Bergen, Norway, for sharing photos from "Come Closer," a musical theatre project produced and performed by adolescents in Children's Welfare (Figures 1.4, 6.6, 7.1, and 8.3).

Maria Logis and Alan Turry, Nordoff–Robbins Center for Music Therapy, New York University, for sharing a photo from a process that led from music psychotherapy to community music therapy (Figure 1.5).

Katrina McFerran, Melbourne University, for sharing a photo from a community music therapy project set up after the Black Saturday fires in 2009, in the bush north of Melbourne (Figure 5.5).

Wang Feng Ng and Jolene Fok, Singapore, for sharing a photo from the music therapy program within the voluntary welfare organization Beyond Social Services, an agency serving disadvantaged children and youth in Singapore (Figure 8.4).

Rii Numata, Kobe University, Kobe, Japan, for sharing photos from The Otoasobi Project, an improvisation collective for musicians with and without intellectual disabilities (Figures 1.3 and 2.4).

Jorunn Bakke Nydal, The Music Therapy Center of the County of Sogn og Fjordane, Førde, Norway, for a photo from your work with Førde Senior Choir (Figure 9.4).

Emma O'Brien, The Royal Melbourne Hospital, for sharing photos from the final installment "avaTara" 2009 of the Opera Therapy project in Melbourne, Australia (Figures 7.6 and 9.6).

Gerd Rieger, Musiktherapie Lebenshilfe Krefeld, Germany, for sharing photos from the Rock am Ring (Rock at the Ring) program developed at the community center (Lebenshilfe) in Krefeld (Figures 4.2, 4.6, 4.7, and 5.7).

Even Ruud and Vegar Storsve, Norwegian Academy of Music, Oslo, Norway, for sharing photos from a music education and community music project in the Palestinian refugee camp Rashedie in Lebanon, under the auspices of Forum for Culture and International Cooperation (Figures 2.5, 4.4, 6.4, 7.3, and 10.1).

Anja Tait, Northern Territory Library, and Catherine Threlfall, Henbury School, Northern Territory, Australia, for sharing photos from the ArtStories and Making Music Being Well initiatives with community building, health promotion, and education through music and the arts (Figures 3.8, 5.10, 6.1, and 8.8).

Katie Whipple and Chesley Sigmon Mercado, Creative Expressions Studio and Gallery and Georgia College & State University respectively, Milledgeville, GA, USA, for sharing photos from a partnership program where a music therapist is engaged to promote creativity and self-expression for artists with developmental disabilities (Figures 6.8, 10.3, and 10.5).

Claudia Zanini, the Federal University of Goiás, Brazil, for sharing photos from your work with groups for people with hypertension and diabetes, which are major public health problems of this country (Figures 3.3 and 10.2).

References

Aasgaard, Trygve (1998). Musikk-miljøterapi: Uvanlig? Uinteressant? Uutforsket! Kommentarer til Nisima Marie Munk-Madsen. [Music Milieu Therapy: Uncommon? Uninteresting? Unexplored! Comments to Nisima Marie Munk-Madsen]. *Nordic Journal of Music Therapy*, 7(2), pp. 168–171.

Aasgaard, Trygve (1999). Music Therapy as a Milieu in the Hospice and Pediatric Oncology Ward. In: Aldridge, David: *Music Therapy in Palliative Care. New Voices*. London: Jessica Kingsley Publishers.

Aasgaard, Trygve (2000). 'A Suspiciously Cheerful Lady.' A Study of a Song's Life in the Paediatric Oncology Ward, and Beyond. *British Journal of Music Therapy*, 14(2), pp. 70–82.

Aasgaard, Trygve (2001). An Ecology of Love: Aspects of Music Therapy in the Pediatric Oncology Environment. *Journal of Palliative Care*, 17(3), pp. 177–181.

Aasgaard, Trygve (2002). Song Creations by Children with Cancer—Process and Meaning. Aalborg, Denmark: Unpublished Doctoral Dissertation, Aalborg University, Department of Music and Music Therapy.

Aasgaard, Trygve (2004). A Pied Piper among White Coats and Infusion Pumps: Community Music Therapy in a Paediatric Hospital Setting. In: Pavlicevic, Mercédès & Gary Ansdell (Eds.). *Community Music Therapy*. London: Jessica Kingsley Publishers.

Abbott, Andrew (1988). *The System of Professions. An Essay on the Division of Expert Labor*. Chicago: The University of Chicago Press.

Abrams, Dominic, Michael A. Hogg & José M. Marques (2005). A Social Psychological Framework for Understanding Social Inclusion and Exclusion. In: Abrams, Dominic, Michael A. Hogg & José. M. Marques (Eds.). *The Social Psychology of Inclusion and Exclusion* (pp. 1–23). New York: Psychology Press (Taylor & Francis).

Abrams, Mark (1951). *Social Surveys and Social Action*. London: William Heinemann's Medical Books.

Aftret, Kari (2005). Samspill. Om musikkterapeuten i kommunen [Interaction and Collaboration. On the Role of the Music Therapist in the Municipality]. Unpublished Master's Thesis. Oslo, Norway: Norwegian Academy of Music.

Aigen, Kenneth (1995). An Aesthetic Foundation of Clinical Theory: An Underlying Basis of Creative Music Therapy. In: Kenny, Carolyn (Ed). *Listening, Playing, Creating: Essays on the Power of Sound*. Albany: State University of New York Press.

Aigen, Kenneth (2002). *Playin' in the Band: A Qualitative Study of Popular Music Styles as Clinical Improvisation*. New York: Nordoff–Robbins Center for Music Therapy, New York University.

Aigen, Kenneth (2004). Conversations on Creating Community: Performance as Music Therapy in New York City. In: Pavlicevic, Mercédès & Gary Ansdell (Eds.). *Community Music Therapy*. London: Jessica Kingsley Publishers.

References Aigen, Kenneth (2005). *Music-Centered Music Therapy*. Gilsum, NH: Barcelona Publishers.

Aigen, Kenneth (2008). In Defense of Beauty: A Role for the Aesthetic in Music Therapy Theory. Part II: Challenges to Aesthetic Theory in Music Therapy: Summary and Response. *Nordic Journal of Music Therapy*, 17(1), pp. 3–18.

Aigen, Kenneth (in press). Community Music Therapy. In: McPherson, Gary & Graham Welch (Eds.). *Oxford Handbook of Music Education*. New York: Oxford University Press.

Aldridge, David (1996). *Music Therapy Research and Practice in Medicine. From Out of the Silence*. London: Jessica Kingsley Publishers.

Aldridge, David (2004). *Health, the Individual and Integrated Medicine*. London: Jessica Kingsley Publishers.

Alvesson, Mats & Kaj Sköldberg (2009). *Reflexive Methodology: New Vistas for Qualitative Research* (2nd edition). London: Sage Publications.

Alvin, Juliette (1966/1975). *Music Therapy*. London: Hutchinson & Co.

Alvin, Juliette (1968). Changing Patterns in Music Therapy—The Mental Patient and Community Care in England. In: Gaston, E. Thayer (Ed.). *Music in Therapy*. New York: Macmillan Publishing.

Amdam, Roar (2010). *Planning in Health Promotion Work. An Empowerment Model*. New York: Routledge.

American Music Therapy Association (2011). What is the Profession of Music Therapy? American Music Therapy Association website. Retrieved February 21, 2011, from: http://www.musictherapy.org/.

American Psychiatric Association (1980). *DSM-III. Diagnostic and Statistical Manual of Psychiatric Disorders*. Washington, DC: American Psychiatric Association.

American Psychiatric Association (2000). *DSM-IV TR. Diagnostic and Statistical Manual of Psychiatric Disorders*. Washington, DC: American Psychiatric Association.

Amir, Dorit (2002). What is the Meaning of Music Therapy These Days? *Voices: A World Forum for Music Therapy*. Retrieved November 26, 2005, from: http://voices.no/?q=fortnightly-columns/2002-what-meaning-music-therapy-these-days

Amir, Dorit (2004). Community Music Therapy and the Challenge of Multiculturalism. In: Pavlicevic, Mercédès & Gary Ansdell (Eds.). *Community Music Therapy*. London: Jessica Kingsley Publishers.

Anderson, Harlene & Harold Goolishian (1992). The Client is the Expert: a Not-Knowing Approach to Therapy. In: McNamee, Sheila and Kenneth J. Gergen (Eds.). *Therapy as Social Construction*. London: Sage Publications.

Ansdell, Gary (1997). Musical Elaborations. What has the New Musicology to Say to Music Therapy? *British Journal of Music Therapy*, 11(2), pp. 36–44.

Ansdell, Gary (2001). Musicology: Misunderstood Guest at the Music Therapy Feast? In: Aldridge, David, Gianluigi DiFranco, Even Ruud & Tony Wigram. *Music Therapy in Europe*. Rome: Ismez.

Ansdell, Gary (2002). Community Music Therapy and the Winds of Change—A Discussion Paper. *Voices: A World Forum for Music Therapy*, 2(2). Retrieved February 23, 2011, from: https://normt.uib.no/index.php/voices/article/view/83/65

Ansdell, Gary (2003). The Stories We Tell: Some Meta-Theoretical Reflections on Music Therapy. *Nordic Journal of Music Therapy*, 12(2), pp. 152–159.

Ansdell, Gary (2004). Rethinking Music and Community: Theoretical Perspectives in Support of Community Music Therapy. In: Pavlicevic, Mercédès & Gary Ansdell (Eds.). *Community Music Therapy*. London: Jessica Kingsley Publishers.

Ansdell, Gary (2005a). Community Music Therapy: A Plea for "Fuzzy Recognition" Instead of "Final Definition." [Contribution to Moderated Discussions] *Voices: A World Forum for Music Therapy*. Retrieved January 17, 2006, from http://www.voices.no/discussions/discm4_07.html.

Ansdell, Gary (2005b). Being Who You Aren't; Doing What You Can't: Community Music Therapy & the Paradoxes of Performance. *Voices: A World Forum for Music Therapy*. Retrieved February 24, 2011, from: https://normt.uib.no/index.php/voices/article/view/229/173.

Ansdell, Gary (2010a). Belonging through Musicing: Explorations of Musical Community. In: Stige, Brynjulf, Gary Ansdell, Cochavit Elefant & Mercédès Pavlicevic (Eds.). *Where Music Helps. Community Music Therapy in Action and Reflection*. Aldershot, UK: Ashgate Publishing Limited.

Ansdell, Gary (2010b). Where Performing Helps: Processes and Affordances of Performance in Community Music Therapy. In: Stige, Brynjulf, Gary Ansdell, Cochavit Elefant & Mercédès Pavlicevic (Eds.). *Where Music Helps. Community Music Therapy in Action and Reflection.* Aldershot, UK: Ashgate Publishing.

Ansdell, Gary & Mercédès Pavlicevic (2005). Musical Companionship, Musical Community: Music Therapy and the Process and Values of Musical Communication. In: Miell, Dorothy, Raymond MacDonald, & David Hargreaves (Eds.). *Musical Communication.* Oxford: Oxford University Press.

Ansdell, Gary & Mercédès Pavlicevic (2008). Responding to the Challenge: Between Boundaries and Borders (Response to Alison Barrington). *British Journal of Music Therapy, 22*(2), pp. 73–76.

Antonovsky, Aaron (1987/1991). *Hälsans Mysterium* [Unraveling the Mystery of Health: How People Manage Stress and Stay Well]. San Francisco: Jossey-Bass Publishers.

Askew, Kelly M. (2002). *Performing the Nation. Swahili Music and Cultural Politics in Tanzania.* Chicago: The University of Chicago Press.

Åslund, Cecilia, Bengt Starrin & Kent W. Nilsson (2010). Social Capital in Relation to Depression, Musculoskeletal Pain, and Psychosomatic Symptoms: A Cross-Sectional Study of a Large Population-Based Cohort of Swedish Adolescents. *BMC Public Health, 10,* pp. 715–724.

Atkinson, Paul, Amanda Coffey, Sara Delamont, Jon Lofland & Lyn Lofland (Eds.) (2001). *Handbook of Ethnography.* Thousand Oaks, CA: Sage.

Bailey, Betty & Jane W. Davidson (2003). Amateur Group Singing as a Therapeutic Instrument. *Nordic Journal of Music Therapy, 12*(1), pp. 18–32.

Bailey, Derek (1992). *Improvisation—Its Nature and Practice in Music.* London: The British Library National Sound Archive.

Baines, Susan (2000/2003). A Consumer-Directed and Partnered Community Mental Health Music Therapy Program: Program Development and Evaluation. *Canadian Journal of Music Therapy, VII*(1), pp. 51–70. Republished in: *Voices: A World Forum for Music Therapy.* Retrieved January 26, 2011, from https://normt.uib.no/index.php/voices/article/view/137/113.

Baker, John, Kathleen Lynch, Sara Cantillon & Judy Walsh (2004). *Equality. From Theory to Action.* Hampshire, UK: Palgrave MacMillan.

Ball, Olivia & Paul Gready (2007). *The No-Nonsense Guide to Human Rights.* Oxford, UK: New Internationalist.

Barcellos, Lia Rejane Mendes (2002). An "Impossible Dream"? In: Chapter 19 of: Kenny, Carolyn & Stige, Brynjulf (Eds.) (2002). *Contemporary Voices in Music Therapy: Communication, Culture, and Community* (pp. 249–251). Oslo, Norway: Unipub.

Barcellos, Lia Rejane Mendes (2005). Juggling with Life. *Voices: A World Forum for Music Therapy.* Retrieved November 26, 2005, from http://www.voices.no/columnist/colbarcellos140205.html

Barnes, John Arundel (1954). Class and Committees in a Norwegian Island Parish. *Human Relations, 7,* pp. 39–58.

Barnett, Adrian G., Jolieke C. van der Pols, Annette J. Dobson (2005). Regression to the Mean: What It is and How to Deal with It. *International Journal of Epidemiology, 34*(1), pp. 215–220.

Barrera, Manuel (2000). Social Support Research in Community Psychology. In: Rappaport, Julian & Edward Seidman (Eds.). *Handbook of Community Psychology* (pp. 215–245). New York: Kluwer Academic/Plenum Publisher.

Barrington, Alison (2005). Music Therapy: A Study in Professionalisation. Unpublished doctoral dissertation. Durham, UK: University of Durham, Department of Music.

Barrington, Alison (2008). Challenging the Profession. *British Journal of Music Therapy, 22*(2), pp. 65–72.

Bartley, Melanie, Jane E. Ferrie & Scott M. Montgomery (2006). Health and Labor Market Disadvantage: Unemployment, Non-Employment and Job Insecurity. In: Marmot, Michael & Richard G. Wilkinson (Eds.). *Social Determinants of Health* (pp. 78–96). Oxford: Oxford University Press.

Barz, Gregory (2006). *Singing for Life. HIV/AIDS and Music in Uganda.* New York: Routledge.

Batt-Rawden, Kari Bjerke (2007). Music and Health Promotion: The Role and Significance of Music and Musicking in Everyday Life for the Long-Term Ill. Unpublished Doctoral Dissertation. Exeter, UK: University of Exeter.

References

Batt-Rawden, Kari Bjerke, Tia DeNora & Even Ruud (2005). Music Listening and Empowerment in Health Promotion: A Study of the Role and Significance of Music in Everyday Life of the Long-term Ill. *Nordic Journal of Music Therapy, 14*(2), pp. 120–136.

Bauman, Zymunt (1993). *Postmodern Ethics.* Oxford: Blackwell.

Bauman, Zymunt (2000/2001). *Flytende modernitet* [Liquid Modernity]. Translated by Mette Nygård. Oslo: Vidarforlaget.

Baumeister, Roy & Mark R. Leary (1995). The Need to Belong: Desire for Interpersonal Attachments as a Fundamental Human Motivation. *Psychological Bulletin, 117*(3), pp. 497–529.

Beck, Ulrich (1986/1992). *Risk Society: Towards a New Modernity* (Translated by Mark Ritter). London: Sage Publications.

Berganza, Carlos E., Juan E. Mezzich & Claire Pouncey (2005). Concepts of Disease: Their Relevance for Psychiatric Diagnosis and Classification. *Psychopathology, 38,* pp. 166–170.

Berkaak, Odd Are (1993). *Erfaringer fra risikosonen: opplevelse og stilutvikling i rock* (Experiences from the Zone of Risks: Experience and Development of Style in Rock]. Oslo, Norway: Universitetsforlaget.

Berkaak, Odd Are & Even Ruud (1992). *Den påbegynte virkelighet. Studier i samtidskultur* [Emerging Reality. Studies in Contemporary Culture]. Oslo, Norway: Universitetsforlaget.

Berkaak, Odd Are & Even Ruud (1994). *Sunwheels. Fortellinger om et rockeband* [Sunwheels. Stories about a Rock Band]. Oslo, Norway: Universitetsforlaget.

Berkman, Lisa F. & Thomas Glass (2000). Social Integration, Social Networks, Social Support, and Health. In: Berkman, Lisa F. & Ichiro Kawachi (Eds.). *Social Epidemiology* (pp. 137–173). Oxford, UK: Oxford University Press.

Berlin, Isaiah (1969/2002). *Liberty* (Incorporating *Four Essays on Liberty*, edited by Henry Hardy). Oxford, UK: Oxford University Press.

Bethlehem, Jelke G. (1999). Cross-Sectional Research. In: Adèr, Herman J. & Gideon J. Mellenbergh (Eds.). *Research Methodology in the Social, Behavioural and Life Sciences* (pp. 110–142). London: Sage Publications.

Bijleveld, Catrien C.J.H., Leo J.Th. van der Kamp & Ab Mooijaart (1998). *Longitudinal Data Analysis: Designs, Models and Methods.* London: Sage Publications.

Bjørkvold, Jon-Roar (1989/1992). *The Muse Within. Creativity and Communication, Song and Play from Childhood through Maturity* (translated by William H. Halverson). St. Louis, MO: Magna-Music Baton.

Black, Douglas (1980) *Inequalities in Health.* Report of a research working group chaired by Sir Donald Black. London: DHSS.

Bohlman, Philip V. (1999). Ontologies of Music. In: Cook, Nicholas & Mark Everist (Eds.). *Rethinking Music* (pp. 17–34). New York: Oxford University Press.

Bordens, Kenneth S. & Bruce B. Abbott (2008). *Research Design and Methods. A Process Approach* (7th edition). Boston: McGraw Hill.

Bourdieu, Pierre (1986). The Forms of Capital. In: Richardson, John G. (Ed.). *The Handbook of Theory: Research for the Sociology of Education* (pp. 241–258). New York: Greenwood Press.

Bowers, Judy (1998). Effects of Intergenerational Choir for the Community-Based Seniors and College Students on Age-Related Attitudes. *Journal of Music Therapy, 35*(1), pp. 2–18.

Boxill, Edith Hillman (1985). *Music Therapy for the Developmentally Disabled.* Maryland: An Aspen Publication.

Boxill, Edith Hillman (1988). Continuing Notes: Worldwide Networking for Peace (Editorial). *Music Therapy,* 7(1), pp. 80–81.

Boxill, Edith Hillman (1997a). Music Therapists for Peace, Inc.: A Global Imperative. Retrieved August 21, 2009, from http://pages.nyu.edu/ehb2mtp.html

Boxill, Edith Hillman (1997b). *The Miracle of Music Therapy.* Gilsum, NH: Barcelona Publishers.

Boxill, Edith Hillman (1997c). Students against Violence Everywhere—S.A.V.E.—Through Music Therapy: A Manual of Guidelines, Music Therapy Interventions, Music Activities, Music Materials. New York: Music Therapists for Peace, Inc.

Boxill, Edith Hillman & Cella Schieffelin Roberts (2003). Drumming Circle for Peace. *Voices: A World Forum for Music Therapy.* Retrieved March 12, 2003, from http://www.voices.no/discussions/discm19_01.html.

Boyd, Kenneth M. (2011). Disease, Illness, Sickness, Health, Healing and Wholeness: Exploring Some Elusive Concepts. *Journal of Medical Ethics, 26,* pp. 9–17.

Bradt, Joke (2009). Hope is Change. *Voices: A World Forum for Music Therapy. Voices: A World Forum for Music Therapy.* Retrieved July 26, 2010, from http://www.voices.no/columnist/colbradt090309.php

Bronfenbrenner, Urie (1979). *The Ecology of Human Development. Experiments by Nature and Design.* Cambridge, MA: Harvard University Press.

Broucek, Marcia (1987). Beyond Healing to 'Whole-ing': A Voice for the Deinstitutionalization of Music Therapy. *Music Therapy, 6*(2), pp. 50–58.

Brown, Julie (2001/2002). Towards a Culturally Centered Music Therapy Practice. *Canadian Journal of Music Therapy, VIII*(1) (Fall 2001), pp. 11–24. Republished in: *Voices: A World Forum for Music Therapy.* Retrieved February 24, from: https://normt.uib.no/index.php/voices/article/view/72/62.

Brown, Timothy A. (2006). *Confirmatory Factor Analysis for Applied Research.* New York: Guilford Press.

Bruscia, Kenneth (1989). *Defining Music Therapy.* Spring City, PA: Spring House Books.

Bruscia, Kenneth (1995). The Process of Doing Qualitative Research: Part I: Introduction. In: Wheeler, Barbara L. (Ed.). *Music Therapy Research. Quantitative and Qualitative Perspectives.* Gilsum, NH: Barcelona Publishers.

Bruscia, Kenneth (1998). *Defining Music Therapy* (2nd edition). Gilsum, NH: Barcelona Publishers.

Buchanan, Jennifer (2009). Fran Herman, Music Therapist in Canada for over 50 years. *Voices: A World Forum for Music Therapy.* Retrieved July 20, 2010, from http://www.voices.no/mainissues/mi40009000311.php.

Bull, Michael (2000). *Sounding Out the City: Personal Stereos and the Management of Everyday Life.* New York: Berg Publishers.

Bull, Michael (2007). *Sound Moves: iPod Culture and Urban Experience.* London: Routledge.

Bunt, Leslie (1994). *Music Therapy. An Art Beyond Words.* London: Routledge.

Burke, Kenneth (1945/1969). *A Grammar of Motives.* Los Angeles: California University Press.

Bygren, Lars Olov, Boinkum Benson Konlaan & Sven-Erik Johansson (1996). Unequal in Death. Attendance at Cultural Events, Reading Books or Periodicals, and Making Music or Singing in a Choir as Determinants for Survival: Swedish Interview Survey of Living Conditions. *British Medical Journal, 313,* pp. 1577–1580.

Byrkjedal, Ingunn (1992). Musikkterapi ved klassemiljøutvikling (Music Therapy for Classroom Climate Development]. *Nordic Journal of Music Therapy, 1*(1), pp. 14–20.

Cahill, Caitlin, Farhana Sultana & Rachel Pain (2007). Participatory Ethics: Politics, Practices, Institutions. *ACME: An International E-Journal for Critical Geographies, 6*(3), pp. 304–318.

Cassel, John (1976). The Contribution of the Social Environment to Host Resistance. *American Journal of Epidemiology, 104,* pp. 107–123.

Centre for Human Rights (1994). Human Rights and Social Work: A Manual for Schools of Social Work and the Social Work Profession. Professional Training Series, No. 1. Geneva: United Nations.

Chagas, Marly (2007). Art along the Path: Art, Society, and Constructions of Subjectivities. *Voices: A World Forum for Music Therapy.* Retrieved January 19, 2008, from http://www.voices.no/mainissues/mi40007000230.php.

Chaney, David (2002). *Cultural Change and Everyday Life.* New York: Palgrave.

Chase, Kristen (2003). Multi-Cultural Music Therapy: A Review of Literature. *Music Therapy Perspectives, 21,* pp. 84–88.

Clarke, Eric (2005). *Ways of Listening: An Ecological Approach to the Perception of Musical Meaning.* New York: Oxford University Press.

Clarke, Eric, Nicola Dibben & Stephanie Pitts (2010). *Music and Mind in Everyday Life.* New York: Oxford University Press.

Clayton, Martin, Trevor Herbert & Richard Middleton (Eds.) (2003). *The Cultural Study of Music. A Critical Introduction.* New York & London: Routledge.

References   Clift, Stephen, Grenville Hancox, Ian Morrison, Bärbel Hess, Günter Kreutz, & Don Stewart (2010). Choral Singing and Psychological Wellbeing: Quantitative and Qualitative Findings from English Choirs in a Cross-National Survey. *Journal of Applied Arts and Health*, 1(1), pp. 19–34.

Cohen, Anthony (1985/1993). *The Symbolic Construction of Community*. London: Routledge.

Cohen, Gene (2009). New Theories and Research Findings on the Positive Influence of Music and Art on Health with Aging. *Arts & Health*, 1(1), pp. 48–63.

Cohen, Sheldon & Jeffrey R. Edwards (1989). Personality Characteristics as Moderators of the Relationship between Stress and Disorder. In: Neufeld, Richard W.J. (Ed.). *Advances in the Investigation of Psychological Stress* (pp. 235–283). Oxford: John Wiley.

Cohen, Sheldon, Benjamin H. Gottlieb & Lynn G. Underwood (2000). Social Relationships and Health. In: Cohen, Sheldon, Benjamin H. Gottlieb & Lynn G. Underwood (Eds.). *Social Support Measurement and Intervention* (pp. 3–25). New York: Oxford University Press.

Cohen, Sheldon & Tom A. Wills (1985). Stress, Social Support, and the Buffering Hypothesis. *Psychological Bulletin*, 98(2), pp. 310–357.

Cole, Michael (1996). *Cultural Psychology. A Once and Future Discipline*. Cambridge, MA: The Belknap Press of Harvard University Press.

Collins, Randall (2004). *Interaction Ritual Chains*. Princeton, NJ: Princeton University Press.

Conrad, Peter (2007). *The Medicalization of Society: On the Transformation of Human Conditions into Treatable Disorders*. Baltimore, MD: The Johns Hopkins University Press.

Cook, Nicholas (1998). *Music. A Very Short Introduction*. New York: Oxford University Press.

Cook, Nicholas & Mark Everist (Eds.) (1999). *Rethinking Music*. New York: Oxford University Press.

Creswell, John & Vicki Plano Clark (2011). *Designing and Conducting Mixed Methods Research* (2nd edition). Thousand Oaks, CA: Sage Publications.

Crook, Stephen, Jan Pakulski & Malcolm Waters (1992). *Postmodernization. Change in Advanced Society*. London: Sage Publications.

Cross, Ian (2003). Music and Biocultural Evolution. In: Clayton, Martin, Trevor Herbert & Richard Middleton (Eds.). *The Cultural Study of Music. A Critical Introduction*. New York & London: Routledge.

Cross, Ian (2005). Music and Meaning, Ambiguity and Evolution. In: Miell, Dorothy, Raymond MacDonald, & David Hargreaves (Eds.). *Musical Communication*. Oxford: Oxford University Press.

Cross, Ian & Iain Morley (2009). The Evolution of Music: Theories, Definitions and the Nature of the Evidence. In: Malloch, Stephen & Colwyn Trevarthen (Eds.). *Communicative Musicality. Exploring the Basis of Human Companionship*. Oxford, UK: Oxford University Press.

Csikszentmihalyi, Mihaly (1990). *Flow. The Psychology of Optimal Experience*. New York: Harper Perennial.

Curtis, Sandra L. & Chesley Sigmon Mercado (2004). Community Music Therapy for Citizens with Developmental Disabilities. *Voices: A World Forum for Music Therapy*. Retrieved February 24, 2011, from https://normt.uib.no/index.php/voices/article/view/185/144

Dahle, Kathrine & Veronica Vågnes Slettebakk (2006). Framføring i samfunnsmusikkterapi—med blikk på roller i framføringssituasjonen [Performance in Community Music Therapy—With a Focus on Roles and Relationships in Situations of Performance]. Sandane: Sogn og Fjordane University College, Norway.

Dalton, James H., Maurice J. Elias & Abraham Wandersman (2007). *Community Psychology. Linking Individuals and Communities* (2nd edition). London: Wadsworth (Thomson Learning).

Darnley-Smith, Rachel & Helen M. Patey (2003). *Music Therapy*. London: Sage Publications.

Delanty, Gerald (2003). *Community*. London: Routledge.

DeNora, Tia (2000). *Music in Everyday Life*. Cambridge, UK: Cambridge University Press.

DeNora, Tia (2003). *After Adorno. Rethinking Music Sociology*. Cambridge, UK: Cambridge University Press.

DeNora, Tia (2006). Evidence and Effectiveness in Music Therapy. *British Journal of Music Therapy*, 20(2), pp. 81–93.

DeNora, Tia (2007). Health and Music in Everyday Life—A Theory of Practice. *Psyke & Logos*, 28(1), pp. 271–287.

De Silva, Mary J., Kwame McKenzie, Trudy Harpham & Sharon R.A. Huttly (2005). Social Capital and Mental Illness: A Systematic Review. *Journal of Community Health*, 59, pp. 619–627.

Diener, Ed (1984). Subjective Well-Being. *Psychological Bulletin*, 95, pp. 542–575.

Dileo, Cheryl (2000). *Ethical Thinking in Music Therapy*. Cherry Hill, NJ: Jeffrey Books.

Dillon, Robin S. (2010). Respect. In: *The Stanford Encyclopedia of Philosophy*. Retrieved July 22, 2010, from http://plato.stanford.edu/entries/respect/

Dissanayake, Ellen (1992/1995). *Homo Aestheticus. Where Art Comes From and Why*. Seattle: University of Washington Press.

Dissanayake, Ellen (2000a). Antecedents of the Temporal Arts in Early Mother–Infant Interaction. In: Wallin, Nils L., Björn Merker & Steven Brown (Eds.). *The Origins of Music*. Cambridge, MA: The MIT Press.

Dissanayake, Ellen (2000b). *Art and Intimacy: How the Arts Began*. Seattle: University of Washington Press.

Dissanayake, Ellen (2001). An Ethological View of Music and its Relevance to Music Therapy. *Nordic Journal of Music Therapy*, 10(2), pp. 159–175.

Dissanayake, Ellen (2009). Root, Leaf, Blossom, or Bole: Concerning the Origin and Adaptive Function of Music. In: Malloch, Stephen & Colwyn Trevarthen (Eds.). *Communicative Musicality. Exploring the Basis of Human Companionship*. Oxford, UK: Oxford University Press.

Dreier, Ole (1994). Sundhedsbegreber i psykososial praksis [Concepts of Health in Psychosocial Practice]. In: Jensen, Uffe Juul & Peter Fuur Andersen (Eds.). *Sundhedsbegreper i filosofi og praksis* [Concepts of Health in Theory and Practice]. Århus, DK: Philosophia.

Dunn, Barbara (2008). Transforming Conflict through Music. Unpublished PhD dissertation. Cincinnati, OH: Union Institute and University.

Durkheim, Emile (1912/1995). *The Elementary Forms of Religious Life* (Translated by Karen E. Fields). New York: The Free Press.

Easterlin, Richard A. (2003). Building a Better Theory of Wellbeing. March 2003. *IZA Discussion Paper*, 2003/742. Los Angeles: University of Southern California. http://ssrn.com/abstract=392043.

Economist (2005). The Economist Intelligence Unit's Quality of Life Index. http://www.economist.com/media/pdf/QUALITY_OF_LIFE.pdf.

Edwards, Jane (2002). 'Music Therapy by any Other Name Would Smell as Sweet' or 'Community Music Therapy' Means 'Culturally Sensitive Music Therapy' in Our Language." *Voices: A World Forum for Music Therapy*. Retrieved October, 15, 2002, from: http://www.voices.no/discussions/discm8_03.html

Edwards, Jane (2007). *Music: Promoting Health and Creating Community in Healthcare Contexts*. Newcastle: Cambridge Scholars Publishing.

Einbu, Torun (1993). Prosjektet 'Aktiv musikk for alle' [The Project "Music Activities for Everybody"]. *Nordic Journal of Music Therapy*, 2(2), pp. 26–28.

Elefant, Cochavit (2010a). Musical Inclusion, Intergroup Relations, and Community Development. In: Stige, Brynjulf, Gary Ansdell, Cochavit Elefant & Mercédès Pavlicevic (Eds.). *Where Music Helps. Community Music Therapy in Action and Reflection*. Aldershot, UK: Ashgate Publishing.

Elefant, Cochavit (2010b). Giving Voice: Participatory Action Research with a Marginalized Group. In: Stige, Brynjulf, Gary Ansdell, Cochavit Elefant & Mercédès Pavlicevic (Eds.). *Where Music Helps. Community Music Therapy in Action and Reflection*. Aldershot, UK: Ashgate Publishing.

Elliott, David J, (1995). *Music Matters. A New Philosophy of Music Education*. New York: Oxford University Press.

Ely, Elisabeth & Miriam A. McMahon (1990). Integration—Where Does it Begin? . . . A Creative Arts Perspective. *Australian Journal of Music Therapy*, 1, pp. 36–44.

Ely, Elisabeth & Karen Scott (1994). Integrating Clients with an Intellectual Disability into the Community through Music Therapy. *Australian Journal of Music Therapy*, 5, pp. 7–18.

Embretson, Susan E. & Steven P. Reise (2000). *Item Response Theory for Psychologists*. Mahwah, New Jersey: Erlbaum Publishers.

References

Empson, Laura (2007). Surviving and Thriving in a Changing World: The Special Nature of Partnership. In: Empson, Laura (Ed.). *Managing the Modern Law Firm. New Challenges, New Perspectives* (pp. 10–36). Oxford: Oxford University Press.

Epp, Erinn (2007). Locating the Autonomous Voice: Self-Expression in Music-Centered Music Therapy. *Voices: A World Forum for Music Therapy*. Retrieved January 19, 2011, from https://normt.uib.no/index.php/voices/article/view/463/372.

Eriksen, Thomas Hylland (2010). *Small Places, Large Issues. An Introduction to Social and Cultural Anthropology* (3rd edition). London: Pluto Press.

Erkkilä, Jaakko (2003). Book Review of *Contemporary Voices in Music Therapy: Communication, Culture, and Community* (Kenny, Carolyn & Brynjulf Stige) [online]. *Nordic Journal of Music Therapy*. Retrieved April 2, 2003, from: http://www.njmt.no/bookreview_2003029.html

Felce, David & Jonathan Perry (1995). Quality of Life: Its Definition and Measurement. *Research in Developmental Disabilities, 16 (1)*, pp. 51–74.

Feldman, Pamela J. & Sheldon Cohen (2000). Social Support. In: Kazdin, Alan E. (Ed.). *Encyclopedia of Psychology, 7* (pp. 373–376). Washington, DC: American Psychological Association.

Finlay, Lindan & Brenda Gough (Eds.) (2003). *Reflexivity. A Practical Guide for Researchers in Health and Social Sciences.* Oxford, UK: Blackwell Publishing.

Folsom, Geneva Scheihing (1968). The Developing Situation. In: Gaston, E. Thayer (Ed.). *Music in Therapy.* New York: Macmillan Publishing.

Fornäs, Johan (1995). *Cultural Theory and Late Modernity.* London: Sage Publications.

Foucault, Michel (1961/1991). *Galskapens historie i opplysningens tidsalder* [Madness and Civilization: A History of Insanity in the Age of Reason. Original title in French: Folie et dêraison. Historie de la folie à l'âge classiquie]. Oslo, Norway: Gyldendal.

Fouché, Sunelle & Kerryn Torrance (2005). Lose Yourself in the Music, the Moment, Yo! Music Therapy with an Adolescent Group Involved in Gangsterism. *Voices: A World Forum for Music Therapy.* Retrieved February 24, 2011, from https://normt.uib.no/index.php/voices/article/view/232/176.

Frank, Jerome D. & Julia B. Frank (1991). *Persuasion & Healing. A Comparative Study of Psychotherapy.* Baltimore: The Johns Hopkins University Press.

Freidson, Eliot (1970/1988). *Profession of Medicine: A Study of the Sociology of Applied Knowledge.* Chicago: The University of Chicago Press.

Freire, Paulo (1970/2000). *Pedagogy of the Oppressed: 30th Anniversary Edition.* New York: Continuum.

Friedson, Steven M. (1996). *Dancing Prophets. Musical Experience in Tumbuka Healing.* Chicago: The University of Chicago Press.

Friedson, Steven M. (2000). Dancing the Disease: Music and Trance in Tumbuka Healing. In: Gouk, Penelope (Ed.). *Musical Healing in Cultural Contexts.* Aldershot, UK: Ashgate Publishing.

Frith, Simon (2004). Why Does Music Make People so Cross? *Nordic Journal of Music Therapy, 13*(1), pp. 64–69.

Frohne, Isabelle (1986). Music Therapy in Social Education and Music Therapy in Psychiatry. In: Ruud, Even (Ed.) (1986). *Music and Health.* Oslo, Norway: Norsk Musikforlag.

Frohne-Hagemann, Isabelle (1998). The 'Musical Life Panorama' (MLP). A Facilitating Method in the Field of Clinical and Sociocultural Music Therapy. *Nordic Journal of Music Therapy, 7*(2), pp.104–112.

Frohne-Hagemann, Isabelle (2001). *Fenster zur Musiktherapie. Musik-therapie-theorie 1976–2001* [A Window to Music Therapy. Music Therapy Theory 1976–2001]. Wiesbaden, Germany: Reichert Verlag.

Furedi, Frank (2004). *Therapy Culture: Cultivating Vulnerability in an Uncertain Age.* London: Routledge.

Gadamer, Hans-Georg (1960/1999). *Truth and Method.* New York: Continuum.

Galtung, Johan (1994). *Human Rights in Another Key.* Cambridge, UK: Polity Press.

Galtung, Johan (1999). The NATO War, the Ethnic Cleansing, Is There a Way Out? [online]. *Transnational Foundation for Peace and Future Research.* Retrieved April 6, 2003, from: http://www.radiobergen.org/serbia/galtung.htm.

Galtung, Johan (2008). Peace, Music, and the Arts: In Search of Interconnectedness. In: Urbain, Olivier (Ed.). *Music and Conflict Transformation. Harmonies and Dissonances in Geopolitics* (pp. 53–60). London & New York: I.B. Tauris.

Garred, Rudy (2002). The Ontology of Music in Music Therapy: A Dialogical View. In: Kenny, Carolyn B. & Brynjulf Stige (Eds.). *Contemporary Voices of Music Therapy: Communication, Culture, and Community* (pp. 35–45). Oslo, Norway: Unipub forlag.

Garred, Rudy (2006). *Music as Therapy: A Dialogical Perspective.* Gilsum, NH: Barcelona Publishers.

Gaston, E. Thayer (Ed.) (1968). *Music in Therapy.* New York: Macmillan Publishing.

Geck, Martin (1972/1977). *Musikterapi. Bot eller bedövning? En kritisk diskussion om musiken i samhället?* [Music Therapy. Remedy or Apathy? A Critical Discussion of Music in Society. (Original title in German: Musiktherapie als Problem der Gesellschaft)]. Stockholm: Wahlström &Widstrand.

Geertz, Clifford (1973/1993). *The Interpretation of Cultures.* London: Fontana Press.

Geertz, Clifford (1983). *Local Knowledge. Further Essays in Interpretive Anthropology.* New York: Basic Books.

Gennep, Arnold van (1909/1999). *Rites de Passage. Overgangsriter* [Transitional Rites]. Oslo, Norway: Pax.

Giddens, Anthony (1991). *Modernity and Self-Identity: Self and Society in the Late Modern Age.* Cambridge, UK: Polity Press.

Gibson, James J. (1979/1986). *The Ecological Approach to Visual Perception.* Hillsdale, NJ: Lawrence Erlbaum Associates, Publishers.

Goffman, Erving (1959/1990). *The Presentation of Self in Everyday Life.* London: Penguin Books Ltd.

Goffman, Erving (1963). *Stigma. Notes on the Management of Spoiled Identity.* Englewood Cliffs, NJ: Prentice-Hall.

Goffman, Erving (1967). *Interaction Ritual. Essays on Face-to-Face Behavior.* New York: Anchor Books.

Gold, Christian (2004). The Use of Effect Sizes in Music Therapy Research. *Music Therapy Perspectives, 22*(2), pp. 91–95.

Gold, Christian, Tor Olav Heldal, Trond Dahle & Tony Wigram (2005). Music Therapy for Schizophrenia and Schizophrenia-Like Illnesses. *Cochrane Database of Systematic Reviews(2)*, CD004025. Retrieved February 19, 2011, from: http://onlinelibrary.wiley.com/o/cochrane/clsysrev/articles/CD004025/pdf_fs.html

Gold, Christian, Randi Rolvsjord, Leif Edvard Aarø, Trond Aarre, Lars Tjemsland, & Brynjulf Stige (2005). Resource-Oriented Music Therapy for Psychiatric Patients with Low Therapy Motivation: Protocol for a Randomised Controlled Trial (RCT-MTPSY). *BioMed Central Psychiatry, 5*:39 http://www.biomedcentral.com/content/5/1/39.

Gold, Christian, Hans Petter Solli, Viggo Krüger & Stein Atle Lie (2009). Dose–Response Relationship in Music Therapy for People with Serious Mental Disorders: Systematic Review and Meta-Analysis. *Clinical Psychology Review, 29*, pp. 193–207.

Gold, Christian, Randi Rolvsjord, Karin Mössler & Brynjulf Stige (forthcoming). Reliability and Validity of a Scale to Measure Interest in Music among Clients in Mental Health Care.

Gonzalez, Paula Alicia Melante, Mariana Cardoso Puchivailo, Sheila Volpi & José Roberto Neves D'Amico (2008). Musica, Educacion y Sociedad, una vision transdisciplinar en Musicoterapia [Music, Education and Society: a Transdisciplinary Vision in Music Therapy]. *Paper at the 12th World Congress in Music Therapy*, Buenos Aires, Argentina, July 2008.

Gouk, Penelope (2000). Sister Disciplines? *Music* and *Medicine* in Historical Perspective. In: Gouk, Penelope (Ed.) *Musical Healing in Cultural Contexts* (pp. 171–196). Aldershot, UK: Ashgate Publishing.

Green, Lucy (2002). *How Popular Musicians Learn. A Way Ahead for Music Education.* Farnham, UK: Ashgate Publishing.

Green, Lucy (2008). *Music, Informal Learning and the School: A New Classroom Pedagogy.* Farnham, UK: Ashgate Publishing.

Groves, Robert M., Floyd J. Fowler Jr., Mick P. Couper, James M. Lepkowski, Eleanor Singer & Roger Tourangeau (2004). *Survey Methodology.* Hoboken, NJ: John Wiley.

References

Guba, Egon G. & Yvonna S. Lincoln (2005). Paradigmatic Controversies, Contradictions, and Emerging Confluences. In: Norman K. Denzin & Yvonna S. Lincoln (Eds.). *The Sage Handbook of Qualitative Research* (3rd edition). Thousand Oaks, CA: Sage Publications.

Gustavsen, Bjørn (2006). Theory and Practice: The Mediating Discourse. In: Reason, Peter & Hilary Bradbury. *The Handbook of Action Research.* (Concise paperback edition.) London: Sage Publications.

Gutheil, Thomas G. & Archie Brodsky (2008). *Preventing Boundary Violations in Clinical Practice.* New York: The Guilford Press.

Gutheil, Thomas G. & Glen O. Gabbard (1993). The Concept of Boundaries in Clinical Practice: Theoretical and Risk Management Dimensions. *American Journal of Psychiatry, 150*(2), pp. 188–196.

Guze, Samuel B. (1978). Nature of Psychiatric Illness: Why Psychiatry is a Branch of Medicine. *Comprehensive Psychiatry, 19*(4), pp. 295–307.

Habermas, Jürgen (1968/1971). *Knowledge and Human Interests* (Original title in German: Erkenntnis und Interesse]. Boston: Beacon Press.

Hadsell, Nancy (1974). A Sociological Theory and Approach to Music Therapy with Adult Psychiatric Patients. *Journal of Music Therapy, xi*, pp. 113–124.

Halldorsson, Mathías, Anton E. Kunst, Lennart Köhler & Johan P. Mackenbach (2000). Socioeconomic Inequalities in the Health of Children and Adolescents. A Comparative Study of the Five Nordic Countries. *European Journal of Public Health, 10*(4), pp. 281–288.

Halstead, Jill (2010). Making Music: Action, Embodiment, Health. Locating Music as Act and Activity in Contemporary Culture. Post doctoral project proposal. Bergen, Norway: The Grieg Academy, University of Bergen.

Hammersley, Martyn & Paul Atkinson (2007). *Ethnography. Principles in Practice* (2nd edition). London: Routledge.

Hancock, Gregory R. & Ralph O. Mueller (2006). *Structural Equation Modeling: A Second Course.* Greenwich, CT: Information Age Publishing.

Hanifan, Lydia Judson (1916). The Rural School Community Center. *Annals of the American Academy of Political and Social Science, 67*, pp. 130–138.

Harkness, Janet A., Fons J. R. Van de Vijver & Peter Ph. Mohler (Eds.) (2003). *Crosscultural Survey Methods.* Hoboken, NJ: John Wiley & Sons.

Hartley, Nigel (2008). The Arts in Health and Social Care: Is Music Therapy Fit for Purpose? *British Journal of Music Therapy, 22*(2), pp. 88–96.

Heck, Ronald H. & Scott L. Thomas (2008). *An Introduction to Multilevel Modeling Techniques.* Mahwah, NJ: Erlbaum.

Helle-Valle, Anna (2011). Restless Children: Who are They, How can They Best be Met, and What can be the Contribution of Music Therapy? Unpublished PhD Proposal. Bergen, Norway: The Grieg Academy, University of Bergen.

Hernes, Helge (2002). Perspektiver på profesjoner [The Professions in Perspective]. In: Nylehn, Børre & Anne Marie Støkken (Eds.). *De profesjonelle* [The Professionals]. Oslo, Norway: Universitetsforlaget.

Heron, John (1992). *Feeling and Personhood: Psychology in another Key.* London: Sage Publications.

Hillery, George A. Jr. (1955). Definitions of Community: Areas of Agreement. *Rural Sociology, 20*(4), pp. 111–123.

Hird, Susan (2003). What is Wellbeing? A Brief Review of Current Literature and Concepts. NHS Scotland, April 2003. Retrieved January 17, 2011, from: http://www.phis.org.uk/doc.pl?file=pdf/What%20is%20wellbeing%202.doc.

Hogg, Michael A. (2001). Social Categorization, Depersonalization, and Group Behavior. In: Hogg, Michael A. & R. Scott Tindale (Eds.). *Blackwell Handbook of Social Psychology: Group Processes* (pp. 56–85). Oxford, U.K.: Blackwell.

Hogg, Michael A. & Deborah J. Terry (2001). Social Identity Theory and Organizational Processes. In: Hogg, Michael A. & Deborah J. Terry (Eds.). *Social Identity Processes in Organizational Contexts* (pp. 1–12). Philadelphia, PA: Psychology Press (Taylor & Francis).

Hollander, Edwin P. (1976). *Principles and Methods of Social Psychology* (3rd edition). New York: Oxford University Press.

Holmes, Thomas A. & Richard H. Rahe (1967). The Social Readjustment Rating Scale. *Journal of Psychosomatic Research*, 11, pp. 213–218.

Honneth, Axel (2003). *Behovet for anerkendelse* [The Need for Recognition]. Copenhagen, DK: Hans Reitzels forlag.

Horden, Peregrine (Ed.) (2000). *Music as Medicine: The History of Music Therapy since Antiquity*. Aldershot, UK: Ashgate Publishing.

House, James S. (1981). *Work Stress and Social Support*. Reading, MA: Addison-Wesley.

Huisman, Martijn, Anton E. Kunst & Johan P. Mackenbach (2005). Inequalities in the Prevalence of Smoking in the European Union: Comparing Education and Income. *Preventive Medicine, 40*, pp. 756–764.

Hunt, Meagan (2005). Action Research and Music Therapy: Group Music Therapy with Young Refugees in a School Community. *Voices: A World Forum for Music Therapy*. Retrieved February 24, 2011, from https://normt.uib.no/index.php/voices/article/view/223/167.

Ife, Jim (2008). *Human Rights and Social Work. Towards Rights-Based Practice*. New York: Cambridge University Press.

Ife, Jim (2010). *Human Rights from Below. Achieving Rights through Community Development*. New York: Cambridge University Press.

Ishay, Micheline R. (2004). *The History of Human Rights*. Berkeley, CA: University of California Press.

Jampel, Peter (2006). Performance in Music Therapy with Mentally Ill Adults. Unpublished Doctoral Dissertation. New York: New York University.

Jampel, Peter (2011). Performance in Music Therapy: Experiences in Five Dimensions. *Voices: A World Forum for Music Therapy*, 11(1). Retrieved March 14, 2011, from: https://normt.uib.no/index.php/voices/article/view/275/440

Janss, Christian & Christian Refsum (2003). *Lyrikkens liv. Innføring i diktlesing* [The Life of Lyrics: Introduction to the Reading of Poetry]. Oslo, Norway: Universitetsforlaget.

Janzen, John M. (2000). Theories of Music in African Ngoma Healing. In: Gouk, Penelope (Ed.). *Musical Healing in Cultural Contexts*. Aldershot, UK: Ashgate Publishing.

Kagan, Carolyn & Mark Burton (2005). Marginalization. In: Nelson, Geoffrey & Isaac Prilleltensky (Eds.) *Community Psychology. In Pursuit of Liberation and Well-Being* (pp. 293–308). New York: Palgrave MacMillan.

Kahn, Robert L. & F. Thomas Juster (2002) Wellbeing: Concepts and Measures. *Journal of Social Issues, 58*(4), pp. 627–644.

Kaslow, Florence W. (Ed.) (1996). *Handbook of Relational Diagnosis and Dysfunctional Family Patterns*. New York: Wiley.

Kasser, Tim (2002). *The High Price of Materialism*. Cambridge, MA: The MIT Press.

Katz, Sharon (2011). The Peace Train. *Voices: A World Forum for Music Therapy*, 11(1). Retrieved March 14, 2011, from: https://normt.uib.no/index.php/voices/article/view/284/439

Kawachi, Ichiro (2000). Income Inequality and Health. In: Berkman, Lisa F. & Ichiro Kawachi (Eds.). *Social Epidemiology* (pp. 76–94). Oxford: Oxford University Press.

Kawachi, Ichiro & Lisa F. Berkman (2000). Social Cohesion, Social Capital, and Health. In: Berkman, Lisa F. & Ichiro Kawachi (Eds.). *Social Epidemiology* (pp. 174–190). Oxford: Oxford University Press

Kawachi, Ichiro, S.V. Subramanian & Daniel Kim (2010). Social Capital and Health—A Decade of Progress and Beyond. In: Kawachi, Ichiro, S.V. Subramanian & Daniel Kim (Eds.). *Social Capital and Health* (pp. 1–26). New York: Springer.

Keil, Charles & Steven Feld (1994). *Music Grooves*. Chicago: The University of Chicago Press.

Kenny, Carolyn B. (1982). *The Mythic Artery. The Magic of Music Therapy*. Atascadero, CA: Ridgeview Publishing Company.

Kenny, Carolyn B. (1985). Music: A Whole Systems Approach. *Music Therapy*, 5(1), pp. 3–11.

References

Kenny, Carolyn B. (1988). A Song of Peace: Dare We Dream? *Music Therapy*, 7(1), pp. 51–55.

Kenny, Carolyn B. (1989). *The Field of Play. A Guide for the Theory and Practice of Music Therapy.* Atascadero, CA: Ridgeview Publishing Company.

Kenny, Carolyn B. (1999). Music Therapy Qualitative Research: How Music Therapy Research Can Influence Social Change. Panel debate, chaired by Carolyn Kenny, at the 9th World Congress of Music Therapy, Washington, DC.

Kenny, Carolyn B. (2002a). Blue Wolf Says Goodbye for the Last Time. *American Behavioral Scientist*, 45(8), pp. 1214–1222.

Kenny, Carolyn B. (2002b). Keeping the World in Balance—Music Therapy in a Ritual Context. In: Kenny, Carolyn B. & Brynjulf Stige (Eds.) (2002). *Contemporary Voices of Music Therapy: Communication, Culture, and Community* (pp. 157–170). Oslo, Norway: Unipub forlag.

Kenny, Carolyn B. (2006). *Music and Life in the Field of Play.* Gilsum, NH: Barcelona Publishers.

Kenny, Carolyn B. & Brynjulf Stige (Eds.) (2002). *Contemporary Voices of Music Therapy: Communication, Culture, and Community.* Oslo, Norway: Unipub forlag.

Kern, Petra (2005). Using a Music Therapy Collaborative Consultative Approach for the Inclusion of Young Children with Autism in a Child Care Program. In: *Jahrbuch Musiktherapie.* Band 1: Forschung und Lehre [Music Therapy Annual, 1: Research and Development, pp. 107–134]. Berufsverband der Musiktherapeutinnen und Musiktherapeuten in Deutschland e.V. (BVM), Wiesbaden, Reichert Verlag.

Kiesler, Donald J. (1991). Interpersonal Methods of Assessment and Diagnosis. In: Snyder, C.R. & Donelson R. Forsyth (Eds.). *Handbook of Social and Clinical Psychology* (pp. 438–468). New York: Pergamon.

Kigunda, Bernard M. (2004). Music Therapy Canning and the Healing Rituals of Catholic Charismatics in Kenya. *Voices: A World Forum for Music Therapy.* Retrieved February 26, 2011, from: https://normt.uib.no/index.php/voices/article/view/186/145.

Kim, Daniel, S.V. Subramanian & Ichiro Kawachi (2010). Social Capital and Physical Health: A Systematic Review of the Literature. In: Kawachi, Ichiro, S.V. Subramanian & Daniel Kim (Eds.). *Social Capital and Health* (pp. 139–190). New York: Springer.

Kirk, Stuart A. & Herb Kutchins (1994). The Myth of the Reliability of DSM. *Journal of Mind and Behavior*, 15(1&2), pp. 71–86.

Kleive, Mette & Brynjulf Stige (1988). *Med lengting, liv og song* [With Longing, Life, and Song.] Oslo, Norway: Samlaget.

Knardal, Solgunn (2007). I songen vi møtest . . . Ein tekst om pensjonistar som syng i kor, basert på medlemmene sine eigne forteljingar [In Singing We're Relating . . . A Text on Senior Choir Singers, Based on Their own Words]. Unpublished master thesis. Oslo/Sandane, Norway: Norwegian Academy of Music/Sogn og Fjordane University College.

Knorth, Erik J., Peter Van Den Bergh, & Fop Verheij (Eds.) (2002). *Professionalization and Participation in Child and Youth Care: Challenging Understandings in Theory and Practice.* Aldershot, UK: Ashgate Publishing.

Korsyn, Kevin (2003). *Decentering Music. A Critique of Contemporary Musical Research.* New York: Oxford University Press.

Kristiansen, Ivar Sønbø & Gavin Mooney (Eds) (2004). *Evidence-Based Medicine. In its Place.* London and New York: Routledge.

Krüger, Viggo (2004). Læring gjennom deltagelse i et rockeband. Et instrumentelt case studie om situert læring i musikkterapi [Learning through Participation in a Rock Band. An Instrumental Case Study on Situated Learning in Music Therapy]. Unpublished master thesis. Oslo/Sandane, Norway: Norwegian Academy of Music/Sogn og Fjordane University College.

Krüger, Viggo (2007). Music as Narrative Technology. *Voices: A World Forum for Music Therapy.* Retrieved January 19, 2011, from https://normt.uib.no/index.php/voices/article/view/492/399.

Krüger, Viggo (forthcoming). Musikk—fortelling—fellesskap. Musikkterapi i en barnevernsinstitusjon [Music—Narrative—Community. Music Therapy in a Children's Welfare Institution]. Unpublished Doctoral Dissertation. Bergen, Norway: The Grieg Academy, University of Bergen.

Kuhn, Thomas S. (1962/1996). *The Structure of Scientific Revolutions* (3rd edition). Chicago: The University of Chicago Press.

Langner, Thomas. S. & Stanley T. Michael (1963). *Life Stress and Mental Health.* London: Free Press.

Lave, Jean & Etienne Wenger (1991). *Situated Learning. Legitimate Peripheral Participation.* Cambridge, UK: Cambridge University Press.

Lazarus, Richard S. & Susan Folkman (1984). *Stress, Appraisal and Coping.* New York: Springer.

Lee, Colin (1996). *Music at the Edge. The Music Therapy Experiences of a Musician with AIDS.* London: Routledge.

Leer-Salvesen, Paul (2002). Preludium: Arven fra Hippocrates [Prelude: The Hippocratic Heritage]. In: Nylehn, Børre & Anne Marie Støkken (Eds.). *De profesjonelle* [The Professionals]. Oslo, Norway: Universitetsforlaget.

Leppert, Richard & Susan McClary (Eds) (1987). *Music and Society. The Politics of Composition, Performance and Reception.* Cambridge: Cambridge University Press.

Logis, Maria & Alan Turry (1999). Singing My Way through It: Facing the Cancer, the Darkness and the Fear. In: Hibben, Julie (Ed.). *Inside Music Therapy: Client Experiences*, pp. 97–118. Gilsum, NH: Barcelona Publishers.

Lopez, Alan D., Colin D. Mathers, Majid Ezzati, Dean T. Jamison & Christopher J. L. Murray (Eds.) (2006). *Global Burden of Disease and Risk Factors.* New York: Oxford University Press.

Lubet, Alex J. (2004). Tunes of Impairment: An Ethnomusicology of Disability. *Review of Disability Studies, (1)*1, pp. 133–155.

MacDonald, Raymond, Gunter Kreutz & Laura Mitchell (Eds.) (in press). *Music, Health and Wellbeing.* New York: Oxford University Press.

MacDonald, Scott & Michael Viega (2011). Hear Our Voices: A Music Therapy Songwriting Program and the Message of the Little Saints. In: Hadley, Susan & George Yancy (Eds.). *Therapeutic Uses of Rap and Hip-Hop.* New York: Routledge.

MacQueen, Kathleen M., Eleanor McLellan, David S. Metzger, Susan Kegeles, Ronald P. Strauss, Roseanne Scotti, Lynn Blanchard & Robert T. Trotter (2001). What is Community? An Evidence-Based Definition for Participatory Public Health. *American Journal of Public Health*, 91(12), pp. 1929–1943.

Maddux, James E. (2002). Stopping the "Madness"—Positive Psychology and the Deconstruction of the Illness Ideology and the DSM. In: Snyder, C.R. & Lopez, Shane J. (Eds.). *Handbook of Positive Psychology* (pp. 13–25). Oxford: Oxford University Press.

Maddux, James E. (2008). Positive Psychology and the Illness Ideology: Toward a Positive Clinical Psychology. *Applied Psychology: An International Review*, 57, pp. 54–70.

Major, Brenda & Collette P. Eccleston (2005). Stigma and Social Exclusion. In: Abrams, Dominic, Michael. A. Hogg & José. M. Marques (Eds.). *The Social Psychology of Inclusion and Exclusion* (pp. 63–87). New York: Psychology Press (Taylor & Francis).

Malekoff, Andrew (1997). *Group Work with Adolescents.* New York: Guildford Press.

Malloch, Stephen & Colwyn Trevarthen (Eds.) (2009). *Communicative Musicality. Exploring the Basis of Human Companionship.* Oxford, UK: Oxford University Press.

Maratos, Anna (2004). Whatever Next? Community Music Therapy for the Institution. In: Pavlicevic, Mercédès & Gary Ansdell (Eds.). *Community Music Therapy.* London: Jessica Kingsley Publishers.

Marmot, Michael, Johannes Siegrist & Töres Theorell (2006). Health and the Psychosocial Environment at Work. In: Marmot, Michael & Richard G. Wilkinson (Eds.). *Social Determinants of Health* (pp. 97–130). Oxford: Oxford University Press.

Martin, Pete J. (1995). *Sounds and Society.* Manchester: Manchester University Press.

Martin, Pete J. (2006). Music and the Sociological Gaze. Art Worlds and Cultural Production. Manchester: Manchester University Press.

Mathers, Colin D., Alan D. Lopez & Christopher J. L. Murray (2006). The Burden of Disease and Mortality by Condition: Data, Methods and Results for 2001. In: Lopez, Alan D., Colin D. Mathers, Majid Ezzati,

References   Dean T. Jamison & Christopher J. L. Murray (Eds.). *Global Burden of Disease and Risk Factors* (pp. 45–240). New York: Oxford University Press.

Mattern, Mark (1998). *Acting in Concert: Music, Community, and Political Action.* New Brunswick, NJ: Rutgers University Press.

May, Elizabeth (1983). *Musics of Many Cultures.* Berkeley: California University Press.

McFerran, Katrina (2009). A Journey into the Heart: Music Therapy after the "Black Saturday" Bush Fires. *Voices: A World Forum for Music Therapy. Voices: A World Forum for Music Therapy.* Retrieved January 3, 2010, from http://www.voices.no/columnist/colMcFerran7*mm*yy.php.

McFerran, Katrina (2010). *Adolescents, Music and Music Therapy: Methods and Techniques for Clinicians, Educators and Students.* London: Jessica Kingsley Publishers.

McFerran, Katrina (in press). Moving out of Your Comfort Zone: Group Music Therapy with Adolescents Who Have Misused Drugs. In: Meadows, Anthony (Ed.). *Developments in Music Therapy Practice: Case Study Perspectives.* Gilsum, NH: Barcelona Publishers.

McFerran, Katrina & Meagan Hunt (2008). Learning from Experiences in Action: Music in Schools to Promote Healthy Coping with Grief and Loss. *Educational Action Research, 16*(1), pp. 43–54.

McFerran, Katrina & Kate Teggelove (2011). Music Therapy with Young People in Schools: After the Black Saturday Fires. *Voices: A World Forum for Music Therapy, 11*(1). Retrieved March 14, 2011, from: https://normt.uib.no/index.php/voices/article/view/285

McGuire, Michael G. (Ed.) (2004). *Psychiatric Music Therapy in the Community: The Legacy of Florence Tyson.* Gilsum, NH: Barcelona Publishers.

McKenzie, Kwame (2006). The State of the Art. In: McKenzie, Kwame & Trudy Harpham (Eds.). *Social Capital and Mental Health* (pp. 151–158). London: Jessica Kingsley Publishers.

McMillan, David W. (1976). Sense of Community: An Attempt at Definition. Nashville, TN: George Peabody College for Teachers (Unpublished manuscript).

McMillan, David W. & David M. Chavis (1986). Sense of Community: A Definition and Theory. *Journal of Community Psychology, 14 (January 1986),* pp. 6–23.

Mechanic, David (1999). Mental Health and Mental Illness: Definitions and Perspectives. In: Horwitz, Allan V. & Teresea L. Scheid (Eds.). *A Handbook for the Study of Mental Health* (pp. 12–28). Cambridge, UK: Cambridge University Press.

Merton, Robert K. (1942/1973). The Normative Structure of Science. I: Merton, Robert K. *The Sociology of Science. Theoretical and Empirical Investigations.* Chicago: The University of Chicago Press.

Metell, Maren (2011). What Can Music Therapy Afford Children with Severe Visual Impairment in Terms of Social Participation? Unpublished Master thesis. Bergen, Norway: The Grieg Academy, University of Bergen.

Milgram, Stanley (1967). The Small-World Problem. *Psychology Today 1,* pp. 61–67.

Mill, John Stuart (1859/2003). *On Liberty* (edited by David Bromwich & George Kateb). New Haven and London: Yale University Press.

Miller, Geoffrey (2000). Evolution of Human Music through Sexual Selection. In: Wallin, Nils L., Björn Merker & Steven Brown (Eds.). *The Origins of Music.* Cambridge, MA: The MIT Press.

Miller, Geoffrey (2001). *The Mating Mind. How Sexual Choice Shaped the Evolution of Human Nature.* London: Vintage, Random House.

Mitchell, Laura, Raymond MacDonald & Christina Knussen (2008). An Investigation of the Effects of Music and Art on Pain Perception. *Psychology of Aesthetics, Creativity, and the Arts, 2*(3), pp. 162–170.

Mittelmark, Maurice, Leif Edvard Aarø, Sigrun G. Henriksen, Johan Siqveland & Torbjørn Torsheim (2004). Chronic Social Stress in the Community and Associations with Psychological Distress: A Social Psychological Perspective. *International Journal of Mental Health Promotion, 6,* pp. 4–16.

Miyake, Hiroko (2008). Rethinking Music Therapy from the Perspective of *Bio-politics. Voices: A World Forum for Music Therapy.* Retrieved February 3, 2011, from https://normt.uib.no/index.php/voices/article/view/413/337.

Moreno, Joseph (1988). The Music Therapist: Creative Arts Therapist and Contemporary Shaman. *The Arts in Psychotherapy*, 15(4), pp. 271–280.

Moreno, Joseph (1995a). Candomblé: Afro-Brazilian Ritual as Therapy. In: Kenny, Carolyn B. (Ed.). *Listening, Playing Creating. Essays on the Power of Sound*. Albany: State University of New York Press.

Moreno, Joseph (1995b). Ethnomusic Therapy: An Interdisciplinary Approach to Music Healing. *The Arts in Psychotherapy*, 22(4), pp. 329–338.

Moreno, Joseph (2003). Music Therapy in the White House. *Voices: A World Forum for Music Therapy*. Retrieved May 9, 2004, from http://www.voices.no/discussions/discm17_01.html.

Murphy, Michael, Martin Bobak, Amanda Nicholson, Richard Rose & Michael Marmot (2006). The Widening Gap in Mortality by Educational Level in the Russian Federation, 1980–2001. *American Journal of Public Health*, 96, pp. 1293–1299.

Naples, Nancy A. (2003). *Feminism and Method: Ethnography, Discourse Analysis, and Activist Research*. New York: Routledge.

Nelson, Geoffrey & Isaac Prilleltensky (Eds.) (2005). *Community Psychology. In Pursuit of Liberation and Well-Being*. New York: Palgrave MacMillan.

Nerheim, Hjördis (1995). *Vitenskap og kommunikasjon. Paradigmer, modeller og kommunikative strategier i helsefagenes vitenskapsteori* [Science and Communication. Paradigms, Models and Strategies of Communication in the Health Disciplines' Theory of Science.] Oslo, Norway: Universitetsforlaget.

Nettl, Bruno (1956). Aspects of Primitive and Folk Music Relevant to Music Therapy. In: *Music Therapy 1955. Fifth Book of Proceedings of the National Association for Music Therapy*. Lawrence, KS: The National Association for Music Therapy.

Newman, Katherine S. (1999). *Falling from Grace. Downward Mobility in the Age of Affluence*. Berkeley, CA: University of California Press.

Ng, Wang Feng (2005). Music Therapy, War Trauma, and Peace: A Singaporean Perspective. *Voices: A World Forum for Music Therapy*. Retrieved November 2, 2007, from http://www.voices.no/mainissues/mi40005000191.html.

Nilsen, Venja Ruud (2007). "Musikk i fengsel og frihet"—et samfunnsmusikkterapeutisk tilbud. ["Music in Custody and Liberty"—A Community Music Therapy Program]. Unpublished Master's Thesis. Oslo, Norway: Norwegian Academy of Music.

Nisbet, Robert A. (1966/2002). *The Sociological Tradition*. New Brunswick, NJ: Transaction Publishers.

Noone, Jason (2008). Developing a Music Therapy Programme within a Person Centred Planning Framework. *Voices: A World Forum for Music Therapy*, 8(3). Retrieved December 6, 2009, from http://www.voices.no/mainissues/mi40008000281.php.

Nordoff, Paul & Clive Robbins (1965/2004). *Therapy in Music for Handicapped Children*. Gilsum, NH: Barcelona Publishers.

Nordoff, Paul & Clive Robbins (1971/1983). *Music Therapy in Special Education*. Saint Louis, MO: Magna-Music Baton.

Nordoff, Paul & Clive Robbins (1977/2007). *Creative Music Therapy*. Gilsum, NH: Barcelona Publishers.

Norman, Rachel, Derek Sellman & Catherine Warner (2006). Mental Capacity, Good Practice and the Cyclical Consent Process in Research Involving Vulnerable People. *Clinical Ethics*, 1(4), pp. 228–233.

Numata, Rii (2009). EinScream! Possibilities of New Musical Ideas to Form a Community. *Voices: A World Forum for Music Therapy*, 9(1). Retrieved January 29, 2011, from https://normt.uib.no/index.php/voices/article/view/363/286.

Oddy, Nicola (2001/2005). Convergences: Possibilities for Therapeutic Intervention in a Large Scale Community Performance. *Canadian Journal of Music Therapy*, VIII(1), pp. 48–63. Republished in: *Voices: A World Forum for Music Therapy*. Retrieved January 26, 2011, from https://normt.uib.no/index.php/voices/article/view/239/183.

O'Grady, Lucy (2005). The Relationship between the Ways that Musicians and Music Therapists Describe their Work in Community Contexts: A Grounded Theory Analysis. Unpublished Master's Thesis. Melbourne: University of Melbourne, Faculty of Music.

References

O'Grady, Lucy (2009). The Therapeutic Potentials of Creating and Performing Music with Women in Prison: A Qualitative Case Study. Unpublished Doctoral Dissertation. Melbourne: University of Melbourne, Faculty of Music.

O'Grady, Lucy & Katrina McFerran (2006). Birthing: Feminist Community Music Therapy: The Progeny of Community Music Therapy Practice and Feminist Therapy Theory. In: Hadley, Susan (Ed.) *Feminist Perspectives in Music Therapy*. Gilsum, NH: Barcelona Publishers.

O'Grady, Lucy & Katrina McFerran (2007). Community Music Therapy and its Relationship to Community Music: Where Does it End? *Nordic Journal of Music Therapy, 16(1)*, pp. 14–26.

Onghena, Patrick (2005). Single-Case Designs. In: Everitt, Brian S. & David Howell (Eds.). *Encyclopedia of Statistics in Behavioral Science, 3* (pp.1850–1854). New York: Wiley.

Oosthuizen, Helen (2006). Diversity and Community: Finding and Forming a South African Music Therapy. *Voices: A World Forum for Music Therapy*. Retrieved February 19, 2011, from https://normt.uib.no/index.php/voices/article/view/277/202.

Oosthuizen, Helen, Fouché, Sunelle & Torrance, Kerryn (2007). Collaborative Work: Negotiations between Music Therapists and Community Musicians in the Development of a South African Community Music Therapy Project. *Voices: A World Forum for Music Therapy*. Retrieved February 19, 2011, from https://normt.uib.no/index.php/voices/article/view/546/407.

Owen, Frances & Dorothy Griffiths (Eds.) (2009). *Challenges to the Human Rights of People with Intellectual Disabilities*. London: Jessica Kingsley Publishers.

Pan American Health Organization (1999). Methodological Summaries: Measuring Inequity in Health. *Epidemiological Bulletin, 20(1)*, 1. Retrieved February 16, 2011, from http://www.ops-oms.org/english/sha/be991ineq.htm.

Pavlicevic, Mercédès (2003). Risk, Indemnity and Social Responsibility in Music Therapy Training. *Voices: A World Forum for Music Therapy*. Retrieved March 17, 2003, from http://www.voices.no/mainissues/mi40003000115.html.

Pavlicevic, Mercédès (2004). Learning from Thembalethu: Towards Responsive and Responsible Practice in Community Music Therapy. In: Pavlicevic, Mercédès & Gary Ansdell (Eds.). *Community Music Therapy*. London: Jessica Kingsley Publishers.

Pavlicevic, Mercédès (2010a). Let the Music Work: Optimal Moments of Collaborative Musicing. In: Stige, Brynjulf, Gary Ansdell, Cochavit Elefant & Mercédès Pavlicevic. *Where Music Helps: Community Music Therapy in Action and Reflection*. Aldershot, UK: Ashgate Publishing.

Pavlicevic, Mercédès (2010b). Crime, Community, and Everyday Practice: Music Therapy as Social Activism. In: Stige, Brynjulf, Gary Ansdell, Cochavit Elefant & Mercédès Pavlicevic. *Where Music Helps: Community Music Therapy in Action and Reflection*. Aldershot, UK: Ashgate Publishing.

Pavlicevic, Mercédès & Gary Ansdell (Eds.) (2004). *Community Music Therapy*. London: Jessica Kingsley Publishers.

Pavlicevic, Mercédès & Gary Ansdell (2009). Between Communicative Musicality and Collaborative Musicing. In: Malloch, Stephen & Colwyn Trevarthen (Eds.). *Communicative Musicality*. Oxford: Oxford University Press.

Pellizzari, Patricia C. & Ricardo J. Rodríguez (2005). *Salud, Escucha y Creatividad. Musicoterapia Preventiva Psicosocial* [Health, Listening, and Creativity. Preventive Psychosocial Music Therapy]. Buenos Aires: Ediciones Universidad del Salvador.

Pettersen, Jarle A. (2008). Musikkterapi i fengsel. Møte mellom musikkerapien og "den totale institusjonen" [Music Therapy in Custody. The Encounter between Music Therapy and "the Total Institution"]. Unpublished Master's Thesis. Bergen, Norway: Department of Administration and Organization Studies, University of Bergen.

Pinker, Steven (1997). *How the Mind Works. The New Science of Language and Mind*. London: Penguin.

Portes, Alejandro (1998). Social Capital: Its Origins and Applications in Modern Sociology. *Annual Review of Sociology, 24*, pp. 1–24.

Powell, Harriet (2004). A Dream Wedding: From Community Music to Music Therapy with a Community. In: Pavlicevic, Mercédès & Gary Ansdell (Eds.) (2004). *Community Music Therapy*. London: Jessica Kingsley Publishers.

Presser, Stanley, Jennifer M. Rothgeb, Mick B. Couper, Judith T. Lessler, Elisabeth Martin, Jean Martin & Eleanor Singer (Eds.) (2004). *Methods for Testing and Evaluating Survey Questionnaires*. New York: Wiley.

Priestley, Mary (1975/1985). *Music Therapy in Action*. St. Louis, MO: MagnaMusic Baton.

Procter, Simon (2001). Empowering and Enabling: Improvisational Music Therapy in Non-Medical Mental Health Provision. *Voices: A World Forum for Music Therapy*. Retrieved February 23, 2011, from https://normt.uib.no/index.php/voices/article/view/58/46

Procter, Simon (2004). Playing Politics: Community Music Therapy and the Therapeutic Redistribution of Musical Capital for Mental Health. In: Pavlicevic, Mercédès & Gary Ansdell (Eds.) (2004). *Community Music Therapy*. London: Jessica Kingsley Publishers.

Procter, Simon (2006). What are we Playing at? Social Capital and Music Therapy. In: Edwards, Rosalind, Jane Franklin & Janet Holland (Eds.). *Assessing Social Capital: Concept, Policy and Practice*. Cambridge: Scholars Press.

Procter, Simon (2008). Premising the Challenge (Response to Alison Barrington). *British Journal of Music Therapy, 22*(2), pp. 77–82.

Procter, Simon (2011). Reparative Musicing: Thinking on the Usefulness of Social Capital Theory within Music Therapy. *Nordic Journal of Music Therapy*. First published March 18, 2011 (iFirst). DOI: 10.1080/08098131.2010.489998.

Putnam, Robert (2000). *Bowling Alone: The Collapse and Revival of American Community*. New York: Simon and Schuster.

Ragland, Zane & Maurice Apprey (1974). Community Music Therapy with Adolescents. *Journal of Music Therapy, XI*(3), pp. 147–155.

Ramsey, David (2002). The Restoration of Communal Experiences during Music Therapy. Unpublished Doctoral Dissertation. New York: New York University, The School of Education, Health, Nursing, and Arts Professions.

Rappaport, Julian (1977). *Community Psychology: Values, Research, and Action*. New York: Holt, Rinehart & Winston.

Reason, Peter & Hilary Bradbury (2006). *The Handbook of Action Research*. (Concise paperback edition.) London: Sage Publications.

Redfield, Robert (1953/1963). *The Little Community/Peasant Society and Culture*. Chicago: The University of Chicago Press.

Reis, Harry T. (1995). Social Support. In: Antony S.R. Manstead & Miles Hewstone (Eds.). *The Blackwell Encyclopedia of Social Psychology* (pp. 608–609). Cambridge, MA: Blackwell.

Rickson, Daphne (2008). The Potential Role of Music in Special Education (The PROMISE). New Zealand Music Therapists Consider Collaborative Consultation. *The New Zealand Journal of Music Therapy, 6*, pp. 76–97.

Rickson, Daphne (2010). Music Therapy School Consultation: A Literature Review. *The New Zealand Journal of Music Therapy, 8*, pp. 59–91.

Rieger, Gerd (1992). Rockmusik mit jungen Aussiedlern [Rock Music with Young Immigrants]. *Musiktherapeutische Umschau, 13*(3), pp. 217–220.

Rieger, Gerd (2006). Musiktherapie und Gemeinwesenarbeit [Music Therapy and Community Work]. *Musiktherapeutische Umschau, 27*(3), pp. 235–244.

Rieger, Gerd (2008). Musik verbindet. Das Lebenshilfe-Bandprojekt *Rock am Ring* und Community Music Therapy [Music Connects. The Life Enhancing Band Project *Rock am Ring* and Community Music Therapy]. *Geistige Behinderung, 47*(3), pp. 257–266.

Rio, Robin (2005). Adults in Recovery: A Year with Members of the Choirhouse. *Nordic Journal of Music Therapy, 14*(2), pp. 107–119.

References

Robson, Colin (2002). *Real World Research.* (2nd edition). Oxford, UK: Blackwell.

Roer, Sten (2001). Performance as Therapy: Chok-Rock New York Tour 1997. Paper at The 5th European Music Therapy Congress. Naples, Italy, April 2001.

Rogers, Wendy Stainton (1991). *Explaining Health and Illness: An Exploration of Diversity.* New York: Harvester Wheatsheaf.

Rohrbacher, Michael (1993). The Ethnomusicology of Music Therapy. Unpublished doctoral dissertation. Baltimore, MD: University of Maryland, Baltimore County.

Rohrbacher, Michael (2008). The Application of Hood's Nine Levels to the Practice of Music Therapy. In: Koen, Benjamin D. (Ed.). *The Oxford Handbook of Medical Ethnomusicology.* New York: Oxford University Press.

Rokeach, Milton (1968). *Beliefs, Attitudes and Values: A Theory of Organization and Change.* San Francisco: CA: Jossey-Bass Inc. Pub.

Rolvsjord, Randi (2004). Therapy as Empowerment: Clinical and Political Implications of Empowerment Philosophy in Mental Health Practices of Music Therapy. *Nordic Journal of Music Therapy, 13*(2), pp. 99–111.

Rolvsjord, Randi (2007). "Blackbirds Singing": Explorations of Resource-Oriented Music Therapy in Mental Health Care. Unpublished Doctoral Dissertation, Aalborg Universitet.

Rolvsjord, Randi (2010). *Resource-Oriented Music Therapy in Mental Health Care.* Gilsum, NH: Barcelona Publishers.

Rolvsjord, Randi, Christian Gold & Brynjulf Stige (2005). Research Rigour and Therapeutic Flexibility: Rationale for a Therapy Manual Developed for a Randomized Controlled Trial. *Nordic Journal of Music Therapy, 14*(1), pp. 15–32.

Rosenwein, Barbara H. (2006). *Emotional Communities in the Early Middle Ages.* Ithaca, NY: Cornell University Press.

Rutter, Michael L., Bridget Yule, David Quinton, Olwen Rowlands, William Yule & Michael Berger (1975). Attainment and Adjustment in Two Geographical Areas: III. Some Factors Accounting for Area Differences. *British Journal of Psychiatry, 126,* pp. 493–509.

Ruud, Even (1980). *Hva er musikkterapi?* [What is Music Therapy?] Oslo, Norway: Gyldendal.

Ruud, Even (Ed.) (1986). *Music and Health.* Oslo, Norway: Norsk Musikforlag.

Ruud, Even (1987/1990). *Musikk som kommunikasjon og samhandling. Teoretiske perspektiver på musikkterapien.* [Music as Communication and Interaction. Theoretical Perspectives on Music Therapy.] Oslo, Norway: Solum.

Ruud, Even (1988). Music Therapy: Health Profession or Cultural Movement? *Music Therapy, 7*(1), pp. 34–37.

Ruud, Even (1991). Improvisasjon som liminal erfaring—om jazz og musikkterapi som overgangsritualer [Improvisation as Liminal Experience—On Jazz and Music Therapy as Rites de Passage]. In: Stige, Brynjulf & Bente Østergaard (Eds.). *Levande musikk. Foredrag og referat fra 1. Nordiske Musikkterapikonferanse* [Live Music. Proceedings from the First Nordic Music Therapy Conference]. Sandane: Høgskuleutdanninga på Sandane.

Ruud, Even (1992a). Improvisasjon som liminal erfaring—om jazz og musikkterapi som overgangsritualer [Improvisation as Liminal Experience—On Jazz and Music Therapy as Rites de Passage]. In: Berkaak, Odd Are & Even Ruud. *Den påbegynte virkelighet. Studier i samtidskultur.* Oslo, Norway: Universitetsforlaget.

Ruud, Even (1992b). Innføring i systematisk musikkvitenskap [Introduction to Systematic Musicology]. Oslo, Norway: Institutt for musikk og teater, University of Oslo.

Ruud, Even (1995). Jazz and Music Therapy as Modern 'Rites de Passage.' In: Kenny, Carolyn (Ed.). *Listening, Playing, Creating. Essays on the Power of Sound.* Albany: State University of New York Press.

Ruud, Even (1997a). Music and Identity. *Nordic Journal of Music Therapy, 6*(1), pp. 3–13.

Ruud, Even (1997b). *Musikk og identitet* (Music and Identity]. Oslo, Norway: Universitetsforlaget.

Ruud, Even (1998). *Music Therapy: Improvisation, Communication and Culture.* Gilsum, NH: Barcelona.

Ruud, Even (2000). 'New Musicology', Music Education and Music Therapy. *Paper at the 13th Nordic Congress of Musicology, Århus, Denmark.* Retrieved March 31, 2004, from: www.njmt.no.

Ruud, Even (2002). Music as a Cultural Immunogen—Three Narratives on the Use of Music as a Technology of Health. In: Hanken, Ingrid Maria, Siw Graabæk & Monika Nerland (Eds.). *Research in and for Higher Music Education. Festschrift for Harald Jørgensen*. Oslo, Norway: NMH-Publications, 2002: 2.

Ruud, Even (2004). Defining Community Music Therapy. [Contribution to Moderated Discussions] *Voices: A World Forum for Music Therapy*. Retrieved January 16, 2006, from http://www.voices.no/discussions/discm4_07.html.

Ruud, Even (2010). *Music Therapy: A Perspective from the Humanities*. Gilsum, NH: Barcelona Publishers.

Ruud, Even (2011). Musikk med helsekonsekvenser. Et musikkpedagogisk prosjekt for ungdommer i en palestinsk flyktningleir [Music with Health Consequences. A Music Education Project for Youths in a Palestinian Refugee Camp]. *Nordic Research in Music Education, Yearbook*. 12, pp. 59–80.

Ruud, Even (in press). The New Health Musicians. In: MacDonald, Raymond, Gunter Kreutz & Laura Mitchell (Eds.). *Music, Health and Wellbeing*. New York: Oxford University Press.

Ryan, William (1971). *Blaming the Victim*. New York: Random House.

Saarikallio, Suvi (2007). Music as Mood Regulation in Adolescence. Doctoral dissertation. Jyväskylä, Finland: University of Jyväskylä, The Faculty of Humanities.

Saracci, Rodolfo (1997). The World Health Organization Needs to Reconsider its Definition of Health. *British Medical Journal, 314* (10 May 1997), p. 1409.

Sarafino, Edward P. (2002). *Health Psychology—Biopsychosocial Interactions*. New York: John Wiley.

Saxbe, Darby (2003). Six Degrees of Separation. *Psychology Today Magazine*, Nov/Dec 2003.

Scheff, Thomas (1966). *Being Mentally Ill: A Sociological Perspective*. Chicago: Aldine.

Scheiby, Benedikte Barth (2002). Caring for the Caregivers: Trauma, Improvised Music and Transformation of Terror into Meaning through Community Music Therapy Training. In: Loewy, Joanne & Andrea Frisch (Eds.). *Caring for the Caregiver: The Use of Music, Music Therapy in Grief and Trauma*. Silver Spring, MD: American Music Therapy Association.

Schullian, Dorothy & Max Schoen (Eds.) (1948). *Music and Medicine*. New York: Henry Schuman.

Schumaker, Lyn (2000). The Dancing Nurse: *Kalela* Drums and the History of Hygiene in Africa. In: Gouk, Penelope (Ed.). *Musical Healing in Cultural Contexts*. Aldershot, UK: Ashgate Publishing.

Schwabe, Christoph (1983). *Aktive Gruppenmusiktherapie für erwachsene Patienten* [Active Group Music Therapy for Adult Patients]. Leipzig: Veb Georg Thieme.

Schwabe, Christoph (1987). *Regulative Musiktherapie* [Regulative Music Therapy]. Leipzig: Veb Georg Thieme.

Schwabe, Christoph (2005). Resource-Oriented Music Therapy—The Development of a Concept. *Nordic Journal of Music Therapy, 14*(1), pp. 49–56.

Schwabe, Christoph & Ulrike Haase (1996). Social Music Therapy in Response to the Changes of Social Conditions. Hamburg: Paper at the 8th World Congress of Music Therapy.

Schwabe, Christoph & Ulrike Haase (1998). *Die Sozialmusiktherapie (SMT)* [Social Music Therapy]. Wetzdorf, Germany: Akademie für angewandte Musiktherapie Crossen.

Schwantes, Melody (forthcoming). Music Therapy's Effects on Mexican Migrant Farmworkers' Levels of Depression, Anxiety, and Social Isolation: A Mixed Methods Randomized Control Trial Utilizing Participatory Action Research. Unpublished Doctoral Dissertation. Aalborg, Denmark: Aalborg University.

Scott, Derek B. (Ed.) (2000). *Music, Culture, and Society. A Reader*. Oxford: Oxford University Press.

Seidel, Almut (1992). Sozialpädagogische Musiktherapie. Anmerkungen zu einem Praxis- und Ausbildungskonzept. [Music Therapy in Social Work: Observations on a Concept for Practice and Training.] *Musiktherapeutische Umschau, 13*(4), pp. 298–306.

Seidel, Almut (1996). Sozialwesen (Sozialarbeit/Sozialpädagogik) [Social Service (Social Work/Social Education)] In: Decker-Voigt, Hans-Helmut, Polo J. Knill. & Eckhardt Weymann (Eds.). *Lexikon Musiktherapie*. Göttingen, Germany: Hogrefe.

Sekeles, Chava (1996). Music in the Traditional Healing Rituals of Morocco. *Paper at the 8th World Congress of Music Therapy*, Hamburg, July 1996.

Selye, Hans (1956). *The Stress of Life*. New York: McGraw-Hill.

References

Sennett, Richard (2004). *Respect: The Formation of Character in an Age of Inequality.* London: Allen Lane.

Shadish, William R., Thomas D. Cook & Donald T. Campbell (2002). *Experimental and Quasi-Experimental Designs for Generalized Causal Inference.* Boston, MA: Houghton-Mifflin.

Shapiro, Noah (2005). Sounds in the World: Multicultural Influences in Music Therapy in Clinical Practice and Training. *Music Therapy Perspectives,* 23, pp. 29–35.

Sherif, Muzafer (1935). A Study of Some Social Factors in Perception. *Archives of Psychology,* 27 (187), pp. 1–60.

Shumaker, Sally Ann & Arlene Brownell (1984). Toward a Theory of Social Support: Closing Conceptual Gaps. *Journal of Social Issues,* 40, pp. 11–36.

Skånland, Marie (2007). Soundescape: En studie av hvordan musikk blir integrert i hverdagen til brukere av mp3-spillere [Soundescape: A Study of How Music is an Integrated Part of the Everyday Life of Users of MP3-Players]. Unpublished Master thesis. Oslo, Norway: University of Oslo, Department of Music.

Skånland, Marie (forthcoming). A Technology of Well-Being. A Qualitative Study of the Use of MP3 Players as a Medium of Musical Self-Care. Unpublished doctoral dissertation. Oslo: Norway: Norwegian Academy of Music.

Skinner, Quintin (1998). *Liberty before Liberalism,* Cambridge: Cambridge University.

Small, Christopher (1998). *Musicking. The Meanings of Performing and Listening.* Hanover, NH: Wesleyan University Press.

Smyth, Marie (2002). Culture and Society. The Role of Creativity in Healing and Recovering One's Power after Victimisation. In: Sutton, Julie P. (Ed.). *Music, Music Therapy and Trauma. International Perspectives.* London: Jessica Kingsley Publishers.

Snow, Charles P. (1959/1998). *The Two Cultures.* Cambridge, UK: Cambridge University Press.

Solli, Hans Petter (2006). Aldri bare syk. Om ressursorientert musikkterapi for en mann med schizofreni [Never Just Sick. On Resource-Oriented Music Therapy for a Man with Schizophrenia]. Unpublished Master's Thesis. Oslo, Norway: Norwegian Academy of Music.

Solli, Hans Petter (2010). Rediscovering Recovery. Music Therapy in Contemporary Mental Health Care. Paper at the 8th European music therapy congress, 5–9 May in Cadiz, Spain.

Stansfeld, Stephen A. (2006). Social Support and Social Cohesion. In: Marmot, Michael & Richard G. Wilkinson (Eds.). *Social Determinants of Health* (pp. 148–171). Oxford: Oxford University Press.

Steptoe, Andrew & Susan Ayers (2004). Stress and Health. In: Sutton, Stephen R., Andrew S. Baum & Marie Johnston (Eds.). *The SAGE Handbook of Health Psychology.* London: Sage Publications.

Stern, Daniel (1985/1998). *The Interpersonal World of the Infant. A View from Psychoanalysis and Development Psychology.* London: Karnack.

Stern, Daniel (1995). *The Motherhood Constellation. A Unified View of Parent–Infant Psychotherapy.* New York: Basic Books.

Stern, Daniel (2004). *The Present Moment in Psychotherapy and Everyday Life.* New York: W.W. Norton.

Stern, Daniel (2010). *Forms of Vitality: Exploring Dynamic Experience in Psychology and the Arts.* New York: Oxford University Press.

Stewart, David (2004). Transformational Contexts in Music Therapy. In: Pavlicevic, Mercédès & Gary Ansdell (Eds.). *Community Music Therapy.* London: Jessica Kingsley Publishers.

Stige, Brynjulf (1983). Ngoma, musirør og anna rør [Ngoma, Music, and Movement]. Oslo, Norway: Unpublished Thesis, Østlandets musikkonservatorium, Section for Music Therapy.

Stige, Brynjulf (1993). Endringar i det musikkterapeutiske 'rommet'—med kulturarbeid i lokalsamfunnet som eit eksempel [Changes in the Music Therapy "Space"—With Cultural Engagement in the Local Community as an Example]. *Nordic Journal of Music Therapy,* 2(2).

Stige, Brynjulf (1993/1999). Music Therapy as Cultural Engagement. Or: How to Change the World, if Only a Bit. Paper at the 7th World Congress in Music Therapy. Vitoria-Gasteiz, Spain. Republished in: Aldridge, David (Ed.). (1999). *Music Therapy Info, Vol. II,* CD-Rom.

Stige, Brynjulf (1995). *Samspel og relasjon. Perspektiv på ein inkluderande musikkpedagogikk* [Interaction and Relationship. Perspectives on Inclusive Music Education.] Oslo, Norway: Samlaget.

Stige, Brynjulf (1996). Music, Music Therapy, and Health Promotion. In: *Report. International UNESCO-conference, Oslo, September 1995.* Oslo, Norway: The Norwegian National Commission for UNESCO.

Stige, Brynjulf (1998). Aesthetic Practices in Music Therapy. *Nordic Journal of Music Therapy, 7(2)*, pp. 121–134.

Stige, Brynjulf (2001). The Fostering of Not-Knowing Barefoot Supervisors. In: Forinash, Michele (Ed.). *Music Therapy Supervision.* Gilsum, NH: Barcelona Publishers.

Stige, Brynjulf (2002). *Culture-Centered Music Therapy.* Gilsum, NH: Barcelona Publishers.

Stige, Brynjulf (2003). *Elaborations toward a Notion of Community Music Therapy.* Doctoral Dissertation. Oslo, Norway: University of Oslo, published by: Unipub.

Stige, Brynjulf (2004a). Community Music Therapy: Culture, Care, and Welfare. In: Pavlicevic, Mercédès & Gary Ansdell (Eds.). *Community Music Therapy.* London: Jessica Kingsley Publishers.

Stige, Brynjulf (2004b). Performance of Community. *Voices: A World Forum for Music Therapy.* Retrieved February 21, 2011, from http://testvoices.uib.no/?q=fortnightly-columns/2004-performance-community.

Stige, Brynjulf (2005a). Ethnography and Ethnographically Informed Research. In: Wheeler, Barbara (Ed.) *Music Therapy Research* (2nd edition) (pp. 392–403). Gilsum, NH: Barcelona Publishers.

Stige, Brynjulf (2005b). Participatory Action Research. In: Wheeler, Barbara (Ed.) *Music Therapy Research* (2nd edition) (pp. 404–415). Gilsum, NH: Barcelona Publishers.

Stige, Brynjulf (2006). Toward a Notion of Participation in Music Therapy. *Nordic Journal of Music Therapy,* 15(2), pp. 121–138.

Stige, Brynjulf (2007). The Grieg Effect—On the Contextualized Effects of Music in Music Therapy. *Voices: A World Forum for Music Therapy.* Retrieved January 19, 2011, from https://normt.uib.no/index.php/voices/article/view/548/409.

Stige, Brynjulf (2008a). The Aesthetic or Multiple Aesthetics? A Response to Kenneth Aigen. *Nordic Journal of Music Therapy,* 17(1), pp. 25–29.

Stige, Brynjulf (2008b). Dancing the Drama and Singing for Life: On Ethnomusicology and Music Therapy. *Nordic Journal of Music Therapy,* 17(2), pp. 155–171.

Stige, Brynjulf (2010a). Musical Participation, Social Space and Everyday Ritual. In: Stige, Brynjulf, Gary Ansdell, Cochavit Elefant & Mercédès Pavlicevic (Eds.). *Where Music Helps. Community Music Therapy in Action and Reflection.* Farnham, UK: Ashgate Publishing.

Stige, Brynjulf (2010b). Practicing Music as Mutual Care. In: Stige, Brynjulf, Gary Ansdell, Cochavit Elefant & Mercédès Pavlicevic (Eds.). *Where Music Helps. Community Music Therapy in Action and Reflection.* Farnham, UK: Ashgate Publishing.

Stige, Brynjulf (2011). The Grieg Effect—On Music Therapy as Source of Knowledge about the Contextualized Effects of Music. In: Solomon, T. (Ed.). *Music and Identity in Norway and Beyond. Essays in Commemoration of Edvard Grieg the Humanist.* Bergen, Norway: Fagbokforlaget.

Stige, Brynjulf (in press). Health Musicking. In: MacDonald, Raymond, Gunter Kreutz & Laura Mitchell (Eds.) (forthcoming). *Music, Health and Wellbeing.* New York: Oxford University Press.

Stige, Brynjulf, Gary Ansdell, Cochavit Elefant & Mercédès Pavlicevic (2010a). *Where Music Helps. Community Music Therapy in Action and Reflection.* Farnham, UK: Ashgate Publishing.

Stige, Brynjulf, Gary Ansdell, Cochavit Elefant & Mercédès Pavlicevic (2010b). When Things Take Shape in Relation to Music. Towards an Ecological Perspective on Music's Help. In: Stige, Brynjulf, Gary Ansdell, Cochavit Elefant & Mercédès Pavlicevic (Eds.). *Where Music Helps. Community Music Therapy in Action and Reflection.* Farnham, UK: Ashgate Publishing.

Stige, Brynjulf & Carolyn Kenny (2002). Introduction—The Turn to Culture. In: Kenny, Carolyn & Brynjulf Stige (Eds.). *Contemporary Voices in Music Therapy. Communication, Culture, and Community.* Oslo, Norway: Unipub forlag.

Stige, Brynjulf, Kirsti Malterud & Torjus Midtgarden (2009). Towards an Agenda for Evaluation of Qualitative Research. *Qualitative Health Research,* 19(10), pp. 1504–1516.

Stjernø, Steinar (2004). *Solidarity in Europe. The History of an Idea.* Cambridge, UK: Cambridge University Press.

References

Støkken, Anne Marie (2002). Profesjoner: kontinuitet og endring [Professions: Continuity and Change]. In: Nylehn, Børre & Anne Marie Støkken (Eds.). *De profesjonelle* [The Professionals]. Oslo, Norway: Universitetsforlaget.

Storsve, Vegar, Inger Anne Westby & Even Ruud (2010). Hope and Recognition. A Music Project among Youth in a Palestinian Refugee Camp. *Voices: A World Forum for Music Therapy*. Retrieved February 21, 2011, from https://normt.uib.no/index.php/voices/article/view/158/246.

Sutton, Julie P. (Ed.) (2002). *Music, Music Therapy and Trauma. International Perspectives*. London: Jessica Kingsley Publishers.

Tait, Anja, & Leonie Murrungun (2010). ArtStories: Early Childhood Learning in Remote Indigenous Australian Communities. *Imagine, 1* (1), pp. 52–54. Retrieved February 21, 2011 from: http://imagine.musictherapybiz/Imagine/imagine_online_magazine.html.

Tarulli, Donato & Carol Sales (2009). Self-Determination and the Emerging Role of Person-Centred Planning: A Dialogical Framework. In: Owen, Frances & Dorothy Griffiths (Eds.). *Challenges to the Human Rights of People with Intellectual Disabilities*. London: Jessica Kingsley Publishers.

Threlfall, Catherine (1998). Community Music and Music Therapy—Partnerships and Possibilities. *Australian Music Therapy Association Network*, November, pp. 10–15.

Trevarthen, Colwyn & Stephen Malloch (2000). The Dance of Wellbeing: Defining the Musical Therapeutic Effect. *Nordic Journal of Music Therapy*, 9(2), pp. 3–17.

Tuastad, Lars & Roar Finsås (2008). Jeg fremfører, altså er jeg. En studie av deltagernes opplevelser i to rockeband tilknyttet musikktilbudet "Musikk i fengsel og frihet" [I perform, thus I am. A study of Participant Experiences in Two Rock Bands Linked to the Project "Music in Custody and Liberty"]. Unpublished Master Thesis. Bergen, Norway: The Grieg Academy, University of Bergen.

Tuastad, Lars & Lucy O'Grady (forthcoming). Music as a "Free Space" in Prison.

Turner, Bryan (2004). *The New Medical Sociology. Social Forms of Health and Illness*. New York: W. W. Norton & Company.

Turner, Victor W. (1967). *The Forest of Symbols: Aspects of Ndembu Ritual*. Ithaca, NY: Cornell University Press.

Turner, Victor W. (1969). *The Ritual Process: Structure and Anti-Structure*. Chicago: Aldine.

Turry, Alan (2005). Music Psychotherapy and Community Music Therapy: Questions and Considerations. *Voices: A World Forum for Music Therapy*. Retrieved February 26, 2011, from https://normt.uib.no/index.php/voices/article/view/208/152.

Tyson, Florence (1959). The Development of an Out-Patient Music Therapy Referral Service. In: *Music Therapy 1958. Eight Book of Proceedings of the National Association for Music Therapy*. Lawrence, KS: The National Association for Music Therapy.

Tyson, Florence (1968). The Community Music Therapy Center. In: Gaston, E. Thayer (Ed.). *Music in Therapy*. New York: Macmillan Publishing.

Tyson, Florence (1973). Guidelines toward the Organization of Clinical Music Therapy Programs in the Community. *Journal of Music Therapy*, 10(3), pp. 113–124.

Twenge, Jean M. & Roy F. Baumeister (2005). Social Exclusion Increases Aggression and Self-Defeating Behavior while Reducing Intelligent Thought and Procosial Behavior. In: Abrams, Dominic, Michael A. Hogg & José M. Marques (Eds.). *The Social Psychology of Inclusion and Exclusion* (pp. 27–46). New York: Psychology Press (Taylor & Francis).

United Nations (1948). Universal Declaration of Human Rights. Retrieved January 24, 2006, from: http://www.un.org/Overview/rights.html

United Nations Development Programme (UNDP) (2005). *Human Development Report 2005—International Cooperation at a Crossroads: Aid, Trade and Security in an Unequal World*. New York: United Nations Development Programme.

United Nations Educational, Scientific and Cultural Organization (UNESCO) (2010). *Reaching the Marginalized. EFA (Education for All) Global Monitoring Report, 2010*. Oxford, UK: Oxford University Press.

Urbain, Olivier (Ed.). (2008). *Music and Conflict Transformation. Harmonies and Dissonances in Geopolitics.* London & New York: I.B. Tauris.

Uricoechea, Ana Sheila (2003). Rethinking Music Therapy with the Mentally Handicapped. *Voices: A World Forum for Music Therapy.* Retrieved November 26, 2005, from http://www.voices.no/mainissues/mi40003000123.html.

Ursin, Holger & Hege Randi Eriksen (2004). The Cognitive Activation Theory of Stress. *Psychoneuroendocrinology, 29,* pp. 567–592.

Vaillancourt, Guylaine (2007). Multicultural Music Therapy as an Instrument for Leadership Listening—Vision—Process. *Voices: A World Forum for Music Therapy, 7*(2). Retrieved February 26, 2011, from https://normt.uib.no/index.php/voices/article/view/493/400.

Vaillancourt, Guylaine (2009). Mentoring Apprentice Music Therapists for Peace and Social Justice through Community Music Therapy: An Arts-Based Study. Dissertation submitted to the PhD in Leadership and Change Program. Santa Barbara, CA: Antioch University.

Veblen, Kari K. (2007). The Many Ways of Community Music. *International Journal of Community Music, 1*(1), pp. 5–21.

Veenhoven, Ruut (1995). The Cross-National Pattern of Happiness: Test of Predictions Implied in Three Theories of Happiness. *Social Indicators Research, 34,* pp. 33–68.

Veenhoven, Ruut (2004). Happiness as an Aim in Public Policy. In: Linley, P. Alex, Stephen, Joseph & Martin E. P. Seligman (Eds.). *Positive Psychology in Practice* (pp. 658–678). Hoboken, NJ: John Wiley.

Vinader, Maria Elena López (2008). Music Therapy: Healing, Growth, Creating a Culture of Peace. In: Urbain, Olivier (Ed.). *Music and Conflict Transformation. Harmonies and Dissonances in Geopolitics.* London & New York: I.B. Tauris.

Völker, Ulrike (2004). Chance zur Teilhabe über die Therapie hinaus. Musiktherapie zwischen kulturtherapeutischen Fragestellungen und (psycho-)therapeutischem Selbstverständnis auf der Grundlage Integrativer Therapie [Possibilities of Participation beyond Therapy. Music Therapy between Cultural Therapeutic Problems and (Psycho)therapeutic Self Understanding in Integrative Therapy]. Unpublished Master thesis, University of Applied Sciences, Magdeburg-Stendal

Vygotsky, Lev (1978). *Mind in Society. The Development of Higher Psychological Processes.* Cambridge, MA: Harvard University Press.

Wagemakers, Annemarie (2010). Community Health Promotion. Facilitating and Evaluating Coordinated Action to Create Supportive Social Environments. Unpublished doctoral dissertation. Wageningen, The Netherlands: Wageningen University.

Wakao, Yu (2002). John Cage and Therapeutic Silence. *Voices: A World Forum for Music Therapy, 2*(3). Retrieved February 26, 2011, from https://normt.uib.no/index.php/voices/article/view/99/76.

Wallin, Nils L. (1991). *Biomusicology. Neurophysiological, Neurospychological and Evolutionary Perspectives on the Origins and Purposes of Music.* Stuyvesant, NY: Pendragon Press.

Wallin, Nils L., Björn Merker & Steven Brown (Eds.) (2000). *The Origins of Music.* Cambridge, MA: The MIT Press.

Walker, Scott (Ed.) (1993). *Changing Community.* Saint Paul, MN: Graywolf Press.

Wampold, Bruce (2001). *The Great Psychotherapy Debate: Models, Methods, and Findings.* Mahwah, NJ: Lawrence Erlbaum Associates.

Warner, Catherine (2005). Music Therapy with Adults with Learning Difficulties and 'Severe Challenging Behaviour.' An Action Research Inquiry into the Benefits of Group Music Therapy within a Community Home. Unpublished Doctoral Dissertation, University of the West of England, Bristol, UK.

Wenger, Etienne (1998). *Communities of Practice: Learning, Meaning and Identity.* New York: Cambridge University Press.

Wenger, Etienne, Richard McDermott & William M. Snyder (2002). *Cultivating Communities of Practice.* Boston, MA: Harvard Business School Press.

Wheaton, Blair (1999). The Nature of Stressors. In: Horwitz, Allan V. & Teresa L. Scheid (Eds.). *A Handbook for the Study of Mental Health. Social Contexts, Theories, and Systems* (pp. 176–197). Cambridge, UK: Cambridge University Press.

References   Wilkinson, Richard (1996). *Unhealthy Societies—The Afflictions of Inequality*. London: Routledge.

Wilkinson, Richard & Kate Pickett (2010). *The Spirit Level: Why Equality is Better for Everyone*. London: Penguin.

Williams, Alistair (2001). *Constructing Musicology*. Aldershot, UK: Ashgate Publishing.

Williams, Colin C. & Jan Windebank (2001). *Revitalising Deprived Urban Neighbourhoods: An Assisted Self-Help Approach*. Aldershot, UK: Ashgate Publishing.

Williams, Kate & Vicky Abad (2005). Reflections on Music Therapy with Indigenous Families: Cultural Learning put into Practice. *Australian Journal of Music Therapy*, 16, pp. 60–69

Williams, Raymond (1961/1971) *The Long Revolution*. Harmondsworth, UK: Pelican Books.

Williams, Robin M. (1979). Change and Stability in Values and Value Systems: A Sociological Perspective. In: Rokeach, Milton (Ed.). *Understanding Human Values, Individual and Societal*. New York: Free Press.

Wills, Thomas A. & Michael G. Ainette (2007). Social Support and Health. In: Ayers, Susan, Andrew Baum, Chris McManus, Stanton Newmand, Kenneth Wallston, John Weinman & Robert West (Eds.). *Cambridge Handbook of Psychology, Health and Medicine* (pp. 202–207). Cambridge: Cambridge University Press.

Wilson, Mitchell (1993). DSM III and the Transformation of American Psychiatry: A History. *American Journal of Psychiatry*, 150, pp. 399–410.

Wittgenstein, Ludwig (1953/1967). *Philosophical Investigations*. Oxford: Blackwell.

Wood, Stuart (2006). "The Matrix": A Model of Community Music Therapy Processes. *Voices: A World Forum for Music Therapy*. Retrieved February 19, 2011, from https://normt.uib.no/index.php/voices/article/view/279/204.

Wood, Stuart, Rachel Verney & Jessica Atkinson (2004). From Therapy to Community: Making Music in Neuro-Rehabilitation. In: Pavlicevic, Mercédès & Gary Ansdell (Eds.). *Community Music Therapy*. London: Jessica Kingsley Publishers.

Woodward, Alpha M. (2002/2004). Finding the Client in Their Environment: A Systems Approach to Music Therapy Programming. *Canadian Journal of Music Therapy*, 9(1), pp. 50–64. Republished in: *Voices: A World Forum for Music Therapy* Retrieved February 26, 2011, from https://normt.uib.no/index.php/voices/article/view/183/142.

World Health Organization (1946). The Constitution of the World Health Organization. Geneva: World Health Organization. See also: http://w3.whosea.org/aboutsearo/pdf/const.pdf.

World Health Organization (1978). The Alma Ata Conference on Primary Health Care. *WHO Chronicle*, 32(11), pp. 409–430. See also: http://www.who.int/hpr/NPH/docs/declaration_almaata.pdf

World Health Organization (1986). Ottawa Charter for Health Promotion. Geneva: World Health Organization.

World Health Organization (2001a). International Classification of Functioning, Disability, and Health (ICF). Geneva: World Health Organization: Fifty-Fourth World Health Assembly.

World Health Organization (2001b). *The World Health Report 2001: Mental Health: New Understanding, New Hope*. Geneva: The World Health Organization.

World Health Organization (2003). *The World Health Report 2003: Shaping the future*. Geneva: The World Health Organization.

World Health Organization (2007a). Achieving Health Equity: From Root Causes to Fair Outcomes. Interim Statement from the Commission on Social Determinants of Health. Geneva: World Health Organization. http://who.int/social_determinants

World Health Organization (2007b). *Social Determinants of Indigenous Health: The International Experience and its Policy Implications*. Report for the International Symposium on the Social Determinants of Indigenous Health, Adelaide, 29–30 April 2007. Geneva: World Health Organization.

Wosch, Thomas (2011). *Musik und Alter in Therapie und Pflege. Grundlagen, Institutionen und Praxis der Musiktherapie bei Alter und Demenz*. Stuttgart: Kohlhammer.

Yalom, Irwin D with Molyn Leszcz (2005). *The Theory and Practice of Group Psychotherapy* (5th edition). New York: Basic Books.

Yin, Robert K. (2008). *Case Study Research: Design and Methods* (4th edition). Thousand Oaks, CA: Sage Publications.

Zanini, Claudia Regina de Oliveira & Eliane Leao (2006). Therapeutic Choir—A Music Therapist Looks at the New Millennium Elderly. *Voices: A World Forum for Music Therapy*, 6(2). Retrieved February 21, 2011, from https://normt.uib.no/index.php/voices/article/view/249/193.

Zatonski, Witold & Prabhat Jha (2000). *The Health Transformation in Eastern Europe after 1990: A Second Look*. Warsaw: Department of Epidemiology and Prevention of Cancer, Centre of Oncology, Marie Sklodowska Curie Memorial Institute in Warsaw.

Zharinova-Sanderson, Oksana (2004). Promoting Integration and Socio-Cultural Change: Community Music Therapy with Traumatised Refugees in Berlin. In: Pavlicevic, Mercédès & Gary Ansdell (Eds.). *Community Music Therapy*. London: Jessica Kingsley Publishers.

Ziman, John (2000). *Real Science. What it Is, and What it Means*. Cambridge, UK: Cambridge University Press.

Author Index

Subject Index

communal (sociocultural) 4, 14, 15, 18, 20, 22–3, 27, 39, 47–8, 82, 103, 106, 112, 136, 139, 146, 150–3, 158–63, 171–2, 175, 180, 187, 195, 206–30, 237–8, 240–2, 266; musical and paramusical 118–22, 138–9, 152, 165; *see also* model of processes in community music therapy; PREPARE

China 84

choir: adolescent 34; adult 10, 61, 100–2, 130, 137, 167, 212, 222, 226, 241–2, 253, 272–3; children 189, 212, 245–6; multi–generational 215; senior 98, 130, 167, 206–7, 212, 250; *see also* community singing

Christian democracy *see* democracy

chronic health problems 75, 77, 83, 99–100, 156, 158, 227

citizen participation 148, 170, 172, 176–7, 220; *see also* human rights; inclusion; marginalization

civil and political rights *see* human rights

classical music *see* Western art music

collaborative musicking *see* musicking

Colombia 50

Commonwealth of Independent States 75–6

communal musicking *see* musicking

communicating and celebrating *see* model of participatory processes in community music therapy

communicative musicality *see* musicality

communitas 47, 90, 127, 141

communities of practice *see* community of practice

community 90–3; geographical notion of (defined by location) 90, 92, 110; musical 26, 92, 16–19; relational notion of 90, 92, 110; *see also* sense of community

community development 5, 31–2, 51, 53, 58, 146, 159, 160, 174, 286

community music 46, 49, 169, 216, 272, 278, 285

community music therapy matrix 213–14

community music therapy processes *see* model of participatory processes in community music therapy

community music therapy: and conventional music therapy 24–6; defined 14–16; history of 31–55; understood as human rights practice 178–99; qualities of 16–20; *see also* PREPARE

community of practice 92–3, 136–7, 141, 151, 195, 214, 229, 276

community psychology 18, 26, 52–3, 58, 65, 159, 201, 280

community singing 155, 159, 212; *see also* choir

community work *see* community development

comparison theory 80–1

conflict resolution *see* conflict transformation

conflict transformation 54, 160, 162–3, 206, 215, 219, 231, 278, 283

context (notion of) 113; *see also* ecological model; environment

coping resources 100

countries in Central and Eastern Europe 76

craft *see* skills

creating critical awareness *see* awareness; model of participatory processes in community music therapy

critique *see* social critique

culture of mutual care 98, 167

culture: and community 90–3; and community of practice 136–8; and definition of music therapy 24–6; and interaction rituals 134–6; and musicking 125–6; and musics 122–5; and the paramusical 118–22; and professional identity 270–4; and relational concept of health 66–8; and social capital 101–6; and social construction 71–3

DALY *see* disability–adjusted life years

dealing with predicaments *see* model of participatory processes in community music therapy

democracy 21, 189, 197, 200, 230, 277; Christian 194; participatory 199, 200, 207; social 181, 194

Denmark 68, 114

deviance 67, 69, 72–3, 83; primary 72–3, 83; secondary 72–3, 83; *see also* labeling theory

diagnosis 22, 71–3, 83, 170–1, 173; DSM 71–3; ICD 69, 71–3

Diagnostic and Statistical Manual of Mental Disorders (DSM) *see* diagnosis

dimensions of health *see* health

direct effect hypothesis of social support *see* social support

disability 29, 60, 65, 69, 71, 77, 80, 109, 123, 161, 278

disability-adjusted life years (DALY) 65

disease 59, 60, 62–3, 65, 69, 71–2, 75–8, 80, 82, 130, 150, 175, 260, 270; Group I, II, and III diseases 76–7, *see also* illness; sickness